D1640971

Hawaiian Language

Hawaiian Language
Past, Present, Future

What Every Teacher and Student of Hawaiian
Might Like to Know about the History
and Future of the Language

Albert J. Schütz

University of Hawaiʻi Press
Honolulu

Printed in the United States of America

25 24 23 22 21 20 6 5 4 3 2 1

Library of Congress Cataloging-in-Publication Data

Names: Schütz, Albert J., author.
Title: Hawaiian language : past, present, and future / Albert J. Schütz.
Description: Honolulu : University of Hawai'i, 2020. | Includes bibliographical references and index.
Identifiers: LCCN 2019033187 | ISBN 9780824869823 (hardback) | ISBN 9780824869830 (paperback)
Subjects: LCSH: Hawaiian language—History. | Hawaiian language—Vocabulary. | Hawaiian language—Alphabet.
Classification: LCC PL6441 .S378 2020 | DDC 499/.42—dc23
LC record available at https://lccn.loc.gov/2019033187

University of Hawai'i Press books are printed on acid-free paper and meet the guidelines for permanence and durability of the Council on Library Resources.

Cover art: *The Discovery* (1928) by Arman Tateos Manookian (Armenian, born Turkey, 1904–1931). Oil on canvas. Courtesy of Collection Elizabeth E. Wong and Isabella N. Wong.

Design by Nord Compo

To the memory of Dr. Karen M. Peacock—dear friend and wayfinder for all scholars in their Pacific odysseys

CONTENTS

INTRODUCTION

As the title suggests, this book promises to describe the past, present, and future of the Hawaiian language. It is not designed to help teach the language but instead to provide a *background* for language teaching and learning by telling teachers and students about the language and its history.

Over the years, writers of Hawaiian textbooks have varied in their philosophy about language teaching. Some have ignored the culture, treating the language as a list of patterns and words to memorize. Others have realized that language and culture go hand in hand. To this end, they have attempted to cover the bare bones of grammatical explanations and vocabulary exercises with the flesh of context, providing a cultural background for the language material in focus.

But even with this broadened view, there are still many questions about Hawaiian that are beyond the scope of a textbook. Here are a few:

- How did Polynesian languages come to be known to the outside world?
- How is Hawaiian related to other Pacific languages?
- How is it different from its closest relatives?
- How was its alphabet developed?
- How were people taught to read and write Hawaiian?
- What were the results of this newfound literacy?
- How were new words formed in the past?
- How and why does Hawaiian borrow words from other languages?
- How is the vocabulary being expanded to supply the words needed for the rapidly growing language immersion programs?
- Has the Hawaiian alphabet changed the language?
- What reference materials are needed for Hawaiian language programs?
- How can existing reference materials be improved?
- What are the main differences between bilingual and monolingual dictionaries?
- How can dictionaries reflect Hawaiian culture?
- What are the advantages of electronic dictionaries?

This book answers these questions, and many others as well—not only for teachers and learners of the language, but for anyone—especially

Hawai'i residents—who would like to know more about this all-important aspect of Hawaiian culture.

ORGANIZATION

Part I combines history and geography, allowing readers to look at Hawaiian not as an isolated language in an isolated island group but instead as an important piece in a large picture puzzle of a family of languages spoken in islands spread throughout the Pacific area and extending to Southeast Asia and Madagascar as well.

Time, as well as space, plays an important role in this discussion, for we try to use our present knowledge of this family to provide clues as to how and when its speakers moved eastward from Asia and Southeast Asia, eventually settling in Hawai'i.

Part II tells the story of how an alphabet was created for a language that had never been written before. It focuses on the solutions to two alphabetic problems: too many letters and too few.

Part III sketches the ways in which Hawaiians used the alphabet to read and write their own language. It also reveals some of the effects that this newfound literacy had on Hawaiian culture.

Part IV takes a basic element of Hawaiian structure that is not usually treated in detail in textbooks and grammars—vocabulary—and elaborates on it.

Part V, necessarily open-ended, examines some of the changes in Hawaiian that have taken place since outside contact, seeking patterns that might suggest the direction of further changes. In addition, it suggests ways to expand existing reference materials so that they can reflect a Hawaiian worldview.

The book as a whole shows that studying Hawaiian can involve much more than just speaking and participating in those areas of the culture that still exist or are being revitalized. Because of its content, it can be used by at least three groups: language learners who want to supplement their textbooks, language teachers who want to understand more about the structure and the history of the language that they're teaching, and residents and visitors who realize how important it is to be better informed about Hawaiian.

Most chapters end with the following section: "Verbatim"—extended quotations about the topic(s) treated in the chapter, directing the reader to sources beyond the text.

ABBREVIATIONS

In the following list, Austronesian language names are abbreviated in the conventional way. Such abbreviations are used in the annotations but not in titles of works or in direct quotations (except for HAW).

ABCFM	American Board of Commissioners for Foreign Missions, Boston
Adm	Admiralty Records, London
BCE	Before Common Era
BP	before present
EAS	Easter Island (language)
ed.	edition
ENG	English (language)
E-P	Elbert and Pukui 1979 (*Hawaiian Grammar*)
HAW	Hawaiian (language)
HMCS	Hawaiian Mission Houses Historic Site and Archives, Honolulu
JBM	Bernice Judd, Janet E. Bell, and Clare G. Murdoch (1978), *Hawaiian Language Imprints, 1822–1899*
k.o.	kind of
LMS	London Missionary Society
MAO	Māori (language)
MQA	Marquesan (language)
ms.	manuscript
mss.	manuscripts
P-E	Abbreviation for Pukui-Elbert, referring to any of the several editions of Hawaiian dictionaries compiled by these authors or to the compilers themselves. See the various entries for Mary Kawena Pukui and Samuel H. Elbert in the references.
PHG	*Pocket Hawaiian Grammar*
PN	Polynesian (languages)
PNP	Proto-Nuclear Polynesian
PPN	Proto-Polynesian
SAM	Samoan (language)

TAH	Tahitian (language)
TON	Tongan (language)
UHM	University of Hawaiʻi at Mānoa, Hamilton Library, Honolulu

ACKNOWLEDGMENTS

LIBRARIES AND ARCHIVES

Sources for learning about the history of Hawaiian and its study are not confined to libraries and archives in Hawaiʻi but are scattered around the world. The geography that the following list represents reflects not only scholarly interests but other enterprises as well.

The formal names of these institutions conceal their colorful contents—including the varied personalities of people who wrote about Hawaiʻi and Hawaiian. They cover a wide range: explorers, beachcombers, sandalwood traders, whalers, missionaries, journalists, novelists, philologists, lexicographers, anthropologists, archaeologists, and linguists. Moreover, they wrote their findings in Dutch, English, French, German, Latin, Russian, and Spanish.

In 1995, I gave a talk for the Friends of the Hawaiʻi Kai Library entitled "Lost in the stacks: My search for Pacific grammars and dictionaries, and the people who wrote them." I won't try to repeat that lecture but will only say that my work in the following collections was a series of adventures and discovery—rather like the first voyages to the Pacific, but without the physical inconveniences. Moreover, in each of the libraries, I had the guidance of well-trained and knowledgeable professionals. Without them, this book could not have been written.

Alexander Turnbull Library, National Library of New Zealand, Wellington
Auckland Institute and Museum Library, New Zealand
Auckland Public Library, New Zealand
Bernice P. Bishop Museum Library, Honolulu
The British Library, London
Cambridge University Library (England)
Cooke Library, Punahou School, Honolulu
Cornwall Free Library, Cornwall, CT
Essex Institute Library, Salem, MA
Hawaiian and Pacific Collections, Hamilton Library, University of Hawaiʻi at Mānoa

Hawaiian Historical Society Library, Honolulu
Hawaiian Mission Houses Historic Site and Archives, Honolulu
Hocken Library, University of Otago, Dunedin, New Zealand
Houghton Library, Harvard University, Cambridge, MA
Kroepelin Collection, Kon-Tiki Museum, Oslo
Mitchell Library, State Library of New South Wales, Sydney, Australia
Peabody Museum Library, Salem, MA
School of Oriental and African Studies Library, University of London
Staatsbibliothek zu Berlin/Preußischer Kulturbesitz
Sterling Memorial Library, Yale University, New Haven, CT
Tozzer Library, Harvard University, Cambridge, MA
Widener Library, Harvard University, Cambridge, MA
Yale Anthropological Library, New Haven, CT
Yale Divinity School Library, New Haven, CT

CHAPTER DECORATIONS

Most of the woodblock prints that begin each chapter are from *O ke Kumumua na na Kamalii* (1835).

PEOPLE

Mahalo to readers, colleagues, and other friends who offered help and advice: Aitor Arronte Alvarez, Puanani Anderson-Fung, John Barker, Robert A. Blust, John Charlot, Kenneth William Cook, Steven Egesdal, Steven Roger Fischer FRS (NZ), Paul Geraghty, Ruth Horie, Gary N. Kahāhoʻomalu Kanada, Jeffrey Kapali Lyon, Alexander Mawyer, Nancy J. Morris, Robert J. Morris, Keao NeSmith, ʻŌiwi Parker Jones, James Rumford, Noenoe Silva, Sigrid B. Southworth, Stephen Trussel, Margo Vitarelli, Mary Walworth, Carol White, and Thomas A. Woods.

Mahalo to the Department of Linguistics secretarial staff for invaluable and always cheerful help with computer problems: Nora Lum and Jennifer Kanda.

Mahalo to the Hawaiian Mission Houses Historic Site and Archives for permission to duplicate the first printing in Hawaiian, *The Alphabet,* and a number of images from their publications.

I am especially grateful to Elizabeth E. Wong and Isabella N. Wong for allowing me to use their beautiful painting, *The Discovery,* on the cover. Mahalo also to SaraLyn Smith, not only for arranging the permission but also for supplying the image itself, with the help of Lesa Griffith, director of communications, and Hathaway Jakobsen, deputy director, Honolulu Museum of Art, for the high-resolution image of *The Discovery.*

And—as always—*mahalo ā nui loa* to the staff of Hamilton Library's Hawaiian and Pacific Collections, University of Hawaiʻi at Mānoa. Listed alphabetically, they are Stu Dawrs, Eleanor Kleiber, Jodie Mattos, Dore Minatodani, Andrea Nakamura, Wesly Poka, Ann Rabinko, and Kāpena Shim.

Hawaiian Language

PART I

HISTORY

CHAPTER 1

DISCOVERING HAWAIIAN'S FAMILY TREE

Because language is such an ordinary part of our daily lives, we usually take it for granted without questioning its past or future. Perhaps its distance from the center of our consciousness explains why no epic tales or chants mark the important milestones in the development of Hawaiian. The only traces of its earliest form are those that we can reconstruct by examining and comparing features of its descendants—but more about that on the next page.

The main physical evidence documenting the history of the Hawaiian language comes in the form of a particular kind of pottery—Lapita, which was first made in New Britain and Mussau[1] about 1,400 years BC (figure 1.1, left). The users of these artifacts can be traced back another two millennia to Taiwan (Robert Blust, pers. comm., 12 July 2010).

Figure 1.1. Left: A Lapita pot from Teouma, Efate Island, Vanuatu, but imported from New Caledonia; right: contemporary Fijian pottery

1. "Mussau Island, W Pacific Ocean, N Bismarck Archipelago, in St. Mathias Group NNW of New Hanover" (*Merriam-Webster's Geographical Dictionary* 1997).

For this period, long before an alphabet was devised for the language spoken by the makers of the pottery, all we can say is that what they spoke was *ancestral* to Hawaiian and its relatives in the Pacific.

How do we know this fact? Not directly; however, the earlier movements of the people who now speak Hawaiian and other Polynesian languages can be reconstructed by using a variety of methods. Some of them are from familiar academic disciplines, such as archaeology (e.g., the Lapita connection), but others are from more recent but well-established procedures such as radiocarbon dating and from even newer fields, such as DNA studies (Borg 1997) and the comparison of bacterial samples from the stomachs of current human populations (Renfrew 2009). In a metaphorical sense, it seems as though modern scientists have taken a soothsayer's array of bones, blood, and guts and have put them under an electron microscope to shed more light on the past.

Still, language provides the most important data for our purposes here: comparing and describing languages rather than tracing the movements of their speakers.

The main footprints that a language leaves over time are the changes that have taken place. But these changes occur so slowly that we don't usually notice them, especially if we're dealing only with spoken language. Still, even in the relatively short time that Hawaiian has been written, we can see that some of the words written down in 1778 no longer match current ones.[2]

But what of the features that changed before the language was written? In order to find these, we begin with evidence from the present and work backward through an increasingly indistinct past. This procedure helps us form a picture of both an ancestral language and a *language family.*

These terms may remind you of genealogy: different generations of children, parents, and grandparents arranged on a family tree. But a language family is different. When we say that Hawaiian, Tahitian, Marquesan, Māori, and other Polynesian languages belong to one family, we mean that these languages that are now different were once the same language, spoken in one community. The same principle holds for the relationship between Polynesian languages and the languages much farther west, such as Malay, Tagalog, Ilocano, Malagasy, and many others: even further in

2. The words were collected by William Anderson, naturalist on Captain James Cook's third voyage. Anderson's work is treated in more detail in chapter 5.

the past, these languages were also spoken in the same community as one language.

To examine the idea that one language has, through the years, split into a number of different languages, we return to the concept of *change.*

Why do languages change? The answer is complicated, for some of the reasons have to do with the very nature of language itself.

But other reasons are simpler, especially when we look at how vocabulary—just one part of language—changes. As people develop new ideas, beliefs, and technology, they have to find words to express these things.

Geography also plays a role in how vocabulary can change. Imagine what New Zealand presented to the voyaging Polynesians who arrived there: high mountains, fjords, volcanoes, snow, ice, and new plants and animals—a host of physical features different from those in many of the Pacific islands, especially those in low-lying atolls nearer the equator.

Sometimes cultural practices prompt change as well. Tahitian once had a word-taboo system, called *pi'i* (or perhaps *pī*), which made it necessary to change words that sounded like a chief's name, or even parts of the name.[3] For example, when the chief Tū took the name Pōmare, the words *pō* 'night' and *mare* 'cough' (cf. Hawaiian *pō* and *male*) were changed to *ru'i* and *hota.* In the same way, the word *vai* 'water' (cf. Hawaiian *wai*) was changed to *pape;* the port village that was once called *Vai'ete* is now *Pape'ete.* But some people resist name changes: Michael Koch reported that a few older people in the Marquesas still referred to the town as *Vai'ete* (pers. comm., May 2016).

Finally, the sounds of a language can change without any apparent stimulus, drifting gradually and imperceptibly from one vowel to another or from one consonant to another. After all, "proper pronunciation" is decided mainly by majority rule, not by any universal standards.

At any rate, linguistic change, in a complex relationship with people's movements (which cut off communication), resulted in a number of different—but related—Polynesian languages spread over a large area of the Pacific. Certainly, people living in various island groups that were in frequent contact were aware of the similarities and differences among

3. Ralph Gardner White (1967), who had firsthand knowledge of Tahitian and wrote a number of articles on the topic of word replacement, thought that the situation was not as simple as this short description would suggest. He quoted a passage from Elbert 1953 (see chapter 2) as representing "the final formulation of a scholarly myth."

their languages. But not until the early eighteenth century did scholars from the outside begin to piece together a larger picture: a family that included languages from Madagascar, Formosa, New Zealand, Easter Island, Hawaiʻi, and many other places—a total of some 900–1,200 languages (estimates disagree).[4]

THE MALAYO-POLYNESIAN LANGUAGE FAMILY: AN IDEA IS BORN

Europeans first became aware of Polynesian languages through their quest for spices—those exotic seasonings that were used to heal the body and the spirit and to enhance the flavor of food, as well as to help preserve it. So highly valued were these condiments that even the words "spice" and "salt" became metaphors for things that added zest to life.

Once trading routes were established in northern and western Europe, salt became more plentiful, for it was mined in several places in that general area (e.g., Salzburg, the Austrian city, means "salt fortification"). But more exotic spices from Southeast Asia, such as cloves, mace, nutmeg, and pepper, were strictly controlled by Venetian merchants, who bought them in Alexandria, sold them at inflated prices, and protected their monopoly with a powerful fleet of ships. It was to break this monopoly that, in the late fifteenth century, other Europeans began to build ships so that they could find an alternate route to the spice-producing countries.

These explorations were later called "voyages of discovery." But because their main purpose was to find and open new trade routes, any other types of discoveries were merely by-products.[5] Still, the voyages gave those merchants and seamen who were interested in the natural sciences a chance to observe and write about the islands, the people, and the languages they encountered in their travels through uncharted waters.

---

4. The simplest reason for the discrepancy is that it is difficult to draw a line between "dialect" and "language." See chapter 2.

5. In his *Exploration of the Pacific* (1966), J. C. Beaglehole named various motives for the voyages: curiosity, profit, trade, proselytizing. In other words, none was ever undertaken with just a single goal in mind. Even those prompted mainly by intellectual curiosity spread their attention across several fields. And, as Beaglehole added, the politician who held the purse strings could shift a largely intellectual focus to commerce and expansion of empire.

LE MAIRE AND SCHOUTEN

The first glimpse that Europe had of a Polynesian language was just this kind of by-product, one that grew out of a Dutch voyage,[6] begun in 1615, to find a passage to the "South Sea"—that is, a new route to the East Indies.[7] The commercial enterprise was a partnership between Willem C. Schouten, an experienced seaman already familiar with the East Indies, and Isaac Le Maire, a merchant from Amsterdam who wanted to see something of the outside world.

The company set out in two ships: the *Eendracht* ('Unity'), and the *Hoorne* (the name of the commune where Schouten was born). The first ship set sail on 25 May 1615, with the second following about a week later. Early in December of that year, on the Patagonian coast of South America, the *Hoorne* burned, and the combined crews were forced to continue their voyage in a single ship, the *Eendracht.*

But losing one of their ships was not the end of their troubles. When the company was further into its voyage, it was plagued by a problem just as serious: disease. Month after month of a diet deficient in vitamin C resulted in the crew's contracting scurvy, a disease characterized by increasing weakness, loose teeth and swollen gums, sore joints, and hemorrhaging.

In April 1616, the captain wrote, "The scurvey [*sic*] affected most of the crew," and on the ninth of that month, Schouten's brother died of the malady. The crew sighted fish, but couldn't catch any, and the occasional small island they were able to land on afforded little in the way of fresh water, meat, or vegetables. It was an urgent need for fresh provisions to help ward off scurvy that provided the Dutch seamen with their first and only close contact with Polynesians in May 1616. Because they hoped to barter goods for the supplies they needed, they spent some time with the people from two clusters of islands just north and northwest of Vavaʻu in the Tonga Group.

---

6. The account of this voyage is from Dalrymple 1771.

7. The purpose of this new route was to avoid restrictions of trade imposed by the Dutch East India Company (an example of a monopoly, mentioned above). Specifically, any other company was prohibited "from trading eastwards beyond the Cape of Good Hope, or westwards through the Straits of Magellan, in any countries within these limits" (Kerr 1814:162).

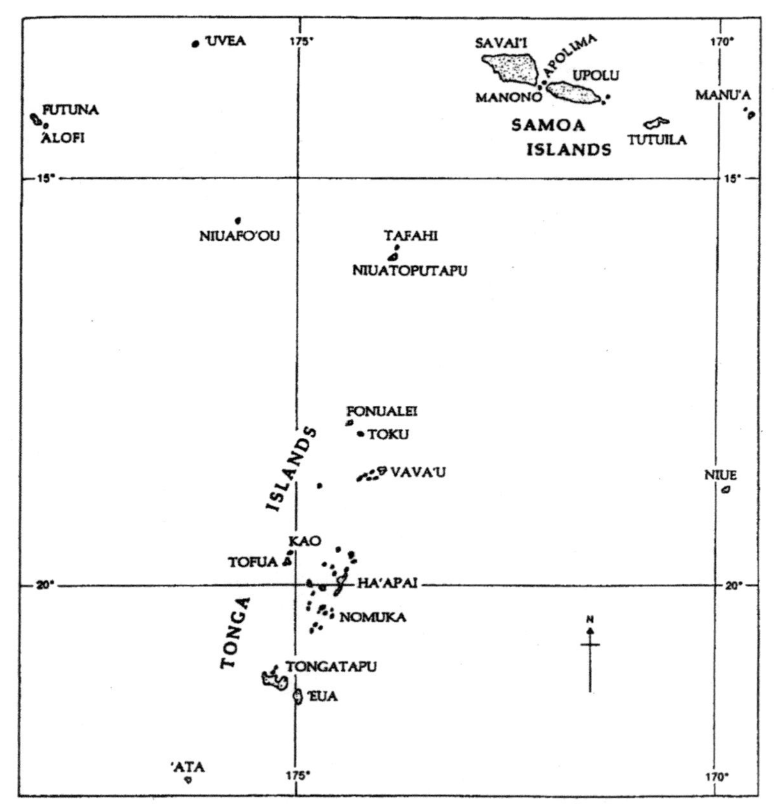

Figure 1.2. Map showing Tafahi, Niuatoputapu, and the Horne Islands (Futuna and 'Alofi) in relation to the Vava'u Group in Tonga

After both the seamen and the islanders made some hostile moves, they established a temporary truce, and, taking time out from more practical chores, Le Maire's son Iacob collected 32 words from Tafahi ("Cocos Island")[8] and 118 words from East Futuna ("Hoorn/Horne Islands," present-day Futuna and 'Alofi). Even though Tafahi is now a part of Tonga, and the inhabitants speak Tongan, the word list shows that their language was closer at that time to Samoan. To add to the confusion of labeling, the Dutch thought that they had rediscovered the Solomons, and for years, the word lists were said to represent "languages of the Salomonis islands." (Actually, the Solomon Islands are much farther to the northwest.)

---

8. Later known as Boscawen Island. Some sources (e.g., Biggs 1971:467; Rensch 2000:57) identify "Cocos" as Niuatoputapu, about six miles from Tafahi.

Figure 1.3. Outrigger approaching the ship, 9 May 1616

Figure 1.4. Cocos Island (Tafahi); Traitor's Island (Niuatoputapu) in distance

Figure 1.5. Horn Island (Futuna)

And what happened to this first sample of a Polynesian language? For a time, later explorers, such as Abel Tasman, who sailed in the Pacific from 1642 to 1644, tried to use the lists to help communicate with speakers of other Polynesian languages—first Māori and then Tongan—but with little success.

From a practical point of view, then, the lists were a dead end. It would have been unrealistic to expect the hastily written words from one Polynesian language, reinterpreted and undoubtedly mispronounced by outsiders, to be understood by speakers of a different language, even though the two were related. But eventually, the lists served another purpose—less practical, but important if we are to understand how the idea of a Polynesian language family was born.

MAKING THE CONNECTION

Even though Le Maire's and Schouten's word lists did not seem to help later explorers to communicate with the Pacific islanders, in 1706 the lists provided the key for a Dutch scholar to open a door not to communication, but to an exciting new idea. The scholar was Hadrian Reland, and his proposal was that the similarities between the language transcribed by Le Maire and the better-known Malayan languages farther to the west were too striking to be coincidental. In other words, languages as distant from each other as that of Tafahi and East Futuna and those in the Malay peninsula and Madagascar belonged to one huge language family, later known as MALAYO-POLYNESIAN, now classified as a branch of AUSTRONESIAN. Figure 1.6 shows how the language family is spread across the Pacific.

Later in the eighteenth century, Captain James Cook's explorations added more detail to Reland's rough sketch of a theory and confirmed it. Fortunately, Cook and his naturalists were interested enough in language to treat it as a matter worth recording. Even though Tahitian and Māori were the only Polynesian languages for which vocabularies were collected on the first voyage, on the second one the range was extended to include Easter Island, Marquesan, and Tongan (Beaglehole 1961). As an appendix to Cook's account (1777, 2, fronting p. 364), William Anderson and Johann Reinhold Forster compared some forty words from these five languages, along with three others from outside Polynesia, noting that the languages were "radically the same" in spite of the great distances among the island groups, especially that between Easter Island and New Zealand.

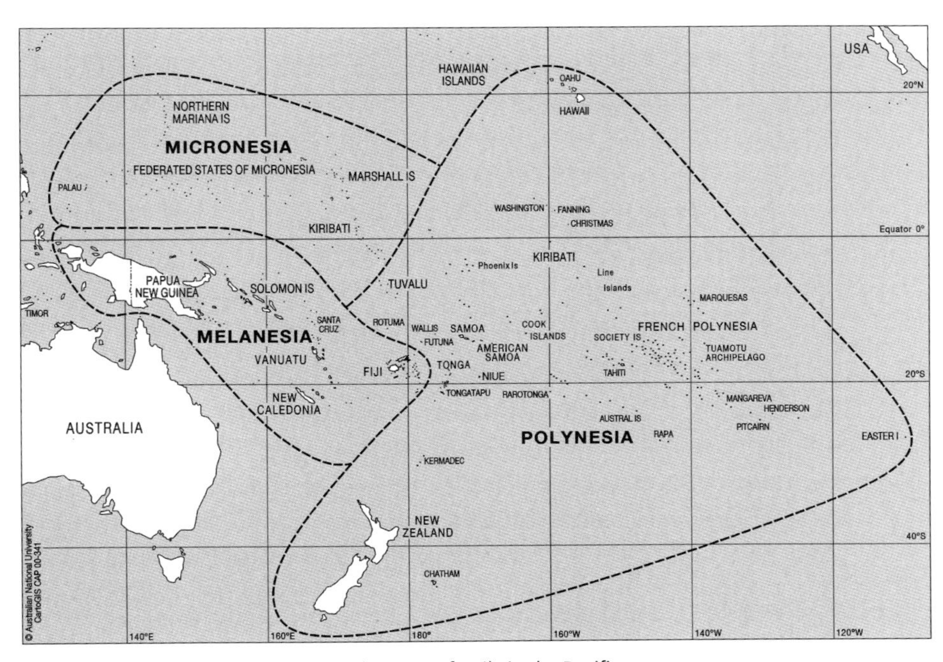

Figure 1.6. Extent of the Austronesian language family in the Pacific

TABLE 1.1. TRANSLATIONS OF NUMERALS

	Hoorn Is.	Malagasy	Tongan	Easter Is.	Hawaiian
1	Taci	Issee, *or* Essa	A Tahaw	Ko Tahai	kahi
2	Loua	Rooe	Looa	Rooa	lua
3	Tolou	Tulloo, *or* Tailloo	Toloo	Toroo	kolu
4	Fa	Efax, *or* Efar	T'Fa	Haa	hā
5	Lima	Lime, *or* Leman	Neema	Reema	lima
6	Houno	One, *or* Aine	Vano	Hono	ono
7	Fitou	Heitoo, *or* Petoo	Fidda	Hiddoo	hiku
8	Walou	Balloo	Varoo	Varoo	walu
9	Ywou	Seeva	Heeva	Heeva	iwa
10	Ongefoula	Foroo, *and* Fooloo	Ongofooroo	Ana Hooroo	anahulu

By this time, Cook's wider contact with Polynesians enabled his naturalists to expand their comparison. In one edition of his narrative, one can find in the appendix, "A comparative TABLE of NUMERALS, exhibiting the Affinity and Extent of Language, which is found to prevail in all the Islands of the Eastern Sea, and derived from that spoken on the Continent of Asia, in the Country of the Malayes."

From the thirty-nine languages on the original chart, I have chosen three—two Polynesian (Tongan and Easter Island) and one outside the Polynesian family (Malagasy). To these, I have added words from Hoorn Island (East Futuna) on the left and Hawaiian on the right, all for translations of the numerals from one to ten (table 1.1). (Although the Hawaiian words are written in the current orthography, the others are in their original spellings.)

If you use your imagination to make the leap from the earlier rough spellings to that of the current Hawaiian words, you can understand how important Reland's discovery was: that these languages, which were so far from each other in distance, were so close in form.

Reland did not give a name to the language family he proposed or to its separate parts. Instead, the credit for inventing the term "Polynesia" goes to Charles de Brosses. In his 1756 *Histoire des Navigations aux Terres Australes,* he divided the "Pacific or Southern Ocean" into three parts. The first two he named Australasia and Magellanic; as for the third, he wrote, "I shall include in the third everything contained in the vast Pacific Ocean, and I shall give this part the name *Polynesia* because of the many islands it encompasses (from 'polus' *multiplex* and 'nèsos' *insula*)" (de Brosses 1756, 1:13, 80; quoted in Tcherkézoff 2003:179).

Even the name he proposed, beyond its transparent Greek etymology, reflected underlying commercial motives. Tcherkézoff explained, quoting from *Histoire,* p. 4: "De Brosses wanted to give the impression with the word 'Polynesia' that, apart from the famous southern continent that would surely be found one day, the Pacific was likely to conceal 'many' lucrative spice islands: 'Apart from the Austral Lands [the proposed southern continent], it is impossible for there not to be, in the immense Pacific Ocean, between Japan and America, *a large number of islands rich in spiceries*'" [emphasis added] (Tcherkézoff 2003:179).

Thus we come full circle—back to commercial motives and the spice trade, not only for the "voyages of discovery" but for the very name of the area itself.

AT HOME IN FIJI: A "TRANSITION ZONE"?

As the previous section shows, research has pushed our knowledge of the origins of the Austronesians farther westward as we go back in time. Now we return to movement in the opposite direction in space and time as certain segments of the group move closer to becoming Polynesians—and eventually, Hawaiians.[9]

If we look at a map of the Pacific to find likely stopping points for eastbound pre-Polynesians—long after leaving Taiwan and mainland China and long before arriving at the Marquesas—it seems likely that eventually the travelers would have encountered the Fiji Islands and spent time there. Straddling the 180th meridian[10] and ranging nearly 4 degrees in both latitude and longitude, the group of over 300 islands would be hard to miss by what must have been a succession of sea voyages. The latest estimates of when Fiji was settled are around 3,100 BP (before present)[11] (Paul Geraghty, pers. comm., October 2014).

---

9. *At Home in Fiji* is the title of one of Constance Gordon-Cumming's best-known books. Cumming Street in central Suva is named after the prolific writer, who visited Fiji in 1875, when her uncle, Sir Arthur Gordon, became governor.

10. In 1879, Governor George William Des Voeux in effect bent the International Date Line around to the east of Fiji to encompass the whole of the group, because the 180th meridian bisected the island of Taveuni (Schütz 1978b:36–37).

11. Generally, the dates referred to have been calculated through the radiocarbon method.

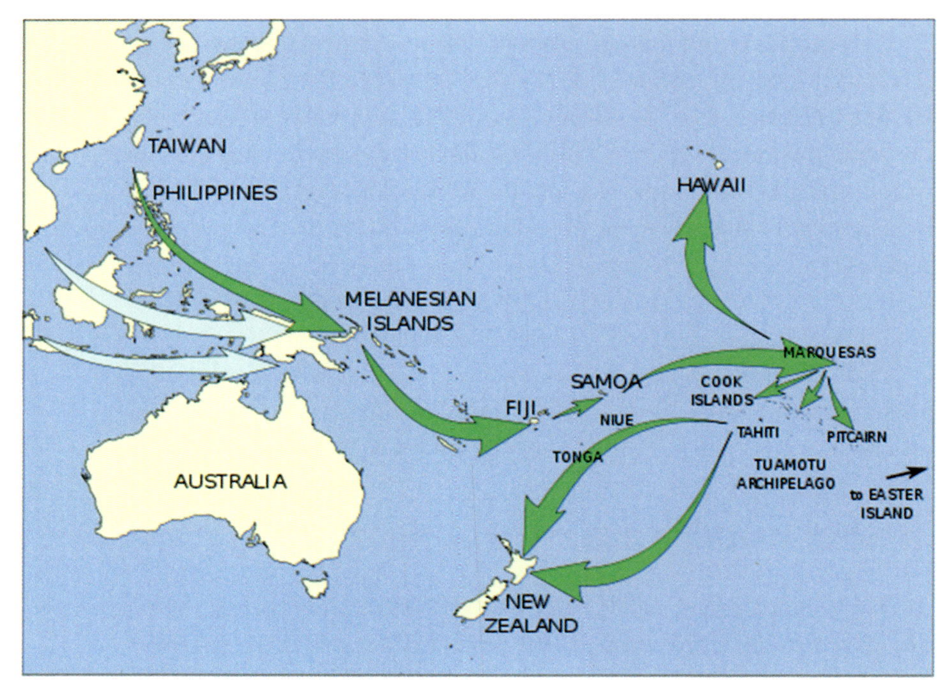

Figure 1.7. Polynesian migration in Oceania

The following quotations, from major studies of the origins of the Polynesians, also link Fiji with the people who became Polynesians:

> Horatio Hale[12] . . . advanced a well-reasoned and carefully documented theory based on a close comparison of Pacific languages. He believed that the Polynesian ancestors had originated in the west, in an ancestral homeland that he called Pulotu (after the Tongan and Fijian [Bulotu] name for the traditional homeland),[13] and had migrated from there to Fiji. From Fiji, these peoples had settled Samoa and Tonga, and then Tahiti, whence the initial colonization of Hawai'i occurred. As we shall see, Hale's theory was in some ways remarkably similar to the picture emerging from modern linguistic and archaeological research. (Kirch 1985:52)

---

12. Hale was a twenty-year-old Harvard graduate when he joined the United States Exploring Expedition (a.k.a. the Wilkes Expedition) and had written an Algonquin grammar at the age of seventeen. His natural talents, along with four years of invaluable experience hearing and describing languages as far-flung as Oceania, Australia, and Native American, resulted in his becoming an outstanding ethnographer, philologist, and linguist.

13. See Geraghty's article on "Pulotu" (1993).

> It should . . . be noted that Polynesian languages show no convincing evidence of substrata from South America or any other parts of the globe, and Polynesia was probably settled only once through the west, by people with a single language derived from Fiji. The present Polynesian languages have all descended from this single ancestor in ways which reflect the major trends of Polynesian culture history. (Bellwood [1978] 1987:30)

> It is possible, but not certain, that Lapita settlers were the first humans to reach Vanuatu (New Hebrides) and New Caledonia, and they were almost certainly the first to reach Fiji . . . The present Polynesians are the direct descendants of these intrepid Lapita voyagers. (Bellwood [1978] 1987:48)

Paul Geraghty (pers. comm., October 2014) added that the current Fijian population is "descended from the Lapita people . . . but with some admixture of later arrivals from Melanesia, especially in the west and centre."

By far the most extensive and rigorous examination of the development of Polynesian within Fiji is Geraghty's *The History of the Fijian Languages* (1983a).[14] Present-day Fiji is well known for its large number of dialects/languages. For example, on Viti Levu, which is only a few square miles smaller than the island of Hawai'i,[15] some forms of speech on the western side are not mutually intelligible with those on the eastern side.[16] Such a degree of diversity points to an early settlement, internal movements, external influences, and—on the basis of Geraghty's comparative research—a long residence by people on their way to becoming Polynesians.

By comparing both content and function forms from a number of *communalects*[17] with those in Polynesian languages, Geraghty (1983a) found that certain areas of Fiji share a closer relationship with Polynesian languages than do other areas. He proposed a dialect chain ancestral to TOKALAU FIJI (Lau and Eastern Vanua Levu) and Polynesian languages and concluded that

---

14. See also Geraghty 1993.

15. With its active volcanoes, Hawai'i does have the advantage of adding to its size.

16. The lowest cognate figures from a "basic" 200-word list are under 60 percent (Schütz 1962, 1972). Moreover, differences in the sound systems and grammars also reduce intelligibility among the so-called "dialects."

17. "A variety spoken by people who claim they use the same speech" (Geraghty 1983a:17–18).

Very little evidence is found for a single language ancestral to all the Fijian and Polynesian languages, but a good deal of evidence to suggest that languages ancestral to those of Eastern Fiji, especially Lau and Eastern Vanua Levu, underwent a period of common development with the language ancestral to the Polynesian languages (348) . . .

It was speakers of this dialect of Tokalau Fiji . . . who settled Polynesia. (381)

RECREATING THE PAST: VOYAGES OF REDISCOVERY

For years it was taken for granted that the principal (or perhaps only) direction for the settlement of the Pacific was west-to-east.[18] However, occasionally minority voices claimed a different origin. For the most part, these ideas were ignored or even ridiculed. But one voice, through a tour-de-force achievement, attracted more attention: Thor Heyerdahl's proposal that Polynesia was settled from South America.

Figure 1.8. *Kon-Tiki* on its voyage

18. The second part of the subheading above is a variation of the title of Ben Finney's excellent book, *Voyage of Rediscovery* (1994).

Heyerdahl's description of his voyage in the *Kon-Tiki*[19] to test his theory is one of the great sea adventure stories of the twentieth century. Scholars at the time, however, noted that although he proved that an east-to-west trip without modern equipment was *possible,* overwhelming evidence from several disciplines showed that it was almost certain that migration to Hawai'i and other Polynesian islands came from the opposite direction.

These findings do not mean that the voyagers from the west had no contact with South America. To paraphrase Robert A. Blust (pers. comm., 12 July 2010), it is hard to imagine that "people sailing into the unknown" would always land on one of the small and far-flung islands or groups of islands and not continue to an inevitable landfall on the continent. Blust continued: "The pre-Columbian presence of *Ipomoea batatas* [sweet potato] in the Pacific is a clear indication of contact with South America, and not of South American contact with the Pacific."

Still, the success of Heyerdahl's voyage encouraged some people to ignore the theory and focus on the vessel itself. For example, Sam Low wrote that as a young boy he had read *Kon-Tiki,* but he questioned why Heyerdahl had chosen "craft so primitive they could neither be steered nor navigated" (2013:xv). Years later, he found a sharp contrast to Heyerdahl's raft in the images of "sleek sailing vessels" in a copy of *Canoes of Oceania* (Hadden and Hornell 1936–38). Why, he wondered, would the ancestors of the Polynesians risk their lives on balsa rafts "when they possessed such graceful and advanced sailing vessels?"

In the introduction to his book, Low used an image from Hawaiian tradition that was reflected in the reality of voyaging:

> The title of this book, *Hawaiki Rising,* has *kaona* or multiple meanings.[20] It is the name of the mythic homeland of the Polynesian people. It refers to the nautical concept of raising land from the sea as when a mariner says, 'We raised O'ahu,' meaning he saw the Hawaiian island rise above the horizon as he approached it from the ocean . . . It also evokes the legend of the Hawaiian demigod Maui, who created the Hawaiian Islands by pulling them from the sea with his magical fish hook, *mānai-a-ka-lani.* And finally it celebrates the raising of the Hawaiian consciousness in their great seafaring heritage—and their pride in it—by voyaging aboard *Hōkūle'a* in the wake of their ancestors. (Low 2013:xi)

---

19. The expedition took place in 1947, the book appeared in 1948, and the film in 1951.

20. For a further discussion of *kaona* and its application to Hawaiian culture, see chapter 16.

Perhaps "raising of the Hawaiian consciousness" was particularly needed to dispute claims that the Polynesians' long-distance voyages had been accidental—an implied slur on "their great seafaring heritage." To counter this argument with a planned voyage, the efforts and skills of many people with different *kuleana* led to the founding of the Polynesian Voyaging Society in 1973, building the *Hōkūleʻa,* and sailing it to Tahiti in 1979. Among its many destinations in the next quarter century were islands as far removed as the other two corners of the Polynesian Triangle: Aotearoa (New Zealand) and Rapa Nui.[21]

Crucial to training navigators in an art lost over time and to honing their skills onboard the craft was Mau Piailug, from Micronesia, an area where navigating skills were still passed on from generation to generation.

Hōkūleʻa put into practice what had been theory and legend by adding a third dimension and reality to maps and myths. After the success of its first voyage, Finney (1994:75) wrote, "Hawaiians were proud of *Hōkūleʻa* as the beautiful sailing vessel that had demonstrated the maritime skills and accomplishments of their ancestors. Social historian George Kanahele [1982] even credits the canoe with helping to ignite a Hawaiian cultural renaissance that burst forth at that time."

In the following years, the *Hōkūleʻa* and crew expanded their domain beyond the Pacific. For example, in May 2014, she and the *Hikianalia* began a three-year sail around the globe, a journey planned to "cover 47,000 nautical miles with stops at 85 ports in 26 countries (Davis 2014)." One of those ports is illustrated in figure 1.9.

This renaissance, which is still flourishing, has extended far beyond sailing to include documenting and conserving the language (e.g., Pūnana Leo and other immersion programs); a growing number of *hālau hula,* culminating in the annual Merrie Monarch Festival and many other performances; the Kamehameha Song Contest and a growing catalog of recordings of Hawaiian music, new and old, by local performers; *hoe waʻa* (canoe paddling) clubs; relearning traditional Hawaiian games; lei making and other activities centered on native plants; and many more.

In summary, what we might call a ripple effect of *Hōkūleʻa* has been a resurgence of Hawaiian activities, scholarship, thought, and pride. This

21. As Steven Roger Fischer pointed out (pers. comm., 11 December 2014), the name "Aotearoa" first appeared in the nineteenth century, "purposely coined to counter the European name." "Rapa Nui" for Easter Island dates from the 1860s.

Figure 1.9. *Hōkūle'a* in New York City, 2016

rebirth—that is, the future of the Hawaiian language and culture—surfaces in Part V of this book: "Changes: Past, Present, and Future."

REACHING FARTHER WEST

As previous sections show, scholarship in various disciplines, supplemented by what we might call the "applied scholarship" of Polynesian voyaging, confirmed a western origin for the people who ultimately became the Polynesians.

But how far to the west? Several decades after the first voyage of *Hōkūle'a,* archaeologists' findings traced the origins of the Austronesians—the pre-Polynesians and their relatives—even farther to the west than had been imagined. The following quotation is from Bob Krauss 2006: "Bishop Museum chairman of anthropology Qianlong Jiao has returned from China with solid evidence that the first voyages of the ancestors of Polynesians were made between the South China Coast across open ocean to the Penghu Islands, 100 miles away in the Strait of Taiwan."

Krauss went on to describe Jiao's findings, based on the isotope analysis of stone tools excavated "at a site called Damaoshan on the small, offshore island of Dongshan on the South China Coast." The analysis showed that the Penghu Islands were the source of the stone. Jiao concluded, "We believe the Damaoshan people went to Penghu and brought back material . . . This is the first evidence of ocean voyaging in the Taiwan Strait. I consider this the first stage of Austronesian seafaring. The evidence indicates continuing contact across the Taiwan Strait, and helps us understand why the material cultures are so similar" (Krauss 2006).

In a later presentation (New Chair Professor of USTC 2013), Jiao added a date to the movements: "Jiao thought that Austronesian probably emerged from the southeast coast of China and Taiwan Strait around 6000 years ago, and then spread to the southwest and southeast regions."

*

This chapter has ranged over the separate but interlocking entities of space and time. The dimension of space is bounded by specific features of geography—the continents or larger island masses that border the Pacific Ocean. The major changes in these boundaries took place in prehistoric times. But although they may have remained relatively stable for the time period covered here, a different kind of change is now taking place more rapidly. Individual small islands are in danger of disappearing,[22] and other land masses within the area may shrink as shorelines recede, if sea levels continue to rise. Still, the continents at the periphery remain more stable. Moreover, new discoveries are moving the western boundary beyond these physical barriers—away from the Polynesian Triangle and farther into Asia.

As for the dimension of time, according to the findings discussed just above, it now spans six millennia, reaching back into a sparsely documented past. Ironically, even the passage of a few decades of time at the other end of the continuum—that is, the present and recent past—has significantly extended our knowledge of the prehistory of Polynesia. This development has grown out of new dating techniques and an expanded interest in the topic stemming from some disciplines that were unknown until recently.

The future of the Hawaiian language has also changed. In the 1960s it was thought that the language would live only through written records.

---

22. For example, note the headline "Remote Hawaiian island largely wiped out by hurricane," referring to East Island, in the northwestern part of the Hawaiian archipelago (Jacobs 2018).

As you proceed through this book more or less chronologically, you will reach times closer to the present and read of the efforts of many dedicated teachers and *kūpuna* to restore and perpetuate the language—a movement parallel in many ways to restoring and preserving the Hawaiians' navigating traditions.

VERBATIM

The following passage, from an edition of Le Maire's and Schouten's journals, describes the Europeans' first impressions of the Polynesians (from Dalrymple [1771] 1967:24–28):

> These people are very handsome men; limbs and body well proportioned, of large stature, quite naked, and without any arms [weapons], having only the obscene parts covered; their heads-of-hair various, some wearing their hair short, others very well curled, some long, others tied in tresses of various kinds. They were excellent swimmers. This island of Cocos is situated in 16°.10′S.
>
> 12th [May, 1616], after breakfast many canoes came aboard again with cocoa-nuts, bananas, yams, and some small hogs, some also with cocoa-nut shells full of fresh water: we exchanged this day full 1200 cocoa-nuts; we had sixty-five [85][23] persons, and each had twelve nuts.
>
> Every one of them wanted to be the first aboard, and swam under each other's canoe to come to our ship to exchange their goods. They brought yams and cocoa-nuts in their teeth, climbing so thick into the ship, that it was necessary to keep them off with sticks: their merchandize being made, they leaped from the ship and swam back to their canoes. They were much astonished at the size and strength of our ship; some went abaft near the rudder, quite under the ship, and knocked with stones on the bottom to try its strength. There came a canoe from the other island, which brought a young boar, which their king sent as a present: we wanted to honor the bearer with something, but he refused it, making signs that the king had forbid him to take any thing.
>
> After noon the king himself came with a large vessel under sail, of the same figure before described, like an ice sledge,[24] and full thirty-five canoes

23. The correction was made in a footnote.

24. That is, a double canoe. Paul Geraghty noted (pers. comm., October 2014) that Hawaiian *hōlua* 'sled' derives from an earlier form *faurua 'double canoe'.

who attended him. This king, or chief, was called by his people, Latou:[25] we received him with drums and trumpets, at which they were very much astonished, as things to them unheard and unknown. They shewed us the highest honour and amity that it was possible to do, bowing the head down, striking their fists on their head, and using many other strange ceremonies. Being a little distance from us, the king began to cry out, and to behave as if he had made a prayer, after this manner, and all those of his company likewise, without our knowing what that meant, only we judged that it was a congratulation of our happy arrival. Immediately after, the king sent us a matt, with three of his servants; to whom we gave in return an old hatchet, a few beads, and a few old nails, with a piece of cloth, which he received very politely, putting it three times upon his head and then bowing the head down in sign of respect and thankfulness. The people who came to the ship threw themselves on their knees and kissed our feet, and were astonished beyond measure at our ship. This king could not be distinguished from the other Indians, for he went also quite naked, except in being treated with respect, and that he was very well obeyed amongst them. We made signs that the Latou should come on board our ship; his son came aboard, whom we treated well, but he himself did not chuse, or at least would not come aboard; but they all made signs for us to go to the other island with our ship, and that he had there plenty of every thing. Amongst other things we exchanged with them three fish-gigs, which were made of reed, like those of Holland, only a little thicker, with barbs of pearl shells. The king's son returned on shore, and the canoe which carried him on the larboard side a large piece of wood, wherewith they kept it upright; on this wood was a fish-gig always ready for use.

SELECTIONS FROM "ESSAY AT A LEXICON OF THE POLYNESIAN LANGUAGE" (HALE 1846:291)

From the previous long quotation, we jump ahead well over two centuries. While serving as the Wilkes Expedition ethnographer and linguist, Horatio Hale spent four years collecting and analyzing data from Polynesian languages (among others)—not only from native speakers, but from manuscripts and books that linguists (mostly missionaries) on various

---

25. Cf. Samoan *lātū* 'person in charge of an undertaking' and Fijian *rātū* (a chiefly title).

islands had produced. In his first long and complex sentence below, one can see how his comments fit into the topics of this chapter.

Note that Hale referred to the "Polynesian language" in the singular. Later comments reflect reasonable assumptions about why the "dialects" have come to differ from one another. Finally, he touched on a matter that is still of concern to linguists who are trying to reconstruct the history of a language family: "imperfect" data because of the lack of comprehensive and accurate dictionaries.

> As in the preceding Grammar an attempt has been made to deduce from a comparison of the various dialects, the general principles of the primitive language to which they owe their origin, it has seemed proper to complete, as far as possible, the view of that language by bringing together, from the different vocabularies, those words which, from the fact of their existence in several dialects, may reasonably be supposed to have formed a part of the original Polynesian idiom. It is evident, from the nature of things, that such a collection cannot be complete, and that it must be liable to errors. Some words may be found in two or three dialects,—as, for example, in those of Eastern Polynesia,—which never formed a part of the primitive tongue, but have come into use since the separation of the Tahitians from the original stock. On the other hand, each dialect has, no doubt, preserved some words of the parent language, which have been lost in all the others, and which we have, therefore, no means of distinguishing from such as are the peculiar property of the dialect. Our materials, moreover, for such a work, though probably more ample than any that have been before collected, are yet very imperfect. When complete dictionaries of all the dialects shall have been formed, no doubt the number of words common to all, or to the greater number, will be materially increased. It is believed, however, that this Lexicon [i.e., Hale's] contains the mass of those vocables which constituted the primitive wealth of Polynesian speech. It comprises the terms for all the most common objects, qualities, and acts, and would probably furnish a sufficient vocabulary for the purposes of ordinary intercourse among a semi-barbarous[26] people.

---

26. This unfortunate term must be viewed in the context of the time in which it was written. It could have meant: "less sophisticated than advanced civilization" (*Webster's New Collegiate Dictionary*). John Charlot added (pers. comm., December 2015) that perhaps "barbarous" was qualified with "semi-" because by now, the Hawaiians had a writing system—one of the marks of "civilization."

CHAPTER 2
POLYNESIAN LANGUAGES

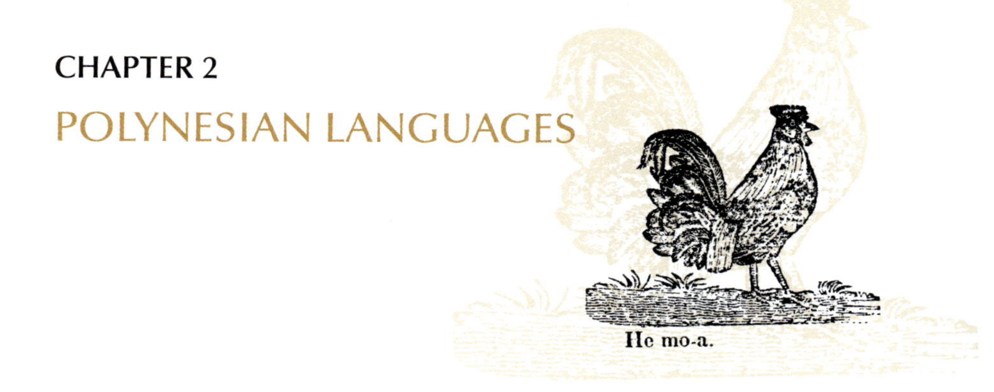

The previous chapter looked at the past of Polynesian languages. This one deals with their present. When one studies these languages as they are today, several questions come to mind immediately: (1) Where are the languages spoken? (2) How many are there? (3) What are their names?

1. *Where?* Figure 2.1 shows the geographical range of most of the languages in the family. Their speakers live in what has come to be known as the Polynesian Triangle, an area of over 2 million square miles (Biggs 1971:466).

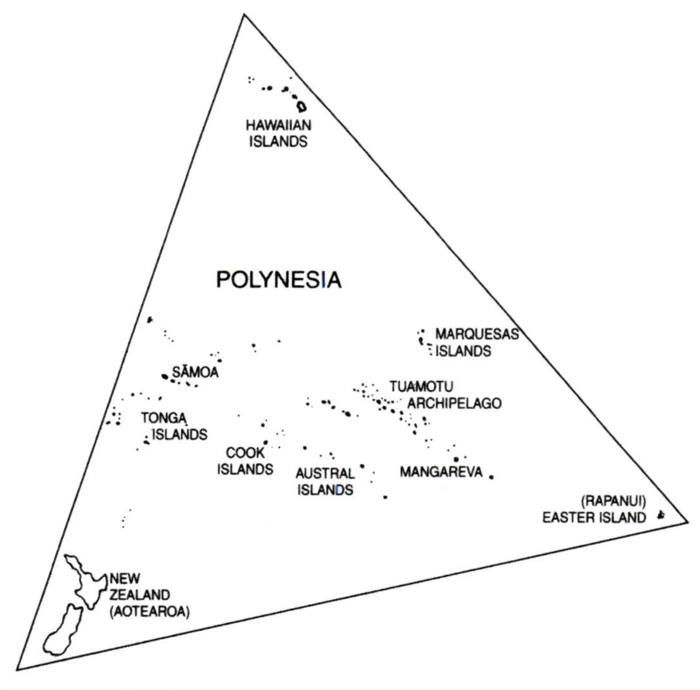

Figure 2.1. The Polynesian Triangle

2. *How many?* Even though this question seems simple, counting languages is actually complicated, as the next section shows. One scholar has suggested that there are some fifty-three speech communities, which can be grouped into twenty-six languages (Biggs 1971:487). But other counts differ.
3. *What are their names?* The list just below, which contains thirty-four language names, provides a possible answer to this question and a rough answer to the first one as well (adapted from Clark 1979:254). It is arranged geographically, thus ignoring the historical relationships among the languages, which will be discussed later.

West Polynesia

Tongan
Tūvalu
Niuean
East Uvea
Samoan
East Futuna
Tokelauan
Niuafoʻou

East Polynesia

Hawaiian
Penrhyn
Marquesan[1]
Rarotongan
Tahitian
Māori
Tuamotuan[2]
Mangareva
Austral[3]
Mōriori (extinct)
Rapanui (Easter Island)

Outliers

These Polynesian languages are spoken on islands outside the Polynesian Triangle, located in Micronesia and Melanesia.

Nukuoro
Kapingamarangi
Pileni
Tikopia
Nuguria
Anuta
Takuu
Mae
Nukumanu
Mele-Fila
Luangiua
West Uvea
Sikaiana
West Futuna
Rennelese

1. Marquesan consists of two distinct dialects, but in general the languages vary from valley to valley.

2. A reviewer pointed out that this name represents an area in which several different languages are spoken.

3. The conditions described in the note just above also apply to the Austral Islands.

Because it is hard to draw a line between the hazy concepts of *dialect* and *language,* different scholars have come up with different numbers and names of Polynesian languages. But, as mentioned above, most early observers spoke of a "Polynesian language" in the singular, not "languages" in the plural. Now I explore that idea further.

DIALECTS OR LANGUAGES?

On 3 July 1769, three months after Cook's *Endeavour* arrived, the ship left Tahiti, bound for New Zealand. Sailing with Cook and the crew, and at his own request, was Tupaia[4]—a Tahitian priest and adviser to the queen and also a skilled navigator with "encyclopaedic local knowledge." Cook wrote, "To have such a person on board, was certainly desirable for many reasons; by learning his language, and teaching him ours, we should be able to acquire a much better knowledge of the customs, policy, and religion of the people than our short stay among them could give us" (Hawkesworth 1773, 2:180). (Page numbers that follow in parentheses are from Hawkesworth).

On their way southwestward, Tupaia explained in detail what he knew of the islands they sighted. In fact, his local knowledge enabled the party to draw a rough map of the area.[5] Eventually, in early October, they reached New Zealand.

Once they were there, the crew's first encounter with the Māori was not a friendly one. But even in the midst of the hostilities, Tupaia tried to communicate with the Māori: "Tupia called to them in the language of Otaheite; but they answered only by flourishing their weapons, and making signs to us to depart" (286).

Later, they found that the Māori could apparently understand what Tupaia said: "Tupia was again directed to speak to them, and it was with great pleasure that we perceived he was perfectly understood, he and the natives speaking only different dialects of the same language. He told them that we wanted provision and water, and would give them iron in exchange, the properties of which he explained as well as he was able" (287).

---

4. Some sources show *Tupaiʻa.* Keao NeSmith (pers. comm., 9 December 2014) reported that the current pronunciation in Tahiti is without the glottal stop.

5. If you google "Tupaia Cook map," you can see images of his map, which are too detailed to display clearly in this book. See also Di Piazza and Pearthree 2007.

Here we see the birth of the idea that Polynesians spoke not many related languages but just *one* language, apparently differing little from dialect to dialect. As for how accurate the account is, we have only the Europeans' opinion that there was "perfect" understanding between the speaker of Tahitian and the Māori.[6] Although this statement may be exaggerated, obviously some communication did take place, for the members of the expedition were able to trade goods for fresh supplies.

Nearly nine years later, Cook's crew (this time on their third voyage) had the same pleasant surprise when they discovered that the Hawaiians at Waimea, Kaua'i, could understand Tahitian, which a number of the crew were familiar with. James King wrote, "What more than all surprisd [*sic*] us, was, our catching the Sound of Otaheite words in their speech, & on asking them for hogs, bread-fruit, yams, in that Dialect, we found we were understood" (Beaglehole 1967:264n.).

David Samwell stated the idea even more strongly, writing that the language was "the same as that of Otaheite."[7]

But was it really "the same?" In spite of the claims of perfect understanding, it now seems clear that it was something less than that—perhaps a communication of simple ideas, enhanced by gestures.

Even scholars who had a longer acquaintance with Polynesia often used the word 'language' in the singular rather than the plural. The Reverend John Davies, the London Missionary Society linguistic pioneer who fashioned an alphabet, a grammar, and a dictionary for Tahitian, was certainly of this one-language opinion. He opened his grammar with this statement: "The inhabitants of most of the numerous Islands of the South Sea, called by modern Geographers by the general name of *Polynesia,* have one common Language, which for that reason may be called the *Polynesian*" (1823:4–5).

When the topic of language versus dialect comes up today, scholars point out that in the two hundred years that have passed since these observations were made, the languages could have changed enough to make it more difficult for a speaker of one Polynesian language to understand

---

6. The story gains more credibility in light of recent statements about the closeness of Māori and Tahitian: "The Maori language of New Zealand is most closely related to Tahitian, reflecting the settlement of New Zealand from the Society Islands" (Kirch 1985:62).

7. The idea expressed in the previous note applies here as well—but for the relationship between Hawaiian and Tahitian.

a speaker of another. For example, Peter Buck (Te Rangi Hiroa) wrote, "The person who says that he can immediately understand all that is said in one Polynesian group because he knows the language of another group lays claim to extraordinary insight. Maori is my mother tongue but I freely admit that I could never understand all that I heard in the Polynesian islands which I visited for the first time" (1938:198). How much more might Polynesian languages have drifted apart in the years that have passed since Buck made this observation?

This view is now the common one: that although the languages were once more similar, they have changed enough through time so that we have moved away from the label of *dialects* toward that of *languages.* Unfortunately, some popular writers seem unaware of the current views, still referring to Hawaiian as a dialect of the Polynesian language (e.g., Helbig 1970).

Still, we know that Hawaiian is more similar to some of these former "dialects" than to others. How can we be more specific about these similarities and differences?

WHICH LANGUAGES ARE HAWAIIAN'S CLOSEST RELATIVES?

One way to approach this topic would be to summarize the latest findings by (1) showing a family tree and (2) giving the current estimates of dates of settlement. However, rather than jumping immediately to the answers, perhaps we can put them in perspective by showing the historical and methodological backgrounds that led to the current conclusions.

First we must revise one of the earliest divisions—that based on geography.

East vs. West?

The list of Polynesian languages shown earlier was accompanied by the caveat that this arrangement was only geographical. But until the mid-twentieth century, it was thought that geography was a major factor in classifying the languages. It seemed logical to propose two major divisions: Nuclear Polynesian—that is, languages within the Polynesian Triangle (see figure 2.1) and Outliers—that is, those languages outside that area. (For the most part, the major features of this division still hold.) Within Nuclear Polynesian, geography also played the principal role. Western Polynesian consisted of Tongan and Samoan; the remainder of the languages within the triangular area were Eastern Polynesian. In 1966, Andrew Pawley, basing his argument on certain grammatical innovations, revised this classification. The Polynesian family tree he constructed (shown in a later section) shows the result of his rearrangement.

METHODS FOR DETERMINING POLYNESIAN RELATIONSHIPS

At first, nineteenth-century grammarians and Bible translators who had some experience with Hawaiian and other Polynesian languages made mainly impressionistic comments about the relationships among them. But the twentieth century gave rise to more formal ways to compare languages, including a systematic treatment of vocabulary, morphology, and grammar. Finally, in the present century we are beginning to see the results of a combination of such areas as linguistics, anthropology, traditional archaeological procedures, and newer archaeological methods.

1. General Impressions

Even while some observers were still debating the dialect-or-language question, others noticed that not all the languages/dialects were equally different from each other. Davies, most familiar with Tahitian, wrote of such unequal relationships (1839). He estimated that among the languages he had studied, Hawaiian, Marquesan, and Māori were closest to each other, with Tahitian coming next. Tahitian differed from the others, he said, by "abridging the words, and dropping a great number of consonants, and in discarding entirely the nasal *ng*, the *g* and *k*."[8] And Tongan differed from them all; in addition to a different sound system (as shown by its larger alphabet), Davies suggested that it might have borrowed many

8. For his evidence, Davies was using methods far ahead of his time. For example (1839:4), he discussed the consonant relationships among several Polynesian languages, as well as Fijian. That is, he didn't merely list similar words but noted that there were relationships between sounds as well, such as *t* and *k*, *h* and *f*, *n* and *ng*, and *l* and *r*.

words from Fijian—a reasonable possibility, considering the long history of contact between the two neighboring island groups.[9]

A comparative linguist might transform Davies's statement into the tree diagram shown in figure 2.2.

We must remember that Davies, even though he recognized that certain consonants changed in a regular way from language to language, was not measuring the differences and similarities in a systematic way but was relying only on his impressions. (However, it is not fair to fault him for his methodology, for the field of comparative linguistics was then in its infancy.)

In 1836, Lorrin Andrews, missionary to Hawai'i, relied just as much on his impressions when he described how certain Polynesian languages were similar to or different from each other: "And a singular circumstance is, that the people at the extreme parts of Polynesia speak dialects of the general language the most resembling each other. It has been said that the dialects of the New Zealanders and the Hawaiians resemble each other more nearly than any of the other dialects" (1836b:12–13).

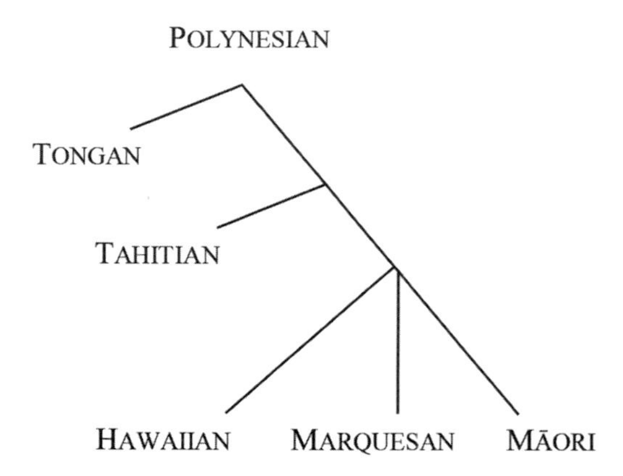

Figure 2.2. Davies's classification of Polynesian

9. There was a reason that Davies chose Fijian as a possible source for borrowings into Tahitian. Temporarily banished from Tahiti in 1809, Davies and his colleagues were bound for Canton via Fiji, but damage to their ship forced them to stay in Fiji for about seven weeks. During this time, Davies—ever the philologist—collected a sample of the language and made observations about its speakers. In 1825, back in Tahiti, he worked with a visiting Fijian speaker and produced an eight-page grammatical sketch of the language (Schütz 1985:8–9, 11–12).

All these remarks lead to the same question: How can we go beyond our impressions to measure the ways in which the languages are the same, the ways in which they differ, and the degree of their relationship with each other? Perhaps one way would be to find out how well speakers of different Polynesian languages can communicate with each other.

2. Mutual Intelligibility

It is not easy to measure how well two people understand each other, for there are many variables involved. The only such study for Polynesian languages was conducted in 1962 by Jack H. Ward, who devised a test to find how well a speaker of one Polynesian language/dialect could understand basic words and short utterances in another. For Hawaiian, some of the scores are as follows (p. 62):[10]

Hawaiian-Marquesan:	41.2%
Hawaiian-Tahitian:	37.5%
Hawaiian-Samoan:	25.5%
Hawaiian-Tongan:	6.4%

Using these figures alone, we might suggest that Hawaiian is closest to Marquesan, but nearly as close to Tahitian, quite a bit further away from Samoan, and not very similar at all to Tongan. It is interesting to see that in a way, these figures confirm some of Davies's impressions of nearly a century and a half earlier (figure 2.2).

Another way to gauge how similar or dissimilar Polynesian languages are is to compare common words in each.

3. Systematic Comparison of Features: Shared Vocabulary

Although comparative linguistics now uses several types of data, as an example of this methodology I will use the most common type: comparing words. The underlying principle here, in its simplest form, is that we count *cognates:* words shared by the two languages that have come from a common source (e.g., Hawaiian *maka* and Māori *mata* 'eye'). This

10. Figures for Māori were not included.

method is based on the assumption that the higher the number of cognates, the more closely related the languages.

In the mid-nineteenth century, the French explorer J. S. C. Dumont d'Urville (1834) used a form of this procedure for Hawaiian and several other Polynesian languages (Hymes 1983:83–93). He proposed a scale of six levels to measure the relationship between two words with the same meaning. Using Ø for the lowest degree (that is, totally different words) and 1 for the highest (that is, words that were identical or nearly so), he arrived at a figure of—for example—0.74 for the relationship between Hawaiian and Tahitian.[11]

Even though Dumont's method is similar to current ones, it differs in one important way. For example, note the following cognates in Hawaiian and Māori (see the longer list at the end of chapter 3):

Hawaiian	Māori	
manu	*manu*	bird
hale	*whare*	house
hala	*whara*	pandanus

Using Dumont's method, we would rank the pair of words for 'bird' at the highest level, because they look identical. The other pairs would be ranked lower, for their consonants are different. However, now we know that *h–wh* and *l–r* are regular correspondences between the two languages. That is, many cognates show these relationships. Thus the words for 'house' and 'pandanus' (above) are just as valid as proof of the closeness between the two languages as the words for 'bird'.[12]

A century later, Samuel H. Elbert conducted a rigorous and extensive test among twenty Polynesian languages (Elbert 1953). Although he compared sound systems and word building as well, he arrived at the following figures for the percentage of cognates that Hawaiian shares with the other languages:

11. Hymes found a minor error in the calculations and corrected the figure to .76.

12. Of course, we must know what sounds the letters represent. For example, the *wh* spelling in Māori might remind readers of that combination in English, the actual pronunciation of which can be either [w] or [hw], depending on the dialect of the speaker. It is likely that the original Māori pronunciation was neither of these, but an *f*-like sound made with both lips [ɸ].

Māori	71	Futuna	58	Sikaiana	60	Rapanui	64
Marquesan	70	Uvea	55	Fila	55	Mangareva	69
Samoan	59	Niue	49	Ongtong Java	56	Rarotonga	79
Tahitian	76	Tikopia	67	Nukuoro	49	Tuamotu	77
Tongan	49	Tūvalu	68	Kapingamarangi	49		

If you examine the percentages in the first column, you can see that in general, neither Davies's early impressions nor Dumont's measurements were very far off the mark.

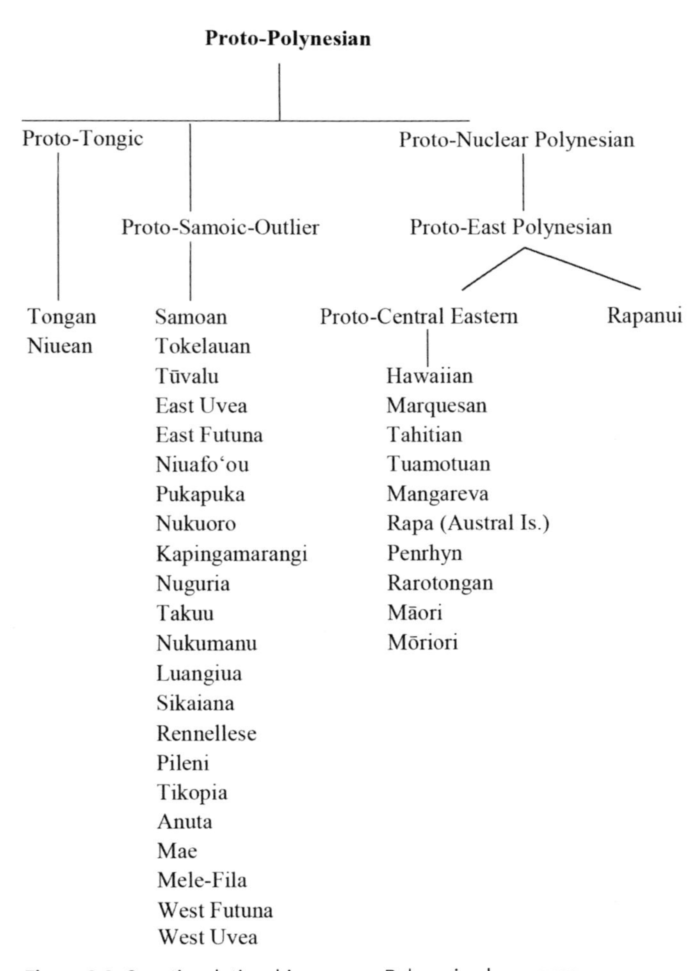

Figure 2.3. Genetic relationships among Polynesian languages

Working with Elbert's and other studies, later scholars have attempted to construct a family tree grouping for the languages. One example is shown in figure 2.3 (Clark 1979:258, based on Pawley 1966). (In this figure, the prefix PROTO- refers to an earlier form of the language that has been reconstructed from present-day evidence.)

To summarize the relationships shown in figure 2.3, working from the bottom up (from the present to the past):

1. Hawaiian belongs to an Eastern branch of the Polynesian family, which is divided into two groups: Rapanui forms one by itself, and Hawaiian, Tahitian, Marquesan, Māori, and six others form the other.
2. One of the other major Polynesian languages,[13] Samoan, is separated from Hawaiian by a longer time span, forming a group together with both close relatives and a number of Polynesian languages spoken in the outlier islands.
3. The last of the major Polynesian languages, Tongan, is separated from nearly all its Polynesian relatives by an even greater time span, making up (along with Niuean) its own branch of the family tree.

In the years since this family tree was presented, various scholars have added their own contributions, usually adding finer detail to one section of the tree or changing some feature of the arrangement.

One such refinement is that of William H. Wilson (1985). In his study he challenged one of the larger subgroups, Samoic-Outlier, proposing instead a relationship between the North Central Outliers and Eastern Polynesian (p. 87). However, from our Hawaiian-centered position here, I will look at only the later and more detailed groupings, shown in figure 2.4.

If you compare this classification with that in figure 2.4, you can see that in the earlier one, Hawaiian appears in a list with nine other languages, and the subtler relationships have not yet been established. In figure 2.4, however, the longer list has been split in two, showing Hawaiian, along with two others, in a small group. Thus, Hawaiian's closest relatives are Marquesan and Mangarevan. Both classifications show Rapanui (Easter Island) out on a limb, as it were, by itself.

A further refinement was proposed by Jeff Marck (1999, 2000). Although the relationships among some other languages were changed

13. That is, in terms of the number of speakers.

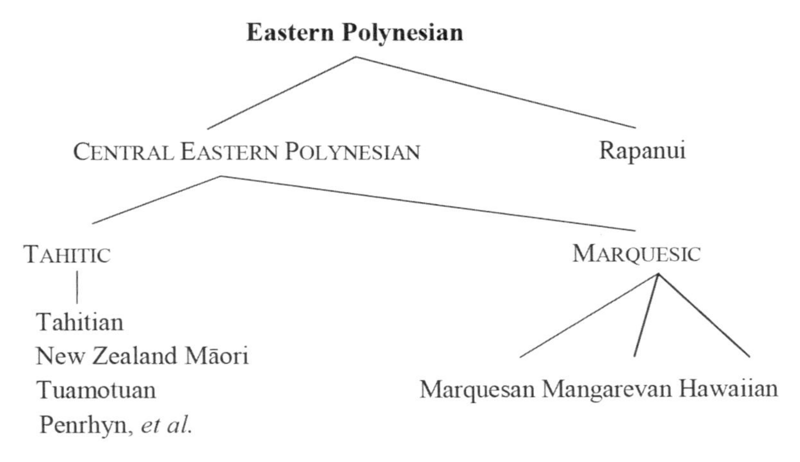

Figure 2.4. Eastern Polynesian relationships

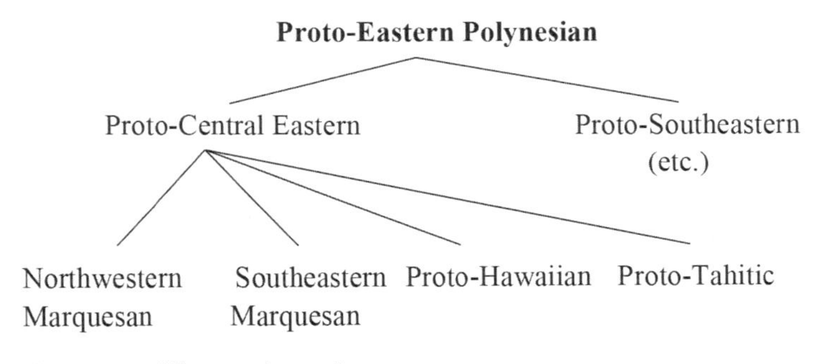

Figure 2.5. A different subgrouping

slightly, Hawaiian was still placed in a group with Marquesan and Mangarevan, with those two languages closer to each other than to Hawaiian.

Steven Roger Fischer (2001:122) argued for a different grouping, dividing Proto-Eastern Polynesian into two subgroups: Proto-Central Eastern and Proto-Southeastern. From our Hawaiian-centered viewpoint, it is the first group that is significant. This part of the family tree is illustrated in figure 2.5.

Mary Walworth (2014:269–71) came to a different conclusion. Citing interdisciplinary research combining the findings of "archaeology, linguistics, and other historical sciences," she found reasons to eliminate the level of Tahitic and Marquesic subgroups from the linguistic tree (see figure 2.5), citing the following ones: "The Tahitic and Marquesic subgroups were based on weak evidence in an attempt to accommodate a long-standing model of settlement derived from both linguistics and archaeology, which involved substantial pauses of proto-language communities and multiple centers of dispersal." Figure 2.6 shows the resultant tree, "new" compared with Marck's work but reverting to the earlier classification shown in figure 2.5.

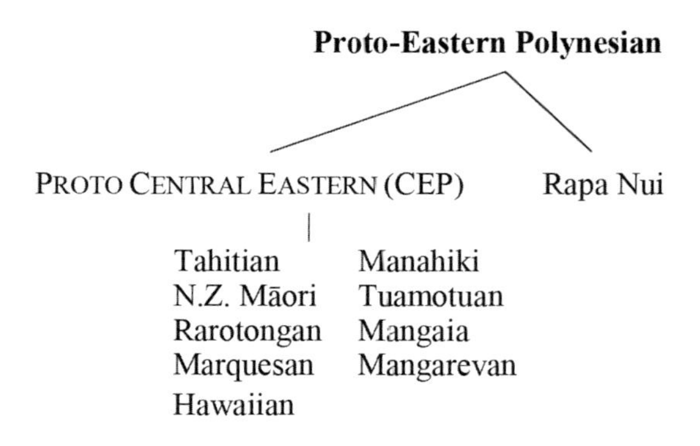

Figure 2.6. Proposed tree for Eastern Polynesian languages

If you compare this structure with that in figure 2.5, you can see that the subgroups of Tahitic and Marquesic have been eliminated. The resultant tree, Walworth wrote,

> independently suggests that the majority of the Eastern Polynesian languages were developed in contact situations with Rapa Nui developing in isolation . . .
>
> This new linguistic tree, while it does not allow for internal grouping of CEP [Central Eastern Polynesian] languages, does mirror the chronology, colonization, and patterns of exchange outlined in the east Polynesian archaeological evidence. Where the previous approaches to Polynesian subgrouping may have provided neat boxes into which to put the Eastern Polynesian languages, in light of the new archaeological evidence the older account was found to be neither convincing nor realistic.

The study just described noted "the value of interdisciplinary cooperation for archaeology, linguistics, and other historical sciences." The following section sketches a range of studies, varying in methodology but all aimed at reconstructing the history of Polynesian languages and their interrelationships.

4. Combination of Fields: Linguistics, Anthropology, Traditional Archaeology, Newer Archaeological Methods

This chapter began by asking three major questions about Polynesian language: Where? How Many? and What? Now we add a fourth: When? In other words, when did the important migrations take place that resulted in forming separate languages—in particular, Hawaiian?

TIME OF SEPARATION

The trees represented in figures 2.3, 2.4, 2.5, and 2.6 deal with time not in an absolute but in a relative sense. That is, it is clear only that the higher splits on the trees took place earlier than the lower ones. Thus, studying language relationships in this way is similar to examining objects from two different levels in an archaeological dig: we assume that objects found at the lower level are older than those at the higher level, but it is not clear how much time separates the two and even less clear just when the objects were made.

Just as archaeology developed some ways to deal with absolute, not just relative, time (such as carbon-14 dating), so did linguistics. In brief, for certain language families whose long written tradition offered a way to check the findings, it was found that after a language splits into two separate languages without contact, common words (which are most resistant to change) do change at a roughly fixed rate (for that language family). It was thought that applying this procedure to languages without a written history would show roughly when one language separated into two.

Based on the findings of this technique, which is called *glottochronology,* it was estimated that Hawai'i may have been settled sometime from AD 930 to 1300.[14] However, language change is too variable for the technique to be considered seriously on its own. For example, the Tahitian practice of *pi'i,* mentioned in chapter 1, changed the vocabulary faster than might have happened otherwise.

Although the varying rates of change among different language families have generally discredited glottochronology as a way to obtain exact dates, still, those derived from the procedure can be combined with others, such as those established by genealogies (AD 1050) or carbon-14 dating (AD 818–1190). Thus, ideally, it provides some tentative dates that need

---

14. Elbert 1953:168.

to be verified—or refuted—by other methods of dating, especially techniques used by archaeologists and other scientists and the tradition of oral genealogies common throughout Polynesia (e.g., Pawley and Green 1971).

Carbon-14 dates from some studies also fall in this range. For example, Pawley and Green (1973:20), based on archaeological evidence presented by Patrick V. Kirch, deduced that Hawaiʻi was settled in the ninth century AD. However, later studies pushed that date back considerably. In 1985, Kirch wrote, "It is probable that the first settlement of Hawaiʻi occurred sometime *before* the fourth to fifth century. At present, it is difficult on strictly archaeological grounds to be more precise as to the date of initial colonization of the Hawaiian Islands. In my own view, given that a number of permanent settlements were distributed throughout all the main islands by the sixth century, it is likely that the first colonization occurred some two or three centuries earlier, perhaps by A.D. 300" (68). (Kirch noted that not all his colleagues agreed with him.)

In 1987, Bellwood wrote, "We also know that the Hawaiian Islands and Easter Island were settled by at least AD 400, both perhaps from the Marquesas" (62).

THE MARQUESAN CONNECTION

As the quotation above suggests, although the immediate source of the migrations to Hawaiʻi was long thought to be Tahiti, linguistic and archaeological research from the mid-1950s onward pointed instead to the Marquesas, with settlement from Tahiti coming later.

Note the use of the plural here with respect to migrations, representing one settlement scenario out of several possibilities. In a section titled "Was Hawaiʻi colonized more than once?" Kirch wrote, "We have now reviewed a wealth of evidence from the perspectives of archaeology, linguistics, physical anthropology, and ethnobotany, all mutually corroborative in pointing to the Marquesas Islands as the immediate homeland of the first Polynesians to settle Hawaiʻi. This does not, however, preclude the possibility of more than one settlement voyage, whether also from the Marquesas, or from some other East Polynesian archipelago, such as the Society Islands" (1985:65–66).[15]

---

15. Sometimes referred to by the name of its largest island, Tahiti.

Bellwood wrote, "It was noted that the islands were settled, possibly from the Marquesas, about AD 300. There is traditional and some archaeological evidence to suggest later influence from the Society Islands, but the significance of this is at present disputed" ([1978] 1987:98).

MORE RECENT RESEARCH: MOVING THE DATES CLOSER TO THE PRESENT

Beginning in 2011, several reports in the media have focused on the research of archaeologist Terry Hunt. It was summarized as follows:

> Recent studies say the people who eventually became known as Polynesians migrated east to Samoa and Tonga in 800 B.C.,[16] then began moving eastward again in A.D. 1100, settling Tahiti and moving into the remaining islands of the eastern Pacific between A.D. 1200 and 1300, including the Marquesas, New Zealand, Rapa Nui and the Hawaiian Islands.
>
> Hunt said according to newly reported radio carbon dating, Polynesians from the Society Islands settled on Rapa Nui and the Hawaiian Islands during the same period, explaining the reason for their similar oral history traditions and languages. (Kubota 2011)

A similar chronology was proposed by Kirch: "Until recently, orthodox opinion put initial Polynesian discovery of Hawaiʻi between ca. AD 300–750. In the past two decades, significant advances in radiocarbon dating and the targeted redating of key Eastern Polynesian and Hawaiian sites have strongly supported a "short chronology" model of Eastern Polynesian settlement. It is suggested here that initial Polynesian discovery and colonization of the Hawaiian Islands occurred between approximately AD 1000 and 1200" (2011:3).

Recent studies that redate and reanalyze archaeological sites have confirmed these results: "This work has led to a revised understanding of the colonization period for Hawaiʻi, with an emerging consensus that the archipelago was settled after AD 800–1000" (Kahn et al. 2014:67).

These possible later settlement dates give us a different view of the "pleasant surprise" that confronted Cook's crew when they found that their knowledge of Tahitian enabled them to communicate with the

---

16. As discussed earlier, because of Fiji's location and size, it is inevitable that the (future) Polynesians spent time there, with linguistic influence in both directions.

Hawaiians. With the advantage of hindsight, we now see that there are two reasons that Anderson and others could easily understand the Hawaiians at Waimea: (1) later settlement of Hawaiʻi and/or (2) continued contact between the Hawaiians and their near relatives to the south. If Kirch's earlier figures (AD 300–400) were accurate and there was no or little contact between Hawaiʻi and Tahiti, we might expect the languages to have drifted much further apart.[17]

Still, not every scholar has accepted this revision of settlement dates. For example, Steven Roger Fischer (pers. comm., 11 December 2014) disagreed with Hunt's late archaeological dates for Eastern Polynesia. Among other reasons, he maintained that 600 years is insufficient time to render the Rapanui language unintelligible to a Mangarevan speaker. Instead, he suggested that the later figures would show that Mangarevan and Rapanui were dialects of the same language. "That they are, in fact, quite separate languages shows that they parted company around AD 600–700."

HOW MANY TIMES WAS HAWAIʻI SETTLED?

Strengthened in recent years by the successful voyages of the *Hōkūleʻa* and the *Hawaiʻiloa,* current opinions on the settlement of Hawaiʻi dismiss the idea that Hawaiʻi was reached on just one occasion and that the Hawaiians remained isolated from other Polynesians.

As for technological advances, the most promising and exciting of these is genetic anthropology, based on the comparison of the DNA[18] makeup of the inhabitants of different Pacific island groups. One finding from such studies suggests that after reaching their island destinations, Polynesians may have continued their voyages to the east, reaching the coast of South America, and then heading back west again. As geneticist Rebecca Cann stated it, "By doing a very fine analysis of the DNA, we've seen that there is in fact one very common cosmopolitan lineage that's spread throughout the Pacific, [which] could only have happened if people were in constant physical contact. The idea that these islands were so isolated is really a foreign invention. The Polynesians used the ocean as a superhighway" (Goodheart 1996:41).

---

17. Suggested by Steven Egesdal, pers. comm., August 2011.

18. Deoxyribonucleic acid.

*

Trying to form a picture of events that took place long ago produces a paradox. While the passage of time sees the voyages and settlements slip further and further away, advanced technologies and ideas bring these events into sharper focus than was possible a century—or even a decade—ago.

One reason is that we now know more about many of the languages than we did several decades ago. At that time, the only materials available for some of the languages were word lists and perhaps a Bible translation. But now that linguists have more accurate information about more features of more languages, they can look beyond vocabulary and sound systems. Thus, increased information has made it possible to change some of the finer details of the classification.

Moreover, studies based on DNA analysis make an interesting addition to the controversy stirred up by Thor Heyerdahl's theory, mentioned earlier. Although the principal settlement was mainly west to east, now we can be reasonably sure that there were occasional voyages in the other direction.

In summary, scholars have compared Polynesian languages, pair by pair, to answer the following questions: (1) How much do speakers of the two languages understand each other? (2) How many basic words do the two languages share? (Here, "basic" refers to those words that are in everyday use and thus least likely to change over time.) This information helps us determine (3) when the languages "split" (in other words, when the speakers of one lost contact with those of the other).

VERBATIM

John Davies, pioneer missionary-linguist in Tahiti, ended up spending over fifty years there. In addition to his work in teaching, translation, and civil administration, he found time to engage in his avocation of comparative linguistics. The following passages are from "The Polynesian Nation," an article he wrote for the *Hawaiian Spectator* in 1839.

> In regard to the aboriginal Polynesians less has been written, yet various opinions have been held, and by some, they also have been supposed "indigenous," and not to be connected with the rest of the human race. Others have supposed "the existence of a vast Continent, which had been submerged in some

tremendous convulsion of nature, and of which the multitude of the isles of the vast Pacific are merely the summits of the sunken mountains." But there is neither a tradition, nor a shadow of probability of such an event having happened. Others, upon more probable and rational ground, have endeavored to trace by means of the affinity of language and customs, the connexion of the Aborigines of the Southern Islands with one or other of the neighboring Continents. It was observed by the great Lexicographer Dr. Johnson,[19] "That similitude and derivation of languages afford the most indubitable proof of the traduction of nations, and the genealogy of mankind: they add physical certainty to historical evidences of ancient emigrations, and of the revolutions of ages which have left no written memorials behind them."

... [I]t may perhaps be of some use to produce evidence of the affinities of the general Polynesian language with the various languages or dialects to the Westward, through the numerous Islands quite to the Asiatic Continent. The affinity of the Polynesian with the general Malay language was observed by Cook and various subsequent Navigators both French and English.[20] Though the modern Malay differs much from the Polynesian, both in its general construction, and the greatest number of its nouns and verbs, yet originally it might not have been so; there are words which both as to sound and sense prove a true affinity; not merely an accidental word or so; this might occur in any language.

19. Samuel Johnson, compiler of *A Dictionary of the English Language* (1755).

20. As mentioned in chapter 1, Reland made this observation much earlier.

CHAPTER 3

HOW DOES HAWAIIAN DIFFER FROM OTHER POLYNESIAN LANGUAGES?

One of the first impressions that speakers of English had of Polynesian languages was that they were "simpler" in their sounds. For example, here is Hawkesworth's version of Captain Cook's description of Tahitian: "Their language is soft and melodious; it abounds with vowels, and we easily learnt to pronounce it: but found it exceedingly difficult to teach them to pronounce a single word of ours; probably not only from its abounding in consonants, but from some peculiarity in its structure; for Spanish and Italian words, if ending in a vowel, they pronounced with great facility (1773, 2:228).

This so-called "peculiarity in its structure" refers to an important difference in the ways consonants and vowels are arranged in English and Polynesian languages. Figure 3.1 compares the structure of a syllable in English and in (most) Polynesian languages. (C stands for a consonant and V for a vowel or a diphthong. A Hawaiian vowel or diphthong may be either short or long. In both types, the consonant is optional, represented by parentheses.)

English	Polynesian
(C)(C)(C) V (C)(C)(C)(C)	(C)V

Figure 3.1. English and Polynesian syllable structure

In other words, an English syllable can have as many as three consonants before and four after the required vowel nucleus. It is hard to find a word that takes full advantage of the pattern in figure 3.1, but *strengths* (CCCVCCC) comes close. (Note that we're not dealing with spelling, but pronunciation. In this word, *ng* represents just one sound, as does *th.*) An example of a word that ends in four consonant sounds is *texts.* In a slow, careful pronunciation, the consonants that follow the vowel are /ksts/).

In contrast, a syllable in Polynesian languages (except for some of the Outliers) consists of just one optional consonant as an onset (i.e., at the beginning of a syllable) and a required vowel or diphthong. For example, the following words consist of just one syllable:

a	‘of’	*ʻoe*	‘you (singular)’
i	‘towards’	*ʻo*	topic marker
au	‘I’	*kū*	‘stand’
ō	‘answer’	*kāu*	‘your (singular)’

Another striking feature of Polynesian languages is their relatively low number of consonants and vowels. As a matter of fact, until a few years ago, Hawaiian was thought to have the world's smallest alphabet.[1]

However, the number of letters in a language's alphabet has no effect on how its speakers can communicate. For example, although English has many fewer vowels and consonants than one of the languages of the northern Caucasus (which has perhaps 75),[2] we still manage to get by with our smaller number. In short, these figures do not tell us that some languages are simpler or more sophisticated than others. Instead, they merely show that although in some ways all languages are similar, in other ways they can be very different from each other.

Beyond statements about syllable structure, many of the early comments about Polynesian languages were simply wrong. For example, at the time of the first European contact with Tahiti, Philibert de Commerson, naturalist on Bougainville's expedition, mistakenly thought that Tahitian had only about four or five hundred words (Rensch 1991:404). It is easy enough to understand why some people made such mistakes: their slight contact with the speakers was not enough to change their preconceived idea that the language was simple.

---

1. The only languages with smaller systems are Rotokas and Mura, each with only eleven vowels and consonants (Maddieson 1984:7). Pirahã is also a contender, but the figure of 10 phonemes does not include tones, which are phonemic—that is, serve as the only distinction between words that are otherwise identical.

2. Hockett 1958:93.

The reason that I've mentioned just two features of language—sounds and words—is that it is impossible to compare one entire language with another. Instead, we try to compare smaller, more manageable pieces. In the next sections, by using sounds and words as gauges, we will show how Hawaiian is like—and unlike—other Polynesian languages.

SOUNDS

When we study different varieties of English, we find that the consonants are rather stable from dialect to dialect, but the vowels are much less so. Polynesian languages, however, are just the opposite: the consonant systems differ, while the vowel systems are nearly identical. Even though in certain Polynesian languages some vowels have changed to become more like or less like surrounding vowels, the *systems* do not vary greatly from one language to another. This fact leads to the obvious conclusion that they have changed little in their development from Proto-Polynesian (PPN).

The Sounds of Proto-Polynesian

Based on present-day languages, the vowel system of the ancestral language can be reconstructed in two ways, depending on one's interpretation of long vowels. The first proposes five short vowels, as in figure 3.2.[3]

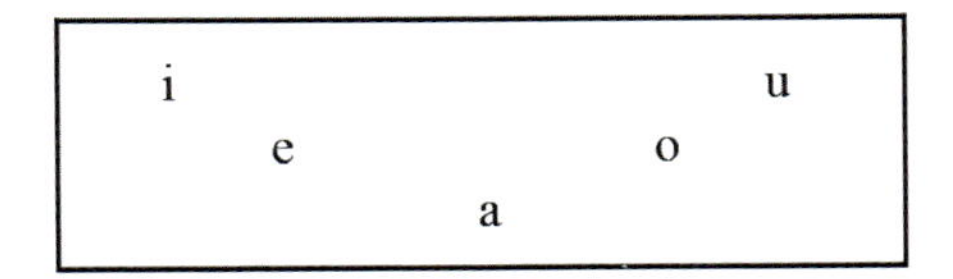

Figure 3.2. PPN vowels

Long vowels are then interpreted as a sequence of identical vowels; for example, *aa, ee, ii, oo, uu.*

Some of these vowel sequences could be the result of losing a consonant that once appeared between them. For example, P-E (Pukui-Elbert)

3. These vowel symbols have roughly the values of those in the International Phonetic Alphabet.

gives the PPN ancestor of *mā* 'faded' as **ma'a*,[4] indicating that a glottal stop between the two vowels has dropped out.

However, not all long vowels can be accounted for in the same way. For example, for *lā* 'sail', P-E cites the PPN form as **laa*, with no intervening consonant. (The notation *aa* presents a problem: some linguists insist that *all* long vowels should be written as two vowels. Thus, it is impossible to know whether *aa* represents a double vowel or a long vowel.)

A second interpretation is shown in figure 3.3.

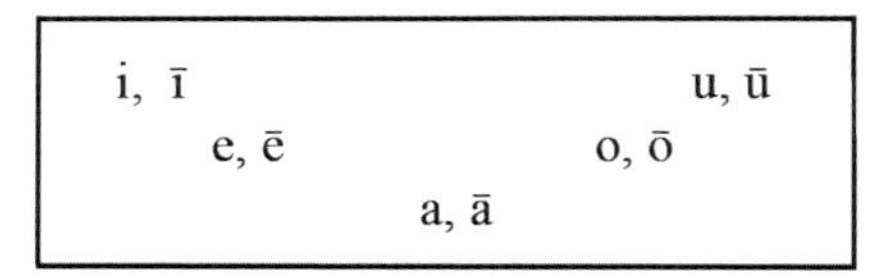

Figure 3.3. PPN vowels

In this study, I take the position that present-day long vowels could stem from either an earlier long vowel (written with a macron) or two identical vowels that were once separated by a glottal stop.

As mentioned earlier, in contrast to the relatively stable vowels, it is the consonants that account for most of the differences among Polynesian sound systems (and alphabets). Figure 3.4 shows what happened to Hawaiian's consonants, as the language changed from its ancestral form, Proto-Polynesian. The phonetic symbol [ʔ] represents an *'okina* (glottal stop), and [ŋ] represents *ng*, as in *si**ng**er* (but not as in *fi**ng**er*, which is [ŋg]).

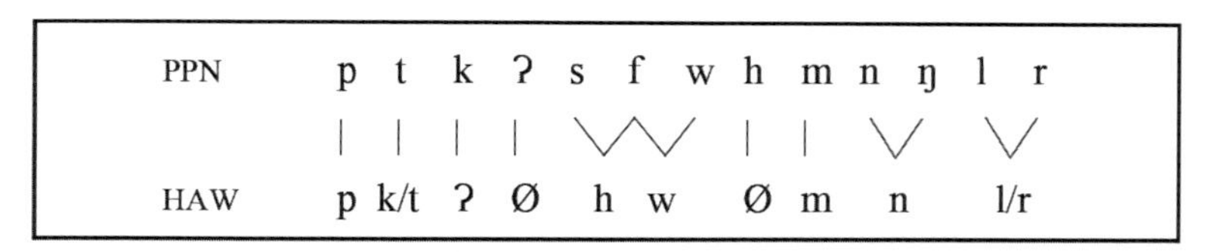

Figure 3.4. Proto-Polynesian and Hawaiian consonants. Note: Two possibly unfamiliar symbols: [ʔ] represents a glottal stop (*'okina*, written as a single opening quote) and [ŋ], a back velar nasal (as in *si**ng***)

Figure 3.4 looks like a simple chart, but there are different ways to interpret this information. First, we could simply state what happened to

4. The "*" before a word indicates that it is either an ancestral form (as in this example) or an incorrect form with respect to the language's grammar or sound system.

each PPN consonant—that is, work from the past to the present. Or we could begin with the present, go backward in time, and trace the history of each Hawaiian consonant. However, it is more useful to try to analyze the changes. In other words, what are the different kinds of changes that took place and what are the results of each?

(But first, readers should realize that PPN consonants are abstractions—reconstructed from present-day sounds in the descendant languages. Next, the row of HAW consonants makes the system look simpler than it actually was. In this figure, *k/t* and *l/r* each represent one distinctive sound, with the second pronunciation in each pair prevalent in Niʻihau Hawaiian.[5] *W* represents a range of pronunciations. Chapter 7 describes not only the alternations but also the phonetic characteristics of these consonants in more detail.)

From Proto-Polynesian to Hawaiian

The following list shows the types of changes that have taken place.

1. Two PPN consonants are unchanged in Hawaiian:

PPN	*p	E.g.,	*paa ʻfence’
HAW	p	E.g.,	*pā*
PPN	*p	E.g.,	*mohe ʻsleep’
HAW	m	E.g.,	*moe*

2. Two PPN consonants changed from one sound to another:

PPN	*t	E.g.,	*mata ʻeye’
HAW	k[6]	E.g.,	*maka*
PPN	*k	E.g.,	*kai ʻeat’
HAW	ʔ	E.g.,	*ʻai*

5. This is not to say that [k] is not spoken on Niʻihau. Instead, the distribution is more complicated—often an alternation between [t] and [k] in the same word. Moreover, more recently one can find minimal pairs for [t] and [k]. See chapter 7.

6. Some varieties of Hawaiian have retained the [t] pronunciation. Standard Hawaiian has [k].

It is important to realize that neither of these two types of change affected the vocabulary. Even though the changes in #2 produced words that sounded somewhat different, no information was lost. In other words, the changes produced no *homonyms*—words that sound the same but have different meanings.

The other changes, however, were not so simple. You can see that the remaining nine consonants in PPN were reduced to four. This reduction took place in three different ways:

3. One pair (two consonants), *ʔ and *h, were lost in Hawaiian.

PPN	ʔ Ø	h Ø
	\ /	\ /
	Ø	Ø

E.g.,	PPN	*faʻa 'stalk'	PPN	*muhu 'silent'
	PPN	*faa 'four'	PPN	*muu 'weevil'
	HAW	*hā* 'stalk, four'	HAW	*mū* 'silent, weevil'

4. Two pairs (four consonants) were reduced to two consonants in Hawaiian.

PPN	n ŋ	l r
	\ /	\ /
HAW	n	l/r[7]

E.g.,	PPN	*nga(a) plural	PPN	*lua 'pit'
	PPN	*naʻa 'settled'	PPN	*rua 'two'
	HAW	*nā* plural, 'settled'	HAW	*lua* 'pit, two'

5. In a more complicated relationship, three consonants, **s*, **f*, and **w*, were reduced to two consonants in Hawaiian.

PPN	s f w
	\ / \ /
HAW	h w

---

7. Anderson wrote *r*, not *l*, in his Waimea word list, discussed in chapter 7.

E.g. PPN *faa, HAW *hā* 'four' PPN *sala, HAW *hala* 'mistake'

PPN *walu, HAW *walu* 'eight' PPN *fafine, HAW *wahine* 'woman'

PPN *fara, HAW *hala* 'pandanus'

(In some cases, nearby sounds played a role in such complications. For example, **f* became HAW *h* under certain conditions, and *w* under others.)

The Results of the Sound Changes

The most important result of changes #3–5 is that unlike #1–2, words that once were kept distinct were now homonyms. For example, see figure 3.5.

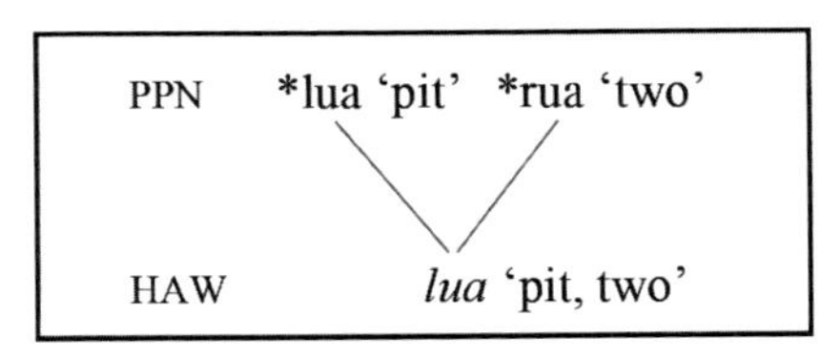

Figure 3.5. PPN l, r > HAW l

Therefore, for *lua* (and many other words), speakers of Hawaiian must rely on context to keep the meanings separate. To an outsider, this feature may seem inconvenient for straightforward communication, but it serves an important stylistic function. Two words that sound the same or similar but with different meanings are the essence of *kaona*—hidden meanings.[8] As P-E defined the term, "Hidden meaning, as in Hawaiian poetry; concealed reference, as to a person, thing, or place; words with double meanings[9] that might bring good or bad fortune." Chapter 16 shows how this important feature is reflected in Hawaiian poetry, sayings, cosmography, and healing.

Some Polynesian languages have been much more conservative in their development. Figure 3.6 shows that the consonant system of

8. Mentioned in Charlot 1983:42; see also chapter 16.

9. This term is incorrect. Homonyms may sound alike, but they are separate words, not words with "double meanings."

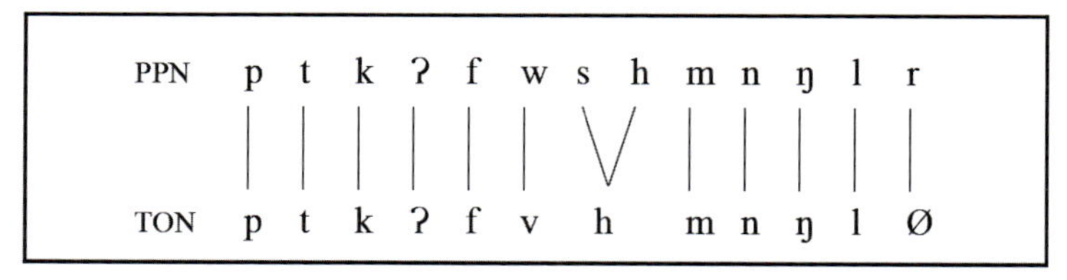

Figure 3.6. Proto-Polynesian and Tongan consonants

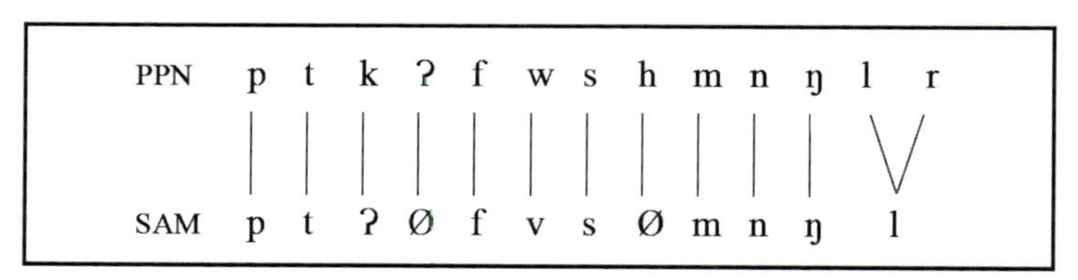

Figure 3.7. Proto-Polynesian and Samoan consonants

Tongan (TON) is much closer to that of Proto-Polynesian.[10] Here, only two changes affected the vocabulary: the merger of *s and *h and the loss of *r.

The consonant system of Samoan is also larger than that of Hawaiian, but it is somewhat smaller than that of Tongan.[11]

WORDS

Polynesian vocabulary can be studied in several different ways. First, as discussed in chapter 2, we use words to determine how close languages are to each other. We assume that if one pair of languages shares a larger number of *cognates* than another pair, the former languages are more closely

---

10. If you're familiar with Tongan, you'll see that *s* is missing. There are two sources for this sound in the present-day language. First, in the words that Tongan inherited from Proto-Polynesian, when /t/ was followed by /i/, it changed first to [č] (as in ENG ***chin***) and later to [s]. But because many words have been borrowed from English or from a nearby relative such as Samoan or Fijian, we now find *s* before other vowels as well. The native speakers I've questioned about *s* don't seem to feel that it is different from the other consonants. In other words, [s] has been accepted as part of the system.

11. This chart represents Formal Samoan, which has a somewhat different system than Colloquial Samoan.

related. In terms of time, such figures mean that they separated later than the members of the other pair.

For example, according to one study, Hawaiian and Māori share 71 percent of items in a list of common words, but Hawaiian and Tongan share only 49 percent. What do these figures reveal? First, they tell us that Hawaiian and Māori are more closely related than Hawaiian and Tongan; second, that Hawaiian and Māori shared a common history much more recently than did Hawaiian and Tongan (see figure 2.3).

Next, we can also study the meanings of shared words, for they might suggest where the ancestral language was spoken. For example, if a word for *mountain range* can be reconstructed for the ancestral language, we can infer that its location was more likely a high island than an atoll. (This idea is discussed at greater length in chapter 13.)

Finally, the meanings of the words can also give us a glimpse of the speakers' lives. For example, a rich vocabulary for sailing terms shows that this activity was important for the speakers.

You can read more about these last two topics in chapter 11.

The list in table 3.1 shows some of the common words that Hawaiian shares with other Polynesian languages—in this example, Māori, Samoan, and Tongan. You should remember, however, that the list does not give a realistic picture of the relationships among the languages, for the words were chosen to illustrate *similarities,* not *differences.* To show how similar these languages are to a closely related language outside the Polynesian family, Fijian cognates have been added. A blank in the Fijian column indicates that the word for this concept is not cognate—that is, it is not related to the others.

TABLE 3.1. COMPARATIVE WORD LIST FOR FOUR POLYNESIAN LANGUAGES AND FIJIAN

ENG	HAW	MAO	SAM	TON	FIJ
afraid	makaʻu	mataku	mataʻu	manavahē	mataku[a]
awake	ala	ara	ala	ʻā	yadra
bird	manu	manu	manu	manu	manumanu
breadfruit	ʻulu	kuru	ʻulu		
canoe	waʻa	waka	vaʻa	vaka	waqa
channel	awa	awa	ava	ava	
chief	aliʻi	ariki	aliʻi	ʻeiki	riki
cry	kani	tangi	tagi	tangi	tagi
cut	mahele[b]	here	sele	hele, tele	sele

Table 3.1 (cont.)

ENG	HAW	MAO	SAM	TON	FIJ
deaf	kuli	turi	tuli	tuli	
dig	ʻeli	keri	ʻeli	keli	keli
ear	pepeiao[c]	taringa	taliga	telinga	daliga
eight	walu	waru	valu	valu	walu
enter	ulu[d]	uru	ulu	hū	curu
fire	ahi	ahi	afi	afi	
fish	iʻa	ika	iʻa	ika	ika
five	lima	rima	lima	nima	lima
fly (n.)	nalo	ngaro, rango	lago	lango	lago
four	hā	whā	fā	fā	vā
gall	au	au	au	ʻahu	
hand, arm	lima	ringa	lima	nima	liga
house	hale	whare	fale	fale	vale
leaf	lau	rau	lau	lau	drau
learn, teach	aʻo	ako	aʻo	ako	
louse	ʻuku	kutu	ʻutu	kutu	kutu
mosquito	makika	namu	namu	namu	namu
mullet	ʻanae	kanae	ʻanae	kanahe	kanace
neck	ʻāʻī	ua	ua		uʻa
net	ʻupena	kupenga	ʻupega	kupenga	
new	hou	hou	fou	foʻou	vou
nine	iwa	iwa	iva	hiva	ciwa
one	kahi	tahi	tasi	taha	
outrigger boom	ʻiako	kiato	ʻiato	kiato	
pandanus	hala	whara	fala	fā	vadra
prohibited	kapu	tapu	tapu	tapu	tabu
rain	ua	ua	ua	ʻuha	uca
road	ala	ara	ala	hala	gaunisala
rock	(pō)haku[e]	whatu	fatu	fatu	vatu
scrape	walu	waru	valu	vau	walu
sea	moana	moana	moana	moana	
sea(water)	kai	tai	tai	tahi	taci*
seven	hiku	whitu	fitu	fitu	vitu
shark	manō	mangō	magō	ʻanga	
sit, stay	noho	noho	nofo	nofo	

Table 3.1 (cont.)

ENG	HAW	MAO	SAM	TON	FIJ
six	ono	ono	ono	ono	ono
sky	lani	rangi	lagi	langi	lagi
sleep	moe	moe	moe	mohe	moce
snare (n.)	hele	here	sele	hele	
spear	kao	tao	tao	tao	
stalk (taro)	hā	whā	fā	fa'a	
stink	hauna	haunga	sauga	haunga	
three	kolu	toru	tolu	tolu	tolu
tooth	niho	niho	hifo	nifo	
turn over	huli	huri	fuli	fuli	vuki[f]
two	lua	rua	lua	lua, ua	rua
voice	leo	reo	leo	le'o	
wind	makani	matangi	matagi	matangi	cagi
woman	wahine	wahine	fafine	fefine	
wrong	hala	hara	sala	hala	cala
yam	uhi	uwhi	ufi	'ufi	uvi
year	kau	tau	tau	ta'u	

a. *Mataku* and *riki* are Western Fijian.

b. Some sources have *māhele*.

c. Keao NeSmith noted that *kalina,* the expected Hawaiian cognate, refers to an ear-shaped fungus that grows on trees (pers. comm. Jan. 2009).

d. As suggested by Kenneth W. Cook (July 2015), one meaning of *ulu* is connected with a spirit "entering" a person.

e. P-E also has *haku* 'stone'.

f. Perhaps not cognate.

Note that spelling conventions may make words look different when they are actually the same. For example, the [ŋ] sound (as in English *si**ng**er*) is written *ng* in Tongan but *g* in Samoan and Fijian. Also, both Hawaiian and Samoan have *k* and *t* dialects; the standard spelling for each obscures this feature. Finally, although the current spelling uses *l,* its earlier pronunciation was more like that of *r* (i.e., [ř]) in related languages.

Traditional Fijian spelling uses these conventions: *b* = [mb], *d* = [nd], *q* = [ŋg], *c* = [ð], *v* = [ß], *g* = [ŋ], and *dr* = [n] followed by an [r] ranging from a tap to a trill.

It was mentioned earlier that because the words were chosen to illustrate similarities, the list gives a skewed picture of the relationships among these languages. In table 3.2, the pairs of Hawaiian and Tongan words[12]—not cognate, but with the same meaning—emphasize the differences.

TABLE 3.2. SELECTED NONCOGNATE HAWAIIAN AND TONGAN WORDS

ENG	HAW	TON
big	nui	lahi
bite	nahu	uʻu, ʻusi
cold	anu	momoko
come	hele mai	haʻu
dog	ʻīlio	kulī
fall	hāʻule	tō
fear	makaʻu	ilifia
flower	pua	matala
mouth	waha	ngutu
not	ʻaʻole	ʻikai
see	ʻike	sio

VERBATIM

This chapter sketches a way to reconstruct the past of Polynesian languages by comparing words from the languages of the present. The method is not new; at nearly the same time that the first missionaries arrived in Hawaiʻi, German scholars began to make systematic comparisons of Indo-European languages.

In 1836, the missionary Lorrin Andrews pondered the origin of Polynesian languages. Of course, we would like to know if Andrews had read the German articles and books, but we have no way of knowing, unless he noted it in his journals or letters. We do know that missionaries in various parts of Polynesia —as well as scholars in Europe—corresponded and shared their ideas about this topic. And Andrews may have been familiar with the findings of the naturalists on the Cook expeditions. At any rate, he wrote the following comments:

> The origin of the language of the Polynesians, divided as it is into several different dialects, is buried in deep obscurity. The people themselves know not

12. Just a few examples from a Swadesh 200-word list.

whence they are, as the fabulous accounts of their own origin sufficiently testify; and yet, on the slightest inspection and comparison of the different dialects, it cannot for a moment be doubted that they had one common origin. And a singular circumstance is, that the people at the extreme parts of Polynesia speak dialects of the general language the most resembling each other. It has been said that the dialects of the New Zealanders and the Hawaiians resemble each other more nearly than any of the other dialects . . . But *whence* came the inhabitants of Polynesia? *How* did they come, or get possession of so many islands scattered over such a vast extent of ocean? *When* did they come? And *why* did they come? are questions that cannot now be answered without much conjecture. Yet, no doubt a careful and thorough examination of the several dialects, and a comparison of one with the other with a view to ascertain the groundwork of the general language, and a comparison with the languages of the neighboring continents, would not only be a subject of inquiry full of interest, but would go far to indicate the probable origin of this people. (Andrews 1836b)

It is interesting that scholars today are still asking these questions.

PART II

THE ALPHABET

He ku-la.

CHAPTER 4

PRELUDE TO THE ALPHABET

So far as we know, until the Europeans arrived, writing was unknown to the Polynesians. (The Rapa Nui [Easter Island] *rongorongo* tablets, once thought to be an exception, were probably inspired by a 1770 Spanish document.)[1]

In Hawaiian culture, apparently the closest equivalents to the *form* of writing were *petroglyphs,* which were indigenous and not based on any Western writing system (see figure 4.2). But does a line drawing on the surface of a rock really represent a written language? The missionary scholar William Ellis begged the question by describing petroglyphs as "first efforts" toward a writing system. He suggested that the rock carvings conveyed limited amounts and types of information, such as the number of people in a party that had traveled nearby, or the kind or size of fish caught in the vicinity (Ellis [1825] 1979:334). Perhaps in time, the petroglyphs might have been developed into a form of writing, just as ancient pictograms did when they came to represent abstract, not just concrete, ideas.

Figure 4.1. A sample of writing from the *rongorongo* tablets

1. Fischer 1997:139–42, 214.

Figure 4.2. Hawaiian petroglyphs

Hawaiians had another form of what we might call "prewriting": *palapala*—that is, *kapa* decoration. But did it communicate? Perhaps it did, but only to the extent that any art or craft form does. William Tufts Brigham, who studied Hawaiian *kapa*[2] in the early 1900s, suggested that the traditional *palapala* was only ornamental and not symbolic in the way that Egyptian hieroglyphics were (Brigham 1911). Still, this is only one opinion; others might argue that the *palapala* decorations did indeed communicate ideas.

A tattoo (*kākau*) is another kind of Native Hawaiian decoration that is similar in form to writing. As a matter of fact, the word is now used in a number of phrases that refer to different kinds of writing. But did *kākau,* before European writing was introduced, communicate in the way that a writing system does?

Without such a system, how did the Hawaiians preserve the memories of important events and people and pass them on from generation to generation? The answer is that they did it through oral tradition—chants and genealogies. To those of us who rely on writing and instant access to data via computers, memorizing so much information seems an amazing feat.

2. The Hawaiian word for *tapa.* The English word was borrowed from Marquesan and Tahitian.

FIRST ATTEMPTS AT WRITING

Hawaiian words were written for the first time when Captain James Cook and his crew arrived in January 1778. If you read Cook's account of his meeting with Hawaiians, the first example of the language you'll find is the word *Hamaite*—which he identified as the Hawaiians' response to the pieces of iron they saw when they came on board the *Resolution.* Cook suggested that the word might refer to "some instrument, in the making of which iron could be usefully employed." But this "word" was actually the phrase *He maita'i!* (*t,* not *k,* was used on Kaua'i then) 'It's good!' Apparently the Hawaiians were familiar with iron from nails and other small pieces of metal they found on wood washed ashore as jetsam from some distant shipwreck.

Some of the other Hawaiian words in Cook's narrative have even made their way into English dictionaries: *taboo* (*kapu*) 'sacred, forbidden' (possibly the first Polynesian borrowing into English; Cook learned the word *tapu* in Tonga and used it in the report on his second voyage),[3] *maro* (*malo*) 'loincloth', and names for such common plants as *tee* (*kī*) and *taro* (*kalo*).

But not everyone spelled these words the same way. For example, Charles Clerke, captain of the *Discovery,* wrote the word *malo* as *Marrow.* In Clerke's short account of his stay in Hawai'i (Beaglehole 1967:1320–23), he also wrote these words: *A'towi* (*Kaua'i*), *O'neehow* (*Ni'ihau*), and *Aree* (*ali'i*).

Even though two people might write the same word differently, these earliest attempts at writing Hawaiian had at least two things in common. First, they reflected the language of the writer. That is, speakers of different languages generally followed the writing conventions of their own language (e.g., see the discussion of Spanish and French word lists in Schütz 1994:76–83). Next, the Hawaiian words, only incidental in the writers' reports, were usually the names of people and places or words for Hawaiian concepts that had no English equivalents. Because consistency wasn't their main goal, the writers probably weren't concerned about writing the same sound with the same letter each time.

---

3. Unaspirated [p] was perceived as [b] by speakers of English. Oddly, Merriam-Webster dictionaries still give the source of *taboo* as Tongan *tabu,* although the word hasn't been spelled with a *b* for over a century.

But as the next chapter relates, one of Cook's crew, Dr. William Anderson, collected a much larger sample of Hawaiian words. And because he had a scientific interest in all the languages he encountered on Cook's second and third voyages, he did try to write words in a consistent way.

VERBATIM

The following paragraphs expand on William Ellis's remarks on Hawaiian petroglyphs (Ellis [1825] 1979:334). As for his unfortunate characterization of the Hawaiians as an "uncivilized people" (along with Hale's term "semi-barbarous" in chapter 1), we should remember that it was common at that time to apply such a label to people of any culture other than one's own.

Hawaiian Rock Carvings

In the course of our tour around Hawaii, we met with a few specimens of what may perhaps be termed the first efforts of an uncivilized people towards the construction of a language of symbols.

Along the southern coast, both on the east and west sides, we frequently saw a number of straight lines, semicircles, or concentric rings, with some rude imitations of the human figure, cut or carved in the compact rocks of lava. They did not appear to have been cut with an iron instrument, but with a stone hatchet, or a stone less frangible than the rock on which they were portrayed.

On inquiry, we found that they had been made by former travellers, from a motive similar to that which induces a person to carve his initials on a stone or tree, or a traveller to record his name in an album, to inform his successors that he has been there.

When there were a number of concentric circles with a dot or mark in the centre, the dot signified a man, and the number of rings denoted the number in the party who had circumambulated the island.

When there was a ring, and a number of marks, it denoted the same; the number of marks shewing of how many the party consisted; and the ring, that they had travelled completely round the island; but when there was only a semicircle, it denoted that they had returned after reaching the place where it was made.

In some of the islands we have seen the outline of a fish portrayed in the same manner, to denote that one of that species or size had been taken near the spot; sometimes the dimensions of an exceedingly large fruit, &c. are marked in the same way.

No written language in Hawaii

With this slight exception, if such it can be called, the natives of the Sandwich and other islands had no signs for sounds or ideas, nor any Pictor[i]al representation of events. Theirs was entirely an oral language; and, whatever view we take of it, presents the most interesting phenomenon connected with the inhabitants of the Pacific.

CHAPTER 5

DR. WILLIAM ANDERSON

Forgotten Philologist

The largest sample of Hawaiian from the report on Captain James Cook's third voyage is the 250-word list collected by William Anderson, surgeon and unofficial naturalist for the expedition.

Anderson, born in Scotland in 1750, was educated at Edinburgh University. In December 1771, he joined Cook's crew for the second voyage, serving as surgeon's mate. On the third voyage, he was surgeon aboard the *Resolution* (Beaglehole 1974).

Because Anderson knew that he had tuberculosis (consumption, as it was called then), he had considered staying in the Society Islands when Cook's ships prepared to sail toward the harsh winter of the northwest coast of North America. Had he done so, he would have missed the expedition's historic encounter with Hawai'i, and we would have been denied his carefully written record of the language.

ANDERSON AT WAIMEA

Shortly before landing at Kaua'i, Anderson had been very ill.[1] But on 21 January 1778, he felt well enough to walk with Cook and the artist John Webber about a half mile[2] up the Waimea River to the Ke'a'ali'i Heiau.

The description of this short excursion shows that each man recorded his impressions of the *heiau* in a different way. Cook, duty bound to keep a journal in which he wrote a detailed account of his observations, no matter whether they were important or trivial, described the scene in words, which you can read in Beaglehole 1967:269–71.

---

1. Beaglehole 1974:574.

2. Samwell wrote that it was a mile upstream. See below.

Figure 5.1. Village of Waimea, Kaua'i

Webber, the artist, recorded his own observations at the site itself. Figures 5.5–5.6 show how his simpler monotone sketches were later rendered into watercolors that showed much greater detail.

While Webber was sketching what he *saw,* Anderson wrote down what he *heard*—the Hawaiian language. His end product—a word list—raises a number of questions.

Figure 5.2. John Webber, RA, *Das Leben Malers Johann Weber aus Bern* (1821), by Sigmund Wagner

How Did They Communicate?

How was Anderson able to elicit and write words from a language he had never heard before? The earlier accounts from Cook's first and second voyages of the first meetings between the crew and the Polynesian islanders suggest that some rather complex ideas were communicated between the two groups. Just how the two groups communicated, however, remains unclear, for writers described the process with such vague phrases as "we endeavour'd to explain as well as we could" or "made signs to us."

The following notes, based on Hawkesworth's account (1773), illustrate how earlier, Cook and his crew had communicated with the Tahitians on first contact. Page numbers are in parentheses.

1. (79–80): The date was 11 April 1769, but it wasn't until the morning of the 12th that any Tahitians were sighted, and these from a distance. Some canoes approached, but no one could be persuaded to come on board. The first sign of communication seems to have been "young plantains, and branches of a tree which the Indians call *E'Midho;* these, as we afterwards learnt, were brought as tokens of peace and amity." The Tahitians wanted them to be placed on board, "which we did not immediately understand; at length we guessed that they wished these symbols should be placed in some conspicuous part of the ship . . . We then purchased their cargoes, consisting of cocoa-nuts, and various kinds of fruits." But how this transaction was conducted was not explained.
2. (81): Owhaw came on board and was recognized by crew members who had landed earlier with Wallis.[3] Might he have recognized a few words of English?
3. (82): A green branch was presented as a "symbol of peace."
4. The Tahitian names written up to this point are *Otaheite, E'Midho, Matavai, Owhaw, Matahah, Tootahah, Tubourai Tamaide,* and *Tomio.*
5. (85): Here we find the first mention of an attempt to speak Tahitian: "We laid our hands upon our left breasts, and pronounced the word *Taio,* which we supposed to signify friend."[4] This sentence is followed by another reference to communication: "The Chief then gave us to understand, that if we chose to eat, he had victuals ready for us."

The meeting between Cook's crew and the Hawaiians contrasted sharply with those earlier encounters with Tahitians, for no such rough sign language was necessary. In spite of the great distance between Tahiti and Hawai'i, the striking similarity between their languages was one of the first things that several journal writers mentioned (see chapter 2). And by this time, some members of the crew were familiar enough with Tahitian to make it easy to talk with the Hawaiians—at least about simple matters. Finally, as noted in chapter 2, it now appears that the split between Tahitian and Hawaiian was more recent than was thought only a few decades ago—another reason for more understanding between speakers of the two languages.

---

3. Samuel Wallis, Captain of HMS *Dolphin,* was the first European on record to spend time at Tahiti. He and his crew stayed there from 17 June to 27 July 1767.

4. ". . . archaic, but used when the first popa'ās [white men] arrived in Tahiti; you can hear the word many times in the 1935 film *Mutiny on the Bounty*" (Wahlroos 2002:226–27).

Figure 5.3. Cook monument in Waimea

Figure 5.4. Poliʻahu Heiau view of Wailua River mouth and Malae Heiau hillside

Figure 5.5. The *heiau* at Waimea, exterior (sketch)

Figure 5.6. The *heiau* at Waimea, exterior (colored engraving)

Figure 5.7. The *heiau* at Waimea, interior

Perhaps because Anderson was interested and trained in the study of language, his ability to speak Tahitian was much more than just basic. David Samwell, his first mate on the *Resolution,* reported that Anderson was better at speaking and understanding Tahitian than anyone else on the expedition. Even a quick look at his word list shows us that he must have used Tahitian to elicit some fairly complicated grammatical concepts that would have been difficult to elicit through gestures.

ANDERSON'S ALPHABET

Those of us concerned with the more technical aspects of Anderson's task would ask this question: What kind of alphabet did he use?

Some critics have called Anderson's alphabet confused and unsystematic. And at first glance, we might agree, for many words are spelled very differently from the way they are today. To find out why, we must first examine his earlier word lists—specifically those for Tahitian and Māori, and next, put them in the broader context of the state of linguistics in the late eighteenth century. Finally, I make use of the obvious (which previous critics missed): a key to his system.

One of the greatest obstacles to understanding these earliest attempts to write Hawaiian was the lack of a standard phonetic alphabet at that time. As a result, visitors to Hawaiʻi wrote words the way they "heard them," which usually meant that they used the conventions of their own language—in this case, English.

However, as anyone who reads and writes English knows, its spelling is only partly regular. To bypass this difficulty, Anderson, in his study of several Polynesian languages (especially Tahitian), had worked out a consistent way to represent their words on paper. He described the system that he had devised, and Cook included it in the official publication of his second voyage (Anderson 1776–77). Its aim was, as Cook wrote, to "help the reader to a proper pronunciation of the different Words."

Anderson's rules illustrate the philological approach that was familiar to him: he explained what each letter of his proposed alphabet represented. In other words, he moved from symbol to sound. You can see the same approach outlined in the introduction to Samuel Johnson's classic *Dictionary of the English Language* (1755):

> *A* has three sounds, the slender, open, and broad.
> *I* has a sound, long, as in *fīne;* and short, as *fĭn.*
> *U* is long in *ūse, confūsion,* or short, as in *ŭs, concŭssion.*

Since the early nineteenth century, however,[5] it has been standard practice for philologists to move in the opposite direction: to begin with the sounds of an unfamiliar language and then choose symbols with which to represent them.

The Tahitian List

For Tahitian, the consonants posed few problems (except for the glottal stop). Instead, it was Anderson's treatment of the vowels that made his spelling system unusual. When he wrote Tahitian words, he used conventions that applied then—and still apply—to English: certain combinations of letters represented simple sounds. For example, *ai, ee,* and *oo* (as in ***rain, see,*** and ***food***) stood for what Tahitian now writes as *e, i,* and *u.* To show that these combinations were units and belonged to one syllable, he linked the letters with a ligature across the top. Dots over vowels showed that each represented a separate syllable (Anderson 1777).

To avoid the complication of using the ligatures in the published version of the Tahitian list, the printer wrote the vowel sequences above in

5. See Schütz 1994:103–4.

TABLE 5.1. ANDERSON'S SPELLING OF TAHITIAN WORDS COMPARED WITH CURRENT SPELLINGS

Anderson's spelling	Respelled words	Current spelling	Gloss
rȯȧ	roa	roa	Great, long, distant
E′reema	e′rima	e rima	Five
ry′poeea	rai′poia	raipoia	Fog or mist
e′h*oo*ra	e′hura	e huri	To invert or turn upside down
par*oo*, r*oo*	paruru	paruru	A partition, division, or screen

italics, as in table 5.1. However, no information was lost in this change, and the accent marks and dots over the vowels remained.

The Māori List

Figure 5.8, showing a portion of the Māori word list that Anderson collected only a few months earlier, illustrates the same conventions.[6]

In the first three words we see that *ai, ou,* and *ee* (with a line over each pair) represented the diphthongs *ae, āo,* and the vowel *i.* As mentioned above, if two vowels represented two sounds (and two syllables as well), he wrote a dot over each (as in *rȯȧ* in table 5.1). It is likely that Anderson marked these vowels in this way so that an English reader wouldn't pronounce *oa* as one vowel, as in ***boat***. Finally, he marked the syllable with the strongest accent in some words or phrases of three or more syllables. An example is *e'wakka* [*he waka*] 'a boat or canoe'.

Although the part of his journal that contains the Hawaiian list has been lost, the Māori list shows that only a few months before reaching Hawai'i, Anderson was using the system that he had originally devised for Tahitian. Thus, it is reasonable to suppose that he would have continued to use these conventions for Hawaiian as well.

However, the printed version of Anderson's Hawaiian list contains *no* diacritics or even a contrast between roman and italic type. As a result, the published list does not accurately reflect what Anderson heard and wrote. As an example, note the difference between the printed spelling and the modern spelling of the common words shown in table 5.2 (Anderson 1784).

6. From the Admiralty Records.

+ Āi . . . . Yes
+ Ka'oure . . . . No
+ Eēka . . . . Fish
He'kaeē . . . . To chew or eat
+ E'wakka . . . . . . A boat or Canoe
Makkaireēdē . . . . Cold
Taoō'my . . . . . Come here
A'gōōanaē . . . . Presently - By and by - To day
+ Tak'ōōpo . . . . . The head
Ekonohēē . . . . The Eye
+ Reenga . . . The hand
Nōōe of Hēē'erahoē . Large
'Whaēro . . . . . Red
Kak'ahōō . . Cloth
x Ōū I
Kōē . . . . . You
'Taōōa . . . . We
E'nāā . . . . Hearh - I say
Ka'haēa . . . . . Where - Where is it or he.
Māāh . . . . . Food of any kind.
Hōmy, or 'Magōō . . . Give me . . . (a)

Figure 5.8. A sample of Anderson's transcription of Māori

TABLE 5.2. SAMPLES OF ANDERSON'S HAWAIIAN SPELLING IN THE PUBLISHED VERSION OF COOK'S THIRD VOYAGE

Printed spelling	Modern spelling	English translation
haire	*hele*	go
haieea	*he iʻa*	it's a fish
ou	*au*	I

Reconstructing the Original

If we could consult the original manuscript, we could easily "translate" Anderson's list into a spelling that would be much closer to the modern one. But the manuscript is missing, perhaps buried in the uncatalogued material in the Admiralty Records.

However, with the help of his Tahitian and Māori lists, we can now look at Anderson's work in a new light, making educated guesses at where the diacritics might have been. Not that his list is entirely accurate, but a knowledge of his intentions changes many confused-looking forms into words that more closely resemble those in today's spelling. This analysis gives us a better look at the kind of Hawaiian spoken on Kauaʻi over two hundred years ago.

First, it shows us that *t* and not *k* was spoken on Kauaʻi as well as on Niʻihau, where that pronunciation is concentrated today. Moreover, the *t* pronunciation was consistent: at least as Anderson chose to represent it, it did not alternate with *k*.

The same holds for *r*, as opposed to the *l* that is written today. The *r*, by the way, was not like the *r* of American English, but a careful reading of the missionary correspondence in the 1820s and later reveals that it was a tap—rather like the *r* in Spanish (as in *pero* 'but', not *perro* 'dog', which is a trill), Tahitian, or Māori.

As noted in chapter 3, one of the ways in which Hawaiian has changed over the years is that, unlike some other Polynesian languages, it no longer has an *ng* sound [ŋ] (see figure 3.3). However, Anderson wrote three words with *ng* (and in two others, he explicitly noted that *ng* alternated with *n*), showing the Hawaiian spoken then (at least on Kauaʻi) still had remnants of that pronunciation (Geraghty 1983b:557).

These three features show us that in the late eighteenth century, the pronunciation of Hawaiian on Kauaʻi, especially certain consonants, was somewhat closer to that of Proto-Polynesian than it is today.

ANDERSON'S DEATH

Anderson's one visit to the *heiau* seems to have been his main contact with native speakers. Bad weather limited the number of trips ashore; even Cook went on land only three times. On 2 February, the expedition left the islands and headed north—toward a climate not only less comfortable than that of Tahiti and Hawai'i, but also, for someone with tuberculosis, fatal.

Anderson continued to write in his journal until 3 June 1778. He died exactly two months later, at the age of twenty-eight. In his own journal, Lieutenant James King wrote the following eulogy, entitled "Portrait of Anderson": "At 1/2 past 3 PM dyed Mr Anderson our Surgeon: his decline was too rapid since our leaving the Society Islands not to be Observable by all; but he himself long before that time knew that his lungs were affect'd . . . he foretold for a year before his death the different stages of his disorder, & knew the time nearly of his Existence" (Beaglehole 1967:1429–30).

King went on to praise Anderson for his unaffected behavior and "equality of temper" in spite of his illness and regretted that his important work would remain unfinished, there being no proper substitute for a naturalist on board either of the ships. He concluded, "If we except our Commander, he is the greatest publick loss the Voyage could have sustaind. The Island which we saw 3 hours after his death the Captain calld after the deceas'd."

RETRACING ANDERSON'S FOOTSTEPS

After over two centuries, information about the Waimea *heiau* visited by Cook, Webber, and Anderson seems as shadowy as Anderson's reputation, showing that even blocks of stone cannot guarantee permanence.

First of all, even the exact location of the *heiau* has been disputed. Samwell wrote that it was about a mile up the Waimea River; another report said a half mile. In the 1930s, archaeologists were cautious about making a positive identification, but singled out Ke'a'ali'i Heiau, said to be behind "the first Japanese temple." More recent studies state that Ke'a'ali'i was definitely the site. However, still other sources disagree. See "Verbatim" at the end of this chapter.

It is difficult to stretch the imagination far enough to step into a Webber engraving and relive Anderson's walk up the Waimea River. Even the river itself has changed: frequent flooding made it necessary to build protective dikes along the banks near the estuary. Along Ala Wai Road on the way to the *heiau*, the scattered thatched houses sketched by Webber have been replaced by modern ones spanning several periods and styles. An occasional abandoned store hints at a more commercial past, contrasting with the current residential nature of the outskirts of Waimea.

The "first Japanese temple," Honpa Hongwanji Mission of Hawai'i, occupies a level grassy area, perhaps 80 × 100 feet, closed in by buildings on two sides. On the *ma uka* side of the main area are a Japanese garden and a stone commemorating the dedication of the new temple in October 1970.

The new temple is said to sit directly on the *heiau* site; apparently it was built slightly behind the old one. A few large stones lie near the entrance, but otherwise, no trace of the original foundations or walls remains. Thomas Thrum identified the site: "At Keaalii, west side Waimea river. Destroyed years ago and its stones used for fences. Fragments of foundation shows [*sic*] it to have been about 60 feet square" (1906:38).

Houses and trees now block the view of the river, but the high bank on the opposite side is still visible. The trees also nearly obscure the outline of the hills that Webber sketched, so that it is difficult to match them with the somewhat softened profiles of his drawings (compare figures 5.6 and 5.9).

An overlay of other cultures seems to pervade the whole area. The temple itself reflects the drastic change in population from late nineteenth-century immigration. To the right of the entrance is a more contemporary symbol of a different culture: the grounds of Waimea Headstart—a small

Figure 5.9. Honpa Hongwanji Mission. Are the stones in the foreground the only remnants of the earlier *heiau?*

playground with, as its focal point, a bright green playhouse decorated with a yellow lion.[7] Even the vegetation is dominated by imports: plumeria, *Nandina domestica,* hibiscus, and ornamental pines and other conifers greatly outnumber the native plants.

Nor does closing the eyes help the imagination: the afternoon quiet is punctuated by the crowing of a nearby rooster and the sound of an occasional car or moped roaring by. The present obliterates the past, intruding through all the senses.

*

By the time much material had been written or printed in Hawaiian, certain features of the language as it was in 1778 had been somewhat altered. For example, the standardized writing system eventually contributed to reducing much (but not all) of the variation that existed before, and many aspects of the indigenous culture (along with their words) were replaced by alien ones.

Ideally, we should like to stock up on batteries and disks, grab our recording devices, step into a Wellsian time machine, and hear and record the language for ourselves. But because that is possible only in the realm of science fiction, we have to make do with what the earliest observers wrote. The important thing—no easy matter—is to try to see through their eyes and hear through their ears. Each piece of evidence is useful in some way; even the words that were misheard or misinterpreted can tell us something.

In addition to being a "first," the word list that Anderson, as linguist and naturalist, recorded makes his pioneering work on Hawaiian extremely important. But Anderson, the person, has all but faded from public knowledge. His name is not well known in Hawai'i. No gravestone marks his resting place, for he was buried at sea. Even "Anderson Island"—a gesture made by Cook just after Anderson's death—was a short-lived memorial, having already been discovered and named by Vitus Jonassen Bering fifty years earlier. Only the botanical genus *Andersonia* bears his name. William Anderson's reputation seems as impermanent as his final resting place, perhaps because the accuracy of his scholarship was

7. These details may have changed since the 1990s.

distorted by a printer's seemingly innocent—but unfortunate—decision to print pages uncluttered by extra symbols.

However, it is clear that Anderson's writing system, reconstructed here by using his "Directions for the Pronunciation of the Vocabulary" (1776–77), represents the first regular, consistent alphabet for Hawaiian.[8]

VERBATIM

The following accounts demonstrate that the precise location of the *heiau* where Anderson collected his word list is still open to question.

> There are several historical accounts of heiau on the east bank of the Waimea River prior to the construction of Fort Elisabeth. A luakini heiau was noted by Captain Cook and sketched by his artist, John Webber, most likely on the west bank and further upstream from the fort. Cook noted another heiau on the east bank, but could not reach it from his position (Beaglehole 1967:270–71). A surgeon with Cook, William Ellis, drew a shipboard sketch of Waimea Bay that he used to make a more detailed sketch at a later date (Forbes 1992:28–29). Both sketches show a heiau on the east bank of the Waimea River slightly upstream from the eventual location of Fort Elisabeth.[9] This may be a heiau 272 feet long by 75 to 81 feet wide, the remains of which Thomas Thrum observed in the early 1900s. (Thrum 1906:39; Mills 1997:160)

> The exact location of this heiau described by Cook is unknown. The lake or pond referred to was probably made by the backing up of the Waimea river. Of the large heiau that Cook mentioned as being across the pond, nothing remains. . . . On the northern side of [p. 43] the river, the supposed site of the described heiau would be in the position of Keaalii heiau (Site 23) [see below], though this is mostly destroyed. The background given by the artist Webber is far different than that seen at Site 23, but it is quite possible that the background was a later addition to the picture, and not one made on the site.[10] (Bennett 1931:42–43)

---

8. Other writers (e.g., Rumford 1993b; Laimana 2011) credit the alphabet devised by ʻŌpūkahaʻia/Ruggles as the first systematic writing system. However, Anderson's work preceded this one by thirty years.

9. Note that the excerpt below (Bennett 1931) places the *heiau* on the west bank.

10. If this supposition is true, it removes the reason for Alison Kay's search, described below.

Site 23. Keaalii heiau, at Keaalii on the west side of the Waimea river, behind the first Japanese temple.

This structure is reported by some to be the heiau described by Captain Cook but, though the location seems about correct, so little remains that the rumor cannot be substantiated. Imbedded in the ground are fragments of its foundation, but the outline is no longer traceable. Thrum says "Fragments of foundation show it to have been about 60 feet square." There are other fragments, however, that would make it over 150 feet in length, and 100 feet in width. (Bennett 1931:104)

AN ALTERNATE VIEW

(*Author's note:* This section was written at my request by Sigrid Southworth in 2016.)

In 2001 a small group of friends who enjoyed going *holoholo* on neighbor islands was planning a trip to Kaua'i. Alison [Kay], longtime University of Hawai'i professor of zoology, was part of the group.

Some years before, Alison had taken a copy of John Webber's drawing of the *heiau* [figures 5.5, 5.6] that he, Captain Cook, and William Anderson saw in Waimea to Kaua'i and had spent a day driving and walking until she found what she was sure was the location of the *heiau.* She matched the mountains in the background of Webber's sketch with the peaks and ridges behind Waimea.

When our group got to Waimea, Alison took us to the site. Waimea Canyon Road climbs above the hospital and then zigzags back and forth until it comes to a group of perhaps a dozen houses clustered on either side of a small street called Panini Place.

A map of the Waimea area, including the river, the road, and Panini Place, confirms that the distance would be within the estimates given by two members of Cook's crew—Webber's (a half mile from the anchorage) and Samwell's (a mile).[11]

*

11. See note 2 above.

If we move back in time, we can compare the passages above with Cook's account of the trek up the Waimea, summarized earlier in this chapter. The source is Beaglehole 1967: 269–72, and the spelling is as in the original.

> As soon as every thing was settled to my satisfaction, I left the command to Mr Williamson who was with me and took a walk up the Vally, accompanied by Dr Anderson and Mr Webber; conducted by one of the Natives and attended by a tolerable train. Our guide proclaimed our approach and every one whom we met fell on their faces and remained in that position till we had passed. This, as I afterwards understood, is done to their great chiefs. Our road lay in among the Plantations, which were chiefly of Tara [*kalo*], and sunk a little below the common level so as to contain the water necessary to nourish the roots. As we ranged down the coast from the East in the Ships, we observed at every Village one or more elevated objects, like Pyramids and we had seen one in this vally that we were desirous of going to see. Our guide understood us, but as this was on the other side of the river, he conducted us to one on the same side we were upon; it proved to be a Morai[12] which in many respects was like those of Otaheite.

Cook continued, giving a detailed description of the *heiau,* images contained therein, and some customs connected with the site. He did not say how long the party stayed, but it was time enough for Webber to make his drawing and for Anderson to collect his word list.

> After having seen every thing that was to be seen about this Morai and Mr Webber had taken a drawing of it, we returned to the beach by a different route to the one we came. Besides the Tara plantations before mentioned we met with some plantations of plantain, Sugar cane and the Chinese paper Mulbery tree or cloth plant, as it is more generally called by us, there were also a few low cocoanut trees, but we saw but one bread fruit tree and but very few of any other sort.

From our language-centered point of view, it is unfortunate that Cook mentioned Webber's activity at the *heiau,* but not Anderson's. Moreover, as noted earlier in this chapter, Anderson's Hawai'i journal had disappeared long before Beaglehole examined the wealth of historical material

---

12. This spelling shows how Cook wrote the Tahitian word *marae,* which referred to a structure similar in form and function to a Hawaiian *heiau.* He used it in his description of Tonga as well.

that underlies his monumental works on Cook. Thus, we have no first-hand account of how and from whom he collected his word list.

Once more, even though Anderson's word list survived through the early printings and is reproduced in Beaglehole's edition, it is only Cook's and Webber's activities that are mentioned. Are explorers and artists always more interesting than linguists?

CHAPTER 6

3s AND 8s

The Unusual Alphabet of ʻŌpūkahaʻia and Ruggles

Even though William Anderson's Hawaiian alphabet was systematic, it still depended solely on what he—an outsider—heard during a short interview, combined with what he could draw on from his extensive knowledge of Tahitian and other Pacific languages. His short contact with Hawaiian did not allow him to analyze it more thoroughly.

The first alphabet for Hawaiian that is based on longer contact with native speakers[1] is the one used in a manuscript grammar written at Cornwall, Connecticut, in 1819 and housed in the collection of the Hawaiian Historical Society since 1892.[2]

FROM KAʻŪ TO CONNECTICUT

Cornwall is important in the history of the Hawaiian language mainly because of a young Hawaiian, ʻŌpūkahaʻia, later christened Henry. (Most of our information about ʻŌpūkahaʻia comes from his *Memoirs.* This inspiring book, compiled by Edwin W. Dwight ([1818] 1968, 1990), grew out of ʻŌpūkahaʻia's journal and his letters and the memories and letters of his friends.)

Born in Kaʻū on the island of Hawaiʻi circa 1787,[3] ʻŌpūkahaʻia arrived at Yale University in 1809, having sailed from Hawaiʻi to New England

---

1. See Schütz 1994:67–69 for a discussion of Archibald Campbell's word list (1816). Campbell spent a little over a year in Hawaiʻi in 1809–10. He recalled enough of the language about five years later for his editor to collect approximately 400 words and adjust Campbell's spelling to his own system.

2. A note attached to the manuscript says that it was found among Queen Emma's private papers.

3. Earlier reports gave 1792.

Figure 6.1. ʻŌpūkahaʻia

as a cabin boy on the *Triumph*, commanded by Captain Caleb Britnall of New Haven, Connecticut.[4] The voyage provided an opportunity for his first English lessons: one of the crew taught him the "letters in [an] English spelling-book," most likely by Noah Webster.[5]

During his years in New England, ʻŌpūkahaʻia studied and worked in various towns in both Connecticut and Massachusetts. In 1815, caught up in the fervor of a widespread religious revival, he converted to Christianity. A year later, he and several others from the Sandwich Islands, as well as other Polynesians and Native Americans, studied at the Foreign Mission School in Cornwall. The object of their training was to equip them to return to their respective homes and share the Gospel with their own people.

Even earlier, ʻŌpūkahaʻia realized how essential the Hawaiian language was for the proposed mission to Hawaiʻi. Once he was familiar with English spelling and grammar and had begun to study Hebrew and Latin, he tried to discover how his own language was constructed. With some assistance from his teachers and the Reverend Eleazar T. Fitch of New Haven, he began work on "a Grammar, a Dictionary, and a Spelling-book," and he also translated the book of Genesis into Hawaiian.

---

4. For more details on how and why this journey was made, see Dwight 1818, 1968, 1990, Schütz 1994, and Lyon 2004.

5. This "English spelling-book" turns out to play an important role in ʻŌpūkahaʻia's story, told later in this chapter.

Figure 6.2. The Foreign Mission School in Cornwall, Connecticut

Figure 6.3. Plaque at the site of the Foreign Mission School

AN OWHIHE GRAMMAR.

The parts of speech, as in most other languages, are nine: the Article, Noun, Pronoun, Adjective, Verb, Adverb, Conjunction, Preposition, and Interjection

The ARTICLE.

The articles are four, O, Ok3, Oke and Ha.
The article O, is placed before the personal pronouns, and also before the names of persons and places; as O-ou, I — O-e, (or O-e-na,) Thou — O-e-3-l3, He, She or It.
O-whi-he   O-mon-3-ha-3 &c.
The article O is declined in the following manner:

N. O.—
P. O-ho.
O. E-3.

The articles O-k3 and O-ke are placed before all nouns, except the names of persons and places, and are declined thus:

N. O-k3.   N. O-he.
P. O-ko.   P. O-ko.
O. E-k3.   O. E-he.

Figure 6.4. The first page of the "grammar" once attributed to ʻŌpūkahaʻia

So far as we know, all these works are lost.[6] And although for the past century, it was thought that the manuscript grammar mentioned above might be ʻŌpūkahaʻia's, in 1993 James Rumford found it to be written in the hand of Samuel Ruggles, one of the First Company of missionaries to Hawaiʻi and a fellow student with ʻŌpūkahaʻia at Cornwall (Rumford 1993b).

Still, ʻŌpūkahaʻia's work lives on through that of Ruggles, who wrote to his sister that his own grammar had been "much assisted by one which Obookiah attempted to form."[7]

Figure 6.5. Samuel Ruggles

Numbers for Letters?

If you look at the first page of the grammar (figure 6.4), you can immediately see that its unusual alphabet, apparently influenced by ʻŌpūkahaʻia's, contains not only Roman letters but also the numbers *3* and *8*. For example, note these common words (from later pages in the booklet):

Ha-h3-la	the house	*8-8-k8*	little
Ha-k3-n3-k3	the man	*3-o-la*	no
Le-m3	hand	*Mi*	from
L8-n3	upward	*O-ou*	I
M3-m8-3	forward	*Wun-na*	presently

This code is no enigma but instead is easily decipherable: all one has to do is to compare these spellings with the current ones:

6. In 1923, Fred W. Beckley wrote, "In the Congressional Library [*sic*] at Washington D.C., authenticated copies of the original translation of the first two chapters of the Bible by Henry Opukahaia, a native Hawaiian, are on file." Ruth Horie, a former cataloger for the University of Hawaiʻi at Mānoa's Hamilton Library, has searched for the manuscript, but so far the staff at the Library of Congress has not been able to find the copies that Beckley referred to.

7. See *Memoirs,* 1990 edition, xv, introduction by A. Loomis: "Of the fourteen Americans who sailed in the Thaddeus, only Samuel Ruggles had ever met Opukahaʻia face to face."

Ha-h3-la	*he hale*	*8-8-k8*	*ʻuʻuku*
Ha-k3-n3-k3	*he kanaka*	*3-o-la*	*ʻaʻole*
Le-m3	*lima*	*Mi*	*mai*
L8-n3	*luna*	*O-ou*	*ʻo au*
M3-m8-3	*ma mua*	*Wun-na*	*auaneʻi*[8]

This comparison shows that the number *3* represents the vowel *a,* and *8* represents *u.* But some of the vowel letters themselves are also used in a way that seems unusual to us now. All in all, the patterns that differ from today's spelling are as follows:

e for *i*   *a* for *e*   *3* for *a*   *u* for [ʌ][9]   *8* for *u*   *ou* for *au*   *i* for *ai*

With very little practice, one could learn to read it, for it shouldn't take long to learn seven simple rules of spelling.

But one is still left with questions about the system. For instance, did ʻŌpūkahaʻia use it in his translation of Genesis? Perhaps so. The following letter suggests that the numbers may have appeared in the Bible translations that existed at that time:[10] "As to elementary books in the language of O[whyhee] something has been done & some passages of scripture have been translated. I do not think the character in which the language is to be written is yet satisfactorily settled. Our alphabet is used with the addition of 3 characters viz. the figure 3 for the sound of the a in father, 4 for a in hail[11] & 8 for oo in room. The fact that these are employed for a different purpose is an objection & another is that they are not used for this in Otaheite"[12] (Bingham 1819:490). Reading between the lines, we might suppose that one "elementary book" might be the 1819 grammatical sketch

8. Thanks to Jeffrey Kapali Lyon for this identification.

9. In Hawaiian, this sound is a variant of *a,* occurring when the following vowel is *i* or *u,* even if it is in the next syllable. It is also a variant of *a* in an unaccented syllable; an example is the first *a* in the phrase *ka hale* 'the house'. In phonetic terms, it is raised from the normally low position of *a,* approaching the sound of the vowel in *cut.*

10. Thanks to Christopher L. Cook for supplying this quotation.

11. The figure *4* is not part of the orthography used in the 1819 sketch. In Webster's system (figure 6.7), *4* represents the vowel in *here,* pronounced [ɪ] in today's American English. However, it is unclear how it was pronounced on the East Coast in the early 1800s.

12. As mentioned elsewhere, it was thought (or at least hoped) that printed material in Tahitian would suffice for Hawaiian, another Polynesian "dialect."

(in Ruggles's handwriting). As for the "passages of scripture," the orthography that Bingham described seems to be the only one in use then.

A more important question is: What is the origin of the system? The answer lies in the history of American education, the backgrounds of the people who trained the Hawaiians in New England in the first two decades of the nineteenth century, and especially "the spelling book."

Noah Webster: The Key to the Puzzle

In the account of ʻŌpūkahaʻia's first English lessons, the spelling book that was mentioned is most likely one volume of Noah Webster's *Grammatical Institute of the English Language*, later known simply as the *American Spelling Book* ([1783] 1800). This work, familiar to nearly every American schoolchild at that time, was used after 1820 to teach English to the Hawaiians. It is also the source of the *3*s and *8*s.

In his book, Webster helped beginning readers by indicating which of several possible sounds the vowel letters represented. His chart, reproduced as figure 6.7, is a guide to the system.

This is how Webster used the letter-number combinations shown in the examples above. Because his first aim was to teach children how to read English aloud from a written text, he tried to show that certain

Figure 6.6. Noah Webster

vowel letters could be pronounced in several different ways (1800:13). On 16 September 1783, he wrote: "The sounds of our vowels . . . are ascertained by the help of figures" (Kendall 2010:91).

For example, the letter *a* could represent one of three sounds, and each of these was distinguished by a small number over the letter. The other vowel letters were treated in the same way.[13]

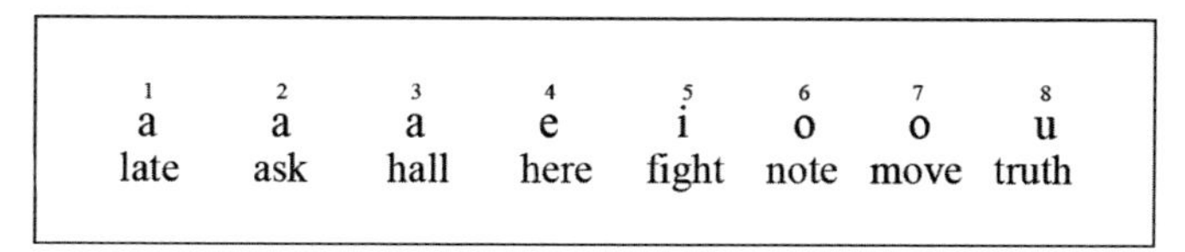

Figure 6.7. Webster's vowel scheme

We can see that for four of the five vowel letters, *a, e, i,* and *o,* the main sound that each represented was the name of the letter itself—that is, what we call the letter when we recite the alphabet. Thus, the letter *a* represents the sound [e] (as in *bait*), *e* [i] (as in *beat*), *i* the diphthong [ai] (as in *bite*), and *o* [o] (as in *boat*). This system is still in place in current Merriam-Webster dictionaries, slightly modified: for these four vowel letters, macrons indicate the "primary values": ā, ē, ī, and ō, illustrated just above.

As for the [a] sound in Hawaiian, as in *lā* 'sun', it is not the name of an English vowel letter, but it is Webster's "third value" of the letter *a.*[14] And because the name of the letter *u* is pronounced [yu] (as in *you*) and not [u] (as in *boot*), *u* with a small *8* over it was used for the vowel in such words as *room* and *true.* The only instance of *u* in Ruggles's manuscript (other than combined with other vowels for diphthongs) is in the word for the time marker, *wun-na* (*auane'i*) 'soon'; here it seems to indicate Webster's "short *u*"—that is, [ʌ], as in *come* or *love.*

At first, Ruggles's use of *ou* for [au] suggests a mistranscription, but for Webster (and others from that era, such as William Anderson—see chapter 5—and the lexicographer Samuel Johnson), *ou* represented the diphthong in ***house*** or ***loud.***

13. About a century later, the McGuffey primer and first three readers ([1879], 1881) used a similar system but with diacritics rather than numbers: for example, wĕnt, fĭsh, sāfe, ärms.

14. Not everyone's pronunciation of this sample word in English will match the Hawaiian sound, for English vowels in this phonetic area show significant dialect variation. In brief, the range of pronunciations is from [a] to [ɔ].

Actually, Webster didn't invent the scheme himself but borrowed it from any of several British English pronouncing dictionaries widely used at the time, intended to promote an "accepted" pronunciation over a "common" one. As for who suggested that the numbers be applied to Hawaiian—not as aids to pronunciation but as actual "letters"—we have no direct evidence. Wayne H. Brumaghim (2011:92–93) was of the opinion that it was the Reverend Eleazar T. Fitch's idea.[15]

In a sense, these numbers were the beginning of the practice in English dictionaries of indicating the pronunciation directly after the headword. Until the missionaries in Hawai'i later abandoned the idea that the names of the vowel letters were their basic sounds, this method was the only means available for showing the pronunciation of Hawaiian vowels.

'Ōpūkaha'ia and Webster: A Personal Connection?

It is difficult—perhaps impossible—to examine the effect of Webster's numerical aids to pronunciation on 'Ōpūkaha'ia's and Ruggles's work without asking if there had been any personal connection among the three men. Here, the birth and death dates of all three are important:

'Ōpūkaha'ia	1787–1818
Ruggles	1795–1871
Webster	1758–1843

Thus, it might have been possible that the three met, for they and some of the First Company of missionaries shared a Yale connection. However, we have no evidence that they did.[16] Instead, their connection need not be personal, but it was definitely scholarly. It was mentioned earlier that 'Ōpūkaha'ia had his first instruction in reading and writing English on the voyage from Hawai'i to New England, when one of the crew taught him the "letters in [an] English spelling-book." Another source identifies this book as Webster's *Blue-backed Speller*. That book is also mentioned in missionary correspondence and in *The Grapes of Canaan* (1966),

15. Fitch and 'Ōpūkaha'ia worked together on "our Grammar" (as 'Ōpūkaha'ia described it) and "translating a few chapters of the Bible" (Dwight ([1818] 1990:41–42).

16. Research on 'Ōpūkaha'ia's life continues, and such a connection may eventually be discovered.

Albertine Loomis's book about her ancestors, the rest of the first companies of missionaries, and their Hawaiian consultants.

To show that ʻŌpūkahaʻia and the missionaries at the Foreign Mission School in Cornwall, Connecticut, were almost certain to have been influenced by Webster's book, we have only to look at its Harry Potter–like book sales. After the book was first published in 1783, "more than 50 impressions of the book appeared before 1800, some of them 25,000-copy runs. Another 100 impressions were run off by 1829 when the number of copies sold throughout the United States reached at least 20 million" (Morgan 1975:48–49). Since the population of the United States in 1820 was a little under 10 million, this means that the Webster speller must have been familiar to nearly every American schoolchild at that time (Schütz 1994:91).

Prelude to Consonant Confusion

The differences between the unusual 1819 alphabet and the one we are familiar with today lie mostly in the vowel system. But later, it was discovered that the consonants posed an even greater problem, apparently unknown to Ruggles. His spelling of Hawaiian words shows that he was not aware that several consonants varied from place to place and from speaker to speaker (which will be discussed in the next chapter). As a result, he and the other missionaries were not prepared for what they found when they reached Hawaiʻi a year later.

It seems strange that the consonant variation was not noticed, for the Hawaiian students at the Foreign Mission School must have spoken different varieties of the language. For example, George Kaumualiʻi came from Kauaʻi and probably spoke a *t*-dialect, different from the kind of Hawaiian that ʻŌpūkahaʻia had spoken on the island of Hawaiʻi. And Ruggles must have been aware that the Hawaiian words in Cook's account were written with *t*.[17] Why didn't his grammar reflect such differences?

One possibility is that the Hawaiians at Cornwall, thrown together after being away from their own dialects for years, had developed a common pronunciation among themselves. As a matter of fact, Kaumualiʻi, who left Hawaiʻi at the age of six, was said to have forgotten his Hawaiian to the extent that ʻŌpūkahaʻia was teaching him his own language.[18]

17. On the other hand, perhaps the missionaries did not have access to Cook's works.

18. James D. Rumford, pers. comm., 20 October 1992.

Another possibility is that Ruggles might have worked exclusively with ʻŌpūkahaʻia, who was most likely a *k*-speaker. If so, he might have influenced Ruggles's choice of letters. In addition, ʻŌpūkahaʻia's own difficulties in pronouncing American English *r* (described in the *Memoirs*) might have prompted him to suggest *l* for his alphabet rather than *r*.

FINAL JOURNEY

ʻŌpūkahaʻia was not able to fulfill his dream of carrying Christianity back to Hawaiʻi, for he died of typhus in February 1818. He was buried in the oldest section of the Cornwall cemetery, which is separated from the village by a winding two-lane highway. His memorial there was a large, horizontal slab resting on a mortared stone platform, perhaps three feet high at the lower end of the slope (figure 6.10, center distance).

Figure 6.8. The Congregational Church (now United Church of Christ) in Cornwall

Figure 6.9. The house in which ʻŌpūkahaʻia died

Figure 6.10. The mown path leading to the grave

Figure 6.11. ʻŌpūkahaʻia's grave at Cornwall.

Figure 6.12. He makana mai Hawaiʻi na ʻŌpūkahaʻia

IN
Memory of
HENRY OBOOKIAH
A native of
OWHYHEE
His arrival in this country gave rise
to the Foreign mission school,
of which he was a worthy member.
He was once an Idolater, and was
designed for a Pagan Priest; but by
the Grace of God and by the prayers
and instructions of pious friends,
he became a christian.
He was eminent for piety and
missionary Zeal. When almost prepared
to return to his native Isle to preach the
Gospel, God took [him] to himself. In his last
sickness, he wept and prayed for Owhyhee
but was submissive. He died without fear
with a heavenly smile on his
countenance and glory in his soul.
Feb. 17, 1818
aged 26.

Figure 6.13. Inscription on ʻŌpūkahaʻia's tombstone

Does ʻŌpūkahaʻia's scholarly work live on? We have no idea of how much of his grammar Ruggles used in his own. Nor can we be sure whose idea it was to use Webster's numbers in place of *a* and *u*.

Its uncertain history notwithstanding, this short work is a remarkable document, being probably the first example of Hawaiian written on other than a hasty and impressionistic phonetic basis, or, as with Anderson's list, on only a very short acquaintance with the language.[19]

As one can see from the first booklet printed in Hawaiian (*The Alphabet* [1822]; see chapter 9), the unusual alphabet was short-lived. Even

19. Archibald Campbell's Hawaiian word list (1816) might be an exception, for the editor attempted to devise a consistent scheme for writing the words. However, Campbell was not a native speaker, having learned the language—to a degree—during a stay of a little more than a year. On the other hand, at that time he may have been totally immersed in the Hawaiian language, leading to a substantial control of the language. For more details, see Schütz 1994:67–69.

before the missionaries set sail for Hawaiʻi, they found it awkward. After all, Webster's numbers were not meant to serve as letters in the alphabet but instead were rather like training wheels on a bicycle: meant only to help beginners and then to be discarded.

But why couldn't the unconventional numbers and letters simply have been adjusted? Putting the unusual orthography aside for the moment and looking more closely at *A Short Elementary Grammar of the Owihe Language,* one might suggest that it was not its alphabet that kept it out of the hands and minds of potential learners in Hawaiʻi but, instead, its contents.

Looking ahead to the 1822 primer that did introduce literacy to the Hawaiians, one finds that these two works are very different in their structure and contents—reflecting two separate series of Webster's textbooks. By comparing them with those works that were available at the time (excluding the dictionaries), it is evident that the 1819 work is closer to Webster's English grammar than to his spellers or readers. Following the Latinate model common in grammars of that period, it describes Hawaiian as if it were a language replete with noun declensions, verb conjugations, parts of speech, and gender. In this sense, it is descriptive, possibly intended to present Hawaiian grammar to the American or European scientific community.

In contrast, the 1822 work is pedagogical—it introduces the concept of an alphabet and how to combine letters into syllables, syllables into words, and words into sentences. It is not a "grammar," but a "primer," designed to teach Hawaiians how to read and write their own language.

*

In July 1993, at the request of his collateral descendants, ʻŌpūkahaʻia's remains were exhumed, flown to Hawaiʻi, and reinterred within the grounds of Kahikolu Church at Nāpoʻopoʻo, Kona, overlooking Kealakekua Bay, on the island of Hawaiʻi.

Although ʻŌpūkahaʻia's scholarly works may be forgotten, the young man is well remembered and revered, for his influence on Hawaiian language history is not confined to a handful of lost manuscripts. Instead, his personality and zeal inspired many others during his lifetime, and—through his *Memoirs*—they continue to do so even after his death.[20]

---

20. See Schütz 1989, a more detailed study of ʻŌpūkahaʻia's work.

Figure 6.14. ʻŌpūkahaʻia's grave at Nāpoʻopoʻo

Figure 6.15. ʻŌpūkahaʻia's grave at Nāpoʻopoʻo

Figure 6.16. ʻŌpūkahaʻia's memorial stone at Nāpoʻopoʻo

VERBATIM

Edwin W. Dwight was a student in the Divinity School at Yale when he found a weeping ʻŌpūkahaʻia on the steps of Yale. Because he was in charge of classes at the Foreign Mission School, he formed a close association with ʻŌpūkahaʻia as his teacher and friend. *Memoirs of Henry Obookiah* appeared only a few months after the young man's death. The following passage is one of several that shows ʻŌpūkahaʻia's interest in language:

His inquisitive mind was not satisfied with pursuing the usual round of study, but he was disposed to understand critically every branch of knowledge to which he attended. For this reason his progress in his studies was not rapid—but, as a scholar, he was industrious, ingenious, and thorough. His mind was also inventive. After having acquired some slight knowledge of the English language in its grammatical construction, he entered upon the project of reducing to system his own native tongue. As it was not a written language, but lay in its chaotic state, every thing was to be done. With some assistance he had made considerable progress towards completing a Grammar, a Dictionary, and a Spelling-book.

He had also translated into his native tongue the whole of the Book of Genesis.

These specimens of his industry and ingenuity, *when seen,* administer severe reproof to the sloth of most persons of much greater age and of advantages far superior to his own.

When Obookiah became a member of the Foreign Mission School, he had attended to all the common branches of English education. In reading, writing, and spelling, he was perhaps as perfect as most young men of our own country, of the same age and with common opportunities. He wrote a legible manly hand, and had acquired the habit of writing with considerable rapidity. He had at this time studied the English Grammar so far as to be able to phrase [parse?] most sentences with readiness. He understood the important rules in common Arithmetic, and had obtained considerable knowledge of Geography. He had studied also one book of Euclid's Elements of Geometry, and of his own accord, without a regular instructor, had acquired such knowledge of the Hebrew, that he had been able to read several chapters in the Hebrew Bible, and had translated a few passages into his native language. He had a peculiar relish for the Hebrew language, and from its resemblance to his own, acquired it with great facility; and found it much less difficult to translate the Hebrew than the English into his native tongue. (Dwight [1818] 1990:77–78)

CHAPTER 7

HOW THE ALPHABET CHANGED FROM 1820 TO 1826

One reader of ʻŌpūkahaʻia's *Memoirs* who was deeply affected by his story was Elisha Loomis, another well-known figure in Hawaiian mission history. He found the account of ʻŌpūkahaʻia's life and death so moving that he resigned his printer's apprenticeship in Canandaigua, New York, and joined the Foreign Mission School. It is perhaps fitting that it was his trained hand that eventually set the type and supervised the printing of the first book in Hawaiian on the secondhand Ramage printing press—the beginning of the literate revolution that changed the path of Hawaiian history.

Loomis was in the First Company of the Hawaiian Mission, the organization that had such a profound effect on written Hawaiian. For this reason, it is impossible to understand how the Hawaiian alphabet developed unless we also know something about the history of the mission as well.

1820–1824

March 1820, which is when the Congregational missionaries arrived in Hawaiʻi, is often cited as the beginning of the Hawaiian Mission. However, the idea itself is older, going back to 1795, when Thomas Haweis, founder of the London Missionary Society (LMS), proposed a mission to the Sandwich Islands.[1] About a decade later, the American Board of Commissioners for Foreign Missions (ABCFM) in Boston expressed a more definite interest in spreading the gospel to Hawaiʻi, which resulted in ʻŌpūkahaʻia, eighteen other Hawaiians, and several American mission-

1. Haweis's proselytizing foray into the Pacific was said to have been inspired by reading the accounts of Cook's voyages (Haweis 1795–1802).

Figure 7.1. The four Hawaiians who returned

aries being trained at the Foreign Mission school in Cornwall.[2]

But it wasn't until 23 October 1819 that the *Thaddeus* set sail from Boston with the First Company of missionaries to the Sandwich Islands, accompanied by Thomas Hopu, John Honoli'i, George Sandwich (Humehume), and George P. Kaumuali'i.

For all these missionary groups in Polynesia and nearby islands—the LMS, which concentrated on Tahiti and Sāmoa;[3] the ABCFM; the Wesleyan Methodist Missionary Society (WMS), which later worked in Fiji and Tonga; and the Church Missionary Society (CMS), which served mainly in New Zealand—language was important because it was the key to conversion. And more than any other missionary contribution connected with language, such as grammars or dictionaries, it was the alphabet that would have the greatest effect on the Hawaiians, for it would enable them to read and write their own language.

For a time, it wasn't even certain that there *would* be an alphabet, for at least two other communication systems were also considered. First, Hiram Bingham, inspired by Thomas Hopkins Gallaudet, a pioneer in teaching the deaf in America, considered sign language as a possible approach.[4] Later, Bingham and the other missionaries discussed both the Russian

2. These numbers are from Nancy J. Morris (pers. comm., 4 April 2018). She elaborated: "By my reckoning there were 19 Hawaiians at the school. Three died while at the school. Twelve came back to Hawaii though not all had any association with the mission. Information on the others is lacking."

3. The Wesleyans were also interested in Sāmoa. See Wood 1975 for details about a territorial conflict between the WMS and the LMS.

4. Hiram Bingham to Samuel Worcester, Salem, MA, from Goshen, CT, 11 May 1819. Bingham family papers, 1-1, p. 4.

alphabet and a syllabary (such as Japanese *katakana* or *hiragana*) as possible writing systems. As a matter of fact, Bingham experimented with a syllabary, and a fragment of the Lord's Prayer written with such a system can be found in his papers at the Hawaiian Mission Houses Historic Site and Archives. Figure 7.3 shows the symbols and their values (Rumford 1997).

Figure 7.2. Hiram Bingham

These modes were eventually ruled out in favor of an alphabet that would be at least somewhat similar to that of English (thus simplifying the teaching of both languages) and to that of Tahitian (because it was believed that the same books could be used for both "dialects").

Still, no uniform alphabet existed. Neither the missionaries nor the long-term foreign residents wrote Hawaiian words consistently. As for the residents, Bingham thought that their abilities in Hawaiian were not to be trusted, for the way they pronounced or wrote the names of places and people was far from what the Hawaiians were actually saying (1847:153).

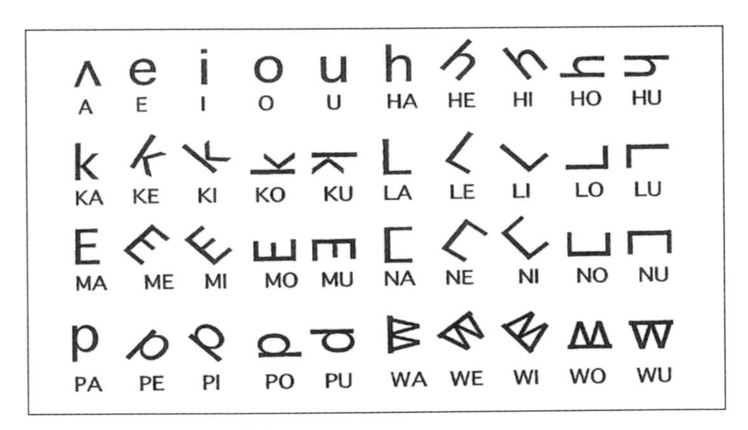

Figure 7.3. Bingham's syllabary

Nor were established spellings reliable; for example, some of the most common names, such as "Owhyhee," were fixed by convention in a form that only suggested an authentic pronunciation. Others, less common, were spelled differently by each person who wrote them.

These haphazard attempts to write the language might have been adequate for some uses, but it was obvious that they could not serve as a foundation for literacy in the Hawaiian language. Thus, with the help and advice of the Hawaiians, the missionaries had to examine the sounds of the language, one by one, and decide on a consistent way to write each one. The results of their decisions are shown on the first two pages of the first book printed in the Hawaiian language.

1822

The Alphabet

The Alphabet is a primer just eight pages long, 16 × 10.5 centimeters: a little smaller than a modern paperback.[5] The printing itself took place early in 1822: "We are happy to announce to you that on the first Monday of January [the 7th] we commenced printing, & with great satisfaction have put the first eight pages of the Owhyhee spelling book into the hands of our pupils, copies of which we now transmit to you for the examination of the Committee, and as little articles of curiosity from these dark Isles. By the next conveyance we hope to send complete copies, with a preface. The edition will be small, about 500 copies,—We should be obliged, if the Committee should suggest alterations & amendments, from a perusal of the first 8 pages" (Missionary letters: 16, Oʻahu, 1 February 1822).

A. Grove Day and Albertine Loomis added some detail to the bare account just above:

> Among the group were the Mission's leader, Rev. Hiram Bingham, traders Butler of Maui and Hunnewell of Honolulu, American ship captains Henry

5. It is not clear why the "spelling book" has the title *The Alphabet*. *Merriam-Webster* does not include 'primer' or 'spelling book' as one of the meanings of *alphabet.* Perhaps the following definition from the *Oxford English Dictionary* comes closer: "The key to any study or branch of knowledge; the first rudiments." However, some children's readers did hinge on the alphabet, but they were organized around words and then sentences featuring *A*, *B*, and so on.

and Masters, and Chief Keʻeaumoku (Governor Cox) of Maui, who happened to be in Honolulu and who would take a leading role in what Bingham called "laying a cornerstone of an important edifice for the nation."

Keʻeaumoku was handed a composing stick and shown how to set a few pieces of lead type in a line. On the bed of the press lay the first two pages of the spelling lesson. Loomis inserted Keʻeamoku's stick, inked the type, put a sheet of paper in place, and rolled the type and paper under the press. He then turned to the chief and motioned to the big lever that worked the giant screw, to press the blank sheet unto the inked type. Loomis said, "huki!" (pull). Keʻeaumoku hauled on the lever.

The first impression from the Mission Press was struck. Carefully, Loomis backed off the pressure and lifted the sheet sprinkled with wet black syllables in two languages. "Maikaʻi" (good!) exclaimed the chief. Later he was quoted as saying he had "made a book." What he had actually accomplished was far more important, for he had printed the first of millions of pages of books and pamphlets in the Hawaiian language. That initial sheet of a schoolbook was the prototype of a hundred and seventy-five years of literacy in the Hawaiian Islands. ([1973] 1997:6)

Another eight pages appeared in late February 1822.[6] Perhaps the most important decision that the missionaries made is shown in the top portion of figure 7.6: a uniform way to write the vowels. In the next section, I discuss the reasons for these choices.

Figure 7.4. Keʻeaumoku striking the first image

6. In chapter 9, the entire work is reproduced and discussed.

Figure 7.5. Interior of the printshop. Photograph by John Barker

Replacing the "English" Vowels

In the first year of the Mission (1820), when the alphabet was at an experimental stage and there were no Hawaiian texts to use in the schools, the missionaries did use "both English and Hawaiian together" (Bingham 1847:103). But the teachers were aware of the irregularities of English spelling, and wished "to avoid an ambiguous, erroneous, and inconvenient orthography, to assign to *every character one certain sound* [emphasis added], and thus represent with ease and exactness the true pronunciation of the Hawaiian language" (Bingham 1847:153).

It is obvious that the first step toward an efficient alphabet was to replace the English way of writing vowels with the Continental (European mainland) system. The problem with English spelling was that it used none of the orthographic ideals listed just above, whereas Latin and Italian used them consistently. Here, coincidence came into play, for the vowel systems of Hawaiian and other Polynesian languages are very similar to that of Latin. In other words, the five vowel letters available in the

THE ALPHABET.

VOWELS.	Names.	SOUND. Ex. in Eng.	Ex. in Hawaii.
A a	â	as in *father*,	la—sun.
E e	a	— *tele*,	hemo—cast off.
I i	e	— *marine*,	marie—quiet.
O o	o	— *over*,	ono—sweet.
U u	oo	— *rule*,	nui—large.

CONSONANTS.	Names.	CONSONANTS.	Names.
B b	be	N n	nu
D d	de	P p	pi
H h	he	R r	ro
K k	ke	T t	ti
L l	la	V v	vi
M m	mu	W w	we

The following are used in spelling foreign words:

F f	fe	S s	se
G g	ge	Y y	yi

1

Figure 7.6. First page of *The Alphabet.* Note: *Ono* [*'ono*] usually means 'delicious', but in the compound *wai 'ono* 'honey' it can mean 'sweet'

Roman alphabet (*a, e, i, o, u*) exactly matched those necessary to write Hawaiian.[7]

The European system was also favored by the New England scholar John Pickering,[8] who recognized the problems that English spelling presented. For example, in an English word, the letter *a* could represent any of four different sounds.[9] Thus, Pickering recommended what he called the "foreign" sounds of the vowels. In other words, Hawaiian should use the five vowel letters that were available, but each letter would represent the Latin or Italian value,[10] not the English one.

Another advantage of using this scheme is that most of the missionaries would have been familiar with Latin, especially those who had trained at a theological seminary.

Finally, this decision brought Hawaiian into line with the Polynesian alphabets already well established—those for Tahitian and Māori.

Naturally, the Latin way of spelling vowels had its critics: one called it a needless innovation and "an affectation of Italicising." But such criticisms usually came from those who did not use the revised alphabet. Those who did use it were both satisfied and pleased with it.

In all their efforts to devise an efficient alphabet, the missionaries, who knew that they were not especially well trained for this task, called on help from the outside—not only scholars from New England but also colleagues from different mission organizations working elsewhere in the Pacific or in North America. For example, they wrote to the ABCFM headquarters that "Any books from you, in the language

---

7. English, which has a greater number of vowel sounds, must use combinations of vowel letters to supplement the basic five. For example, *ea* in English is often used to indicate one vowel sound, as in *beat.* In Hawaiian, *ea* represents two vowels, as in *kea* 'white'. English also uses double letters to represent different vowels: for example, *ee* for /i/ and *oo* for /u/.

8. John Pickering, of Salem, Massachusetts, was already well known as the author of *Essay on a Uniform Orthography for the Indian Languages of North America* (1820).

9. As described in chapter 6, this distribution was one of the reasons for using the numeral *3* for one of the *a* sounds. Incidentally, Webster apparently recognized only three different values.

10. That is, the Continental pronunciation of Latin, not the one commonly used in the British Isles (Jeffrey Kapali Lyon, pers. comm., 2014).

of Otaheite, New Zealand, or of the Indian tribes of America would be acceptable to us."[11]

And timely help did come from one of these sources: a Māori grammar and dictionary (Kendall and Lee 1820), which arrived in Hawaiʻi just a few days before the first Hawaiian booklet was printed on 7 January 1822. Because the Māori vowels were written in the Continental, not the English way, it helped confirm the Hawaiian missionaries' decision to do likewise.

Except for the *kahakō* (macron, which marks vowel length), the vowel letters in *The Alphabet* were used as they are today. (By the way, in figure 7.3, note "ex. in Eng." just after the boldfaced uppercase and lowercase letters. Wouldn't such examples assume that readers knew English?)

As a corollary to the list of vowels, a list of seven diphthongs[12] also appears (figure 7.4). Its large type suggests that this class of sounds was just as important as single vowels were.

Diphthongs

Some linguists have claimed that Hawaiian does not have diphthongs, maintaining that if *ai* and *au,* for example, are to be considered diphthongs, the second element in each must be a glide—that is, *y* or *w*—not a vowel. This argument may hold for English, but not for Hawaiian. Although *w* exists, there is no *y* in the Hawaiian alphabet. Next, not only do *i* and *u* serve as the second element in a diphthong, but *e* and *o* can have that function as well. Accounting for this pattern would require inventing two more consonants (or semivowels) that would have a very limited distribution.

Another argument claims that unlike English diphthongs, Hawaiian diphthongs do not exist in the underlying phonological structure. A counterclaim (Rolle and Starks 2014:278) neutralizes the two arguments; thus, the "underlying structure" is irrelevant.

Differences of opinion such as this one, as do so many, hinge on definition. *Merriam-Webster's Collegiate Dictionary, Eleventh Edition,* defines "diphthong" as follows: "a gliding monosyllabic speech sound (as the

11. Missionary letters, Oʻahu, 25 November 1821, Bingham, Thurston, Chamberlain, Loomis (13–14).

12. Note the spelling in the heading in figure 7.7. The *Oxford English Dictionary* gives *dipthong* as a variant. Moreover, some pronunciations reflect this spelling.

vowel combination at the end of *toy*) that starts at or near the articulatory position for one vowel and moves to or toward the position of another." Certain vowel combinations in Hawaiian fit this definition perfectly.

The word "monosyllabic" in the definition above leads us to an important topic that the opposing point of view apparently does not consider: *function.* In short: certain Hawaiian vowel combinations are diphthongs because each functions as a *single unit* in one defining position: the second-to-last vowel in a two-syllable unit, such as ***'ai**na* 'meal'. The reasoning is straightforward: if *ai* were not a diphthong, the accent in the word would be on *i*—the second-to-last vowel. The same vowels in the opposite order—*ia*—do not form a diphthong, but two separate syllables, as in *ia* 'he, she, it'. Any account of Hawaiian vowels must account for this important patterning.

Figure 7.7 shows how the missionaries interpreted Hawaiian diphthongs.[13] Note the unsuccessful attempt to illustrate the differences between *-e, -i,* and *-o, -u* with English examples.[14]

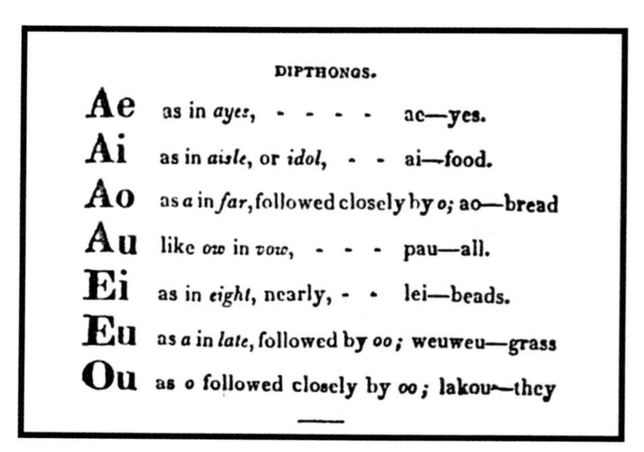

DIPTHONGS.

Ae as in *ayes,* - - - - ae—yes.
Ai as in *aisle,* or *idol,* - - ai—food.
Ao as *a* in *far,* followed closely by *o;* ao—bread
Au like *ow* in *vow,* - - - pau—all.
Ei as in *eight,* nearly, - - lei—beads.
Eu as *a* in *late,* followed by *oo;* weuweu—grass
Ou as *o* followed closely by *oo;* lakou—they

Figure 7.7. Diphthongs

13. Hawaiian also has long diphthongs. For example, *'āina* 'land', contrasting with *'aina* 'meal'. Because the missionary analysts were unaware of vowel length, they missed such contrasts. See Schütz 1981 and Schütz, Kanada, and Cook 2005.

14. The explanations for *-o* and *-u* are more accurate, because they do not attempt to give English words to illustrate the difference.

The Phonetics of Hawaiian Diphthongs

From the list of diphthongs in figure 7.7, one can observe that, although all Hawaiian diphthongs are falling (i.e., the level of prominence "falls" from the first vowel to the second),[15] the examples in the figure can be arranged into phonetic types based on vowel height:[16]

1. *A* (a low vowel) followed by *i* or *u* (high vowels): *ai, au.*
2. *A* followed by *e* or *o* (mid vowels): *ae, ao.*
3. *E* (a mid vowel) followed by *i* or u (high vowels): *ei, eu.*
4. *O* (a mid vowel) followed by *u* (a high vowel): *ou.* Table IX (page 13 of *The Alphabet*) contains one example of the diphthong *oi* (missing from figure 7.7), in *oia* (now written as *ʻo ia*).

One combination, *eo,* not listed above, may function as a diphthong in some dialects (Keao NeSmith, pers. comm., 2014).

Finally, it should be noted that the pronunciation of *a* changes significantly when it is followed by *i* or *u*—not only in a diphthong, but when a consonant separates the two vowels. In this position, /a/ approaches [ə] (as in *cut*).[17]

The sequences that are missing from the list can be described as vowel combinations at the same height on a vowel chart. Such horizontal sequences are as follows:

high: *iu, ui* mid: *oe, eo*

Of these four combinations, *iu*[18] and *oe* are diphthongs, proven by accent patterns when these sequences are in penultimate position.

---

15. Some scholars have misinterpreted this term. Samuel H. Elbert, in the grammatical introduction to *Hawaiian Dictionary,* had the mistaken impression that "rising" and "falling" with respect to diphthongs referred to vowel height, not prominence.

16. That is, tongue and jaw height.

17. See *Pocket Hawaiian Grammar* (Schütz, Kanada, and Cook 2005:xiv–xv).

18. Because the relative sonority of these vowels is similar, sometimes it is difficult to determine where the accent is when the combination is in penultimate position. For example, note the borrowings *Iune* 'June' and *Iulai* 'July'. In those words, *i* seems not to be the peak of the syllable but more like an on-glide—that is, a [y]-like consonant. Similarly, in *uila* 'wheel', *u* sounds rather like [w].

Native Speaker Reactions to Diphthongs

In 1838, Lorrin Andrews, who arrived in Hawaiʻi in 1828 and later became the mission's most accomplished grammarian, wrote, "Until lately, the most intelligent Hawaiians would never admit that two vowels ever coalesced so far as to make but one sound: and in a Hawaiian's ear, both vowels in a diphthong are distinctly and separately heard. But since some of the scholars in the Seminary[19] have gotten more perfectly the idea of what is intended by the term diphthong, by a little attention to the Greek and English languages, they are not only ready to admit that there are diphthongs in their language, but that there are a great many of them"[20] (Andrews 1838:394).

However, Andrews's comments on diphthongs cannot be taken at face value. First, he did not use the functional test sketched above—to note which vowel in the sequence was accented when the combination was in penultimate position. Next, his mistaken concept of the *ʻokina* 'glottal stop' was that it was a means to prevent two vowels from forming a diphthong.

Consonants

Figure 7.8 shows *The Alphabet*'s list of consonants. The first anomaly that strikes one is that the list includes five consonants—*b, d, r, t,* and *v*—that are missing in today's alphabet. Four more—*f, g, s,* and *y*—are explained, in smaller print, as letters "used in spelling foreign words."

Even though speakers of Hawaiian didn't usually pronounce a "foreign" consonant in a borrowed word but instead used a Hawaiian sound closest to it, the missionaries felt that it was necessary to keep the spelling (if not the pronunciation) distinct from that of native words. To them, two words with identical spellings but different meanings could sometimes be embarrassing. For example, Andrews thought that if the borrowing *rama* 'rum' were spelled *lama,*[21] it would be confused with *lama*

---

19. The "seminary" refers to Lahainaluna, a high school established on Maui in 1831 by the ABCFM. Because Andrews was the head of the school at its founding, he was familiar with the school, its courses, and its students.

20. Because we do not know how these results were obtained, it is possible that the students' opinions were influenced by their instructors. See Schütz 1981:11–12.

21. See more on *lama* in chapter 16.

CONSONANTS.	Names.	CONSONANTS.	Names.
B b	be	N n	nu
D d	de	P p	pi
H h	he	R r	ro
K k	kẹ	T t	ti
L l	la	V v	vi
M m	mu	W w	we

The following are used in spelling foreign words:

F f	fe	S s	se
G g	ge	Y y	yi

Figure 7.8. Consonants

'torch',[22] or if *mare* 'to marry' were spelled *male,* it would be confused with *male* 'to spit'. (Hiram Bingham's justification for this policy is quoted in full in the "Verbatim" section of chapter 13.)

However, the falling together of certain pairs of consonants in the ancestral language (see chapter 3) had produced many homonyms in the native vocabulary, useful for the poetic feature *kaona* (see chapter 16) and other functions as well. Perhaps the only homonyms that Andrews wanted to avoid were those with meanings that he considered awkward or risqué.

Returning to the five extra consonants, one needs to ask: How were they used? A closer examination of the booklet shows that the missionaries, perhaps assisted by native speakers, seem to have chosen a fixed spelling for some common words.

For example, the word for 'good', now written as *maikaʻi,* is regularly spelled here with a *t: maitai,* but *Akua* 'god' is spelled as it is today—with a *k. Lani* 'heaven' and *hele* 'go' are spelled with *l,* but *aroha* 'love' and *roa* 'long' with *r. ʻAwa* 'kava' is spelled with a *v,* but *wai* 'water' and *kiwi* 'horn' with *w.* (See further discussion in chapter 9.)

Although certain words used these fixed spellings, this practice concealed problems that were soon obvious—and disturbing—to the missionaries. Long before 1820, explorers and traders had noticed that sometimes a word could be pronounced with one consonant and other times with a different one. One of the first examples of this alternation is

22. For example, Psalm 27:1 reads, "Jehovah is my light and my salvation." Interpreting *lama* 'light' as 'rum' would give an awkward meaning to the passage.

from the journal of David Samwell, surgeon on the *Discovery* on Cook's third voyage, who wrote in 1779 that different dialects used different sounds: "These people [of Ni'ihau and Kaua'i] constantly make use of the T, where the others use the K, such as in the Name of the island Atowai which is called Akowai at Ouwaihee" (Beaglehole 1967:1230–31). (However, the missionaries to Hawai'i did not have easy access to such observations in early explorers' and traders' accounts. Moreover, they could not have known of Samwell's findings, for his journal remained unpublished until 1967.)

Soon, however, the framers of this oversized alphabet discovered for themselves similar disturbing patterns among the consonants. They found that words could be written with any letter within each of the following groups without changing the meaning: *b* or *p; l, d, r,* or sometimes *n; t* or *k; v* or *w.* This was a serious problem, and the missionary-linguists spent the next four years looking for a way to solve it. The following sections give some details of their struggles.

How the Consonants Varied

In 1824, the missionary Artemas Bishop wrote to a colleague describing the difficulties that the interchangeable consonants posed: "You must know then, that the use of an L, or an R, in any word when one of these letters is used, conveys precisely the same meaning,—thus to say, a*l*oha or a*r*oha, (love), either will be equally well understood. The same may be said with regard to the letters k & t.—and also v & w. "thus: *t*abu or *k*abu (forbidden) Ha*v*aii or Ha*w*aii, (proper name of this Island)—in the use of either method there is no difficulty in being understood.—The B. & the P. are likewise synonymous, thus we may say, *pure* or *pule, bure* or *bule* (prayer)" (Bishop 1824). Note that this last two-syllable word (now spelled *pule*) could be spelled four different ways; longer words containing all the problem consonants increased the possibilities exponentially.

It is unlikely that any part of the missionaries' training in New England could have prepared them for these apparently unstable consonants. Possibly their experience with English had led them to expect that once the vowels were settled, the rest of the alphabet would fall into place. Even Samuel Ruggles's manuscript grammar showed no hint of the problems that lay ahead.

Nor did the descriptions of Tahitian and Māori help. The Tahitian alphabet contained extra consonant letters, but like the foreign consonants in the Hawaiian alphabet, they were used mainly for writing such words as *Jehovah, Jesus Christ,* and *Adam.*[23] The Māori alphabet of the early 1820s reflected a similar problem, for it used both *r* and *d* for what was actually one sound. But it would have been difficult for a casual reader to notice this pattern, described in figure 7.9.

Figure 7.9. Artemas Bishop

At first the safest plan was to use all these letters, for, as with Tahitian, they could all prove useful for writing foreign terms. Besides, it was felt that words should be written "as they sounded"—that is, to an English ear.

However, although this larger alphabet could give the phonetic detail that the missionaries desired, the spelling and pronunciation of individual words became a problem that was impossible to solve. For example, if *kapu, tapu, kabu,* and *tabu* all meant 'sacred, forbidden', which one was the "correct" spelling? How could the Hawaiians quickly learn to read and write if the relationship between sound and spelling was not constant? How could scholars write a dictionary if so many words had several spellings?

Time after time, the missionaries sought the advice of native speakers. But they found that the Hawaiians, for whom the differences were not significant, could not hear them.

And this was rightly so, for it wasn't necessary to hear them. The principle is this: so long as *kapu* and *tapu,* for example, mean the same thing, it doesn't matter whether you write *k* or *t.* But random spelling is not efficient. And to insist that both spellings are necessary is

23. "Mainly" is used here because of the occasional *b* and *d* that reflect the way speakers of English heard (relatively) unaspirated /p/ and /t/.

to impose the English sound system on Hawaiian. In other words, in English, it is necessary to distinguish between *t* and *k,* because these two sounds keep words distinct (for example, *tin* and *kin*). But *t* and *k* don't function that way in Hawaiian. The same explanation holds for the other groups as well.

Actually, each of the sets of troublesome consonants is slightly different in nature. And it would be more accurate to call some of the groups a *range* rather than an *alternation* of pronunciations. Here is a detailed description of each group:

1. For the so-called *p/b* pair, there probably wasn't much variation at all. English speakers tend to hear Hawaiian *p* as a *b* sound because it doesn't have as much *aspiration* (a strong puff of air) at the beginning of a word as English does. For example, if you pronounce the English words *pin, spin,* and *bin* while holding your hand in front of your mouth, the *p* in *spin* sounds (and feels) more like the *b* in *bin* than like the *p* in *pin.* However, early records show a tendency for some foreign writers to hear *b* more often in the middle of a word (and hence, between vowels).
2. *K* versus *t* was largely (but not entirely) a matter of geography. Speakers from Kaua'i and Ni'ihau usually used *t;* those from other areas usually used *k.* In terms of history, *t* was probably still in the process of changing to *k,* and this change was heading through the chain of islands from the southeast to the northwest. Moreover, as people moved from one area to another, the dialects became mixed. Such a mixing of dialects in some parts of Hawai'i is reflected in early word lists that show both *k* and *t.* Adding to the complexity, speakers from Ni'ihau now use both *t* and *k.*[24]
3. The *l/r/d* problem was somewhat different. The evidence from some nineteenth-century reports suggests that the sound was actually a tapped *r,* similar to the *r* in Spanish (as mentioned in chapter 5), Tahitian, or Māori. Hearing this sound as a *d,* as well as *l,* is also common for speakers of English. As noted above, the compilers of the first Māori dictionary wrote both *r* and *d.* However, the letters did not alternate at random but in a nearly regular way.[25] Table 7.1

24. See Newbrand 1951 and Piccolo 2005 for more details.

25. The written words are our only evidence of what the analysts heard.

TABLE 7.1. *D* AND *R* WRITTEN IN MĀORI IN 1820

da	0, 0	***ra***	50, 123
de	1, 5	***re***	23, 84
di	18, 89	*ri*	1, 14
do	0, 0	***ro***	21, 90
du	25, 74	*ru*	1, 5

shows how these letters were distributed—that is, which vowels they occurred before. In the columns with numbers, the first shows the frequency at the beginning of a word, and the second shows the frequency in the middle. As this distribution shows, the missionaries in New Zealand apparently heard the consonant more often as a *d* before *i* and *u* and as an *r* before any of the other three vowels. For example, the 1820 Māori dictionary contains the entries *duku* 'dive' and *didi* 'anger', now written as *ruku* and *riri*. But the compilers of the dictionary didn't notice the pattern at the time and considered *d* and *r* separate sounds. It wasn't until later that *r* was chosen and *d* discarded. For Hawaiian, however, only a few early writers heard *d*. And although some wrote both *r* and *l*, there were no clear patterns of distribution as there were in Māori.

4. Finally, *w* most likely represented a range of pronunciations as well: a sound made with both lips but heard more like a *v* when the lips were more tightly closed and more like a *w* when they were more relaxed. (See Schütz 1981.)

These were the problems that faced the missionary-linguists. How could they be solved?

1824–1826

Vote for Your Favorite Letters!

In early 1824, after the mission had been using its alphabet for about two years, a committee was formed to examine the problems that the fuller set of consonants presented. They stated their task in the form of two questions: (1) Should they change the existing alphabet? (2) If so, how could they make the spelling system uniform?

This phrasing summarizes a theme that runs through all the missionaries' correspondence on the matter: it was not their intent to change the Hawaiian language but only the way it was spelled. For example, on one occasion they wrote, "Now it is not for us to establish a uniform pronunciation of the language, for this would be impossible."

But a uniform spelling system *was* possible—and essential. To this end, members of the mission, scattered on various stations throughout the Islands, were asked for their recommendations.

Most of the responses were received by July 1826. One surprising result was that William Ellis, the LMS missionary visiting from Tahiti, who has been given so much credit (mistakenly, as it turns out) for the final form of the alphabet, voted to keep all the letters. Indeed, in his writings on Hawai'i, he continued to use his own system, ignoring the decisions of his brethren. If Ellis had had his way, Hawaiian would still be encumbered with an awkward and irregular spelling system.[26]

But Ellis was alone in his opinion. The majority agreed to drop several consonant letters, although they would continue to use them for foreign words.

Some of the missionaries' comments show an insight about language that was far ahead of their time, especially those about the arbitrariness of letters. For example, Joseph Goodrich wrote that even though the letter *t* might be dropped in favor of *k,* in those places where the *t* pronunciation was common, it would be easy to "give the sound of the *t* to the *k.*" His prediction matches what happened on Ni'ihau. Despite over 190 years of reading books that use *k,* the Hawaiian speakers there have not lost their *t* pronunciation.

To counter the argument that words should be written the way they sounded (to speakers of English), William Richards wrote wisely that having too many letters in the alphabet was just as much a fault as having too

---

26. See Schütz 1994:132–33 for examples of how Ellis's influence on the orthography was misinterpreted by a number of scholars. One of the first was Ralph S. Kuykendall ([1938] 1957), who wrote: "By reason of his [Ellis's] knowledge and experience[,] his cooperation was especially helpful in the important work of reducing the Hawaiian language to written form." The first problem with this statement is timing: by the time Ellis arrived in Hawai'i, the first primer had already appeared, showing that the vowel letters had settled into their final form. As for the controversy over the consonant letters, the discussion above shows that Ellis argued on the losing side.

TABLE 7.2. VOTES FOR WHICH LETTERS TO DROP

B	9			P	0
D	8	R	6	L	2
T	8			K	0
V	9			W	0

few. (About 120 years later, the linguist Kenneth L. Pike [1947] called these two faults “over-differentiation” and “under-differentiation.”)

The missionaries who responded were nearly unanimous in their choice of which consonants to eliminate and which to retain. The results (table 7.2) show that *l* was the only letter of today’s alphabet that had to overcome any opposition. As a matter of fact, it was reported that King Liholiho preferred *r* for the spelling of his name. But to speakers of American English, whose *r* is very different from the tapped sound that they heard in Hawaiian, apparently the *l* sounded closer.[27]

At any rate, *p, l, k,* and *w* were kept, and the rest of the problematic letters discarded. The time it took for the decision and the amount of correspondence it produced show the attention that the missionaries gave to the problem. No one could accuse them of taking their task lightly or making hasty judgments.

The efforts of the missionaries, along with those of their Hawaiian advisors, through more than four years of struggling with an unwieldy, cumbersome alphabet, produced the intended results. At last it was possible for Hawaiians to learn to read and write without memorizing individual spellings. In their journal, Elisha and Maria Loomis wrote a simple summary of the years of study, frustration, experimentation, and discussion (18 August 1826): “We have rendered the orthography of the language much more simple by removing from the alphabet one of each of the interchangeable letters, and now hope to have uniformity of spelling” (Loomis and Loomis, 1819–27).

Even after the orthography was fixed by vote, there were still ripples of discontent with the pared-down system. Records show that such objections were mainly from speakers of English, who seemed to scorn an alphabet that was smaller than their own. Richards defended the decision against the fuller alphabet: “It would be very difficult indeed, if not quite

27. Remember that ʻŌpūkahaʻia found the American English *r* hard to pronounce.

impossible for common people to learn to write it uniformly, even though we should adopt a uniform system in all our books" (1828).

He also discounted the possibility that the revised (and more limited) alphabet would change the pronunciation of the language: "There is no probability however that the pronunciation would ever be thus limited, although it might be less varied than it is now."

Perhaps the highest praise for the streamlined alphabet was that it fulfilled its original intent: it made it easier for Hawaiians to become literate in their own language. Richards stated it simply: "But with our present alphabet a boy of fourteen, with common intelligence may in one month become a perfect master of the orthography of his language and be able to read and write the whole of it with correctness" (1828).

*

From a linguistic point of view, the missionaries fulfilled the following goals. Using only a practical, commonsense approach, they found a solution that follows linguistic principles that were not explicitly stated until a century later: they realized that it was important to write only those sounds that allowed hearers (and readers) to distinguish different meanings. In other words, the alphabet reflects the Hawaiian system, not the English one.

VERBATIM

Even though reshaping the Hawaiian alphabet was a serious matter, at least one of the missionaries approached his task with a sense of humor. Abraham Blatchely was a member of the Second Company, which arrived in Honolulu on 27 April 1823. He was stationed in Honolulu for the first three years of his service in Hawai‘i, the only mission doctor there at the time (*Missionary Album* 1969:50). His letter on the controversy of the extra consonants is a parody based on medical terms (Orthography of the Hawaiian Language 1826:3–4).

Abraham Blatchely
upon the orthography
July 11 1826
Rev Hiram Bingham
&
Levi Chamberlain
Present

Honolulu Oahu 11th [July] 1826

Gentlemen

Having been consulted upon the case of the orthography of the Hawaiian language I beg leave to state that I consider the present state in which it lies to be a diseased one and that as the disease has already become chronic something ought to be administered or some course of treatment adopted immediately to remove it. In exam[in]ing the causes of the derangement to say nothing of the Remote & Predisposing I find as a proximate cause five separate extraneous or foreign substances in the Alphabet (viz)

1st one called in the English language a Be
2nd " ———— do ———— a De
3rd " ———— do ———— a Er
4th " ———— do ———— a Te
5th " ———— do ———— a Ve

These cannot remain without producing a constant morbid invitation and (as experience proves) these bodies are equally affected by heat & cold by a humid and dry atmosphere hence it is easy to perceive that they cannot remain connected with a Hawaiian Constitution without producing their consequent evil in any climate or country.

Some may sup[p]ose that these extraneous substances ~~have~~ are connected to the surrounding parts by adhesion but in my opinion the adhesion if any is so slight that ~~that~~ they may be removed without the least injury. And as no radical & permanent relief can be expected without I should recommend most decidedly that they should be removed without delay.

As to the best way of removing them I am not anxious for one made in preference to another equally effectual & would only say that I think that blistering externally would only pal[l]iate & should be afraid that effect of <u>irritants</u> or <u>alternatives</u> administered interternally [sic] would fall into the channel of the disease & aggravate all the symptoms. <u>Query?</u> Would not an Emetic to remove the two uppermost & this followed by a Cathartic to discharge the other three be as good as any?

After the cause is removed & the effect begins to abate I should recommend for a while that a healthy regimen should be strictly adhered to & maintained.

1st It will be highly necessary to avoid all <u>prejudice</u> for this will produce a determination to the brain and effect the sensorium.

2nd Every possible means of ~~producing~~ increasing the stren[g]th & accuteness [sic] of the <u>auditory</u> nerves & enabling them to perform their office in the best manner will be very beneficial.

3rd Above all to restore the tone & keep up healthy action by a free use of <u>candour</u> will be most necessary.

Yours Respectfully
Abm. Blatchely M.D.

One persistent criticism of the missionaries' revised alphabet is that native speakers had no part in the exercise. The following quotation, from William Richards, shows that such a criticism was not valid.

> In my own mind, the question takes precisely this form. Shall we adopt an extremely intricate system of orthography and one which is to natives inexplicable and in every respect arbitrary, with a hope and for the purpose of making the people apprehend distinctions in sound, which the most delicate ear among them is now unable to do?
>
> That this is a fair statement of the question I have never heard denied, and I do not think that any candid person could ever deny it. I of course leave out of account those natives who have learnt to talk English, although very few even of them can pronounce all the interchangeable letters, and I venture to say there is not one to be found even of those who have spent years in America, who uniformly would do it. I will mention a trial which I made in the presence of several members of the reinforcement. A large circle of natives were present. I selected a word where in the last syllable I most frequently hear

a sound approach to the sound of d. I turned to one of the company and said is the word dido? He said, "yes". I asked again, is the word dilo? He answered as before, "yes". I proceeded and said, is it diro? The answer was "yes". Did you say the word was lido? Answer "yes". Is the word lilo? Answer, "yes". Is the word liro? Answer, "yes". Is the word rido? Answer, "yes". Is the word rilo? Answer, "yes". Is the word riro? Answer "yes".[28]

I then inquired of the next one in the circle who answered in the same way. Thus I went around the circle, not one of which perceived but that I asked the same question nine times. I give you this as a correct specimen of which would occur respecting all the interchangeable letters.

In another instance I asked a native to pronounce the word himself. Among the seven listeners there were four opinions as to the answer given. Three thought he pronounced the word lilo; two thought he said lido; one thought he said liro and one thought he said rilo. All however were of opinion that the sound was rather a medium one and not the full sound of the English letters. (Richards 1828)

In other words, it is clear that developing the official alphabet was a cooperative effort between the missionaries and their Hawaiian advisors.

28. Another version of this exchange appears in Loomis (1951) 1966:117.

CHAPTER 8

MISSING PIECES

The *Kahakō* and the *ʻOkina*

Stranger still, that prevalent Polynesian sound, the so-called catch, written with an apostrophe, and often or always the gravestone of a perished consonant.

—Stevenson, *In the South Seas*

The previous chapter examined the matter of too many letters in the alphabet. I now look at the opposite situation—not enough letters.[1]

Even after the Hawaiian vowels were written in the European fashion and the alphabet was purged of its extra consonants, there still remained two subtle but difficult problems to be solved. First, scholars often didn't hear long vowels and glottal stops. Next, when they did hear them, they either misinterpreted them or didn't think that it was necessary to include them in the alphabet. These problems are discussed in detail in the following sections.

LONG VOWELS

Although teachers and lexicographers still use the adjectives "long" and "short" to describe English vowels, those terms now have little to do with actual length.[2] For example, many dictionaries mark the *a* vowel in the

---

1. The names for the items pictured at the top of the page illustrate the two missing letters/diacritics in the alphabet at the time. The phrases are actually *He iʻa* 'A fish' and *He ʻō* 'A fork'. The first noun is missing an *ʻokina* 'glottal stop'; the second, both an *ʻokina* and a *kahakō* 'macron'.

2. In Old English, vowel length was significant—that is, *phonemic*. However, many of the long vowels changed to diphthongs, making vowel *quality* more important than *quantity*.

word *mate* as long (māt) and that in *mat* (măt) as short. Despite these labels, however, those terms describe mainly a difference in vowel *quality*.

In contrast, Hawaiian short and long vowels differ mainly in *quantity*—that is, one lasts longer than the other. In the following examples, as in the official writing system, the long vowel is marked with a *kahakō* 'macron'; the short vowel is unmarked:

(1) *káne* skin disease *kā́ne* male

In this position (i.e., second-to-last syllable), a long vowel is hard to distinguish from a short vowel, for each is accented (as shown). Thus, often *kāne* is pronounced as *kane,* which, as you can see above, has a quite different meaning.

On the other hand, a long vowel in any other position is much easier to hear, because it is always accented. For example:

(2) *Ka*ʻū́ (place name)

(3) wā́*híne* women

Here, the accent patterns are different from those commonly heard in two- and three-syllable words (with only short vowels), which are accented as follows (that is, on the second-to-last syllable):

máka 'eye, face'

moána 'sea'

Today, we know these facts about the language. But in the 1820s, 1830s, and 1840s, vowel length in such pairs as (1) was ignored altogether and in (2) and (3) was mistakenly interpreted as only a change in accent.[3]

Because some writers were unable to hear the length itself but could hear the obvious change in the accent pattern, they marked a long vowel in certain positions with an acute accent. For example, in 1819 Ruggles wrote the plural of *kanaka* 'person' as *kánaka,* which is how he heard *kānaka,* with one of its two accents on the first syllable. In 1825 William Ellis wrote the word for 'star' (*hōkū*) as *hokú.* This particular spelling is

3. For example, on page 4 of his sketch (1819), Ruggles wrote, "There is no distinction between the singular and plural of nouns, unless it is by giving the plural a different accent." Thus he interpreted *kānaka* 'persons' as *kánaka,* ignoring the secondary accent on the following *na* syllable. There is no word in Hawaiian with the accent pattern as he described it.

interesting, because it shows—in one word—the position in which a long vowel was hard to hear (the first) and that in which it was heard but misinterpreted (the second). That is, the first long vowel was overlooked because it *didn't* change the accent pattern, but the final long vowel was noticed because it *did* change the accent pattern. The reason for the confusion can be stated briefly: *every long vowel is accented, but not every accented vowel is long.*

Because of that lopsided arrangement, when vowel length *was* noticed, it was interpreted as accent. And because we don't mark accent when we write English (for example, we don't distinguish between *permít* [verb] and *pérmit* [noun]), the developers of the Hawaiian writing system apparently thought it unnecessary to do so for that language as well. Besides, it was thought that even though the spelling of some words might be ambiguous, those who knew the language could determine the proper pronunciation and meaning through context.

That is exactly what a reader must do now in order to understand most of what has been written in Hawaiian, especially the older translations of the Bible and the wealth of material in the Hawaiian newspapers of the nineteenth and early twentieth centuries.

Still, the missionaries felt that the pronunciation of words should be shown in a detailed way, because they planned to write a Hawaiian grammar and dictionary. With this goal in mind, Hiram Bingham and Elisha Loomis wrote to the ABCFM in 1823 requesting special type, including the five vowels marked with macrons, breves, circumflexes, and acute and grave accents (see figure 8.1). As Lorrin Andrews explained later, "As the Hawaiian books have been printed almost entirely for the use of Hawaiians, it has not been thought necessary to use any marks for accents, but if they should be used by those who wish to acquire the language, it would be very convenient for such to have certain classes of words accented"[4] (1854:21).

But because the ABCFM was unable to supply the type fonts that were requested, the plan was never carried out.

4. This explanation is not as straightforward as it might seem, for Andrews's grammar and his dictionary show that he was never able to hear the *ʻokina* or distinguish between accent and vowel length. However, his statement foreshadows the need for such symbols today, when "those who wish to acquire the language" far outnumber the native speakers.

a	7,300	e	3,000	i	3,450	o	4,440	u	3,180
b	900	d	600	h	1,930	k	2,040	l	1,020
m	2,070	n	1,600	p	1,050	r	1,000	t	630
v	700	w	900	c	600	f	600	g	600
s	660	x	130	y	600	z	600	__	50

Roman lower case letters

ā	210	ē	234	ī	150	ō	150	ū	150
ă	210	ĕ	150	ĭ	150	ŏ	150	ŭ	100
â	120	ê	60	î	60	ô	60	û	60
à	120	è	60	ì	60	ò	60	ù	60
á	120	é	60	í	60	ó	60	ú	60

Accented letters

Figure 8.1. Bingham's and Loomis's list of diacritics requested

SHORT VOWELS: Ă, Ĕ, Ĭ, Ŏ, Ŭ

Even had the typefaces been supplied,[5] we can't be sure that words would have been marked accurately, for vowel length and accent are difficult features to handle, mainly because of the complicated relationships described on the previous page. For example, when Henry H. Parker revised Andrews's dictionary (1922), he used all the symbols necessary to show accent and vowel length, but he used them incorrectly.[6] And in at least three editions of the *Hawaiian Dictionary* (P-E), and in the current edition of the *New Pocket Hawaiian Dictionary* (Pukui and Elbert 1992), long vowels and glottal stops are carefully marked, but the description of accent is wrong. Not until the 1986 edition of the larger dictionary was the statement corrected and a system introduced to show the accent(s) in each headword. In Judd, Pukui, and Stokes's 1945 *Introduction to the Hawaiian Language* (reprinted without corrections in 1995 and renamed *Handy Hawaiian Dictionary*), the vowel marking in the English-Hawaiian section is unreliable, for the authors

5. It is not clear what vowel qualities some of these symbols would have marked.

6. For example, he wrote a macron over *every* vowel in an accented position, short or long. For more examples, see chapter 15.

Figure 8.2. W. D. Alexander

proposed three (rather than two) degrees of vowel length. In the Hawaiian-English section, "limitations of the linotype machines" made it impossible to include any macrons at all.

In summary, there were three main reasons that vowel length was not incorporated into the alphabet in the early years of the mission. First, and most important, it was confused with accent and, perhaps unconsciously, compared to English, in which accented vowels are not marked. For example, even though W. D. Alexander wrote, "It is important to observe the distinction between long and short vowels," his "List of Similar words distinguished by the Accent" (22 pairs) missed the important fact that all his accented vowels in unexpected positions are also long. Moreover, marking long vowels was confined to a few examples (1864:6–7).

Next, it was felt that although those who were learning the language would benefit from such aids to pronunciation, native speakers and readers of Hawaiian needed no such help. A similar feeling still exists today among some native speakers of Ni'ihau Hawaiian.

Finally, the ABCFM was unable to send the proper type for pronunciation guides in grammars and dictionaries. However, using them correctly would have been a challenge, as proven by Parker's obvious failure a century later, described just above.

THE *'OKINA*

The second missing symbol in the 1826 official orthography was the glottal stop—now called an *'okina* in Hawaiian. The sound is made in much the same way that a *p* or *k* is, but instead of the lips or tongue blocking the passage of air, the vocal cords do so. When the air is released, we can hear the sound that results. A common example of the sound in English (which does not use it as a consonant) is in the expression "*Uh-oh,*" in which it separates the two vowel sounds. As a matter of fact, the sound almost always separates the vowels when they are repeated: if you say "*a-a-a,*" a glottal stop precedes each vowel.

In English, we automatically pronounce a glottal stop before a vowel in this position. Thus, most people don't think of it as a consonant but merely a signpost that sometimes marks vowels at the beginning of a word or sometimes separates them in the middle of a word.[7] What it *doesn't* do in English is to keep meanings separate in the way that, for example, *p* and *t* do in the words *pack* and *tack.*

In Hawaiian, however, the sound has a different status: it is definitely a consonant, just like *p* or *k.* Proof is offered by pairs such as *mai* 'hither' and *ma'i* 'ill' or *ano* 'awe' and *'ano* 'variety'—and many more examples. In all such pairs, it keeps meanings apart.

Today, we know this fact about the glottal stop. But in the 1800s, the situation was much different. For the early analysts of Hawaiian, there were two separate but related problems connected with the glottal stop: how to recognize the sound and how to interpret it.

Recognizing the *'Okina*

The dozen or so word lists collected before 1820 show no evidence that their compilers noticed the *'okina.* However, in *The Alphabet* (1822), the first book printed on the mission press, we can find two types of evidence that the sound was heard. The first (p. 3), implicit, is a list of "Double vowels pronounced separately," consisting of words such as *waa* (*wa'a*) 'canoe' and *puu* (*pu'u*) 'hill'. The second, explicit, is *ia'u* 'to me', written with an apostrophe.[8] For a more detailed study of the work, see chapter 9.

7. For example, some English speakers pronounce the word *naïve* with a glottal stop separating the two vowel sounds. Moreover, I have noticed that more and more speakers do not use *an* (indefinite article) before a noun that begins with a vowel but instead pronounce the word with an initial glottal stop and precede it with *a* rather than *an.*

8. A few other words that were written with apostrophes are contractions—or words thought to be contractions.

Figure 8.3. Hiram and Sybil Bingham

In 1823, Sybil M. Bingham, an experienced teacher, realized that unless marked somehow, such words as *ko'u* 'my' versus *kou* 'your' would be ambiguous if they were both spelled *kou,* because they can appear in exactly the same context. Thus, in her phrase book, *Select Hawaiian Phrases & Sentences Rehearsed at Table* (Rumford 1996), she was careful to mark the difference with an apostrophe. Later the entire mission followed this practice, and for over a century these possessives, certain pronouns (such as *a'u* 'to me'), and a few place names were the only Hawaiian words in which the *'okina* was written.

It seems clear from these examples that nonnative speakers could hear the sound between vowels. Where they could seldom hear it was before a vowel at the beginning of a word. Their inability to hear the sound in this position is not because they were poor phoneticians; instead, they were hindered by their native language.

As mentioned above, when speakers of English say a word that begins with a vowel, they actually precede the vowel with a glottal stop. Thus, it is very hard for them to hear a contrast such as the following pair of Hawaiian words:

awa	harbor	*'awa*	kava

However, one mid-nineteenth-century English-speaking observer, William D. Alexander, wrote the following: "There is in many words a guttural break or catching of the breath, *sometimes at the beginning* [emphasis added], but more often in the middle of [a] word" (1864:5).

Why was Alexander able to notice what his predecessors, and even his contemporaries, had missed? It turns out that he had some cross-linguistic help. From the preface of his grammar, we know that he was aware of Pierre Gaussin's work on Tahitian, Marquesan, and Polynesian in general

(1853). Gaussin spoke French, and because a French word beginning with a vowel does not have a strong *'okina* preceding it (see the comments above about English), he was better able than a speaker of English to hear the difference between Tahitian words that began with a vowel and those in which an *'okina* preceded the vowel (see Schütz 1994:145).

So at least in theory, Alexander was aware of *'okina* at the beginnings of Hawaiian words. In practice, however, he did not always accurately represent them. For example, in his grammar (1864:7), he wrote the words in the example above (*awa* versus *'awa*) as ăwa versus *āwa*. Of sixteen words written with an initial vowel but illustrating a medial *'okina,* four actually begin with an *'okina* as well.

From the latter group, one example is interesting from several points of view: "a-í, neck, Polynesian *kaki.*"

1. The actual word is *'ā'ī,* with an *'okina* before each long vowel, both accented, with the second one emphasized. Chapter 9 notes that this pattern fits into a category described as "words of two syllables, having no certain distinction of accent."
2. In the same chapter, the hyphen is explained as a sign that a two- or three-syllable word has an unexpected accent pattern. For example, *pi-a-pa* 'alphabet' actually represents *pī'āpā*—all syllables accented-again, with emphasis on the last.
3. Because he was familiar with Gaussin's work, Alexander should have known that the "Polynesian" *k* would appear as an *'okina* in Hawaiian.

Interpreting the *'Okina*

The previous section concentrated on *perception*. Accepting the *'okina* as a real consonant is another matter if it doesn't *function* that way in one's own language. Andrews (1838:394) seemed to think that it simply showed that two successive vowels in a Hawaiian word belonged to separate syllables—that is, did not form a diphthong. Bingham (1847:152) explained the sound in a different way: he called *'okina* "abrupt separations or short and sudden breaks between two vowels in the same word."[9]

Only later was it realized that the sound was actually a consonant. We don't know exactly when this idea was born, but in his grammar, William

9. Of course, it can occur between any two vowels, not just identical ones.

D. Alexander made the following groundbreaking assertion, a continuation of the quotation above (1864:5): "This guttural is properly a consonant, and forms an *essential* part of the words in which it is found."

Unfortunately, he didn't take the logical next step: to write the sound regularly. Instead, he retreated to the custom of writing it only to avoid ambiguity.

The next stage in recognizing the sound as a real consonant (and not merely the echo or trace of one) was reached by Judd, Pukui, and Stokes, the compilers of the 1945 dictionary and grammatical sketch, *Introduction to the Hawaiian Language,* referred to above. In this work, the sound was not merely mentioned but was also given status as part of the alphabet. Interestingly, the word they used for the glottal stop was not *'okina,* but *'u'ina.*

However, in that work (as in earlier ones), the *'okina* is marked only in the set of possessives, in which, as mentioned earlier, context could not guide the reader to the difference between, for example, the words *kou* 'your' and *ko'u* 'my'.

Because of the continuing distance between theory and practice, the *'okina* in this position was usually ignored until 1957, when the first P-E dictionary appeared.

Writing Vowel Length and the *'Okina*

Even though long vowels and the *'okina* are now recognized as essential parts of the Hawaiian alphabet, many people seem reluctant to give them equal status with the traditional set of consonants and vowels. Even in the academic community, scholars outside the disciplines of linguistics or Hawaiian language studies have often resisted change, apparently considering it affected or trivial to use the symbols.

The same holds true for most areas that deal with Hawaiian words in their written form. In the field of journalism, some publications have ignored modern spelling. Others have been careful in their spelling of Hawaiian names, place names, and expressions used in an English context. On 22 October 2000, the *Honolulu Advertiser* announced that after experimenting with using what it called "diacritical marks," it was now "committing to the use of the kahakō and 'okina on all of our pages." The *Honolulu Star-Bulletin* did not follow this practice. (However, beginning in 2002, it printed a weekly Hawaiian news and opinion column (Kauakūkalahale), using the necessary symbols.) In 2010, the newspapers merged into the *Honolulu Star-Advertiser.* Even though it continued printing the Hawaiian articles in the modern orthography, the rest of the paper reverted to the *Star-Bulletin*'s general practice of ignoring the *kahakō* and the *'okina.* As a result, because I am accustomed to the modern orthography, I interpret many familiar words as misspelled and have little chance of pronouncing an unfamiliar written word or name correctly.

Moreover, pairs of familiar words, kept distinct through their proper spelling, fall together. For example, I find it nearly impossible to see the common (misspelled) phrase "Preserve the *'aina*" without thinking of saving a meal (*'aina*) rather than the land (*'āina*). A similar kind of confusion, one that involves a bit of backpedaling to understand, arises from the following paragraph, the ending of an op-ed piece on the purchase of most of the island of Lanai (i.e., Lāna'i) by Larry Ellison: "A waif from Jersey said it best, perhaps, when she hoped that Ellison didn't think he owned every lanai in Hawaii. I couldn't ask him. He wasn't hanging out on my lanai" (Laccetti 2012). In nineteenth-century spelling, the two words—Lāna'i (island name) and *lānai* 'veranda'—look the same and are often pronounced the same by the uninformed. The pun works only for the written language—and written incorrectly at that.

Hawai'i Public Radio's announcers can handle some Hawaiian words, proper names, and place names adequately, but none is consistent. Even the writers of "Hawaiian Word of the Day" sometimes refer to the *kahakō* as a "stress mark."

So far, the state government has adopted a policy of making it acceptable, but not mandatory, to use the official spelling. After some resistance, the symbols are now used on most new street signs. Maps, however, are another matter; policies vary.

Even the University of Hawai'i administration has seemed curiously naive about the problem. In 1982 the Department of Linguistics had to have the covers for its *Working Papers* printed privately, because the office in charge of such matters refused to print "University of Hawai'i at Mānoa."[10] In the 1990s, the University's name was engraved on each of the marble structures at the Maile Way and East-West Road entrances—

10. On the covers of earlier issues you can find the hypercorrection *Hawai'ian. Hawaiian* is an English word and never pronounced with an *'okina.*

without the *kahakō* or *ʻokina,* which had to be put in as crowded afterthoughts. In early 2003, it was noted that a sign showing the name of the newly renovated Hawaiʻi Hall was misspelled—without the *ʻokina,* of course.

Similarly, in 2003, Hawaiʻi's public television station unveiled its new logo and new name: "PBS Hawaii"—with the two *i*'s facing each other (a design feature that is scarcely noticeable), but with the *ʻokina* missing. The head of the organization at that time vaguely labeled the *ʻokina* as "grammatically[11] and politically correct but a creative distraction." Thus "branding" triumphed over common sense and accuracy. More recently, the branding vanished, and the name reverted to Hawaiʻi.

In late 2007, University of Hawaiʻi Centenary banners flying over the Mānoa campus included the *ʻokina* in *Hawaiʻi* but omitted the *kahakō* in *Mānoa.*

In his otherwise admirable *Garner's Dictionary of Modern American Usage* (2003), under the entry **Hawaii** [*sic*], Bryan A. Garner described the *ʻokina* as a diacritical mark inserted in Hawaiian names "usually between repeated vowels . . . but occasionally between vowels not repeated." In addition to a bizarre statement that the words *ʻokina* and *ʻuʻina* (both spelled without the *ʻokina,* naturally) were pronounced the same, Garner argued against using the sound (or the symbol) in words in an English context. Among other reasons, he suggested that "it smacks of a provincialism that resists linguistic assimilation to standard AmE [American English]," "most speakers would be at a loss to know how to say it," and most Hawaiian names represent a "usage [that] has been long settled, and the okina [*sic*] simply unsettles it." Perhaps users of this reference work are lucky that the *kahakō* seems to have escaped his notice altogether (Schütz 2009).

Fortunately, others have not been so easily influenced by minority opinions. In 2008, the local magazine *Hawaii* officially became *Hawaiʻi,* illustrating its new policy of using modern spelling for Hawaiian words. On the downside, the writer of the article explaining the change (strangely and incorrectly entitled "How Hawaiian Should Sound") apparently understood few of its underlying principles. For example, notwithstanding a suggested correction, he called the *kahakō* "a straight line that indicates stress." Moreover, he quoted extensively a teacher of Hawaiian who also seemed to misunderstand the relationship between the sound system of a

---

11. Of course, using the *ʻokina* has nothing to do with grammar.

language and the alphabet that represents it. For example, she was quoted as saying, "Adding diacriticals . . . heightens the shift in the language from an auditory medium to a visual one. In Hawaiian, when two like vowels appear together, each is pronounced separately. *Kama'āina* (local people) know that the word Hawai'i is pronounced with two distinct "i" sounds. *Pu'u* (hill, mound, or heart) is pronounced 'Pooh-ooh', with a break between the two vowel sounds; it is not a protracted 'pooooh'."

This quotation illustrates two main misconceptions. The first is that the "diacriticals" are something other than letters of the alphabet. The second is that the *'okina* appears only between like vowels.

Using the symbols in people's names seems to be a matter of personal preference. For example, the well-known scholar Mary Kawena Pukui preferred to spell her surname without a *kahakō* and an *'okina,* although it is actually *Pūku'i* (Elbert 1989:132).

There are a number of reasons why many people have been slow to accept the revised spelling:

- They don't realize why it is important to spell and pronounce words properly.
- They are resistant to change.
- They have found that the necessary type fonts are not available (once a serious problem, but less so as computer technology advances).
- They mistakenly think that the symbols are simply "punctuation marks" or "marks to show the proper pronunciation of words."
- Those accustomed to older versions of the Bible or to Hawaiian language newspapers find the extra marks distracting.
- Readers feel that the language of the Bible (i.e., as printed in the nineteenth century, with an *'okina* in only a few words and no *kahakō* at all) represents "true" Hawaiian.

Still, the official policy continues to change, as people become more aware of the importance of writing the language correctly. For example, the last sentiment in the list above may still be felt by some *kūpuna,* but the official position can be illustrated by these headlines (*Honolulu Advertiser,* 4 August 2003): "Hawaiian Bible joins modern age. Electronic version to add diacriticals." As a matter of fact, some of the statements above may already be outdated by the time you read them, which would be welcome signs of such changes. For example, 2014 saw the publication of a bilingual edition of the New Testament, Psalms, and Proverbs "in the modern orthography that uses complete diacritical markings" (New Edition of Bilingual Bible Available 2014).

A technological advancement connected with this topic is the relative ease now (compared with only a decade or two ago) of using *ʻokina* and *kahakō* on a keyboard, suggested in the list above. For several years leading to the publication of *The Voices of Eden* (Schütz 1994), I had to rely on computer gurus to develop a macro that changed other symbols into vowels with *kahakō*. Now a number of Hawaiian fonts, some highly decorative, are available.

Occasionally, a different kind of problem crops up: an *ʻokina* in an unexpected place. For example, the October 2008 issue of *Homescape* (pp. 34, 35), featuring entries in the 52nd Annual Parade of Homes, shows two houses from a development called "Waiʻnani at Poipu." Even if we ignore the misspelling of Poʻipū, we're left with Waiʻnani, an impossible spelling, because it indicates an *ʻokina* between a vowel and a consonant.

Such well-meaning but uninformed uses of the *ʻokina* remind one of Samuel H. Elbert's letter to the editor of one of Honolulu's newspapers sometime in the 1960s. His reaction to the multiple mistakes in the Hawaiian words in a Waikīkī restaurant's menu was that *ʻokina* had been scattered over the words like salt and pepper.

But there are encouraging signs of progress. In its report of President Barack Obama's newest "national monument," the name of the ocean reserve containing nearly 300 million acres northwest of Hawaiʻi,[12] the *New Yorker* correctly spelled Papahānaumokuākea, complete with *kahakō* in the right places, and a pronunciation guide: "Papa-ha-now-moh-koo-ah-kay-ah" (Kolbert 2016).

In summary, even though the *ʻokina* and *kahakō* were recognized as essential elements as early as 1864, that view did not extend beyond short descriptions in the few grammars that followed. As for teaching materials, Elbert's *Conversational Hawaiian* (1951) was the first to use the symbols in exercises and dialogs. The Pukui and Elbert dictionary (1957) made it possible for a slow increase through the following decades in other media's use of modern Hawaiian spelling.

Finally, as for those who object to the modern alphabet because the two additional symbols are "distracting," is that opinion not an example of clinging to the past and ignoring the needs of future speakers?

---

12. Spelled "Hawaii" in the original, perhaps following the *New Yorker's* style sheet.

VOWEL LENGTH, THE *'OKINA,* AND MERRIAM-WEBSTER'S TREATMENT OF HAWAIIAN BORROWINGS IN ENGLISH

Most of the discussion above is related to the spelling of Hawaiian words, sometimes in a Hawaiian context, other times in an English context. How to pronounce Hawaiian words borrowed into English is another problem.[13]

The last line in a well-known *hapa-haole*[14] song contains what is undoubtedly the longest Hawaiian borrowing in English: "Where the *humuhumunukunukuāpua'a* go swimming by."[15]

If you were a singer, unfamiliar with Hawaiian and learning this song from a printed source, how could you find out how to pronounce the word? The standard advice is: look it up in a dictionary. And the word does indeed appear in the online Merriam-Webster Unabridged (2018) with the pronunciation transcription below, followed by the word divided into measures:[16]

\ˌhüməˈhüməˌnükəˈnükəˌäpəˈwäˌä\
humu humu nuku nuku ā pua'a

Auē! Do the four unstressed u vowels really turn into [ə] (i.e., the sound of the first vowel in ***a**bove*)? And what happened to pua'a 'pig'? It's nearly unrecognizable. Is the first vowel in that word really pronounced [ə]? Does the last syllable really have secondary accent?

Two more common borrowings into English refer to types of lava: *pāhoehoe* and *'a'ā.* The Merriam-Webster Unabridged transcription and the measure divisions follow:

\pəˈhōēˌhōē\ and \ˈäˌä, ˌäˈä\
pā hoe hoe 'a'ā

---

13. The following paragraphs are excerpts from Schütz 2009.

14. As a musical genre, *hapa haole* refers to a song whose lyrics are on Hawaiian themes but are mainly in English, usually with a few Hawaiian words or phrases included.

15. Cogswell, Harrison, and Noble 1933.

16. *MW* should definitely indicate a glottal stop in this word. A supporting argument is that its pronunciation guide includes French nasalized vowels and German umlauted vowels. Hawaiian deserves the same consideration. Moreover, the symbol is necessary to indicate the pronunciation of the English expression *uh-oh.* (In my current *MW* dictionaries, the pronunciation of the last word is explained by a phrase: "*usually with strong glottal stops before the vowels.*")

The first pronunciation is recognizable, but it would be closer to the original if the first syllable ([pā]) were transcribed as \ˌpä\ (with a secondary accent) and the final vowels in the next two syllables as \ā\ or \e\. Moreover, the final syllable has primary accent.

As for the rendering of *ʻaʻā,* the first transcription is quite wrong. The second alternate better represents the final long and stressed vowel of the original, but neither of the two forms, as written, is pronounceable without an *ʻokina* before each vowel.

Contrary to *Merriam-Webster*'s treatment of many Hawaiian words borrowed into English, it is easy to indicate a close approximation to an accurate Hawaiian pronunciation. Major sociolinguistic changes in the position of Hawaiian since 1961 have made it not only desirable but necessary to do so. However, it will be more difficult to decide which words also have a pronunciation that is not authentic but fixed by common usage.

*

All in all, the question of whether or not to write the *kahakō* and the *ʻokina* can be summarized this way: unless we make a conscious effort to write the symbols, both the standard pronunciation and the meaning of a significant part of the language may be changed or lost forever.

VERBATIM

It seems odd that people who are not trained in linguistics often react strongly to a particular speech sound—the *ʻokina.* After all, have you ever heard an argument over, say, the letter *m* and the sound it represents? The following quotations illustrate some of the strange comments people have made about the *ʻokina.* (Somehow, long vowels haven't prompted such bizarre reactions.) "Nobody understands them (glottal stops) except the linguists . . . Even the kupunas don't understand what you're talking about." "Old time Hawaiians are sometimes offended to see pronunciation marks above Hawaiian words . . . They aren't used to it. They'd say, 'Ah—that's university Hawaiian'" (*Honolulu Star-Bulletin* 28 May 1986).

Turn back to Stevenson's comment at the beginning of this chapter. His point of view is easy enough to understand; he was probably more interested in turning a clever phrase than in describing a speech sound. But the comments just above reflect an unfortunate situation that is all too common—but hard to excuse. For those seriously interested in Hawaiian, easily accessible sources, spread over nearly a century, explain clearly the status of the *'okina.*

The following quotation gives us some idea of the prevalent attitude of the time about marking vowel length: "The slight variation in quantity, though not in quality, of sound in the vowels requires no mark of distinction, any more than in the variation of the sound of *a* in the English words *art* and *father.* Here the quantity may differ slightly though it is not necessary to put a distinctive mark, or make a different character" (Bingham 1847:153).

Here is W. D. Alexander's full treatment, referred to earlier in the chapter (1864:5–6):[17]

> Besides the sounds mentioned above, there is in many words a guttural break or catching of the breath, sometimes at the beginning, but more often in the middle of a word. This guttural is properly a consonant and forms an *essential* part of the words in which it is found. It almost invariably takes the place of the Polynesian *k.* Thus the Polynesian *ika,* fish, becomes *i'a* in Hawaiian. This guttural consonant is represented by an apostrophe, in a few common words, to distinguish their meaning, as *ko'u,* my, *kou,* thy.

The following is Pukui, Judd, and Stokes's explanation, also referred to earlier (1945:8–9):

> The glottal closure, known to the early Hawaiians as **'u'ina**, we recognize as a consonant and include in the alphabet. It is represented by an inverted comma ('),[18] as is done regularly for the Samoan dialect, and is being done now by the Bishop museum in Hawaiian manuscripts. It represents the Polynesian (not the Hawaiian) "K," attenuated until almost completely elided. Not only by the Hawaiians was this Polynesian "K" so treated, but also by the Samoans and Tahitians, while it was retained in full volume by the other Polynesians in New Zealand, Tonga, Cook, Marquesas, Tuamotu and Easter Islands.
>
> The **'u'ina** is still part of Hawaiian speech, but has not previously been indicated in writing except to distinguish between **a'u** "my" and **au** [āu]

17. Here, an apostrophe represents the *'ōkina.*

18. It is less confusing to call it a single opening quotation mark.

> "thy" and in a very few other words. It has been treated largely as a diacritical mark, although Alexander noted in his grammar: "This gutteral [*sic*] is properly a consonant, and forms an essential part of the words in which it is found." Its presence or absence in Hawaiian words marks distinct terms. For instance, three such words have been written **ai**, although pronounced differently. The correct forms would be **'a'i**, meaning "neck," **'ai**, "food," and **ai**, sexual intercourse."
>
> For clarity, we believe that the **'u'ina** should be indicated when writing. But, whatever the student may choose to do, we afford him the opportunity of knowing the words he uses, and thus of avoiding possible slips.

But although careful to note the *'u'ina* (*'okina*), the authors missed the two *kahakō* in the word for 'neck', which is actually *'ā'ī*.

PART III

THE EFFECTS OF WRITING

CHAPTER 9

KA PALAPALA

Chapter 4 asked whether certain traditional Hawaiian images (petroglyphs, *kapa* decoration, and tattooing) might be defined as writing. Now let's consider the possibilities for naming the new activity and its result. Perhaps it could be a word connected with the *form* of writing—*kiʻi* 'picture, image', *kākau* or *uhi* 'tattoo'; or for the *act* of writing—perhaps *kaha* 'scratch', *helu* 'scratch, count, list',[1] or *heluhelu* 'chant words in a rhythmic way'.[2] Another term might focus on the *function* of writing—communication. Here, a new term might be based on *ʻōlelo* 'speech, language'.

The word that the Hawaiians chose is *palapala,* which originally referred to the printing of tapa designs. The word was already in use by the time the missionaries arrived; its earliest appearance found so far is from Archibald Campbell's word list, recalled from the years 1810–11 (Schütz 1994:154). It also came to mean education in general—that is, the type of education that was introduced from the outside.

As for the first effects of the *palapala,* many Hawaiians reacted as if it had a *mana* (roughly, 'supernatural power') of its own that would be transferred to them once they had learned its mysteries. For a time, this belief made it difficult for some to separate the symbol from the thing that it symbolized.

Records from the period bounded by Cook and the Calvinists occasionally refer to certain Hawaiians wanting to learn to read and write. But these were mainly just a few people, especially chiefs, who had had extended contact with outsiders. And it appears that it was literacy in English that they wanted most, for that was the language more closely

1. Thanks to Keao NeSmith for the previous two examples.

2. The last word was suggested by William H. Wilson, pers. comm.18 June 2012.

connected with the tangible signs of power and wealth—ships, weapons, metal, and other goods.

However, it was the official policy of the mission to encourage the Hawaiians to become literate not in English but in their own language, a policy practiced by other missions in the Pacific and elsewhere as well.

THE PRINTED WORD?

Even though the phrase "printed word" is common, people can be literate without mechanical or electronic printing, for handwriting can have the same effect. (After all, writing systems predate mechanical—and now electronic—printing by thousands of years.) Soon after the Hawaiians began to read and write, letter writing became popular, and by the mid-1830s it had become routine. Lorrin Andrews reported that it was one way that news circulated throughout the islands (Andrews 1836b:15; see also chapter 10).

Nor were printed books absolutely necessary for education, for the missionaries could have taught the Hawaiians to read and write without books or paper by using a technique that was part of an important contemporary educational movement in Britain, called the Lancasterian method.[3]

Such an approach to teaching differed from others in two ways, both aimed at teaching a large number of pupils at a small cost. First, older pupils were trained to teach younger ones.[4] The advantage of this method was that fewer professional teachers had to be employed. On the downside, those in charge of the schools were often forced to use relatively untrained teachers in most of the classrooms.

Next, instead of using individual books, notebooks, or slates, students read from large sheets of paper hung on boards at the front of each classroom, and they practiced writing on thin layers of sand on their desktops.

Missionaries in some parts of the Pacific had tried Lancaster's scheme, but only as a makeshift measure until they could print enough books to satisfy the demand. Although the teachers connected with the mission in Hawai'i knew of the system, their students used slates and paper from

---

3. Joseph Lancaster (1778–1838) was the leader of perhaps the most important of such movements.

4. Andrew Bell (1753–1832) originated the system of using monitors—that is, older pupils who instructed the younger ones.

the beginning, and mission historians did not mention sand writing at all. One reason may have been that the Hawaiian students were intrigued not only by writing and the message it contained but also by its permanent physical manifestation—the books themselves. For example, Hiram Bingham wrote of the Hawaiians' fascination with books in the mid-1820s, "An interesting youth begged of me a book. 'My desire to learn, my ear to hear, my eye to see, my hands to handle; from the sole of my foot to the crown of my head I love the *palapala*'" (1847:257).

A decade later, Asa Thurston and Artemas Bishop reported from Kailua, "Books in a pamphlet form have lost their value in the eyes of the people, but bound books are in good demand, and are sought after even by those who have left the schools" (*Missionary Herald* 31 [1835]:376). Is it any wonder then that the *mana* attached to books enabled them to win over the economical but ephemeral sand writing?

A CLOSER LOOK AT *THE ALPHABET*

If the First Company of missionaries had arrived in Hawai'i with all their teaching and reading materials in place, they could have begun their schools immediately.[5] But in spite of preparatory work at the Foreign Mission School in Cornwall, that was impossible. As explained in previous chapters, even creating the most basic tool for literacy—an efficient alphabet—was no simple matter. Moreover, the missionaries found that it took much longer than expected for them to become fluent enough in Hawaiian to a level necessary for translating the Bible.

They soon realized how serious these problems were. Drawing on material in the journals and letters of Elisha and Maria Loomis, her great-grandparents, Albertine Loomis wrote, "It would have been foolish to go to press with an imperfect orthography, more than foolish to print Bible passages so badly rendered that they promised earthly riches when they meant to proffer heavenly. So the printing waited, and the only school-books at the Mission were Webster's speller and the English Bible" ([1951] 1966:147).

It was obvious that these two works—the speller and the Bible, both in English—could not possibly satisfy the Hawaiians' need for books. Thus,

5. Some of the material in this section appeared in Schütz 2017.

the missionaries had to make a start at printing Hawaiian books—even with an "imperfect" orthography.

Chapter 7 described the first book printed in Hawaiian in terms of the letters it used and the adjustments that needed to be made to the list of consonants in order to produce an efficient alphabet. Chapter 8 showed the importance of two items missing from the first alphabet—the *kahakō* and the *ʻokina.*

A few bibliographic details can be added to the earlier account. This version of *The Alphabet* (as the booklet was named) consisted of only eight pages; another eight were added in February 1822. There were 500 copies in that edition, but 2,000 more copies were printed in September. As an indication of how great the demand was for the book (or, for that matter, *any* book), 20,000 copies of an eight-page version (called *Ka Be-a-ba* [later changed to *Pīʻāpā*]) and 41,000 copies of a work called simply *A E I O U a e i o u* were printed in 1825 (Judd, Bell, and Murdoch 1978).

In this chapter, I analyze the content of the primer beyond the consonants and vowels, showing how its organization stemmed from English models that the missionaries were familiar with (and had perhaps been taught from). I also "translate" some of its terms into more modern ones, showing how they actually describe features of the language that the missionaries were unaware of. On the following pages you'll find a complete copy of *The Alphabet* (figure 9.1), about 50 percent enlarged. In the original, the printed area on each page is only approximately 3 × 5 inches—somewhat smaller than today's average paperback—and in the first version, only eight pages long.

By using your imagination, try to place yourself with other pupils in a classroom, or an open area, experiencing your first encounter with the written language.

THE ALPHABET.

VOWELS.		SOUND.	
	Names.	*Ex. in Eng.*	*Ex. in Hawaii.*
A a	---â	as in *father*,	la—sun.
E e	--- a	— *tele*,	hemo—cast off.
I i	--- e	— *marine*,	marie—quiet.
O o	--- o	— *over*,	ono—sweet.
U u	--- oo	—*rule*,	nui—large.

CONSONANTS.	*Names.*	CONSONANTS.	*Names.*
B b	**be**	**N n**	**nu**
D d	**de**	**P p**	**pi**
H h	**he**	**R r**	**ro**
K k	**ke**	**T t**	**ti**
L l	**la**	**V v**	**vi**
M m	**mu**	**W w**	**we**

The following are used in spelling foreign words:

F f	fe	S s	se
G g	ge	Y y	yi

1

Figure 9.1. Facsimile reproduction of *The Alphabet*

2

DIPTHONGS.

Ae	as in *ayes*, - - - -	ae—yes.
Ai	as in *aisle*, or *idol*, - -	ai—food.
Ao	as *a* in *far*, followed closely by *o*;	ao—bread
Au	like *ow* in *vow*, - - -	pau—all.
Ei	as in *eight*, nearly, - -	lei—beads.
Eu	as *a* in *late*, followed by *oo*;	weuweu—grass
Ou	as *o* followed closely by *oo*;	lakou—they

TABLE I.

LESSON 1.

Ba	be	bi	bo	bu
da	de	di	do	du
ha	he	hi	ho	hu
ka	ke	ki	ko	ku
la	le	li	lo	lu
ma	me	mi	mo	mu
na	ne	ni	no	nu

Fig. 9.1 (cont.)

3

pa	pe	pi	po	pu
ra	re	ri	ro	ru
ta	te	ti	to	tu
va	ve	vi	vo	vu
wa	we	wi	wo	wu

LESSON 2.

Double vowels pronounced separately.

Aa	ee	ii	oo	uu
waa	kee	lii	hoo	puu

LESSON 3.

Dipthongal syllables.

Ae	lae	nae	pae	tae
ai	hai	kai	mai	wai
ao	hao	kao	mao	nao
au	mau	nau	rau	wau
ei	lei	nei	pei	rei
eu	heu	peu	teu	weu
ou	kou	hou	mou	tou

Fig. 9.1 (cont.)

4

TABLE II.

Words of one syllable.

Ae	kae	lau	no
ai	kai	lei	pa
ao	kao	lu	pae
au	kau	ma	pai
ha	ke	mai	pau
hae	ki	mau	pe
hai	ko	me	po
hao	kou	mu	pu
hau	ku	na	ta
he	la	nau	tu
ka	lae	nei	wai

TABLE III.

Words of two syllables, accented on the first.

A a	a ka	a mo	a pu
a e	a ke	a mu	a ra
a i	a ki	a na	a re
ai a	a ko	a ne	a ro
a u	a ku	a ni	a ru
au a	a la	a no	a ta
a ha	a le	a nu	a to
a he	a li	a pa	a tu
a hi	a lo	a pe	a va
a ho	a lu	a pi	e a
a hu	a ma	a po	e e

Fig. 9.1 (cont.)

5

ei a
ei la
e hu
e te
e ve
i a
i e
i i
i o
i ha
i he
i ho
i hu
i ki
i la
i li
i lo
i mi
i mo
i mu
i na
i no
i nu
i pu
i ti
i wa
i wi.
o a

o e
o i
o o
o u
o ha
o he
o hi
o hu
o ka
o ke
o ki
o ko
o la
o le
o li
o lo
o lu
o ma
o mo
o na
o ne
o ni
o no
o nu
o pa
o pe
o pi
o pu

o ra
o re
o ri
o ro
o ru
o te
o ti
o to
u a
u ha
u hi
u ka
u ki
u ku
u la
u lu
u ma
u me
u mi
u na
u ne
u nu
u pa
u pe
u pi
u pu
u tu
ha a

ha i
ha o
ha u
hau na
ha hi
ha ka
ha ki
ha ko
ha ku
ha la
ha le
ha lu
ha mo
ha mu
ha na
ha ni
ha no
ha nu
ha pa
ha po
he a
he e
he hi
he hu
he ka
he ku
he le
he li

Fig. 9.1 (cont.)

6

he lu
he ma
he mi
he mo
he mu
he na
he va
hi a
hi o
hi u
hi hi
hi la
hi li
hi lo
hi lu
hi na
hi ne
hi no
hi nu
hi pu
hi ti
hi tu
ho a
ho e
ho i
ho o
ho u
hou po

ho ka
ho ku
ho la
ho le
ho lo
ho lu
ho ma
ho ni
ho nu
ho pe
ho po
ho pu
hu a
hu e
hu i
hu ka
hu ki
hu la
hu li
hu lu
hu me
hu mu
hu na
hu ne
ka a
ka u
ka ha
ka he

ka hi
ka hu
ka ke
ka la
ka na
ka ne
ka ni
ka no
ka nu
ka wa
ka wi
ke a
ke e
ke u
ke hu
ke ko
ke ku
ke le
ke na
ke pa
ki a
ki i
ki ha
ki he
ki hi
ki ke
ki ki
ki ko

ki lo
ki lu
ki mo
ki na
ki no
ki pa
ki pi
ki ni
ki wi
ko a
ko e
ko i
ko o
ko u
ko ho
ko hu
ko ke
ko ko
ko le
ko lo
ko lu
ko me
ko mi
ko mo
ko na
ko pe
ku a
ku e

Fig. 9.1 (cont.)

7

ku i
ku u
ku he
ku hi
ku ko
ku ku
ku la
ku li
ku lu
ku mu
ku na
ku nu
ku pu
lau la
la ka
la ko
la lo
la ni
la pa
la pu
la we
le a
le e
le o
le ha
le hu
le le
le lo

le pa
le pe
le ve
li a
li o
li u
li ha
li hi
li ke
li ki
li ko
li ma
li mu
li no
li pi
lo a
lo i
lo u
lo ha
lo he
lo hi
lo ko
lo li
lo lo
lo ma
lo mi
lo na
lo no

lo nu
lo pi
lu à
lu u
lu he
lu hi
lu ku
lu pi
lu na
lu nu
ma a
ma e
mai a
mai hi
mai ta
ma o
ma ha
ma hi
ma hu
ma ka
ma ke
ma ki
ma ko
ma la
ma le
ma li
ma lu
ma ma

ma mo
ma na
ma no
ma nu
ma pu
ma ro
ma wa
me a
me o
me ha
me ko
me lu
me ne
me ri
mi o
mi hi
mi ki
mi ko
mi na
mo a
mo e
mo o
mo ho
mo ku
mo li
mo mi
mo ni
mu a

Fig. 9.1 (cont.)

8

mu u	ne ma	nu ku	pe lu
mu ku	ne mo	nu nu	pe no
mu le	ne no	pa a	pe nu
mu mu	ne pu	pa e	pe pe
mu ri	ne va	pa i	pi a
na e	ni u	pa o	pi i
nai a	ni hi	pa ha	pi o
nai o	ni ho	pa hi	pi ha
na o	ni ni	pa hu	pi he
na u	no a	pa ku	pi hi
na ho	no e	pa la	pi ko
na hu	no o	pa le	pi li
na ka	no u	pa li	pi lo
na ku	no ho	pa lo	pi pi
na lo	no hu	pa lu	po i
na lu	no ko	pa na	po o
na mu	no lu	pa ne	po u
na na	no na	pa ni	po he
na ne	no ni	pa pa	po ho
na ni	no no	pe a	po hu
na pa	no pa	pe e	po ka
na pe	no pu	pe o	po ke
ne e	no wa	pe u	po ki
ne u	nu a	pe ha	po la
ne he	nu i	pe hi	po li
ne hu	nu u	pe hu	po ni
ne ko	nu ha	pe ku	po no
ne le	nu ka	pe le	po po

Fig. 9.1 (cont.)

9

po wa	ro no	to i	we he
pu a	ru a	wa a	we hi
pu e	ru li	wa e	we la
pu u	ru na	wai u	we lo
pu hi	ru nu	wai ho	we lu
pu ka	tau a	wai wai	we mi
pu ke	tau la	wa u	we na
pu ku	ta bu	wa ha	wi i
pu la	ta hi	wa he	wi u
pu le	ta pa	wa hi	wi ki
pu lu	ta ro	wa ho	wi la
pu na	tu ha	wa le	wi li
pu ni	ti po	wa li	wi lu
ro a	ti tu	wa wae	wi ni

TABLE IV.

First exercise in reading.

E hele mai oe.

E noho marie oe i loko o ka hale.

E hana pono, a ore hana heva iti.

E hoo lohe i ka mea a ko kumu i i mai la.

TABLE V.

Words of two syllables, having no certain distinction of accent.

A a	ao ao	au hao	a he
ae o	au au	au we	a ke

2

Fig. 9.1 (cont.)

10

e i	hei au	lu ai	pa lau
ou kou	ho ho	mae mae	pa pa
u pa	ho mai	mai au	pe la
u pe	hu hu	mai tai	pe ne
ha ai	kau lai	ma o	pi nai
hae hae	ka kou	ma ma	po ai
hai hai	ka ku	ma nei	po po
hau hau	ke ke	nae nae	pu o
ha ha	la au	nai nai	pu ha
ha nai	lau lau	nao nao	pu pu
ha pai	la la	na na	ra nai
he i	la kou	ne ne	wa wa

TABLE VI.

Words of two syllables, accented on the second.

Ai e	u pe	hi nai	ma nao
a ha	ha hai	ho ai	ma no
a nae	ha hau	ho ha	na au
a nei	ha ke	ho lo	na ha
a no	ha mau	ho tu	na na
o mau	ha na	ki he	ni au
o pa	ha nau	ku lai	ni nau
u ha	ha lau	ma kau	pa pai
u ka	hi hi	ma mae	pi lau

Fig. 9.1 (cont.)

11

TABLE VII.

E hele ana oe ihea?
Hele ana au i ke Heiau.
Manao i ka la tabu, o ke Akua.
E hele mai kakou e pule i ke Akua:
Oia no ka maitai roa.
E makau kakou ia Iala:
Oia no ke Akua nui roa.

TABLE VIII.

Words of three syllables, accented on the second.

A a a	a o he	a li a	i kai ka
a a e	a o no	a li ma	i ki ki
a a hu	a o re	a lu a	i li o
a a ki	au he a	a pa na	i mai le
a a ko	au mo e	a na na	i nai na
a a la	au pu ni	a ro ha	i ni ki
a a lu	a ha a	e a ki	i no a
a a ma	a he a	e a lu	o o pa
a a pa	a hi tu	e ka li	o o pu
a a pu	a ka hi	e nu he	o hi a
a a wa	a ke a	i a ko	o hu le
ai ka ne	a ko lu	i o le	o ka a
a i wa	a ku a	i he a	o le a

Fig. 9.1 (cont.)

o le lo
o le na
o mo le
o no hi
o pa la
o pu u
u a hi
u u ku
u u mi
u ha ne
u ha lu
u hi ni
u ka li
u la na
u mi ki
u ne a
u na hi
u pe na
u wa la
ha a wi
ha ha na
ha ku i
ha ma ma
he a ha
he a lu
he he na
he ki li
he le lo

hi na lo
ho a na
ho a wi
ho i ke
ho ho la
ho ho nu
ho ka nu
ho lo i
ho nu a
ho pu pu
ho wa ha
hu hu ki
ka a we
kai kai na
kau lu a
kau ma he
ka hi ko
ka hi li
ka hu na
ka ka ka
ka le pa
ka lu a
ka na ka
ka ne a
ke i ki
ki a ha
ki ke ke
ki ko ko

ki lo hi
ko ko ke
ko ko lo
ko lo a
ko ro he
ko na li
ko na ne
ku o no
ku ki ni
ku ku i
ku ku lu
ku ku ni
ku li na
la la ne
lo a a
lo i hi
ma o na
ma ha na
ma hi na
ma ho la
ma ka na
ma ka ni
ma ki lo
ma ko le
ma ko lu
ma ku na
ma lo lo
ma lu a

ma ma o
ma ma lu
ma ne o
ma ni ni
ma wai na
mo a na
mo e na
mo mo ku
mo mo na
mu ki ki
mu ma hu
mu mu ku
na e le
na hi li
na ke ke
na lu lu
na na hu
ni ni ni
pa a ne
pa i na
pa he e
pa he lo
pa ka a
pa ke ke
pa ko le
pa lu a
pa lu le
pa pa le

Fig. 9.1 (cont.)

13

pa pa pa	pi pi li	po lo li	pu li ki
pe a hi	po i na	pu a a	pu na na
pe he a	po ha ku	pu e o	pu pu ka
pe pe hi	po hi na	pu e hu	wa hi e
pi la li	po ho o	pu i wa	wa hi ne

TABLE IX.

UA olioli au, i ka olelo mai a lakou ia'u, E hele kakou i loko o ka hale o Iehova.
E malama kakou i ke pono a ke Akua:
Oia no ke Akua nui o ka lani.
Oia no ko kakou mea i ola'i.
I nui ko manao i ka la o ke Akua.
I nui ko makau i ke Akua nui.
I nui ko hoolono i tanawai hemolele a Iehova.

TABLE. X.

Words of three syllables, having a slight accent on the first, and the full accent on the third.

A ka mai	he le lei	ma na ka	pe pei ao
a la la	ho pu pu	mo lo wa	po lo lei
a po po	ka pu ai	mu li wai	pu na wai
ha ka ka	ko ho la	ne hi ne	ta na wai
ha la wai	lu a wai	pe le leu	ti po pou

Fig. 9.1 (cont.)

14

TABLE XI.

MAI ke kumu mai i hanaia e Iehova ka lani a o ko honua.

Aore oau e ike ia Iehova, aka o Iehova ke ike ia'u.

Iehova aia no i loko o ka lani, ina no i na motu a puni.

Iesu Kraist keiki maitai na ke Akua, i make no i ke kina o kakou.

E pule kakou ia Iehova, a e makemake kakou i kana olelo.

Ke Akua makemake i kanaka maitai, a o kanaka maitai he aroha i ke Akua.

I mai la ke Akua, "E nana mai ia'u i ola oukou, pau roa kalau o ko honua, aka oau no ke Akua, aohe me e ae."

TABLE XII.

Words of four syllables, accented on the first and third.

A hi a hi	a mu a mu	a va hi a
a ki a ki	a ni a ni	a va ke a
a ka a ka	a no a no	e ka e ka
a la ka i	a po a po	e le e le
a lu a lu	a pu a pu	i li hu ne
a mo a mo	a va a va	i li ko le

Fig. 9.1 (cont.)

15

i pu a la
o o le a
o li o li
o lu o lu
o pe o pe
u ku le le
u ma u ma
u me u me
u mi u mi
u wa u wa
ha a ha a
ha na pi lo
ha no ha no
ha nu ha nu
he e na ru
li i li i
he le u ma
he mo le le
hi da hi da
hi nu hi nu
ho e u li
ho o lo he
ho o me a
ho o pi li
ho o wa li
ho he wa le
ho lo ho lo
ho lo wa a

ho pu i ho
hu mu hu mu
ka la ka la
ka ma li i
ka ni ka ni
ke e ke e
ki i ki i
ki ni ki ni
ko o ko o
ku e ku e
ku i he va
ku i ma ka
la hi la hi
la le la le
le a le a
le he le he
le hu le hu
li hi li hi
li ma nu i
ma hi o le
ma ka ma ka
ma li hi ni
ma li ma li
ma na ma na
me ha me ha
me le me le
mi li mi li
mi na mi na

mi no mi no
mi ti o e
mo a ta ta
mo ko mo ko
na he na he
ni hi ni hi
ni ho mo le
no o no o
no lu no lu
pa hu pa hu
pa la pa la
pa lu pa lu
pa pa li na
pa pa wa ha
pe la pe la
pi i pi i
pi li ki a
pi ni pi ni
po e po e
pu u pu u
pu ka pu ka
pu na he le
pu na he lu
pu ni pu ni
ti e ti e
tu hi tu hi
we lu we lu
wi ni wi ni

Fig. 9.1 (cont.)

TABLE XIII.

A o Iesu Kraist ka hiapo a ka Makua a ke Akua.
Iesu Kraist he Akua no kanaka maitai.
Oia no ka i hooku a kanaka.
Iho mai kela e hea i kanaka kina e mihi.
I hele mai kela i lalo nei e make i ola kanaka kina.
I hele mai kela i ka lono i tanawai a kona Makua, a hana'i kela i makemake nona.
Ahonui wale ia i ke ao ia kakou i akaka ko kakou ola, a i haawi ia kakou mai ka heva nui.,
I hoomake kela no kakou.
Ai Ierusalema kahi pepehi ai o Iesu Kraist a kanuwaiho no i loko o kepao.
Po akolu i lalo o ka lepo oia no; a ala hou mai.
Hookahi iako la ona i ike'a e lalo nei, mai ke ola hou ana mai.
Hoi ai i luna i ka lani i kona wahi no manuna.
Kokoke e hoi i luna i ka lani, Iesu Kraist hele aku la i na haumana ana, a i aku ia lakou la, e, "Pau aenei ka mana, i loko o ka lani a o ko honua, i haawi ia mai ia'u.
E hele oukou, e ao a pau na motu.
E hele oukou i na motu a puni, a e hai i ka olelo hou maitai a ke ola.
E hai aku ia lakou i ke aroha make a Iesu Kraist: *Baptaise* ia lakou i loko o ka inoa o ka Makua, a o ke Keiki, a o ka Uhane Hemolele e

Fig. 9.1 (cont.)

Analyzing *The Alphabet*

In order better to understand how Hawaiians, both children and adults, learned to read, I now take a careful look at the book that had such a profound effect on thousands of new readers in the 1820s.

Having already discussed consonants, vowels, and diphthongs, we can examine the remainder of the book, looking for clues that will tell us something about how the writer(s) viewed the language at that time.

First, it is clear that despite its title, the book is far more than just a list of the letters of the alphabet.[6] As soon as students were able to recite the alphabet and match each letter with its correct sound, they were expected to proceed to units larger than just consonant and vowel letters. As a matter of fact, the whole book is organized on the principle of moving from smaller units to successively larger ones, as the following abbreviated section heads show:

1. Vowels and consonants
2. Diphthongs
3. A syllable containing a short vowel
4. A syllable containing a diphthong
5. Two-syllable words
6. Three-syllable words
7. Four-syllable words

Also included are four short passages for reading.

Such an organization of a "first reader" may seem unusual to us today, but its emphasis on syllables would have been familiar to any student or teacher in the 1820s. Even vowels and consonants seem to be viewed equally as individual units and the building blocks of syllables.

Although the practice has disappeared, the classroom exercise of spelling aloud also focused on syllables: pupils first pronounced each letter of the syllable and then put the sounds together and pronounced the result, repeating the process—syllable by syllable—until the complete word was spelled.

When Hawaiian students performed this exercise, they began by pronouncing the first consonant, *bē*.[7] Next, they pronounced the first vowel, *ā*. Finally they pronounced the syllable that the sequence produced: *bā*. In

6. The title is puzzling. As mentioned in chapter 7, neither *Webster's Third New International Dictionary* (1961) nor the *Oxford English Dictionary* shows 'primer (introductory reader)' as one of the meanings of *alphabet*.

7. The name of each consonant letter was pronounced with a following vowel. The vowel is long because a minimum utterance must be a "heavy" syllable—that is, containing either a long vowel or a diphthong.

other words, they recited this pattern: "*bē, ā—bā.*" By 1824, this particular sequence of syllables had become the Hawaiian word for 'alphabet'; note the title *Ka be-a-ba* (Judd, Bell, and Murdoch #5). The title appeared on at least two more primers or alphabet tables printed before the spelling was regularized in 1826. Then, after *b* had been eliminated from the alphabet, *p* took its place in the new coinage. From that time on, the word for 'alphabet' has been *pī'āpā,* first appearing (as *Pi-a-pa*) in a book title in 1828 (Judd, Bell, and Murdoch 1978:14).

The hyphens between the syllables in the title may show that the compiler of the primer was aware that the word was not pronounced as most three-syllable words were—that is, with the second-to-last syllable accented—as in, for example, *kanáka* 'person'.[8] Instead, *pī'āpā* is pronounced with the syllables nearly equally accented but with a slight emphasis on the last one.

It is clear that the purpose of all these first exercises was to teach the mechanics of pronouncing words, one by one. Not until page 9 does one find short sentences, labeled "First exercise in reading." These short sentences were all commands; note the imperative *E* beginning each sentence. They were meant to instruct students how to behave in the classroom.

A passage on page 14 illustrates Albertine Loomis's point, made earlier in the present chapter, that the missionaries were not yet capable of translating accurately into Hawaiian. In this particular selection, although one of the sentences is grammatically adequate, several are borderline (although still intelligible), and one is nearly unintelligible.[9] It would appear that the compilers were not aware of the problem: a second edition printed in September 1822 shows no changes to those sentences. This piece of evidence supports the idea that although the missionaries praised the Hawaiians' ability to learn quickly to read, was there much meaning attached to units larger than individual words if they were grammatically garbled? Moreover, the ambiguities of the word "read" and the problems later voiced by Lorrin Andrews (both topics discussed in the next chapter) were already evident.

To see that American students at that time were learning to read in the same way, study the selection from an 1829 edition of *Webster's Speller*

8. In several other places, *pi-a-pa* was printed just as written here—with hyphens between the accented syllables. In an 1835 (figure 9.2) version, the hyphens are lowered.

9. Noted by Noenoe Silva (pers. comm.) and also by William H. Wilson (pers. comm., 18 June 2012).

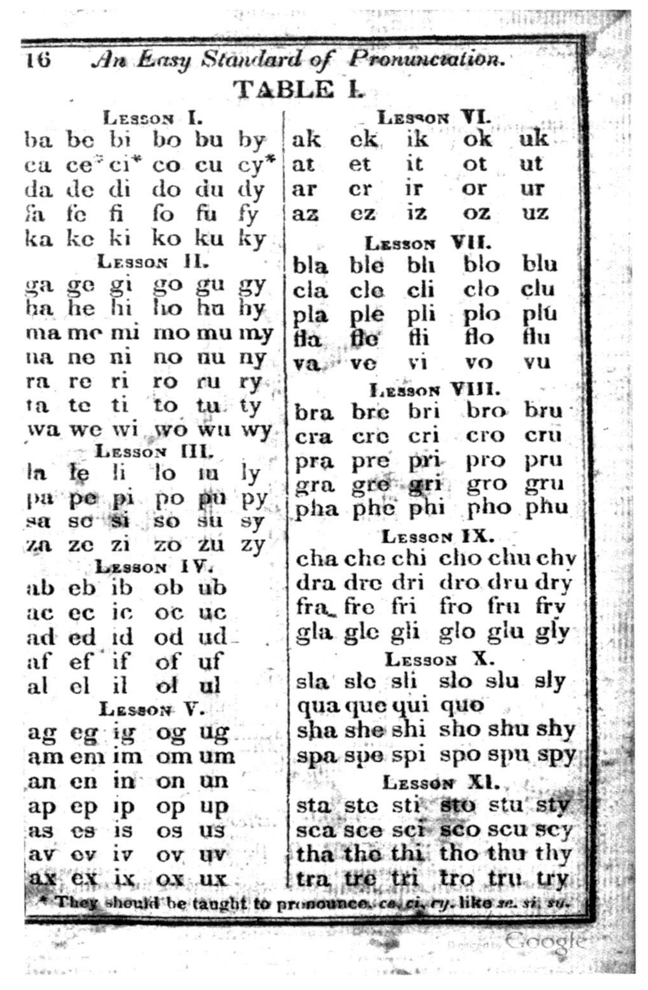
16 *An Easy Standard of Pronunciation.*

TABLE I.

LESSON I.

ba be bi bo bu by
ca ce* ci* co cu cy*
da de di do du dy
fa fe fi fo fu fy
ka ke ki ko ku ky

LESSON II.

ga ge gi go gu gy
ha he hi ho hu hy
ma me mi mo mu my
na ne ni no nu ny
ra re ri ro ru ry
ta te ti to tu ty
wa we wi wo wu wy

LESSON III.

la le li lo lu ly
pa pe pi po pu py
sa se si so su sy
za ze zi zo zu zy

LESSON IV.

ab eb ib ob ub
ac ec ic oc uc
ad ed id od ud
af ef if of uf
al el il ol ul

LESSON V.

ag eg ig og ug
am em im om um
an en in on un
ap ep ip op up
as es is os us
av ev iv ov uv
ax ex ix ox ux

LESSON VI.

ak ek ik ok uk
at et it ot ut
ar er ir or ur
az ez iz oz uz

LESSON VII.

bla ble bli blo blu
cla cle cli clo clu
pla ple pli plo plu
fla fle fli flo flu
va ve vi vo vu

LESSON VIII.

bra bre bri bro bru
cra cre cri cro cru
pra pre pri pro pru
gra gre gri gro gru
pha phe phi pho phu

LESSON IX.

cha che chi cho chu chy
dra dre dri dro dru dry
fra fre fri fro fru fry
gla gle gli glo glu gly

LESSON X.

sla sle sli slo slu sly
qua que qui quo
sha she shi sho shu shy
spa spe spi spo spu spy

LESSON XI.

sta ste sti sto stu sty
sca sce sci sco scu scy
tha the thi tho thu thy
tra tre tri tro tru try

* They should be taught to pronounce ce, ci, cy, like se, si, sy.

Figure 9.2. Page from Webster's *American Spelling Book* (1829)

(figure 9.2). This representative sample shows us that the organization of the Hawaiian speller was not original. Instead, the missionaries were simply following a familiar pattern from their own schooling in New England in the late eighteenth or early nineteenth century.

Comparing the English and Hawaiian materials also shows that there was uniformity in the reading materials used in the United States at that time. In contrast with countless teaching texts now available, Noah Webster's consciously "Americanized" reader served a large portion of the American student population.

The following sketch takes us through the tables and lessons, reinterpreting some of the comments based on syllables into more current linguistic terms.

Table I, Lesson 1 represents a *syllabary:* each of the twelve consonants is followed by each of the five vowels, making a total of sixty syllables. Missing are syllables that consist of a vowel alone, and—because the *'okina* was not recognized as a consonant—syllables consisting of a vowel preceded by that sound. Moreover, any syllable could occur both short and long, but that difference wasn't noticed until much later. Lesson 3 shows each of the seven diphthongs alone and combined with various consonants.

Table II, "Words of one syllable," shows the pattern (C)V, with (C) indicating an optional consonant and V a short vowel, long vowel, short diphthong, or long diphthong (e.g., *kau* could be either *kau* or *kāu*). Because all content words must be at least a long syllable in length, if the short syllables refer to actual words, they are function forms, such as *he* (indefinite, existential marker) or *ka/ke* (definite marker).

In view of a continuing (but uninteresting) disagreement about whether or not Hawaiian has diphthongs, Table II provides implicit support for the concept: because the words above with *ae, au, ai,* and *ei* were described as having one syllable each, this feature satisfies one part of the definition of "diphthong."

Table III, "Words of two syllables, accented on the first," shows the most common type of root words—that is, ˈ(C)V(C)V—an accented syllable (containing a vowel or a diphthong) followed by an unaccented one.[10] Examples from the table are *helu* 'count' and *houpo* 'diaphragm'.

Less common (and not from the table) are words with a long vowel or long diphthong in the first syllable, such as *kāne* 'male' and *'āina* 'land'.

As these examples show, the first syllable can be a simple vowel or diphthong, each either short or long. The final vowel must be short. In the list, the diphthongs in the first syllable are *ai, au,* and *ou.*

Two words that should not be in the list are *waiwai* and *wāwai.* In these words, both syllables are accented, with a slightly stronger accent on the second. These forms belong in Table V.

Table IV consists of sentences, discussed below.

---

10. For some forms, the second consonant cannot be optional; certain vowel combinations would produce a diphthong and thus only one syllable. For example, removing the consonant from *aku* (two syllables) would produce *au* (one syllable).

Table V, "Words of two syllables, having no certain distinction of accent," consists of disyllables in which each syllable is long or a diphthong. The confusion about which syllable is accented rests on context. When the words are pronounced as citation forms, we hear phrase accent, which emphasizes the last diphthong or long syllable. In another context—that is, not in isolation or as the last word in a phrase—each syllable is accented, more or less equally.

In this list, each word consists of two measures.[11]

Table VI, "Words of two syllables, accented on the second," shows forms in which the vowel in the second syllable is long or a diphthong (short or long). For example, because it appears in this list, *mano* has to represent *manō* 'shark'. Some of the forms may not belong on the list. *Nana* could represent *nanā* 'snarling', but if it is meant to be the more common *nānā* 'look', both syllables are accented. *Uha* could be one of four words (because long vowels and the *'okina* are not written), but none of them consists of a short vowel followed by a long vowel.

Each of the words in the list consists of one measure each, because there is only one accent.

Table VII consists of sentences, discussed in the next section.

Table VIII, "Words of three syllables, accented on the second," shows another common pattern for roots. In these forms, the vowel in the accented syllable can be short, long, or a diphthong (short or long). As an example of an accented long vowel, note *aikāne.* Words with *ai* or *au* within one syllable show that these sequences were analyzed as diphthongs. Moreover, in *aikāne,* both syllables are accented, with the second more prominent.

Table IX consists of sentences, discussed in the next section. It contains a word, *oia,* with the diphthong *oi,* but perhaps in a slow, careful pronunciation, the missionaries heard *o ía.*

Table X, "Words of three syllables, having a slight accent on the first, and the full accent on the third," should consist of two measures: a disyllable followed by a long syllable. *Akamai,* accented aka•mai (*àkamái*), fits this description. Some others don't fit. For example, *kapuai* is actually kapu•a'i: two measures and four syllables.[12]

---

11. For an explanation of this term, see chapter 8, note 13, and chapter 11.

12. This example illustrates the confusion caused by the inability of the English-speaking hearers to recognize a glottal stop between vowels. Also, see the explanation of "measure" in chapter 11.

What is written as *a po* provides an example of how older written records might shed light on a current spelling problem. In this instance, the problem is a disagreement about vowel in the first syllable: Is it short or long? P-E writes the word as *ʻapōpō* (two accents; thus two measures); *Māmaka Kaiao* writes it as *ʻā·pōpō* (three accents; thus three measures). If the writers of *The Alphabet* heard the word correctly, the *Māmaka Kaiao* spelling is the correct one.

Table XII, "Words of four syllables, accented on the first and third," consists of words that can be divided into two measures, each consisting of an accented syllable followed by an unaccented one. It is significant that more than half of these words are reduplicated forms.

Are the Sentences Grammatical?

Jeffrey Kapali Lyon offered the following analysis of the sentences in *The Alphabet* (pers. comm. 25 February 2015):[13]

> Many of the sentences of *TA* contain awkward and difficult phrases as well as non-native grammar. Following is a list of the main problems.
>
> Possible typographical errors (especially where the mistake is not repeated elsewhere . . . There seem to be an unusually large number of these in the Hawaiian sentences, probably due to both inexperience in the language and the inexperience of the printer.
>
> English word order used for some Hawaiian sentences
> Misuse of *a/o* possession
> Incorrect prohibition marker[14]
> Odd word choice
> Experimental word choice
> Insufficient understanding of the anaphoric marker *ai*
> Awkward use of conjunctions and prepositions
> Omission of noun markers: *ike'a e lalo nei* [*ʻikea e ko lalo nei*]
>
> The list could be expanded, but the reader can see that the Hawaiian is far from "correct" as the composers of these sentences would have understood

---

13. These examples are an abbreviated version of his comments in Schütz 2017.

14. For example, sentence 3 on page 9 uses *a ore* [*ʻa ole*] 'not' instead of *mai* 'don't' (Lyon, pers. comm., March 2016).

the term. The errors also indicate that the missionary writers had inadequately communicated their wishes to the Hawaiians who were helping them with this publication.[15]

Topics of the Sentences

The later reading exercises in *The Alphabet* (from page 11 on) were aimed toward presenting Christianity to new readers, young and old alike, and instilling in them the rudiments of Christian behavior.

The book was not unusual in its moralistic content; writers of contemporary primers and reading books for English chose their content with the same goals in mind. For example, McGuffey's readers, widely used in the United States in the nineteenth century, in addition to treating religious topics, emphasized that children obey and respect their elders, be kind to animals, and be neat.

The first Hawaiian primer was no exception. For example, it commanded that student readers (*kahakō* and *ʻokina* added) "*E noho mālie ʻoe i loko o ka hale*" ('Sit quietly inside the house'). These instructions are kinder than those suggested by the following passage from one of Webster's primers. He wrote, "As for those boys and girls that mind not their books, and love not the church and school, but play with such as tell tales, tell lies, curse, swear and steal, they will come to some bad end, and must be whipt till they mend their ways." For the Hawaiian situation, because they were instructing mainly adults, including chiefs, the teachers must have decided that such an action just might be counterproductive!

LATER EDITIONS OF *THE ALPHABET*?

Naturally, the missionary teachers were reluctant to print more primers, alphabet tables, hymnals, and other material with only an interim alphabet.[16] Still, the Judd, Bell, and Murdoch bibliography (1978) shows that through 1826, at least 150,000 copies of such works were printed. (This figure is, by necessity, low: for some of the items, there were no records

15. Lyon plans to expand this topic as an article.

16. Hawaiian Historical Society #4281/P57/JBM #135. JBM refers to Judd, Bell, and Murdoch (1978); the number is the item number (on page 48).

showing how many copies were printed.) Nor does it accurately reflect the number of readers, for books were in short supply and were often shared.

Eventually, however, the primer was revised, using the more efficient alphabet of 1826. Figure 9.3 shows one example. The primer differs from *The Alphabet* in several important ways. First, note the change in the title: the English was replaced by the Hawaiian equivalent, representing the word now spelled *pīʻāpā*.

Next, the list of consonants and the syllabic exercises reflect the modified alphabet. On the following pages one finds that a spelling once fixed with *t* (*maitai* 'good') is now *maikai* (i.e., *maikaʻi*), with *k*. Similarly, words formerly spelled with the extraneous consonants now have their normal spelling (but without the *ʻokina* and *kahakō*), and the deleted consonants *b, d, r, t,* and *v* are now added to the 1822 list labeled "used in spelling foreign words" (minus *y*).[17] There are fewer pages of meaningless syllables, and sentences begin on page 4.

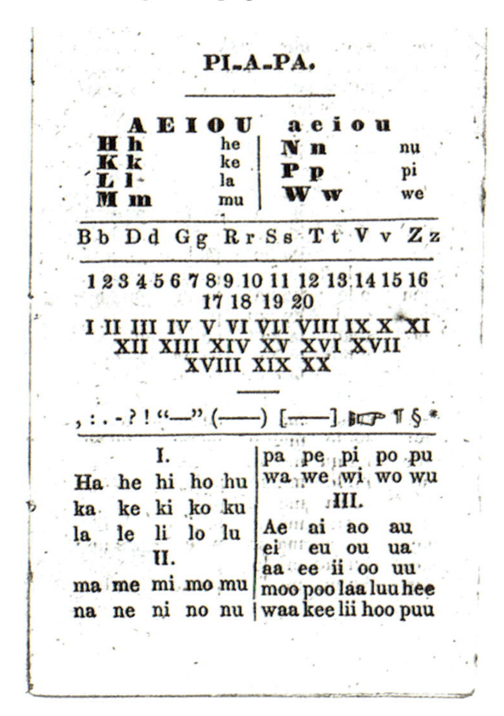
PI-A-PA.

AEIOU aeiou

Hh	he	Nn	nu
Kk	ke	Pp	pi
Ll	la	Ww	we
Mm	mu		

Bb Dd Gg Rr Ss Tt Vv Zz

1 2 3 4 5 6 7 8 9 10 11 12 13 14 15 16
17 18 19 20

I II III IV V VI VII VIII IX X XI
XII XIII XIV XV XVI XVII
XVIII XIX XX

, : . - ? ! "—" (—) [—] ☞ ¶ § *

I.
Ha he hi ho hu
ka ke ki ko ku
la le li lo lu
II.
ma me mi mo mu
na ne ni no nu

pa pe pi po pu
wa we wi wo wu
III.
Ae ai ao au
ei eu ou ua
aa ee ii oo uu
moo poo laa luu hee
waa kee lii hoo puu

Figure 9.3. 1835 *Pī-ʻā-pā*

17. At some point it must have been realized that an unaccented *i,* as in *iaka* 'yak', sounded much like a [y], thus eliminating the need for an initial *y* in borrowings.

Just as the word for 'alphabet' was coined from students' oral spelling of *ba* (later changed to *pa*) from the table of syllables, reciting the first four syllables in the left-hand column inspired more recent word coiners to invent a word for 'syllabary': *ha-ka-la-ma.*[18]

Interestingly, the content, although heavily sacred, is not entirely so. Although a dozen personal names listed are all biblical, borrowed names of months also appear, and among a dozen place names are four that do not appear in the Bible:

A SI A 'Asia'

A FE RI KA 'Africa'

E U RO PA 'Europe'

A ME RI KA 'America'

The work ends with what appear to be four verses of a hymn.

This short sample from one of the first primer's successors shows how drastically the alphabet had changed. However, I have been unable to find in mission histories any discussion of the Hawaiians' reactions to the changes. The lack of such information is surprising, for the spelling of many common words had to be relearned. However, that would have been more of a burden for writing than for reading: readers could adjust quickly to such changes as *maitai* → *maikai.* But how did writers react to such a change?

After all, many readers were probably already familiar with the dialectal differences spread over the chain of islands. Finally, with more examples of the language in context, the spelling changes would have been less of a burden to readers than isolated words out of context.

It seems illogical, then, that some current native speakers resist the minor changes produced by writing the *'okina* and the *kahakō,* finding the symbols "distracting." Moreover, the symbols are *adding* information, not *changing* it (as, for instance, replacing *b* with *p*). It is obvious that familiarity, context, and resistance to change are elements in such attitudes.

---

18. From the first four consonants in the alphabet? See the entry for *hakalama* in *Māmaka Kaiao.* In this word, however, unlike the coining for 'alphabet', the vowels are short. Although P-E already provided translations for 'syllable' (e.g., *hakina 'ōlelo, hopuna 'ōlelo*), perhaps the coiners preferred *hakalama* because it is shorter.

Visible Kaona?

It is only fair to add an argument from the other side. Noenoe Silva has suggested (pers. comm., July 2014) that written Hawaiian, especially as represented in the rich literature found in Hawaiian-language newspapers, could reflect *kaona* in a way that spoken language couldn't—in a sense, *kaona* of the eye, not the ear. Silva expanded on her idea:

> The words "pua," "puaʻa," and "pūʻā" serve as examples; before the use of the macron [and glottal stop] to distinguish them from each other, they were homographs, that is, they looked identical on the page. "Pua" can refer to a blossom, a child, the young of a fish, or the act of issuing or emerging, among other meanings; "puʻa" can be a whistle or to excrete; and "pūʻā," a herd or flock, a sheaf or bundle, to pass food from mouth to mouth, and more. The possibilities for punning and allusion using this one collection of letters in its unmarked form are endless. (Silva 2017:12)

For other examples, see the list of "Poetic Vocabulary" in Elbert and Mahoe 1970:20–24. Before the *ʻokina* was written, *moi* 'threadfish' could also represent *mōʻī* 'king'. The word *ua* 'rain', very common in poetic language and with positive, even sexual connotations, in written Hawaiian at that time could also represent *ʻuʻa* 'useless, unproductive'—a contrast in meaning that could be used to represent irony.

In summary, looking closely at *The Alphabet* and its contemporary models helps us better understand the book that was for many Hawaiians in the 1820s their only contact with the newly written language. In short, it is the most important document available to help us trace the birth of Hawaiian literacy—and education in general.

VERBATIM

The Syllabarium

The introduction to Thomas Dilworth's *New Guide to the English Tongue* ([1740] 1788), a possible model for Noah Webster's works, describes the organization of the book. As reflected in Hawaiian primers, the syllable seems to be the foundation of the teaching methodology:

> I. Words, both *common* and *proper*, from *one* to *six Syllables:* The several sorts of *Monosyllables* in the *common* Words being distinguished by Tables, into Words of *two, three,* and *four* Letters, &c. with six short Lessons at the End of each Table, not exceeding the order of Syllables in the foregoing Tables. The several sorts of *Polysyllables* also, being ranged in proper Tables, have their Syllables divided, and Directions placed at the Head of each Table for the *Accent,* to prevent *false Pronunciation;* together with the like Number of Lessons on the foregoing Tables, placed at the End of each Table, as far as to Words of *four* Syllables, for the easier and more speedy Way of teaching Children to Read.

Webster's speller and, in turn, the contemporary methods of language teaching were just as closely tied to the concept of the syllable. As E. Jennifer Monaghan described it, the main goal of the spelling book was to teach reading, for which spelling—in particular, spelling aloud—was a prerequisite. "As far back as one can trace the history of reading methodology, children were taught to spell words out, in syllables, in order to pronounce them" (1983:14, 31).

Webster himself wrote, "Let a child be taught, first the Roman letters, both small and great—then the Italics—then the sounds of the vowels; not pronouncing the double letters *a* and *u,* &c separately, but only the sound that those letters united express—then the double letters. All this a child should know before he leaves the Alphabet and begins to spell" ([1783] 1800:28).

In the edition just quoted from, Lesson 1 (page 29) begins with a "syllabarium" to be spelled aloud and then pronounced as units: *ba be bi bo bu by.*[19] Thus, students began to learn to read by reciting the names of the letters and then pronouncing the syllable the letters spelled: *be, a: ba.*[20] After this exercise, students could proceed to the lessons.

Lorrin Andrews's *A Dictionary of the Hawaiian Language* is proof that the syllable was still important for language reference materials in 1865. For example, note the following entries, representative of the whole work:

HA LE LA AU	'wooden house'
KA MA AI NA	'native'

19. This example differs from that in Dilworth's primer ([1740] 1789) in including *y* as a vowel. Of course, the letter *y* was not necessary for Hawaiian.

20. Monaghan (1983:14) noted that not until the *McGuffey's Readers* appeared in 1836 did American children begin to learn to read from a "reader" rather than a "speller."

However, in pedagogical readers for students, the emphasis on the syllable as an organizing unit seems to have waned or disappeared entirely by the second half of the nineteenth century. The following quotations show that a different approach was recommended (*McGuffey's First Eclectic Reader* 1879:ii).[21] Note that the word *syllable* is not used.

> This FIRST READER may be used in teaching reading by any of the methods in common use; but it is especially adapted to the Phonic Method, the Word Method, or a combination of the two.
>
> PHONIC METHOD.—First teach the elementary sounds and their representatives, the letters marked with diacriticals, as they occur in the lessons; then, the formation of words by the combination of these sounds. For instance, teach the pupil to identify the characters ă, ŏ, n, d, <macron>g r, and ŧh, in Lesson I, as the representatives of certain elementary sounds; then, teach him to form words by their combination, and to identify them at sight . . . Having read a few lessons in this manner, begin to teach the names of the letters and the spelling of words, and require the groups, "a man," "the man," "a pen," "the pen," to be read as a good reader would pronounce single words.
>
> WORD METHOD.—Teach the pupil to identify at sight the words placed at the head of the reading exercises, and to read these exercises without hesitation. Having read a few lessons, begin to teach the names of the letters and the spelling of words.
>
> WORD METHOD AND PHONIC METHOD COMBINED.—Teach the pupil to identify words and read sentences, as above. Having read a few lessons in this manner, begin to use the Phonic Method, combining it with the Word Method, by first teaching the words in each lesson as words; then, the elementary sounds, the names of the letters, and spelling.

In addition to the unusual characters listed above, *First Reader* also used diacritics to show other unpredictable relationships between symbol and sound, such as when *s* was pronounced as [z] or *c* as [s], and various sounds indicated by the five available vowel letters.

---

21. The first four readers appeared in 1836–37.

CHAPTER 10
HOW LITERACY SPREAD

He ku-la.

Having her eye directed to the first class of letters—the five vowels, she was induced to imitate my voice in their enunciation, a, e, i, o, u. As the vowels could be acquired with great facility, an experiment of ten minutes, well directed, would ensure a considerable advance. She followed me in enunciating the vowels, one by one, two or three times over, in their order, when her skill and accuracy were commended. Her countenance brightened. Looking off from her book upon her familiars, with a tone a little boasting or exulting . . . the queen exclaimed, "Ua loaa iau! [Ua loaʻa iaʻu] 'I've got it! [lit., it's gotten by me]" . . . She had passed the threshold, and now unexpectedly found herself entered as a pupil. Dismissing her cards,[1] she accepted and studied the little book, and with her husband, asked for forty more for their attendants.

—Hiram Bingham (1847:164–65)

This is Hiram Bingham's account of Kaʻahumanu's breaking the literacy barrier in 1822. For a time after the *Pīʻāpā* was printed, the powerful High Chiefess Kaʻahumanu "had not yet deigned to give her attention to a book" (Bingham 1847:163), but eventually she too joined the surge toward learning how to read and write. That one simple phrase above—*Ua loaʻa iaʻu!* 'I've got it!'—justified all the effort, sacrifices, and countless hours of instruction on the part of both the Hawaiians and their teachers.

1. The missionaries didn't approve of Hawaiians "wasting their time" by engaging in such activities. See Bingham's longer quotation later in the chapter.

It is sometimes said (without supporting evidence) that the Hawaiian alphabet and the literacy it facilitated changed the Hawaiian language. It is more likely that literacy changed the Hawaiian *people.*[2]

Kaʻahumanu's enthusiasm did not wane. Later that year, she asked the missionaries to send 800 more books. "We are much pleased to learn the *palapala,*" she wrote. "By and by, perhaps, we shall be *akamai,* skilled or wise" (Bingham 1847:172).

The eagerness to learn to read, on the part of children and adults, of chiefs and commoners, had some of the elements of a religious revival:

> A few copies of the book for the children were ready to be presented before the prayer-meeting of the mothers and their offspring closed. They were received with great eagerness. The next day, troops of children came for more, as fast as they could be made ready for them, at the office. Within the two months after the presentation of this juvenile offering, we had, at the station, 1144 children cheerfully turning its neatly printed pages, more or less embellished with cuts, and learning its spelling, reading, and catechetical lessons, and juvenile songs.[3] This was a specimen of the gladness with which it was received, at the different stations.
>
> . . . At the weekly lecture, on Wednesday, the 6th [January, 1830], about 300 children, were present, and many of them, doubtless, with the hope of obtaining one of the new books. More than a thousand women attended the Friday prayer-meeting on the 8th.
>
> . . . The next day, our houses were thronged, from before breakfast, till the darkness of a rainy night set in . . . The number of readers and learners in the islands, at this time, was estimated at 50,000. (Bingham 1847:369–70)

There are two main reasons that Hawaiians were able to learn the basics of reading and writing very quickly. First, they found printed books intriguing and were eager to learn.[4] Next, after the spelling was adjusted in 1826, the

---

2. Some of the material in this chapter appears in Schütz 1994.

3. From this description, especially its mention of [wood]cuts, it is obvious that the book in question was not the 1822 version of *The Alphabet.* It could possibly be a book from 1830, *He Palapala Mua na na Kamalii e Naauao ai i ko Lakou Wa Opiopio* [A first book for children, to educate them in their youth . . .] (Judd, Bell, and Murdoch 1978, item 6l), which contains woodcuts.

4. As the previous chapter demonstrates, "intriguing" might have had more to do with the novelty of reading than the content of the material.

Hawaiian writing system was extremely efficient. Once pupils learned the relationship between a letter and a sound, they could read and write new material immediately, for other than the missing *ʻokina* and *kahakō,* every word was spelled as it was pronounced, and vice versa. In other words, there were no stumbling blocks in Hawaiian similar to English *b**ough***, *thr**ough***, *r**ough***, *th**ough***, and *th**ough**t*, in which the same combination of letters—***ough***—represents five different vowel sounds.

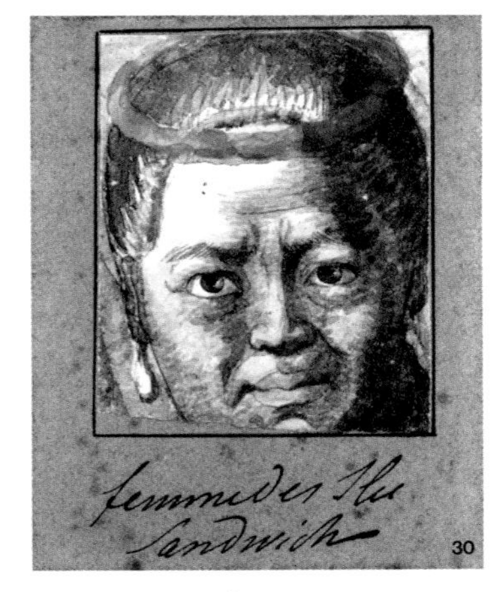

Figure 10.1. Kaʻahumanu

Even though the *ʻokina* and the *kahakō* weren't written in the 1820s (see chapter 8), omitting them was not a major obstacle, for those who already knew the language could usually resolve any ambiguous spellings through context. For example, although the word written as *makau* could represent either *makau* 'fishhook' or *makaʻu* 'fear', context usually made the meaning clear: in the sentence *E makau kakou ia Iala* 'We should fear Him', the reader could see that the meaning had nothing to do with fishhooks.

Figure 10.2. The queen at Waimea, Oʻahu, recommending Christianity

One impediment that persisted, however, was the grammatical errors in written sentences in the lesson books. Still, as the missionaries' skills in the language improved, so did the books—but not immediately.

Several missionary accounts of this period mention that part of the Hawaiians' fascination with reading and writing had to do with the high value they placed on books. But what books were available? From 1822 through 1826, the period during which the alphabet was in a state of flux, only twenty titles were printed. And ten of these were variations on the first primer, *The Alphabet.*

With so little printed material available, what made reading and writing so popular? The following sections reveal that it was not one factor but a combination of them that boosted literacy in Hawai'i.

WHAT HAPPENED AFTER THE FIRST PRINTING

It is hard to look at literacy in Hawai'i without looking at schooling as well. Reading and writing, two of the traditional "Three R's," were closely linked with the schools that the missionaries established—so closely, in fact, that they were considered the foundation on which to build formal education.

Early Schools

In his sketch of the beginnings of Western education, Lorrin Andrews reported that the first schools were established in 1822, with the missionaries as teachers (1832:156). And the only Hawaiian-language book available was *The Alphabet*—that is, the *Pī'āpā.*

Figure 10.3. Chief Kuakini

At first, the student body was made up only of chiefs and people closely connected with them. One of the most notable of these chiefly students was Kuakini, a high chief who as early as 1809 had expressed an interest in learning to read and write English.

Shortly after the first speller was printed, he requested a copy, and only a few days later he sent the missionary Hiram Bingham a letter written in Hawaiian. As Bingham wrote, "Epistolary correspondence, thus commenced in that language, suddenly opened to the chiefs and people a new source of pleasure and advantage, of which hundreds soon availed themselves" (Bingham 1847:157).

Letter Writing

By the mid-1830s, letter writing had apparently become routine. Andrews wrote that many Hawaiians, chiefs and commoners alike, were quick to use the new medium for both "legal proceedings" and the circulation of news (1836b:15).

In the following decades, such active correspondence was to provide a rich source of language data for Andrews, the mission's most active and productive grammarian. He was far ahead of his time in using as the basis for his grammar the writings of native speakers, not of outsiders, no matter how skilled they might be at translating.

Charles Wilkes, commodore of the United States Exploring Expedition (a.k.a. the Wilkes Expedition), which called at Hawaiʻi in 1840 and 1841, was intrigued by another kind of correspondence—love letters. In his account of the Ladies Seminary at Wailuku, Maui, he reported that one courtship had already been carried on through the medium of writing. (Respect for privacy does not seem to have been considered: Wilkes was anxious to obtain the originals or copies, and the missionaries were able to vouch for the innocent nature of the contents.)

In the introduction to his 1854 grammar, Andrews wrote, "The materials for the following grammar have been taken almost entirely from native manuscripts or from documents printed from native manuscripts . . . It is possible that some of the works written by the missionaries might be of equal authority; but as so much has been written by the natives themselves, it was thought best to appeal to them for authority in every case."[5] Although not stated explicitly, some of the "native manuscripts" might well have been letters written to the mission.

In spite of its popularity, letter writing on its own did not contribute directly to achieving the goals that the missionaries had in mind. It continued in its own direction, largely ignored in mission accounts once it was first mentioned. Most of the mission's attention was focused on

---

5. It is fortunate that Andrews was not using sentences from the *Pīʻāpā* as the basis for his grammar.

the *printed* word; one might suggest that the reason was that the content could be controlled and directed toward the ultimate aim of converting the Hawaiians to Christianity.

Convincing the *Ali'i*

Although the rapidly growing student body at the time represented a cross-section of Hawaiians, the missionaries (judging from what they wrote) expended more of their energies on the chiefs. Such a focus was to be expected, for once leaders became interested in reading and writing, they could influence a great number of followers. For example, Bingham wrote, "Kamamalu [Kamāmalu] applied herself . . . with renewed vigor to learn, both in English and in her own language, and exerted an influence, on the whole, favorable to the cause of instruction, and soon had a school-house built for the benefit of her people. Liholiho requested a hundred copies of the spelling-book in his language to be furnished for his friends and attendants who were unsupplied, while he would not have the instruction of the people, in general, come in the way of their cutting sandal-wood to pay his debts" (1847:163).

Figure 10.4. Kamāmalu

In the Classroom

Figure 10.5. Samuel Kamakau

Aside from the personal attention given to the chiefs, however, most of the teaching took place in the classrooms. What actually happened there? Try to imagine yourself in a schoolroom of the period, with the *Pīʻāpā* for a text. Andrews described how the primer was used in class: "The teacher[6] takes a Pia-pa, sits down in front of a row or several rows of scholars, from ten to a hundred perhaps in number, all sitting on the ground, furnished perhaps with Pia-pas, perhaps not. The teacher begins: says *A*. The scholars all repeat in concert after him, *A*. The teacher then says *E*. They repeat all together, as before *E*, and so on, repeating over and over, after the teacher, until all the alphabet is fixed in the memory, just in the order the letters stand in the book; and all this just as well without a book as with one" (1832:159). The phrases "fixed in the memory" and "just as well without a book" are significant, as will be seen later.

Samuel Kamakau, who entered the school at Lahainaluna in about 1832, gave a former pupil's view of the curriculum of that period. As for those activities connected with reading, he confirmed Andrews's report of how spelling was taught orally, syllable by syllable. The only reading materials cited specifically were "portions of the books of Matthew, Psalms, Acts of the Apostles, and Luke." But he seems to have included all the activities of the school in his closing statement: "These were some of the many things taught in old days which gave reading such prestige" (Kamakau [1866–1871] 1961:270).

Through the decade of the 1830s, the list of different books available in Hawaiian grew rapidly. In fact, this period was the press's most productive one.[7] Now I discuss these books in more detail.

---

6. Likely a "monitor"—that is, a recently literate Hawaiian, not one of the missionaries.

7. Here are the number of titles printed for five decades (Judd, Bell, and Murdoch 1978): 1830s: 149; 1840s: 107; 1850s: 65; 1860s: 79; 1870s: 37.

MATERIALS

Often literacy is treated as a skill that can exist on its own. It is easy to forget that the target or object of literacy is to assimilate or transmit the information contained in written material. The sections that follow look at written Hawaiian from three points of view: its availability, its variety, and its content. The role of the Hawaiian-language newspapers in all three of these topics will also be highlighted.

Wanted: More Books

In the letters and reports written during the 1820s and early 1830s, a recurring theme is that in some schools, the *Pīʻāpā* was the only printed matter available for students to read. To make matters worse, there were not enough copies to supply students with their own books. As an extreme example, Andrews (1832:159) reported that in one school, the teacher had only his own copy of the book, and as a result, all his students learned their letters upside down!

In 1825 (three years after the first printing), Bingham (1847:256) wrote that there were thousands of students spread over the islands, and the numbers were increasing. But the demand for books and writing paper was far greater than the mission's supply.

The same year, the printer Elisha Loomis complained that the main problem was (as he repeatedly wrote to the mission headquarters in Boston) that there was not enough paper to keep the press in constant operation. Moreover, because the distribution of letters in Hawaiian is very different from that in English, Loomis needed far more *a*'s and *k*'s than he was supplied with.

Perhaps the most emotional plea from the missionaries to the ABCFM in Boston was this one: "Do, sir, send us *stationery* as well as *bread:* we cannot live without" (Bingham 1847:258).

What was the reason for the constant lack of materials? The answer is one often heard today as well: finances. The ABCFM was in debt, and the Hawaiʻi mission was forced to become more nearly self-sufficient. However, achieving this goal was hindered by an increase in the cost of living, caused—ironically—by the growing presence of Western "civilization," so eagerly desired by many missionaries when they first arrived. As Hawaiians became more interested in foreign goods, they needed more cash with which to purchase them. As a result of this economic spiral, the missionaries could not live as cheaply as before.

One solution was to sell or barter their most valuable commodity: books. But the problem was circular: money could be made by selling books, but there wasn't enough money to buy the materials with which to print them.

Not Enough Variety

It has already been noted that it was impossible to provide enough copies of the first primer, *The Alphabet,* for students to learn the rudiments of reading and writing Hawaiian. But the small number of books available lacked variety as well. Surely students' enthusiasm was dampened if the only textbook available for several years (in extreme cases) was a sixteen-page speller with an imperfect alphabet and a mixture of a few grammatical and ungrammatical sentences.

What else was there to read? We can find the most detailed answer to this question in Judd, Bell, and Murdoch 1978 and Forbes 1999–2003,

Figure 10.6. Early printing of the Bible. Note its size. A later edition has 1,598 pages. Note also the *Pīʻāpā* open to the first page.

which, for most titles, give complete bibliographic information, including the number of copies printed. However, in response to questions from the ABCFM (1834), the mission itself listed the following titles to show what was available, in addition to the *Pī'āpā,* in the 1820s:

1823	A hymnal
1825	Another speller, with extracts from New Testament translations; Scripture extracts, a catechism
1826	The Ten Commandments, the Lord's Prayer, etc.
1827	The Sermon on the Mount
1828	The history of Joseph, an arithmetic text, an enlarged hymnal, the four Gospels
1829	Acts, and parts of Genesis, Exodus, and Leviticus

The press increased its production markedly in the 1830s. For instance, in 1835, the year in which the press was most active, twenty-five titles in Hawaiian appeared: 73,200 books in all, with a total of about 7,960,000 pages. Scattered among the religious titles are a few school texts, including books on arithmetic and penmanship, a spelling book, and three primers (Judd, Bell, and Murdoch 1978).

To show what happened in the next decade, Bingham summarized the output from the press to the middle of 1845: "Twenty thousand Bibles, thirty thousand New Testaments, and more than seventy other works, prepared, written, translated, or compiled by the missionaries, have issued from our mission presses. The printing from January, 1822, to June, 1845, amounted to 149,911,383 pages" (1847:615).

In short, in just ten years (from 1835 to 1845), the number had increased from about 8 million to nearly 150 million pages. The list in figure 10.7 shows the press's publications in Hawaiian (Bingham 1847:615).

Comparing this catalog with the books available to students in America, Laura Fish Judd suggested that it was "a wider range of literature than constituted the library of many happy children in New England forty years ago" (1880:78–79).

Content

If one looks at Judd's evaluation more closely, one must ask what the phrase "wider range" really means. What kind of information did these millions of printed pages contain? As might be expected, it leaned more

Title	Pages
Elementary lessons; 4, 8, and 16 pp.,	100,000 copies
Decalogue and Lord's Prayer	4
Scripture doctrines, a Catechism	8
Thoughts of the chiefs	16
Sermon on the Mount	16
Hawaiian Hymns	60
First Book for children	36
Universal Geography	216
New Testament	520
Fowle's Child's Arithmetic	66
Animals of the earth, with a chart	2
Catechism on Genesis	56
Geometry for Children [Holbrook's]	64
Tract on Marriage	12
Sacred Geography [Worchester's]	100
Geographical Questions	44
Bible Class Book, Abbot & Fisk's, vol.i	62
Colburn's Intellectual Arithmetic	132
History of Beasts	192
Lama Hawaii [Newspaper]	100
Hawaiian Almanac	16
Vocabulary	132
Compend of Ancient History	76
Sacred Geography	84
Union Questions, vol. I	156
Colburn's Sequel	116
History of Beasts for Children	84
Hawaiian Teacher, 4 vols, 4to	420
Child's teacher	96
Daily Food, for 1835, with Notes	36
Hawaiian Grammar	32
First Reading Book for Children	48
Tract on the Sabbath	12.
Universal Geography [Woodbridge's]	203
Daily Food, for 1836, with Notes	36
Maps of U. Geography	9
Scripture Chronology and History	216
Hymns revised and enlarged	184
Hymns with tunes	360
Linear Drawing	36
Little Philosopher [Abbot's]	40
English and Hawaiian Grammar	40
First Teacher for Children	32
Tract on Astronomy	12
Maps of Sacred Geography	6
Sixteen Sermons	144
Tract on Lying	8
Attributes of God	2
First Book for teaching English	36
Moral Science	12
Key to Colburn	76
Heavenly Manna	72
Hymns for Children	122
Hawaiian History	116
Algebra [Colburn's]	44
Anatomy	60
Scripture Lessons	152
Mathematics, Geometry, Trigonometry, Mensuration, Surveying, & Navigation	168
Tract on Intemperance	28
Bible Class Book, Vol. II	36
" " " Vol. III	40
Child's Book on the Soul [Gallaudet's]	66
Natural Theology [Gallaudet's]	178
Nonanona [Newspaper]	00
Articles of Faith and Covenant	00
Church History	340
Moral Philosophy [Wayland's]	215
Pilgrim's Progress	324
Tract on Popery	23
Keith's Study of the Globes	80
Volume of Sermons	296
Sandwich Islands' Laws [by Government]	92
English and Hawaiian Lessons	40
Keith on the Prophecies	12
Dying Testimony of Christians and Infidels	40
Algebra [Bailey's]	160
Reading Book for Schools	340
Messenger, semi-monthly	8
History of the Sandwich Islands in English	464
Hawaiian Bible	000[1]

Figure 10.7. Catalog of Hawaiian Books and Tracts. Several entries omit the number of pages. For the last entry, Bingham might have intended to add the total number in the Bible.

heavily toward the sacred than the secular. In the late 1830s, Sheldon Dibble considered that "everything connected with instruction was inseparably connected in the minds of the people with Christianity" (Westervelt 1912:20).

Dibble himself organized and edited what seems to be the first publication in book form of Hawaiian literature, as opposed to that which was introduced from English. *Ka Mooolelo Hawaii* (*The History of Hawai'i,* 1838) was written by a number of students at Lahainaluna High School and went through several editions, the latest of which appeared in 2006.

However, such works were rare. In a period of nearly fifty years, the mission press printed only three books on Hawaiian history and culture, with a total number of pages under 650.[8]

NEWSPAPERS

The medium that was most successful in broadening the range of reading in the Hawaiian language was the newspapers, the first of which, *Ka Lama Hawaii,* was printed at Lahainaluna in February 1834.[9] During the next 114 years, 106 different newspapers were published.[10] At the beginning of this period, two newspapers appeared, and by the last five years the figure had dwindled to one. But in the peak years (e.g., 1896), the number was as high as fourteen (Mookini 1974).

These newspapers contained a mixture of sacred and secular themes, and they covered news both from Hawai'i and from the outside world. More important, they sometimes represented a point of view different from that of the mission.

However, such open-mindedness caused some disagreements within the mission. In the late 1830s, one missionary resigned because of the policy of the headquarters in Boston to censor all materials, and in 1841, Charles Wilkes, mentioned earlier, criticized what he called the "restriction on the liberty of the press" (Wilkes 1852).

---

8. Because the famous McGuffey books for beginning readers in America were nearly contemporaneous (starting in 1836), it is tempting to compare their wide-ranging contents with the output of the Mission Press. But such a comparison is unfair. First, the compilers of the graded McGuffey series had hundreds of years of printed material to draw on. Next, the collections were aimed at primary school pupils, while the majority of the Hawaiians learning to read were adults.

9. Esther T. Mookini has translated some of the secular articles and arranged them in a collection: *O Na Holoholona Wawae Eha O Ka Lama Hawaii,* or *The Four-Footed Animals of Ka Lama Hawaii* (1985). The work is described in Sachdeva 1985.

10. The list of titles contains a few cross-references, so perhaps the figure is somewhat lower (Mookini 1974:1–41).

Nor were the newspapers free from internal controversy. For example, because people knowledgeable about traditional texts were becoming fewer in number, some Hawaiians were in favor of transcribing those works. But others objected to making such information public, foreseeing the loss of prestige customarily due the traditional expert (Charlot 2005:499).

The subject matter raised other questions as well. One school of thought was that it would be best to ignore pre-Christian history, considered at that time a "period of darkness." An opposing view encouraged such writings, not because they preserved valuable cultural information, but because they would underscore how enlightened the new beliefs were. Whatever the consensus, a great amount of historical and cultural information reached the reading public through the medium of these newspapers (Charlot 2005:499–500).

The current role of the nineteenth-century newspapers in providing reading material is discussed in chapter 15.

Summary

In searching through bibliographies for printed works in Hawaiian, one finds that from 1822 through 1899 there were over 650 titles available. However, as the discussion above shows, in the early years aspiring readers were held back by a lack of books, both in variety and number. And even a half century or more later, books focusing on Hawaiian culture were rare.

LITERACY: SUCCESS OR FAILURE?

How successful were the efforts to turn nineteenth-century Hawaiians into a literate people? In trying to answer this question, one should be aware that for the missionaries, literacy was a means to an end—mainly a tool for conversion and a way to modify behavior.

How many people were literate? Most of the mission reports from the 1820s, 1830s, and 1840s gave high estimates of the number of pupils who had learned to read and write. But what does a figure of, for instance, "30,000 pupils in the 1830s" mean? Do we really know how "literate" these pupils were?

To answer that question, we must first examine the concept itself. What does it mean if we say that someone can read and write?

Degrees of Literacy: From Mechanics to Meaning

Some of these favorable reports seem to have treated literacy as a simple matter: either people know how to read, or they don't. But is it really so simple? Perhaps it is more realistic to view different kinds of literacy as points on a continuum, beginning with the most basic skills—recognizing letters and the sounds they refer to (1 and 2 below) and proceeding (not necessarily in the order below) to the highest level (9), understanding the content. Thus, I suggest that with respect to reading, a literate person can

1. recognize letters and recite the alphabet
2. associate letters with sounds
3. associate a whole written word with a spoken word[11]
4. "sound out" an unfamiliar word from its spelling
5. read isolated common words aloud
6. read sentences aloud
7. develop a style of "oral interpretation"[12]
8. read "silently"
9. understand the content of any written matter.

Several of these levels of literacy alternate between silent and oral reading. As chapter 9 noted, classroom reading exercises usually focused on the latter, perhaps because teachers were better able to track their pupils' progress when they read orally.

The problem with testing this particular activity should be obvious: oral reading might be considered primarily a mechanical skill—rather like an opera singer's ability to perform works in several different languages without necessarily understanding the content of the libretto. Where does meaning enter the picture, and how can it be measured?

Moving from mechanics to meaning could actually span a range of levels listed above. Moreover, number 9—the last in the series—might extend over a lifetime of reading, reflecting a steady process of expanding

11. Note the current (and continuing) controversy about how to teach reading: using phonetics ("phonics") versus a whole-word approach. Thus, #4 and #5 represent different approaches to reading.

12. For some of us, this topic seems a thing of the past. Today, many radio and television announcers seem to have had little or no training in disciplines such as phonetics, oral interpretation, or drama that would result in a more professional use of spoken language.

one's knowledge. It is not easily measured; note Andrews's comments about lack of understanding under "Opposing Opinions" below.

As you read the comments that follow—some positive, others negative—keep in mind that the writers might have had different levels—or definitions—of literacy in mind when they expressed their views. Moreover, few people viewed the topic dispassionately.

Supporting Opinions

As noted before, most firsthand observers agreed that the main reason pupils learned to read so quickly was that the Hawaiian orthography is regular and efficient. It is important to remember that these observers were probably comparing Hawaiian spelling with that of English, with its much less regular system.

The missionary Sheldon Dibble referred specifically to the simplicity and regularity of the Hawaiian spelling system: "The Hawaiian language contains but 12 articulate sounds, and of course the missionaries introduced but 12 letters . . .[13] They adopted also the simple method of avoiding all arbitrary spelling. Every word is spelt precisely as it is pronounced, so that to teach spelling is scarcely an object. Every one who can combine two letters in a syllable, and put two syllables together, can both read and spell with readiness. The art of reading, therefore, is very easily acquired. I think I am safe in saying, that the children of Hawaii learn to read their language in a much shorter time than our children do the English" ([1839] 1909:80).

In the same vein, Artemas Bishop wrote, "About half of the scholars can read with facility in any of the tracts, and all who have passed through the elementary sheet can spell any word in the language, so simple is the syllabic construction of words" (5 September 1828, Missionary Letters, p. 651).

Laura Fish Judd also implied a connection between the structure of the language and the apparently high rate of literacy: "The construction of the Hawaiian language is so simple, when compared with the English,

13. At the time, of course, the glottal stop and vowel length were not considered "articulate sounds." Note that the number twelve (five vowels and seven consonants) refers to the streamlined alphabet of 1826, not the fuller one of 1822.

that it is no marvel that so many of the natives acquired the art of reading and writing it" (1880:78).

One must remember, however, that these assessments were made after 1826, when the orthography was significantly altered. By this time, many Hawaiians had already been taught to read using the fuller (and inefficient) orthography, so they had to relearn the skills of reading and writing—or at least modify them (see chapter 7). Moreover, all the material produced from 1822 to 1826 had to be revised.

As for describing the construction of the language as simple, perhaps, as with Dibble's and Judd's assessments, it was the syllable structure and the one-to-one correspondence between letter and phoneme that were meant, not the grammar.

Other observers were more general in their accounts. For example, Bingham wrote, "The introduction of printing in the language of the country, not only awakened curiosity among the chiefs and people, but gave a new and decided impulse to our schools and the cause of education. From sixty to seventy pupils were at once furnished with copies of the first sheet, as they could not wait till the work was finished. They found the lessons easy. They not only soon mastered them, but were able to teach them to others. In a few months, there were not less than five hundred learners" (1847:160).

Literacy for its own sake was not its only drawing power, at least in the minds of the missionaries. Bingham was pleased with the Hawaiians' newfound fascination for the printed word, for it diverted them from activities that he considered morally degrading: "It has afforded, to a great extent, by the pen, slate, pencil, and book, a substitute for the pleasure which the people once derived from games of chance, and of skill, and strength, connected with staking property; and in many cases instruction imparted by dictation and the exercise of joint recitation or cantillation of moral lessons by classes, has been a happy substitute for the heathen song and dance" (1847:471).

Bingham was not alone in his opinion. Many other writers as well described this new development in glowing terms. For example, Judd, writing about the 1830s and 1840s and amplifying on her comment above, praised the high rate of literacy, estimating it as "greater than in any other country in the world, except Scotland and New England" (1880:78).

Dibble was extremely optimistic in his appraisal, estimating that perhaps a third of the whole population could read. Printing presses, binderies, newspapers, hymnals, schoolbooks, and such activities as writing letters and demonstrating theorems—all these were forces for the good, diverting the people's attention from "vile amusements." He also commented on the extent of this influence: "Every station has had at times from 50 to 150 district schools connected with it. Under my own care at Hilo at one time, there were 87 schools, and not far from 7,000 learners. When collected at the centre at a quarterly examination, they formed an immense crowd, no house could contain them" ([1839] 1909:114–15). As for the extent of literacy in Hawai'i as a whole in the late 1830s, Dibble reported there were at least 30,000 readers (p. 150).

All these assessments are from people connected with the mission. Some opinions from the outside as well echoed these paeans. One example is that of Richard H. Dana (author of *Two Years Before the Mast*), writing in the 1870s. He implied that the whole population of Hawai'i could read and write, and he listed, as gifts from the mission to the people, the alphabet, a grammar, a dictionary, schools, and colleges. Moreover, he maintained, these efforts had preserved the language from extinction and given them a literature. In summary, he wrote, "I visited among all classes, chiefs and the common people: sought information from all, friendly and unfriendly sources, and my conclusion is that the men best acquainted with the history hold in high esteem the labors and conduct of the missionaries" (Dana n.d., ca. 1870s).[14]

In short, according to many reports, the efforts to introduce literacy to the Hawaiians was an unqualified success.

But perhaps some of the most glowing reports ignored the question of whether or not students understood what they were reading but focused merely on students' ability to read aloud the letters, syllables, words, and simple sentences from the *Pī'āpā*. The following section reports the opinions of some observers who had serious doubts about the new readers' ability to understand what they were reading.

Opposing Opinions

As with most matters, not everyone agreed with the enthusiastic reports of how successful the mission's efforts were and how literate the Hawaiians

14. Published in the *New York Tribune*, 5 June 1860, but in a somewhat different form.

had become. Lorrin Andrews, who was closely involved in the system through his work at Lahainaluna, offered a point of view that differed from that of his colleagues: he criticized Hawaiian education in general and questioned the success of Hawaiian literacy.

One of Andrews's complaints was that in some schools, students hadn't progressed beyond the first reader. This unfortunate situation was, he suggested, the fault of the teachers, the methods, and the materials. For example, in many cases, the *Pīʻāpā* was all that the teachers knew how to teach, and they showed little interest in adding to their knowledge.

Andrews also suggested that the additional materials that did exist lacked variety: "In 1830, the *Pia-pa kamalii,* or child's spelling book, was published, since which time no visible change has taken place in the schools. Other books have been added, such as a historical catechism of the Bible, a part of the Epistles, Exodus, and Joshua. These are all the books of an Hawaiian student's library, when he has been so successful as to obtain them all. But probably one half of all the schools on the islands have at this day nothing to read but the Pia-pa. These books may all be termed religious books, except the Arithmetic and the *Ho-pe,*[15] or supplement to the Pia-pa" ([1832] 1834:157).

Moreover, he thought that the students, young and old, were more interested in the mechanics and novelty of reading than in the content. Perhaps overstating his case, Andrews suggested that a set of logarithmic tables, if printed as a book, would be as greatly desired as any other book that had been printed. He continued: "The truth is, a palapala is a *palapala;* it is all new to them, and all considered good. They have been told, that the perusal of these and similar books constitutes the difference between them and ourselves; that they are able to make people wise."

Andrews was especially critical of students' lack of interest in content. The worst thing, he wrote, was that students gleaned no ideas from their reading. "Indeed a great many think there is a kind of mystery, or perhaps magic, in reading . . . I have spent hours at a time in the High School trying to make the scholars believe that a word written on paper or printed in a book, meant just the same thing as when spoken with the mouth" ([1832] 1834:166).

---

15. For example, *He Hope no ka Pi-a-pa* (1830); Judd, Bell, and Murdoch #51.

Nor did the parents escape blame. A mission report in 1833 said that parental laxity resulted in children who were unmanageable by the time they were old enough to attend school (*Missionary Herald* 29 [1833]:456).

Andrews also noted that the number of Hawaiians "who were able to read with more or less facility" had decreased because of the lack of books ([1832] 1834:89).

Occasionally, the missionaries commented on the Hawaiians' phenomenal ability to memorize. It was well known that many Hawaiians could recite genealogies or legends of what outsiders considered an incredible length. Andrews noted the effect that this ability had on reading: "*Committing to memory.* At this the natives have ever shown themselves very skilful; but the ability to repeat and the fact that they do repeat the Pia-pa and the Ui [catechism], and the Mataio [the gospel of Matthew], and other books from beginning to end, does not imply that they can read a word" ([1832] 1834:157). In short, he concluded that "Oral instruction is better understood."

All in all, those who criticized the Hawaiians' progress toward literacy during this period had a number of targets: the teachers, the pupils, the parents, the materials, the administration, the lack of funds, and the Hawaiians' oral culture.

Conclusions

Sometimes, as a result of time and distance, even the severest of critics can change their minds. Nearly thirty years after Andrews sketched his unflattering picture of the state of Hawaiian education and literacy, he had already resigned from the mission and was serving in his new capacity as a judge in Honolulu.[16] From this stance, he looked back on his early years as a teacher:

> In the summer of 1828, I commenced teaching, or rather hearing Hawaiians read, in their own language. That was about the time that the desire to learn to read became prevalent throughout the nation, and schools were established in almost every district on the Islands, and the great *mass* of the people, (adults,) began to *read* in their own language. It is true, they did not read very fluently, nor had they much in their language then to read. But a great many learned to

16. "Mr. Andrews was so strongly opposed to slavery that he resigned as a missionary in 1842 because funds for mission support were received from some of the slave states" (*Missionary Album* 1969:25).

read, and in some measure understood what they read . . . As before, it is not pretended that the adult Hawaiians, as a general thing, became good or fluent readers; but they did read, were anxious to get books, and got ideas from reading.

Again, simultaneously with reading, the people learned *to write,* just as far as they could get the apparatus; that is, pen, or pencil and paper, (the ink they manufactured, or got from the cuttle fish,) or slates and pencils . . . Letter-writing, even at that time, was considerably practiced, and would have been much more, but for want of materials.[17] (Andrews 1864:96)

As the earlier sections show, the question of how successful the missionaries' efforts were to change the Hawaiians' oral culture into a literate one has no clear answer. Contradictions abound. For example, the extremely efficient alphabet made the mechanics of reading simple. But did "reading" mean only pronouncing aloud the words printed on a page, without understanding the content? How many students were actually reading, and how many had memorized the contents through countless oral recitations of the material?

Figure 10.8. Principal characters in *Lāʻieikawai.* Kauʻi Kaina, left, Ioane Goodhue, and Wailana Simcock are locked in a love triangle in *Laʻieikawai,* Kennedy Theatre's first full-length Hawaiian-language play. *HSA* 20 February 2015. The play was performed in February–March 2015.

17. John Charlot pointed out (pers. comm., May 1993) that because of the shortage of writing materials, many Hawaiians learned to read but not to write.

Even for those pupils who did learn to read (without the intrusion of memorizing), understand, and synthesize, there remained a problem: the type and number of books in the Hawaiian language available to readers. There were few Hawaiian-language books printed that did not deal with instruction, whether sacred or secular. For those Hawaiians born after the acceptance of Christianity, the opportunity to learn about their own past through reading was limited to just a few books and the numerous—but more ephemeral—articles in the Hawaiian-language newspapers.

It is also clear that literacy did not turn out to be a sure path to power and prosperity.

However, we can be grateful that nineteenth-century Hawaiians were able to write, leaving records of the language and culture in a period when both were in decline. In large measure, these records are the basis for the reference materials—readers, primers, dictionaries, grammars, and histories—that serve as a firm foundation for the current Hawaiian renaissance. Without them, our knowledge of the past would be very limited indeed, and it would be a much harder struggle to build for the future.

We can also be encouraged by recent efforts toward literacy in a different medium: drama. The year 2015 saw the performance of a Hawaiian-language play, *Lāʻieikawai,* by Tammy Hailiʻōpua Baker. One reviewer began, "For the first time in its 51 years, Kennedy Theatre's mainstage will be filled with the sound of ʻōlelo Hawaiʻi, the native tongue of Hawaiʻi" (Dell 2015:12).[18] Another wrote that the play combined *hula, mele, oli, hula kiʻi,* and Hawaiian martial arts, enhancing the story (Reyes 2015:28).

Baker adapted the play from the 1864 Haleʻole and 1888 Bolster & Meheʻula, both from the *Nupepa Olelo Hawaii.* With a cast of 40, it opened on 20 February 2015.

In September and October 2019, Baker's next production, *ʻAuʻa ʻIa: Holding On*, played to full houses for its run of five three-hour performances. The plot focused on four students studying their history through archival materials. Baker, serving as both playwright and director, used a *Time Machine* approach to present her story. The students observed and reacted to (but were unable to affect) the important events that were portrayed, ranging from precontact conflict to present-day controversies. Integrated

18. Jean Charlot wrote a Hawaiian-language play that was performed locally in 1964. The published version appears in *Two Hawaiian Plays* (Charlot 1976; pers. comm., April 2018, Nancy J. Morris).

into the plot were dance and music performances, and the costumes moved chronologically from *malo* through Victorian splendor to modern dress.

As with Baker's earlier play, described above, the Kennedy stage was filled with *'ōlelo Hawai'i*. But for this performance especially, the *'ōlelo* spilled into the audience. As a linguist, I couldn't help but marvel at the contrast between this occasion and my first contact with Hawaiian, when one instructor taught four courses, with a total of 27 students. In 1962, it was nearly impossible to use the language outside the classroom. But on this Sunday afternoon, in contrast, much, perhaps most, of the audience, 620-strong, obviously knew what was happening, as reflected by their reactions to spots of humor . . . and tragedy.

As reflected by the play and the audience's reactions, the present of Hawaiian language policy seems much more encouraging than its past.

A FINAL WORD: SPEECH VS. WRITING?

Parts of the present work, especially discussions of how the writing system evolved, concern the complicated relationship between spoken and written Hawaiian. It is a topic that recurs repeatedly: in other words, our focus moves back and forth from the spoken word to the written word.

Looking back to a time when Hawaiian culture was flourishing, some writers emphasized the importance of the spoken word. The following quotation illustrates this point: "Hawai'i was a culture without written languages; the spoken word was all important. Thus word sound itself could become almost more symbolic than the object it referred to" (Pukui, Haertig, and Lee [1972–1979] 2002:178).

But even when they were describing this situation, these authors noted the precarious position of cultural knowledge, apparently the property of the elders: "Today, only the older Hawaiian is apt to remember or use word symbolism in speech or healing practices." Now (i.e., 2018), more than thirty-five years have passed since the "today" in the quotation. As the body of native speakers has dwindled to the small number of Ni'ihauans and students from immersion projects,[19] it is crucial to gather cultural material and put it in a form that makes Hawaiian's past accessible to future generations.

Ironically, even relatively recently, some critics of the Hawaiian alphabet considered it to be a cause of the decline of Hawaiian. However,

---

19. Suggested by Kenneth W. Cook (pers. comm., July 2015).

the alphabet—and all it entails—may turn out to be the savior, not the destroyer, of the Hawaiian language and culture.

VERBATIM

The following passage is from the "Annual Report—Mission to the Sandwich Islands": "The demand for books may easily be misapprehended by the unthinking reader of statements on this subject. Nothing could be a greater novelty to a Sandwich islander, than a book, and the art of reading it. This novelty and the curiosity which it awakened, are of course gradually passing away; and that, too, before the people have acquired so much knowledge as to realize its value, and to love and desire it for its own sake" (*Missionary Herald* 29 [1833]:455).

This quotation, even though it comes from a missionary publication, presents an opinion less enthusiastic than many of those in the glowing reports from the 1820s and 1830s. In the present work, I have tried to treat the missionary contributions to the Hawaiian people and their culture in an evenhanded way, showing both its good and bad aspects. In any activity, especially one so controversial and far-reaching as those of the ABCFM, opinions are bound to vary, swinging (albeit slowly) from one extreme to another. Andrews's own opinions, changing over several decades, are an example of such changes.

Nearly a century later, it was fashionable to criticize the missionaries. The following passage is an extreme example:

> It is well to keep history in mind when working on these matters. It is a fact that English was brought into Hawaii as the language of sailors and missionaries. Sailors and missionaries have many things in common, for they both go after the natives hammer and tongs. The missionaries are after their souls (and sometimes their lands); the sailors, after more temporal goods. With Bible and bottle they achieve their respective ends, and English is introduced before you know it. The missionaries are the more abiding influence, for they come and stay and usually set about training a native clergy in the language which they have brought with them as well as in their religion. After the undermining of the old religion and tribal mores in general, sovereignty usually changes hands, and often, as in Hawaii, the language is rapidly supplanted by that of the Bible-and-bottle bearers. (Carr 1951:15)

PART IV

WORDS AND WORD BOOKS

CHAPTER 11

WORDS

Introduction

Although words are only one kind of linguistic building block, they often come to mind first when we're trying to learn a new language. It may be considered old-fashioned to memorize lists of words out of context, but it is still unusual to find a teaching text without some kind of vocabulary exercises. And a dictionary—a "wordbook"—is one of the most valuable tools a language learner can have.

For Hawaiian, individual words (including personal names and place names) were the first parts of the language that outsiders recorded. Moreover, vocabulary lists were among the earliest teaching materials that the missionaries used to learn the language. But when they began to concentrate on Bible translation, these otherwise reasonable scholars felt it necessary to comment on mismatches between Hawaiian and English vocabularies.

It is no surprise that the vocabularies reflecting two cultures as dramatically different as Hawaiian and European/American would not match very well in certain areas. Some missionary translators felt that Hawaiian's vocabulary was too small. On the other hand, another observer complained that Hawaiian's vocabulary was too large, cluttered "with a vast number of useless expressions" (Donne 1866:87–88). Neither of these points of view is very useful, for it is impossible to prove or disprove it. Moreover, each is "linguacentric": it judges another language in terms of its own.

In spite of the general interest in Hawaiian words and many sweeping statements about the nature of the vocabulary, this topic has never been systematically studied. In the present chapter, I look at words from several different points of view.

WHAT'S A "WORD"?

Asking such a question may seem a strange way to begin a discussion of words, but something I will *not* do in the chapter is define the term itself. The reason is that there are two main criteria that people use to determine what a word is in Hawaiian. One is *sound,* and the other is *meaning.* Usually these criteria coincide, and it is easy to decide whether a particular form is one word or two. For example, no one would try to argue that *hale* 'house' is either more or less than one word.[1]

However, sometimes the criteria pull in different directions, making it harder to determine whether a form is one word or two. As an example, consider the Hawaiian expression, widely used in local English as well, that means 'toward inland, toward the mountains'. In terms of meaning, it is made up of two parts: *ma* (locational, directional marker) and *uka* 'inland, interior'. Because *ma* is used in the same way in many other phrases (e.g., *ma Honolulu*), it seems reasonable to write the expression as two separate words: *ma uka.*

On the other hand, pronunciation supports writing it as one word, for the *a* and *u* unite into a diphthong. Thus, the "phrase" is usually pronounced as one unit: *máuka* (two syllables), not *ma úka* (three syllables).[2]

As another example, the translation for 'he, she' was formerly written as one word: *ʻoia.* This practice seems to have been based on sound. As in the example above, the first two vowels form a diphthong, resulting in a two-syllable word, with the accent on the first vowel: *ʻóia.* Using different criteria, in 1978 a committee on spelling decided that it should be two words: *ʻo ia,* probably because *ʻo* is written as a separate word before names: *ʻo Pua, ʻo Keola* (Wilson 1978). Although *ʻo ia* is still pronounced the same, to the eye it looks like a three-syllable word. Thus, this example matches the *mauka/ma uka* dilemma—that is, it stems from a mismatch between sound and meaning. It should be obvious, then, that there is no ideal solution to the problem.

---

1. However, some amateur etymologists have attempted to break the word *haole* into component parts: *hā* 'breath' and *ʻole* 'without', ignoring the long vowel and the glottal stop.

2. Cf. the term *crasis:* "A contraction of two vowels or diphthongs at the end of one word and the beginning of an immediately following word into one long vowel or diphthong" (*Webster's Third New International Dictionary* 1961). This process makes one word out of two.

Difficulties with dividing words go back to the earliest days of writing Hawaiian. Often, the collectors of the first word lists wrote an article (e.g., *he* or *ka/ke*) and a noun with no space between—e.g., *hehale* 'a house'. As for the Hawaiian perception of word division, Laura Fish Judd, who wrote about her life in Hawai'i from 1828 to 1861, reported, "Mrs. B[ingham?] spends two hours more in giving them lessons on the slate, and teaching them how to divide words and sentences. Their preference is to join words together in continuous lines across the page, without stops or marks" (1880:30). Judd's observation suggests that the concept of dividing phrases into words was foreign to the Hawaiians—an oral pattern made visible by writing.

Nor is Hawaiian the only language for which word division is a problem. Compare these three entries from an English dictionary (*Merriam Webster's Collegiate Dictionary,* 11th ed., 2003): *school board; school-leaver; schoolboy.* Although the accent pattern is the same in each case (a particular accent pattern is the phonological criterion for defining a *compound* in English[3]), and each form is somewhat *idiomatic* (having a special meaning that cannot be predicted by knowing the meaning of each part), there is no way to predict how such forms will be written.

It is possible that over time, the pattern moves from left to right in the examples given: two words, one word with a hyphen, and finally, one word with neither a space nor a hyphen. Such a progression is described in the following quotation: "The compound *trade mark* is first attested in 1838. Later in the nineteenth century it appears as a hyphenated compound, and later still as the solid compound we use today" (Hargraves 2015:90).

In summary, when we deal with word division, there are two main areas that cause disagreement among Hawaiian readers and writers:

1. How to write certain grammatical markers or function forms in combination with root words. For example, *ma uka* or *mauka?*
2. How to write forms that might be interpreted as compounds: For example, *makua kāne* or *makuakāne* 'father, uncle'?

Because there are no strict formal arguments to support either solution, language scholars have to rely on arbitrary decisions to establish authority, thus leading to individual variations among teachers and writers—sometimes agreeing with the spelling in P-E, sometimes not.[4]

---

3. See the section on compounding in chapter 12.

4. Thanks to Keao NeSmith for this observation.

HOW TO STUDY WORDS

In addition to deciding how to divide connected speech into words, there are other ways to study Hawaiian words. The most important of these are based on a word's (1) form and (2) its meaning.

Form

One way to analyze a word is to examine its form (that is, its sound). Excluding function words consisting of one short syllable, most simple words are made up of the following combinations:

one long syllable: *kū* 'stand'; *kai* 'sea'; *kāu* 'your'
two short syllables: *ma-ka* 'eye, face'
three short syllables: *wa-hi-ne* 'woman'
one short syllable followed by a long one: *ma-nō* 'shark'; *ha-hau* 'strike'
one long syllable followed by a short one: *kā-ne* 'male'; *'āi-na* 'land'

However, simple words consisting of two short syllables are probably the most common. Take, for example, the numbers from one to ten (without the *'e* or *'a* prefix):

kahi	one
lua	two
kolu	three
hā	four
lima	five
ono	six
hiku	seven
walu	eight
iwa	nine
'umi	ten

With the exception of *hā* 'four', all are two-syllable words. This feature was noticed by Andrews: "Most radical words in Hawaiian, or those from which others are formed, consist of two syllables" (1838:395). (The description is valid only if the syllables contain short vowels.) Later,

Alexander made a similar comment: "Most of the roots in Hawaiian as well as in the other Malayo-Polynesian languages are dissyllabic" (1864:25).[5]

The list of numerals above is an extreme example, for in longer lists of common words, the percentage of two-syllable words is not so high.

Each of these types listed above—one-, two-, and three-syllable words—has just one accented syllable. In the examples just given, the peak of the accented syllable is a short vowel, a long vowel, a short diphthong, or a long diphthong. The following list shows the range of possible shapes for words (and phrases) containing just one accented syllable:

kū́	stand
máka	eye
Kaʻū́	(place name)
kanáka	person
láu	leaf
kā́ne	male
piláu	rotten
ke kā́ne	the male
kā́u	your
ʻáina	meal
ʻo kā́u	your
ka ʻáina	the meal
ʻā́ina	land
ka ʻā́ina	the land

Each of these forms illustrates a different type of accent group, or *measure,* the basis of indicating the accent patterns of the entries in P-E (1986) and *Māmaka Kaiao* (1996, 2003).[6] It follows, then, that longer words are

5. See the extended quotations in chapter 12, "Verbatim."

6. I developed this system for showing the accent in headwords in the Fijian monolingual dictionary (although it was dropped when I was no longer director). When I explained the system to Sam Elbert, he agreed to incorporate it into the 1986 edition of P-E. Pila Wilson supported the idea.

made up of combinations of measures. Here are some examples (raised periods separate the measures):

kapa·kahi	'crooked'
mali·hini	'newcomer'
mā·lama	'care for'
makua·kāne	'father'
hoʻo·nani	'beautify'
pā·hoe·hoe	'lava'

Some words are made up of only one short syllable, but these are all function words—that is, they have only grammatical meaning and never occur as the head of a phrase. For example:

he	class-member, existential, or indefinite marker
ke/ka	common noun marker
i	object marker
e	agent marker

All these short function words have one feature in common: when they are pronounced in isolation, the vowel is lengthened. For example, if you ask speakers to tell you the Hawaiian word for 'at', they'll answer not *ma* but *mā*. As mentioned earlier, the letters of the *pīʻāpā* (Hawaiian alphabet) show this feature as well: each is pronounced as a long syllable: *ʻĀ, ʻĒ, HĀ,* and so on. In other words, a word that consists of just one short syllable can never serve as an utterance on its own.

These qualities of Hawaiian words are all connected with their basic form (sound). Another way to analyze words is to divide them into parts that have meaning.

Meaning

Every Hawaiian word, of course, means something. Here, because I'm describing Hawaiian grammar in English, the meaning of a word is expressed by giving an English translation (i.e., gloss); for example:

lohe 'hear'.[7] This particular word can't be divided into smaller meaningful parts, for *lo* and *he* are just syllables without any meaning of their own.

But many words are composed of smaller pieces that do mean something. Expanding on the example above, we can build related words by adding such pieces—in the following example, first a prefix and then a suffix:

***ho'o**-lohe*	heed, (to) mind (causative)
*lohe-**a***	be audible, be heard (passive)

These words are built by combining *morphemes*—that is, minimum units of meaning. Thus, *ho'o-lohe* consists of two morphemes: one that means roughly 'to cause to' and one that means 'hear'. *Lohe-a* also consists of two morphemes: one that means 'hear', and one that makes the word a passive.

Here's a more transparent example of the causative prefix:

maka'u	fear	*ho'o-maka'u*	frighten (lit., cause to fear)

(Here, and in the next chapter, I highlight these units of meaning by separating them with hyphens, even though the official spelling system doesn't follow this practice.)

In the next section, I take a brief look at the words that Hawaiian has inherited from earlier forms of the language.

WHERE DID THE MOST COMMON HAWAIIAN WORDS COME FROM?

Many Hawaiian words can be traced back to a time when what are now separate Polynesian languages were just one language, spoken in a single community. (This idea was discussed in chapters 1 and 2.)

Anyone who has studied several Pacific languages soon notices that some words are identical or similar across those languages. That is, they seem more resistant to change than others. The word list in chapter 3 illustrates this observation, and table 11.1 repeats some of the most common of these, adding cognates from a more distant relative, Malay.

---

7. When a form and its gloss appear in a paragraph, by linguistic conventions the form is italicized and the gloss appears in single quotes. To show a focus on the sound system, the form appears in slant lines and no italics: /lohe/.

TABLE 11.1. COMMON WORDS IN PACIFIC LANGUAGES

English	Hawaiian	Tongan	Fijian	Malay
eye	*maka*	*mata*	*mata*	*mata*
rain	*ua*	*ua*	*uca*	*hujan*
water	*wai*	*wai*	*wai*	*ayer*
fish	*iʻa*	*ika*	*ika*	*ikan*
leaf	*lau*	*lau*	*drau*	*daun*

P-E gives the Proto-Polynesian (abbreviated as PPN) etymology of words for which reconstructions have been made. For example, the entry for *maka* 'eye' includes the PPN form *mata. As discussed in chapter 3, this convention shows that based on the forms of present-day Polynesian languages, the ancestral (proto-) language most likely had a form **mata* 'eye' (among other meanings). It also shows that the Hawaiian word *maka* has been inherited directly from earlier forms of the language and not borrowed.

Such knowledge helps to argue against occasional suggestions from language amateurs that certain words are related to those in, say, Spanish or Latin. As an example, in the late nineteenth century, a visitor to Hawaiʻi wrote that the word *mauna* 'mountain' had been borrowed from the Latin *mons* (Lobschied 1872:4). A comparison with other Polynesian languages shows instead that *mauna* is a legitimate Polynesian word that developed from an earlier form *maunga.

What Do We Know about Proto-Polynesian Vocabulary?

Some scholars have used the meanings of reconstructed words to form a picture of how Proto-Polynesian speakers lived. For example, the terms that can be reconstructed for various parts of the outrigger canoe show that the Proto-Polynesians had already developed this technology and were not sailing on rafts.[8]

A study by Andrew Pawley and Kaye Green (1971) sorted some 400 reconstructed Proto-Polynesian words into semantic groups. The following list shows both the categories and the number of members of each:

1. Inanimate environment (40)
2. Land fauna (17 birds, 4 mammals, 3 reptiles, 18 insects, 1 other)

8. See various studies by Bruce Biggs and Ross Clark.

3. Land flora (81)
4. Sea life (53 fish, 14 Mollusca, 8 Crustacea, 3 Echinodermi, 8 others)
5. Sailing and navigation (24)
6. Fishing (13)
7. Gardening (17)
8. Garden products (10)
9. Domestic animals (3)
10. Cooking and food preparation and storage (25)
11. Houses and structures (16)
12. Tools (5)
13. Clothing and adornments (11)
14. Sewing and weaving (14)
15. Hunting, weapons (7)
16. Other material culture items (7)

The meanings of these reconstructed forms helped Pawley and Green to make some generalizations about the daily lives of the people who spoke this language. It seems logical to suggest that if a culture had a large number of words for a certain topic, then that topic was important to them. From the list above, you can pick out the richest categories: plants, sea life, the inanimate environment, gardening, sailing and navigation, and the essentials of everyday life, particularly the production and preparation of food.

Specific words add further clues: words for *weave, sennit, sew, tie, thread, plaited coconut leaf,* and others add detail to our picture of material culture, as do the terms connected with houses, such as *thatch, rafter, inner room,* and *post.*

A scarcity of terms can also tell a story: for example, domestic animals were limited to dogs, fowl, and pigs.

Moreover, the vocabulary can give us clues that point to the location of the Proto-Polynesian homeland. From the forms that have been reconstructed so far (as of August 2013, 4,868, from 68 languages),[9] scholars have been able

9. Stephen Trussel, pers. comm., August 2013. These data can be accessed at POLLEX (Polynesian Lexicon Project Online (http://pollex.org.nz), retrieved 26 August 2013). P-E includes roughly 2,000 reconstructions of earlier forms. As of June 2018, about 700 forms have been added. See chapter 15.

to draw some conclusions about the origin of the Polynesians (see Clark 1979; all the following discussion is based on his article). The large number of words relating to the sea point to a coastal rather than a landlocked origin. Other words—such as those reconstructed for *mountain, ridge,* and *river*—suggest high islands rather than atolls. Some widespread plant names as well give further clues about the homeland: the persistence of the terms for *coconut-palm, pandanus,* and *citrus* imply a tropical region, and a number of other reconstructed plant names (especially for such trees or plants as the mangrove, nettle, Polynesian chestnut, sandalwood, and Malay apple) further support the theory that the homeland was a high island. All in all, such comparative studies reveal something of Hawaiian's legacy from Proto-Polynesian.

The next chapters show us how the language can add to its store of inherited words.

VERBATIM

When the missionaries to Hawai'i found that the vocabulary was especially rich in certain areas, they often commented on this feature of the language. The following description is from W. D. Alexander's introduction to Lorrin Andrews's *Dictionary of the Hawaiian Language* (1865).

> So in Hawaiian everything that relates to their every-day life or to the natural objects with which they were conversant is expressed with a vivacity, a minuteness and nicety of coloring which cannot be reproduced in a foreign tongue. Thus the Hawaiian was very rich in terms for every variety of clouds. It has names for every species of plant on the mountains or fish in the sea, and is peculiarly copious in terms relating to the ocean, the surf and waves. The ancient Hawaiians were evidently close observers of nature. For whatever belonged to their religion, their wars, their domestic life, their handicrafts or their amusements, their vocabulary was most copious and minute. Almost every stick in a native house had its appropriate name. Hence it abounds in synonyms, which, however, are such only in appearance, and on which a volume might be written.
>
> Besides the language of every day life, there was a style appropriate to oratory, and another to religion and poetry. The latter is known to but few natives of the present generation, and is fast disappearing.

Over a century later, in *Nā Mele o Hawai'i Nei* (1970:19), Samuel H. Elbert and Noelani Mahoe discussed some surviving features of this poetic language:

THE POWER OF THE WORD[10]

The early Hawaiians spoke no language other than their own, and may not have known of the existence of other languages. When they heard English they called it *namu* (gibberish). So, like the Stoic Greeks, they thought their names were universals with inherent nonarbitrary meanings. The meanings had power and explained the universe.

This was especially true in the religious chants, and efforts were made to preserve them unchanged throughout the centuries. A mistaken syllable might change the word and the new word might have connotations distasteful to a god, who might then cause the chanter's death. Many of the chants were sacred to the gods, including the family gods, and to the family. For this reason they were not freely imparted to passing strangers. They, as priceless heirlooms, were passed down to rightful heirs . . .

The word . . . is still powerful, and the composer even today must consider double meanings. Many composers avoid such words as *uli* (dark, foreboding) and *hala* (pandanus, pass away), but not all composers have these restrictions or we would not have so many songs about pandanus.

Figure 11.1. Cover of *Nā Mele o Hawai'i Nei: 101 Hawaiian Songs* (cover drawing by Jean Charlot)

10. This phrase, or variations of it, is also the theme of chapter 16.

Another interesting discussion in this work contains a list of different semantic categories in poetic language and examples for each (20–24). The categories are as follows:

- birds
- chiefs
- coolness
- fragrance
- fish and sea creatures
- flowers, plants, trees
- love-making
- mountains
- rains
- sea
- height
- mist
- wetness
- winds

CHAPTER 12

MAKING NEW WORDS

TABLE XII.

Words of four syllables, accented on the first and third.

A hi a hi	a mu a mu	a va hi a
a ki a ki	a ni a ni	a va ke a
a ka a ka	a no a no	e ka e ka

Chapter 11 noted that some Hawaiian words (especially those used often enough to resist change) were inherited from an earlier form of the language. But these words account for only part of the vocabulary. From the time of the earliest settlement in the Hawaiian Islands, the Polynesians and successive generations have added to their vocabulary in a number of different ways. This chapter shows some of the ways that words can be added to the Hawaiian language from within—that is, without borrowing from other languages.

TOTALLY NEW FORMS

One way to add words to a language is to coin totally new ones. But some early critics thought that Hawaiian's potential vocabulary was limited by its relatively small number of consonants and vowels. For example, Lorrin Andrews wrote, "From the fewness of the letters and syllables in the language, it must necessarily be that many words of the same letters must have different significations; and so it is, but is greatly remedied in Hawaiian . . . by different tones, accents, or pronunciations . . . making . . . a different word to the ear, though not to the eye" (1854:19).

From what we know now, it is obvious that Andrews was referring to words that were spelled the same (in the system that was used then) but were actually pronounced differently because of an *'okina* or especially vowel length, which could affect the expected accent. He added that these modifications were very difficult for an adult foreign learner to master. (On the other hand, a later writer criticized Andrews because he did not have a "musical ear" and was unable to hear *'okina* and long vowels.)

Even including the *'okina* and long vowels in the inventory of sounds doesn't allow a very large number of potential words. For example, increasing the number of consonants from seven to eight (i.e., adding the *ʻokina*) and the vowels from 5 to 10 (i.e., adding long vowels) would yield only 8,100 potential two-syllable words.[1] Adding diphthongs, short and long, increases the number to 50,625.

Another way to view diphthongization is that it is one way (among several) to shorten forms. For example, it can reduce underlying three-syllable words to two syllables. In this way, the inventory of the more favored pattern is significantly increased. The process can also change an original four-syllable word (e.g., **ha-na-u-ma*) to a three-syllable one (e.g., *ha-nau-ma*).[2]

Working with these components—eight consonants and 25 different vowels and diphthongs (both short and long)[3]—we find that the language has a potential of 225 one-syllable words (8 x 25 syllables that begin with a consonant, plus 25 that consist of a vowel or diphthong alone). Using the formula n^2, n^3, and n^4 for two-, three-, and four-syllable words, we can arrive at these figures:

1-syllable words:	225
2-syllable words:	50,625
3-syllable words:	11,390,625
4-syllable words:	2,562,890,625

Clearly, there is no danger of running out of potential new words!

Because some words are unique to Hawaiian (i.e., not found in the vocabularies of its closest relatives), it is obvious that during Hawaiʻi's period of relative isolation from most other Polynesian languages, the vocabulary has been enriched with totally new words.[4] As a matter of fact,

---

1. That is, two short syllables.

2. Here, as in some earlier examples, meaning and sound are at war with each other. In *Hana+uma,* the last vowel in the first form combines with the first vowel of the second to form the diphthong *au.*

3. This figure includes some long diphthongs that are questionable (speakers may separate them into two syllables). But theoretically, they could be used in new words. Some sequences of consonants in successive syllables are traditionally prohibited or rare, but sometimes new words do not follow these patterns. Thus, the figures give an idea of what would be possible.

4. Or it retained words lost in all related languages.

according to Adelbert von Chamisso, who visited Hawai'i in 1816 and 1817, Kamehameha I made up a new vocabulary of such words, which although popular for a time, eventually died out (Kratz 1986:257). (Incidentally, no one seems to know the reason for this curious practice.)

Without written records before 1778 or evidence from oral tradition, it is impossible to trace the history of those words that are unique to Hawaiian, except for the most recent introductions. That is, we cannot say that they were coined by a certain person on a certain date. We can, however, analyze other types of new words.

The first of these is words that are, in a sense, metaphors—existing words with new meanings added.

EXPANDING THE MEANING OF EXISTING WORDS

Because we know something of Hawaiian culture before European contact, it is easy to look at the headwords in an English-Hawaiian dictionary and pick out those that refer to concepts that were introduced. Some of these turn out to be borrowings, and they are the topic of the next chapter. But for many of the new concepts, existing words were used, but their meanings were expanded. The following are just a few examples:

	ORIGINAL MEANING		ADDED MEANING
ola	live, life	→	salvation
pāhoehoe	smooth lava	→	satin
pūpū	shell	→	beads

For these examples, the old meanings weren't replaced; they were simply expanded. For example, *nalo* still means 'housefly', but it can also mean 'bee'. In such cases (as with so many words), only the context can make the meaning clear.

MODIFYING THE FORM OF EXISTING WORDS

Another way to coin a word for a new concept is to change or add to an existing word. The word for 'horse' is an example of such a process. With their inventory of four-legged land mammals restricted to rat (*'iole*), pig (*pua'a*), and dog (*'i, - lio*), the Hawaiians chose to refer to 'horse' as 'big dog’; in Archibald Campbell’s word list (collected in 1809–10), he wrote the word for ‘horse’ as *edea nooee,* which we would now write as *‘īlio nui.* Apparently the first syllable eventually dropped, as did the modifier *nui,* leaving *lio.*

This etymology is not without its critics. One far-fetched competing explanation is that it was from *lī‘ō* ‘wide-eyed’, describing horses as they were led off ships. This story may have gained support from two contiguous entries in Andrews 1865:

> Li-o, s[ubstantive]. A name given to foreign animals generally when first introduced into the islands. See the verb.
> Li-o, v[erb]. To open the eyes wide, as a wild affrighted animal.

The relationship suggested above may satisfy the eye, but not the ear. Because Andrews did not write the *‘okina* or *kahakō,* the words look identical. But they are actually *lio* and *lī‘ō*—quite different in pronunciation, especially in their accent patterns.

A more transparent example, also from Campbell’s list, is the Hawaiian word for ‘limpet’—*opeehii* [*‘opihi*], which took on an additional meaning, ‘button’.[5] Next, *‘opihi* apparently lost the first syllable, resulting in *pihi.*[6]

WORD BUILDING

Longer words in Hawaiian can be formed by combining shorter ones (*compounding*), adding a prefix or a suffix (*affixation*), or repeating part or all of the form (*reduplication*).

Compounding

A compound in Hawaiian consists of a root (usually a noun or a verb) followed by a modifier (“<” means “modified by”):

a‘a	<	*lolo*	=	nerve
vein		brain		

5. At this time, most buttons were made of shell.

6. Perhaps *‘o* was reinterpreted as a grammatical marker.

moku	<	*lele*	=	airplane
ship		fly (v.)		
nalo	<	*meli*	=	honey bee
fly (n.)		honey[7]		

This process is very common. For example, P-E contains about three dozen compounds made from the root *helu* ‘count’, most of which are terms introduced for the study of arithmetic. Some samples are:

helu ‘ano hui	uneven totals	*heluhana*[8]	factor
helu ‘ano like	even numbers	*helu kanaka*	census
helu hana ‘ia	composite no.	*helu komo*	divisor

As examples of even more productive roots, there are more than 80 compounds from *palapala* ‘writing’ (an expansion in meaning itself; see the discussion in chapter 9) and more than 160 based on *hale* ‘house’. Here are some examples—first, compounds made from *palapala:*

palapala‘āina	land document
palapala hānau	birth certificate
palapala hō‘ike manawa	timetable
palapala hō‘ike waiwai	financial report
palapala lima	manuscript
palapala male	marriage certificate
palapala pī‘āpā	alphabet book
palapala ui	catechism

Next, the following examples show just a few of the compounds made from *hale:*

hale ‘aina	restaurant
hale ali‘i	palace

7. See Schütz 1976:78–79 for speculation regarding the missionaries’ choice of *meli* (from Greek) for ‘honey’ rather than a borrowing from English.

8. The inconsistent word divisions in these forms show that in Hawaiian (as well as in English), often there are no strict criteria for deciding whether a form is one word or two.

hale hana	workshop
hale hana uila	powerhouse
hale hōʻikeʻike iʻa	aquarium
hale inu kī	tearoom
hale kilo hōkū	star observatory
hale maʻi	hospital
hale paʻi	printshop
hale wili kō	sugar mill

In these compounds, *hale* is the first element. For examples of compounds with *hale* in the second position, see the *Combined Hawaiian Dictionary* (see chapter 15), which conveniently shows all such forms in one list. Here are a few examples:

ʻelua hale	bicameral
haku hale	landlord
hoʻolaʻa hale	dedication of a house
ʻimi hale$_1$	to establish, as a dynasty
ʻimi hale$_2$	to form a friendship
kaʻa hale	trailer
kaha kiʻi hale	architect
kahua hale	house foundation
kahu hale kūʻai	storekeeper
kala hale	house gable

As mentioned in chapter 11, in most varieties of English, a compound, such as *greenhouse,* is accented differently from a simple adjective-noun combination, such as *green house.* Test the idea yourself by saying the following two sentences: (1) *He works in a greenhouse.* (2) *He works in a green house.* In (1), *house* is said with less emphasis than it is in (2).[9] However,

9. Some varieties of Hawaiʻi Creole English do not make this distinction. Also, in a contrastive context, *house* could be accented in (2).

compounds in Hawaiian show no such difference in accent: phrase accent always emphasizes the final measure.

For some compounds, the meaning cannot be predicted from the meaning of its parts—the main semantic defining feature of an *idiom*. Thus, because their meanings are unpredictable even if we know what all the pieces mean, the first two examples in this section—*a‘alolo* and *moku-lele*—are idioms. Another example is *hale li‘ili‘i* ‘outside toilet’: its literal meaning is ‘little house’. Finally, the archaic term *kanaka lele* ‘angel’ makes sense only if the hearer or reader has seen traditional images of angels as human forms with wings.

Nor does spelling identify compounds, for some are—by convention—written as two words, while others are written as one:

hale moe	dormitory (house < sleep)
halepā	cupboard (house < dish)

Compounds can also grow beyond two roots. Note how the following simple form grows to one that contains four pieces:

wai	water
wai < ū	milk (water < breast)
wai < ū < paka	butter (water < breast < butter)
wai < ū < paka < pa‘a[10]	cheese (water < breast < butter < solidified)

Affixation

Another way to build words is to add prefixes or suffixes that change the meaning of a root word. A very common prefix is *ho‘o-*, used as a causative (one of several functions). For example, compare the meanings of the following pairs:

mākaukau	ready
ho‘o-mākaukau	to prepare (lit., make ready)
piha	full

10. Today, the shorter form *waiūpa‘a* serves for ‘cheese’, although both forms appear in P-E (pers. comm., Keao NeSmith, January 2009).

ho'o-piha	to fill (lit., make full)
nani	pretty
ho'o-nani	beautify (lit., make-pretty)

How common is *ho'o-*? One proof of its frequency is the 266 *ho'o-* entries in P-E. To show that it is productive, note the following—its use with borrowings:

male	marriage, marry
ho'o-male	perform the marriage ceremony

Among the many suffixes in Hawaiian, there are three important groups (Elbert and Pukui 1979:79):

1. those that make nouns from other forms:

moe	to sleep	*moe-na*	a mat
hana	to work, do	*hana-na*	an occasion, event

2. those that show passive verbs:

'ike	to know	*'ike-a*	be known
'ai	to eat	*'ai 'ia*	eaten

3. those that show that some verbs are transitive:

ala	path	*ala-ka'i*	to lead
kilo	to gaze	*kilo-hi*[11]	to observe

None of these affixes is entirely productive; that is, they attach to some but not all appropriate words. (It would be interesting to see if any of these affixes occur with borrowings, as *ho'o-* does.)

Reduplication

The decoration that begins this chapter is not a woodcut but words from *The Alphabet* (1822) that illustrate a particular pattern. A close look at the examples below shows that most of them consist of two-syllable forms that are repeated: for example, *ahi-ahi* 'evening', *amu-amu* 'reviling'. Such

11. P-E describes *-hi* as a "rare transitivizer."

a method of forming new words is called *reduplication*.[12] Here are some examples, first, with the whole word repeated:

pala	daub, smear	*pala-pala*	writing
hoe	to paddle	*hoe-hoe*	to paddle continuously
niho	tooth	*niho-niho*	notched
huli	search	*huli-huli*	search repeatedly
huki	pull	*huki-huki*	pull frequently
hema	left side	*hema-hema*	awkward

Next, here are examples with only part of the word repeated (usually just one syllable):

nui	large	*nu-nui* (used with plural)
make	die	*ma-make* (used with plural)
kau	placed	*ka-kau* (used with plural)

Reduplicating some longer words involves other types of changes as well:

ʻāpana	part, piece	*ʻāpana-pana*	1. cut into pieces 2. assemble something, work (e.g., on a car)

The second meaning of *ʻāpanapana* is common on Niʻihau (pers. comm., NeSmith, January 2009).

Hawaiian, like many other Pacific languages, uses reduplication extensively and for a number of different purposes. One of the most common of these is to show that the action or state of a verb has been repeated:

haʻi	say	*haʻi-haʻi*	recount a story
maʻi	sick	*maʻi-maʻi*	chronically sick

Reduplication can also shift the meaning in a less regular way. Returning to an earlier example, *helu* 'count', we find a reduplicated form with a somewhat different (but still related) meaning:

helu-helu	read

12. The reduplicated base is almost always a content, not function morpheme.

Borrowed words can also be reduplicated (Schütz, Kanada, and Cook 2005:183):

kula	school	*ku-kula*	go to school

The types just mentioned are examples of the main categories. See Elbert and Pukui 1979:65–66 for a discussion of seven types of reduplication.

*

In summary, what these various ways of building words have in common is that they use forms that are already in the language. The next chapter shows how Hawaiian goes outside its own vocabulary to make up new words.

VERBATIM

By 1838, Lorrin Andrews, now a teacher and administrator at Lahainaluna Seminary, had already compiled his *Hawaiian Vocabulary* (1836a) and had translated both sacred and secular material into Hawaiian. Although his grammar did not appear until 1854, he was already collecting material for that study—mostly from "native manuscripts or from documents printed from native manuscripts." The following passage is from Andrews's 1838 article entitled "Peculiarities of the Hawaiian language," from the *Hawaiian Spectator* 1(4):392–420:[13]

> Most radical words in Hawaiian, or those from which others are formed, consist of two syllables. In this respect the Hawaiian has a great resemblance to the Hebrew. This, however, would not be so apparent on a superficial view as on a more familiar acquaintance.
>
> Though the roots of most words may be found consisting of only two syllables, yet, like the Hebrew, other syllables may be prefixed or suffixed,—one or both may be repeated, etc., to almost any extent . . . and each of these forms may be used as a verb, a noun, an adjective or adverb, according to its place in the sentence.—Thus; *hoopohihihiia,* to cause to be bewildered, (in thought).[14] The termination *ia* is a passive termination of the verb. *Hihi* is the root, sig-

13. The opening sentences of each passage were quoted earlier.

14. Original punctuation.

nifying to branch out thickly as vines. The other *hihi* is a mere reduplication of the root, and gives a frequentative or intensive sense. *Po* is a syllable often prefixed to words, and is intensive in its meaning. *Hoo* is causative of the root, and resembles in meaning the Hiphil conjugation in Hebrew verbs.

Besides this, another form from the same root may be *hihia,* and may take the causative prefix and suffixes, and passive termination, etc., as before; and all these forms may be used as verbs, nouns, adjectives or adverbs, as above stated.

In W. D. Alexander's grammar (1864:25–26), the author described word formation in Hawaiian rather briefly:

> Most of the roots in Hawaiian as well as in the other Malayo-Polynesian languages are dissyllabic. A great many words are formed from others by doubling either the first or second or both syllables of the root. This reduplication, which is common to nouns, adjectives and verbs, expresses the idea of plurality, intensity or repetition.
>
> Other derivative words are formed by prefixing some formative syllable as *pa, ka, ha, na, ma,* and *ki, po, pu,* &c. For the meaning of these formative syllables see Andrews' Dictionary. The verbal noun [ending] in *ana* has been mentioned . . . It expresses the action signified by the verb. Other verbal nouns are formed by suffixing *na,* which more often refers to the result or the means of the action than to the action itself. E.g., *hakina,* a broken piece, a fraction, from *haki,* to break; *mokuna,* a dividing line, from *moku,* to be broken or cut; *haawina,* a gift, from *haawi,* to give; *huina,* an angle, a junction, from *hui,* to unite, &c. Some of these forms are peculiar, as *komohana,* the west, from *komo,* to enter, to sink into, that is the going down of the sun; and *kulana,* a place where many things stand together, as a village, &c., from *ku,* to stand.

CHAPTER 13

BORROWING

With regard to new words in a language just reduced to writing and where improvements, or what is the same thing, where new ideas are brought in, there are two methods of proceeding. One is to introduce new words from other languages to express new ideas.

—Lorrin Andrews, "Remarks on the Hawaiian Dialect of the Polynesian Language"

Some of the examples of word building discussed in the previous chapter are words for concepts that were not native to Hawai'i but were introduced by foreigners—especially words connected with writing, Christianity, laws, and material culture. Thus, new words were built out of pieces that already existed in the language.

In many cases, however, the borrower didn't attempt to construct a new word out of native elements but took the foreign word, along with the concept, and adapted it to fit into the Hawaiian sound system. We call such words *loanwords*, or *borrowings*.[1]

THE EARLIEST BORROWINGS

There are no records of foreign ships calling at any port in Hawai'i for seven years after Captain Cook's expedition left. However, in 1786 there

---

1. Both the names and the animals pictured in the woodcuts heading the chapter represent borrowings. *Hoki* 'mule' is from *horse; pipi* 'cow' is from *beef.*

began a steady flow of visitors, mainly explorers and traders, on ships of British, French, American, and Spanish registry.[2]

Fortunately, some of the crew aboard these ships were interested enough in the Hawaiian language and culture to collect word lists. Between the time of Cook's visit and the arrival of the missionaries (1820), at least nine lists were compiled.

It would be illogical to expect to find loanwords in the very earliest of the word lists. Our first evidence of borrowing comes from Manuel Quimper's list, gathered in 1791. The words are as follows:[3]

tropi (?*ta ropi*)	rope	*tenu* (*tenū* 'canoe')	boat
llepe	ship	*paura*	powder
guine	wind	*aripi*	sleepy

During the next two decades, the non-Hawaiian population in Hawai'i increased markedly: by 1810, it was estimated that about 60 foreigners lived on O'ahu (Kuykendall [1938] 1957:27). Thus, there were more opportunities for foreign commodities and concepts to affect the culture and for the words representing them to affect the language. A list compiled by Archibald Campbell, who was in Hawai'i in 1809–10, contains the following borrowings:

Merikana	American	*bikete*	biscuit	*Itseeke*	Isaac
Pritane	Britain	*tabete*	cabbage	*Keone*	John
Lookeene	Russian	*lumma*	rum	*peepe*	sheep
oila	tallow (oil)	*Keeme*	James	*Williama*	William
tokeine	stocking	*haneeka*	handkerchief	*pockaka*	block, pully
teakete	jacket	*teaboota*	?tippet	*bobokee*	cat (poor pussy?)

As Alfons Korn noted in his article on the origin of *palaka* (1976), the words refer "to a set of items or objects, innovations, and circumstances closely bound up with the material culture of the Hawaiians." As for the

2. See the listings for this year and the following years in Judd and Lind 1974.

3. The last four examples are from Drechsel 2014:144.

proper nouns included, he wrote, "The historical problem of which individual Hawaiianized English names became stabilized before the arrival of the missionaries in 1820 . . . remains a mystery."

In addition to its dramatic effect on Hawaiian culture, that date was also a significant turning point for the growth of Hawaiian vocabulary. With the missionaries' need for terms for the many unfamiliar concepts in the Bible, loanwords poured into the language. The following quotation, certainly an understatement, summarizes the mission's feelings about adding to Hawaiian's store of words: "When we attempt the preparation of books, we find the language very deficient in words proper to convey ideas which lie at the foundation of morals, religion, science, & the arts" (Extracts from a General Letter of the Missionaries 1834:285).

Other than scanning the voluminous missionary reports and correspondence for discussions of individual words, the most convenient record of the effect of Christianity on Hawaiian's vocabulary is, of course, a dictionary.[4]

LOANWORDS FROM ANDREWS'S 1865 HAWAIIAN-ENGLISH DICTIONARY

Figure 13.1. Lorrin Andrews, ca. 1865

In his 1865 Hawaiian-English dictionary, Lorrin Andrews included over four pages of borrowed words. However, his list does not represent all the borrowings in the dictionary, for it includes only those that *begin* with the "foreign" consonants. For example, *mare* 'marry' and *Maraki* 'March" appear in the main part of the dictionary, as do borrowings with only native consonants: *laiki* 'rice', *pena* 'paint', *peni* 'pen', and *waina* 'wine'. Nor would a borrowed word beginning with a vowel appear on the list.

In his introduction to the list, Andrews mentioned an important process that will

4. A Bible concordance might yield more data, but the advantage of using a dictionary is that it includes secular terms as well as religious ones.

be discussed later—adding vowels where necessary to fit Hawaiian syllable structure. He also explained a policy mentioned in chapter 7—that the missionaries thought it necessary to include several "foreign" consonants in the alphabet so that borrowings would stand out from indigenous words.

Because Andrews identified the source for each word, one of the first things one discovers is that they come from six different languages: English, Greek, Hebrew, Latin, Chaldean, and Syrian.

The section is divided into groups beginning with B, D, F, G, J, R, S, T, V, and Z.[5] The following sample includes only words beginning with B. Identical forms for different parts of speech have been deleted. Brackets enclose current spellings, according to P-E. Many of the definitions have been shortened. Biblical abbreviations can be found in P-E, xxvi.

B.

Bai-ba-la [Paipala], s. Eng. Bible

bai-la [paila], v. Eng. To boil; to seethe. Note.—The corresponding hawaiian word is *hoolapalapa.* Ezek. 24:5.

ba-ka [paka], s. Eng. Tobacco; *e puhi baka,* to smoke tobacco.[6]

ba-ke-ke [pākeke], } s. Eng. A bucket.[7] [ba-ke-ke and ba-ke-te are alternates.]
ba-ke-te,

ba-le [pale], s. Eng. Barley. Oihk. 27:16.

ba-le-sa-ma [palakama, palekama], s. Eng. Balsam. Ezek. 27:17.

ba-ma [pāma], s. Balm. Kin. 43:11.

ba-pe-ti-so, } [papekiko] v. Gr. To baptize.
ba-pe-ti-zo,

ba-ra-ni [palani], s. Eng. Brandy.

ba-re-ka [paleka], s. Heb. A carbuncle.

ba-ta, } [paka][8] s. Eng. Butter. Kin. 18:8; Hal. 55:21.
ba-te-ra

---

5. This list does not match the extra consonants on p. 1 of *The Alphabet;* see chapter 9.

6. This common construction focuses on the activity rather than on what appears to be an object. Like *inu pia* 'beer drinking', it uses a borrowed word in an existing pattern.

7. *Pakeke* (i.e., with *p* rather than *b*) appears in the main body of the dictionary. The alternate showing both *k* and *t* is interesting; that pattern is common in Niʻihau Hawaiian today. The current spelling is *pākeke;* the long first syllable produces a different accent pattern than the spellings *bakeke* or *pakeke* would suggest.

8. The alternating forms show the difference between borrowing by ear (without *-r*) and by eye (with *-r*). They also show dialect differences in the model.

ba-to [pako?], s. Heb. A bath, a Hebrew measure. 1 Nal. 7:26.

be-a [pea], s. Eng. A bear. 2 Nal. 2:24; Lam. Haw. 18:1 and 19:1.

be-a-va, } [piwa] s. Eng. A beaver.
be-a-wa, }

be-ka [peka], s. Heb. A half shekel. Puk. 38:26.

be-le [pele], s. Eng. A bell; *bele gula.*[9] Puk. 28:33.

be-lu [polū], adj. Eng. Blue; Ezek. 23:6.

be-re-na [pelena], s. Eng. Bread; food generally. Mat. 4:4. *Berena maka,*[10] dough.

be-re-na-ho-i-ke, s. Eng. with *hoike* [*hōʻike*]. Show bread. Puk. 25:30.

be-re-na-hu, s. Eng. with *hu* [*hū*]. Leavened bread. Puk. 23:18.

be-re-na-hu-o-le, s. Eng. with *hu ole* [*hū ʻole*]. Unleavened bread. Puk. 23:15.

be-re-na-ku-la-la-ni, s. Eng. with *kulalani.*[11] The twelve loaves of bread set by the Jewish priest every Sabbath on the golden altar. Oihk. 24:5, 6.

be-ri-la [pelulo] s. Gr. A beryl.[12] Hoik. 21:20.

be-ri-ta [pelika], s. Heb. A covenant. Kin. 9:9.

be-ru-lo [pelulo], s. Gr. A beryl. See *berila.* Puk. 28:20.

be-ru-mi [pūlumi], v. Eng. To broom. Note.—The Hawaiian equivalent is *kahili.* [*nīʻau kāhili*]

bi-pi [pipi], s. Eng. The Hawaiian pronunciation for *beef,* and should properly be written *bifi. bipi kane,* an ox or bull; *bipi wahine,* a cow; *bipi kaulua,* a yoke of oxen; *bipi kauo* [*kauō*], a draft ox; *bipi wahine hou,* a heifer.[13] Nah. 19:2.

bi-pi-ku-a-puu, s. Eng. *Bipi* with *kuapuu* [*kuapuʻu*], humpback. The bison, buffalo. Lam. Haw. 8:1.

bi-tu-me-na [pikimana], s. Eng. Bitumen. Kin. 11:3.

bo-la [pola], s. Eng. A bowl. Lunk. 6:38. The Hawaiian word is *ipu.*[14]

bu-bo [pupo], s. Heb. A species of owl. Kanl. 14:16.

bu-ke [puke], s. Eng. A book. Puk. 24:7.

---

9. *Gula* 'gold'.

10. *Maka* 'raw'.

11. *Kulalani* 'standing in a row'.

12. P-E has *pelulo.*

13. Several examples of a borrowed word modified by a native word.

14. Another example of a borrowing supplementing a native word.

bu-fa-lo [pāpulō], s. Eng. A buffalo. Haw. 9:1.
bu-ni-be-ti [punipeki], s. The name of a game.[15]
bu-se-la [pūkele], s. Eng. A bushel. Ana Hon. 60.

If one examines the list carefully, nearly every word piques the curiosity. For example, the entry for *baila* 'to boil' tells us that it corresponds to an indigenous word *hoolapalapa* (*hoʻolapalapa*). This information leads to the obvious question: if there was already a word for 'boil', why borrow another one?[16] Did the existing word refer to a particular method of boiling, rather than a general one? (As mentioned earlier, Bible translators often complained about a lack of general as opposed to specific terms.) On the other hand, did it merely provide a synonym? In this case, as so often, we would like to be able to go back in time and ask for an explanation.

Some words could well inspire short essays on their own. Take *beava/beawa* 'beaver', for example. First, one can study the form of the word. The presence of two different spellings shows that even in 1865, nearly forty years after the extra consonants were trimmed from the alphabet, some words had alternate spellings. Why? As we saw earlier, the missionaries encouraged the use of "foreign" consonants in the spelling of some borrowings, apparently so that they would show at least a trace of their origin. Here, *b* identifies the word as a borrowing, as does *v*. But the alternate spelling with *w* shows a tendency to move away from these non-Hawaiian consonants.

Next, note the *-ea-* in the word (where we would expect *-i-* instead). The spelling shows that the form of the word was influenced more by the eye than the ear—in other words, the spelling rather than the pronunciation.

If you look up *beaver* in the English-Hawaiian section of P-E, you'll find that the current translation—*piwa*—has been completely assimilated—that is, it contains no foreign consonants, and it has an accented vowel that matches the English pronunciation, not the spelling. Thus, the current word is much closer to the English model (at least in a New

15. Said to be borrowed from *Bonaparte.*

16. In the English-Hawaiian section of P-E, the entry for "boil" includes *paila* and *kupa,* both borrowed from English. *Kupa* took a more indirect path: its first definition in this semantic domain is 'soup'; 'to boil' seems a secondary meaning.

England or British dialect without a postvocalic [r]), especially if the *w* is given its common [v]-like pronunciation.

What can one study in the list beyond the spellings of the words? Let's return to the word for *beaver*. The entry in the Hawaiian dictionary also contains another translation: *'īlio hulu pāpale,* lit. 'dog [related to] hat fur'. This phrase leads us down a fascinating etymological trail. First, it illustrates the use of *'īlio* 'dog' as the general word for four-legged animals, a topic discussed in the previous chapter. Next, it shows the now-vanished importance of beaver fur felt as a material for hats. For example, according to *Funk and Wagnall's New Encyclopedia* (1973), Geoffrey Chaucer mentioned a beaver hat in his writings. (In that encyclopedia, you can also find the following statement under the heading "Fur": "In the 14th century beaver, used for making headwear, was the only fur worn by common people.")[17]

What else can we learn from these borrowings? Even in this sample, several words have alternate spellings, reflecting a pattern in the complete list. Beyond the sample, *sapphire* offers the most spellings, with four alternates. Much of the fluidity of spelling is connected with the choice of the vowel that has been inserted between consonants or added at the end of a word. For example, *farai/ferai* 'fry' shows alternate inserted vowels *-a-* and *-e-*, and the forms for *sapphire* show three different added vowels: *-a, -e,* and *-o.*

But there was disagreement about the choice of other vowels as well. For example, the words for 'gold' show three different ways to reflect the vowel in the model: *g**o**la/g**ou**la/g**u**la.*

All in all, the short list gives us a glimpse, even though a hazy one, of what lies behind the complex process of borrowing a word from one language to another. In the next sections, I will take a more detailed look at the form of borrowed words.

---

17. Going beyond etymology, one can find another connection between beaver fur and Hawai'i. This commodity was so valuable that England and Spain nearly went to war over who would control the North American fur trade. Some of the first ships that called at Hawai'i after Cook's third voyage, beginning in 1786, were involved in trade between the Pacific Northwest and China. Interested parties aboard the ships, both English and Spanish, collected some of the first Hawaiian word lists after Anderson's (chapter 5).

SOUND PATTERNS

One of the principles we assume for borrowing is that a "Hawaiianized" word should sound as much like the model as possible. How successful this attempt is depends on which language is the donor. For example, if Hawaiian borrows a word from another Polynesian language, say Tahitian or Samoan, it is easy to make it sound like the model, for the sound systems of the languages are very similar. But with English as the main donor, the principle is stretched to its limit because of two important differences between the sound systems of Hawaiian and English. The first is the sounds themselves, and the second is the way in which they're arranged (see figure 3.1).

Sound-to-Sound Correspondences

The most striking difference between the Hawaiian and English sound systems is that English has many more vowels and consonants. As a result, several different sounds in English may be borrowed as one sound in Hawaiian. Figure 13.2 shows the closest Hawaiian equivalents of the English sounds, as evidenced by the borrowings.[18]

As you can see, the most lopsided equation is that for Hawaiian *k*. When you find it in a borrowed word, it could have come from any of twelve English consonants.

English		Hawaiian	English		Hawaiian
p, b, f	→	p	y, i, ɪ	→	i
v, w	→	w	e, ɛ	→	e
hw	→	hu[1]	æ, ɒ, ɜ, ə, ʌ	→	a
s, h, š, f, č	→	h	ɔ, o	→	o
l, r	→	l	u, ʊ	→	u
m	→	m			
n, ŋ	→	n			
t, d, Θ, ð, s, z, š, ž, k, g, č, ǰ	→	k			

Figure 13.2. The most common patterns for borrowing an English word into Hawaiian. Many speakers of English do not use /hw/, but /w/. For example, they do not distinguish between ***wh****ich* and ***w****itch* or ***wh****ere* and ***w****ear*.

18. Adapted from Carr 1951 and P-E 1957:xvii.

š	**show**	θ	**thin**	č	**chess**	ŋ	sin**g**
ð	**then**	ž	lei**s**ure	ǰ	**j**am	ɪ	b**i**t
ɛ	b**e**t	æ	b**a**t	ɒ	**a**h	ɜ	s**ir** (Brit. Pron.)
ə	**a**bove	ʌ	ab**o**ve	ɔ	b**ough**t	ʊ	p**u**t

Figure 13.3. Key to the phonetic symbols

Figure 13.4 shows examples for each sound. As you read through them, please keep two things in mind. First, these patterns aren't entirely regular. Next, because some sounds are relatively uncommon in English, they may not be reflected in a borrowed word. The most obvious example is English [ð] (as in ***th**e*), a low-frequency sound except in several function words. I could find no instance of a word with this sound borrowed into Hawaiian.

Note that no long vowels are listed in the table. The list that follows shows long vowels reflecting two conditions in the English model. First, a long vowel in the Hawaiian form reflects the vowel in an English monosyllable of the CV shape; for example, Hawaiian *kī* from English *key.* Next, a long vowel in a form such as *kāmano* 'salmon' reflects an accented vowel in the model. (See a later section in the present chapter, "Matching Accents.")

A raised period separates accent measures, explained in chapter 11.

A Return to Foreign Consonants?

In the various editions of P-E, the headings under the foreign consonants follow the following pattern:

> **B**
>
> All loan words from English sometimes spelled with initial *b-* are entered under *p-*. For example: *Baibala,* see *Paipala,* Bible; *balota,* see *pālota,*[19] ballot; *bele,* see *pele,* bell; *bila,* see *pila,* bill; *bipi,* see *pipi,* beef; *buke,* see *puke,* book.

The current spellings of words (from older sources) beginning with *D, F, G, J, R, S, T, V,* and *Z* are explained

19. A misprint for *pāloka*.

SOUNDS		EXAMPLES	
ENG	HAW	ENG	HAW
Vowels and diphthongs			
i	i	key	*kī*
ɪ	i	deer	*kia*
e	e	ace	*'eki*
	ei	May	*Mei*
ɛ	e	tennis	*kenika*
æ	a	ham	*hame*
a	a	heart	*haka*
ə, ʌ	a	putty	*pake*
ɔ	o	mosque	*mokeko*
o	o	aroma	*'aloma*
u	u	boom	*pumi*
ʊ	u	book	*puke*
ay	ai	island	*'ai·lana*
aw	ao	town	*kaona*
	au	out	*'auko*
oy	oe	boy	*poe*
	?oi		
iw[1]	iu	mule	*miula*
Consonants			
p	p	pie	*pai*
b	p	butter	*paka*
t	k	tar	*kā*
d	k	dollar, money	*kā·lā*
k	k	collar	*kala*
g	k	gum	*kamu*
č	k	charge	*kāki*
ǰ	k	major	*mekia*
	i	jackal	*iā·kala*
f	h	fa	*hā*
	p	frog	*poloka*
v	w	veto	*wiko*
θ	k	Methodist	*Meko·kiko*
ð	k?	————	
s	k	salmon	*kā·mano*
z	k	tsar	*kā*
š	k	share	*kea*
	h	sheep	*hipa*
ž	k	cashmere	*kaki·mea*
h	h	half	*hapa*
l	l	liter	*lika*
r	l	rye	*lai*
m	m	May	*Mei*
n	n	note	*noka*
ŋ	n	furlong	*pale·lona*
w	w	wine	*waina*
	u	wire	*uea*
hw	hu	wheel	*huila*
y	i	you	*iū*

[1] This sequence might also be interpreted as *yu*.

Figure 13.4. Examples for each sound.

similarly. Note that only the spelling, not the pronunciation, is mentioned. In each case, the spelling that contains a foreign consonant is treated as an alternate form, not as a headword. Another clue that the alternate form represents the written and not the spoken language is the absence of glottal stops, macrons, and measure divisions.

In some written material, the Hawaiian and not the foreign pronunciation of such introduced letters was hinted at in the choice of article (*ka/ke*). For example, in *Nupepa Kuakoa,* 14 August 1924, one finds in an ad for motor oil the phrase *ke Zerolene, ke* (not *ka*) showing that the introduced *Z* was pronounced as [k] (see figure 13.2).[20]

In theory at least, *Māmaka Kaiao* represents a return to the approach taken in the early dictionaries and reflected in Andrews (1865) 2003. Embedded in the entries within the native letters are examples of the foreign consonants, once pruned from the alphabet. Within the main part of the Hawaiian-English section, headword examples are rare; for example:

Kolorado/Kololako	Colorado
Misisipi	Mississippi
Kolomebia/Kolomepia	Colombia
Paraguae	Paraguay

However, in the last few pages of the Hawaiian-English section (echoing the organization of Andrews 1865), following the words that begin with an *ʻokina,* we find words that begin with a foreign consonant. The following list shows the number of words for each consonant and one example for each:

B-	25	*Bahama*	Bahamas
C-	1	*CD*	CD
D-	11	*Dakota Hema*	South Dakota
F-	17	*ferousa*	ferrous
G-	4	*galai·sine*	Glycine
R-	7	*Rūsia*	Russia

20. Example and analysis supplied by Keao NeSmith, pers. comm., August 2011.

S-	43	*Saudi ʻAlapia*	Saudi Arabia
T-	28	*Tonga*[21]	Tonga
V-	2	*Vere moneta*	Vermont
Z-	4	*Zāire*	Zaire

Many of the introduced words refer to place names or chemical elements and compounds. Many also have alternate forms that contain only native consonants. Those that don't (e.g., *Suazilana* 'Swaziland') raise an interesting question: How are these words actually pronounced—in a geography class, for example?

The following answer is from Keao NeSmith (pers. comm., 2 February 2009):

> These are the typical "Hawaiian" pronunciations for the foreign alphabet, as based on native speakers' pronunciation:

b [p]	c [s] [k]	d [t] [k]	f [f] [p]	g [k]
j [i] [k]	q [k]	r [r, Am.] [l]	s [s] [k]	t [t] [k]
v [w, Hawn.]	x [k] [s]	y [i]	z [s] [k]	

NeSmith added, "One disagreement I had with the members of the Committee . . . is their insistence that the foreign letters be pronounced just like they are in American English, I disagree sharply on that one because . . . the native speakers [should be] role models, and not L2s [second-language learners]. It is true that at times native speakers, mostly those from the islands other than Niʻihau, will pronounce the [b] and [d] and maybe [z] as in English, but usually they follow the above key and these sounds are considered 'nicer' to hear."

It will be interesting to see if these new introductions follow the pattern of earlier loans: that is, eventual assimilation to the Native Hawaiian consonant system, with the foreign sounds preserved in only a few words.[22]

---

21. Note that here *ng* represents [ŋ]. Without an explanation, readers might think that it represents [ŋg], a common mispronunciation of *Tonga*.

22. For example, *tūtū* 'grandparent', *ua sila* 'sealed' (from the song "Ke Kali Nei Au"), *Kristo* 'Christ', et al. Keao NeSmith (pers. comm., January 2009) reported that Niʻihau speakers regularly pronounce the name of a store, *Ishihara,* as *Isihala.*

English Vowels and the *'Okina*

If you look at the English words in figure 13.2 that begin with vowels,[23] you'll see that the Hawaiian versions of most of them begin with an *'okina*. This pattern shows that the words were indeed borrowed by ear and not by eye. The reason for the *'okina* is that when we pronounce an English word that begins with a vowel, either alone or at the beginning of a phrase, we precede it by a perceptible glottal stop. Because the sound in English is predictable, it isn't part of the consonant system but rather an introduction to an initial vowel sound (see chapter 8). But Hawaiian speakers hear it and reinterpret it as a consonant in their system, for native words are kept distinct by the sound in this position. For example, *ala* 'way' and *'ala* 'fragrance' are obviously two different words.

How the Sounds Are Arranged

A sound-to-sound approach, such as that illustrated in the list above, only begins to show what happens when Hawaiian borrows an English word, because it doesn't take into account the differences between the two syllable systems. Stated briefly, every consonant in a Hawaiian word must be followed by a vowel. In other words, there can be no consonant clusters or final consonants. To achieve this result in a borrowing, a cluster in the English model either has to be (1) split up by inserting a vowel between the consonants or (2) simplified by dropping one or more consonants. Moreover, a vowel must be added to any word-final consonant.

Adding Vowels

When a vowel is inserted into or added to a borrowed word so that it conforms to Hawaiian syllable structure, it presents a challenge to analysts: Can we predict which vowel will be added? Here, Hawaiian differs from some other related languages. For example, Tongan and Fijian

23. In the list, the vowels that begin the words *uwea* 'wire' and *iū* 'you' are unaccented and reflect the glides *w* and *y*, not vowels.

show certain strong patterns in the choice of vowel—such as *i* after alveolar consonants (made with the tip of the tongue on the gum ridge), *u* after bilabial consonants (made with both lips), *a* after *k,* and *o* after *l.*[24] Although we don't usually think of consonants and vowels as being similar to each other, they do share certain acoustic and articulatory characteristics, and sometimes these features are reflected in the choice of added vowels.

Although the data are limited, some earlier borrowings (as represented in lists collected before 1820) tend to show patterns similar to those in Tongan and Fijian. However, words borrowed later often differ, the result of a conscious decision on the part of the Bible translators. As Hiram Bingham wrote (1847:155), for the words that they introduced, the missionaries in Hawaiʻi decided to insert an *e* between consonants and add an *a* after an English final consonant. This practice disrupted the earlier pattern (apparently unnoticed by the missionaries) and became a pattern in itself.[25]

Figure 13.5 shows how the first of these changes—splitting up consonant clusters—affects the form of borrowed words. (The English words are written according to their sound, not their spelling. A raised period separates English syllables and Hawaiian measures.)

Note first that *kalikimaka* and *kanikela* differ slightly from Bingham's imposed rule, with *ki* and *ni* (rather than *ke* and *ne*) as syllables containing inserted vowels. This feature is interesting in that it may show the original pattern: *i* inserted after alveolar sounds in the models (*s* and *n*).

At first glance, the Hawaiian form for *Christmas* seems rather long: a five-syllable word corresponding to a two-syllable English word. But perhaps the forms match in another way: in each of these examples, the number of English syllables corresponds to the number of Hawaiian measures. The match is represented in figure 13.5, in which brackets enclose English syllables and a raised period separates Hawaiian accent units for the three examples above.

24. See Schütz 1970, 1978a.

25. See Schütz 1976.

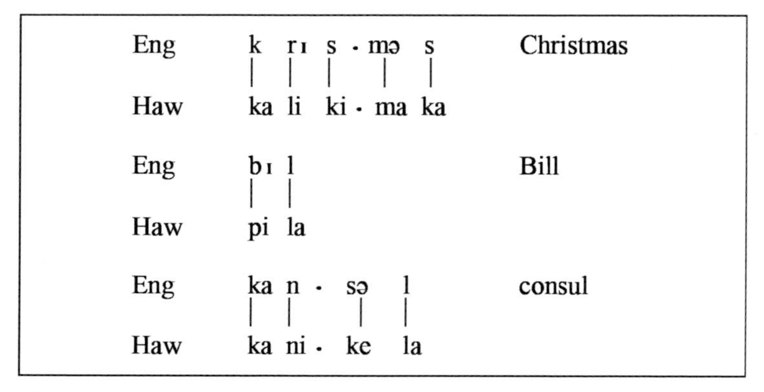

Figure 13.5. Comparing structure of syllables and measures

English Syllables		Hawaiian Measures	
[krɪs][məs]	(2)	kalíki·máka	(2)
[bɪl]	(1)	pila	(1)
[kan][səl]	(2)	kani·kela	(2)

Figure 13.6. Comparing number of syllables and measures

Dropping Consonants

To illustrate the second change mentioned above—dropping a consonant—note that the *nd* cluster in the following example is simplified:

Eng ay lə **n d** island[26]

| | \ /

Haw ai la **na**

And the *sk* cluster is simplified in the following example:

Eng **s k** rey pɜ scraper

\ / | |

Haw **ka** le pa

---

26. Why borrow a word for 'island'? See a later section, "Loanwords as Generalizers?"

The advantage to dropping one of the consonants in a cluster is that it allows the final form to be shorter—and thus more similar to the English model. Simplifying *nd* to *n* follows the English model in another way: often that same sound change occurs in a casual or dialectal English pronunciation.

Matching Accents

We have just seen that when an English word is adapted to the Hawaiian sound system, it is changed in two important ways. First, the English consonants and vowels are replaced by their closest matches in Hawaiian. Next, vowels are added or consonants dropped so that the new word has Hawaiian, not English syllable structure.

Another way to change the Hawaiian word so that it resembles the English model more closely is to try to match the accented syllables in the loanword to those in the model. To achieve the fit, a vowel is usually lengthened so that it will be accented. Compare the examples in the following two columns; only the first column shows lengthening to "attract" the accent:

lā·paki	rabbit	*kalapu*	club
ʻā·kena	agent	*kaluna*	saloon
kā·pena	captain	*kanela*	canal
kā·piki	cabbage	*ʻomeka*	omega
ʻē·poni	ebony	*palola*	parole

In the word for 'rabbit', if the first vowel were not long, the word would be accented *lapáki, which does not match the accent pattern of the English model very well. But no such lengthening is necessary in *kalapu,* for the form already has the accent on the appropriate vowel: *kalápu.*

Even though *lāpaki* is a better accent match than **lapaki,* the stronger accent on the second measure makes it less than ideal. *Ailana* 'island' is another example. However, within the Hawaiian accent system, one cannot eliminate the primary accent on the final measure (ài·lána).

In spite of such limitations, Hawaiian uses vowel length to make a better match with the accent pattern in the English model. But there are some borrowings that don't seem to fit the sound of the English model as closely as possible. Here are some examples:

PRESENT FORM		PROPOSED FORM
kelaki	celery	**kela·kī*
ʻepane	apron	**ʻē·pane*
ʻenemi	enemy	**ʻene·mī*
palo·meka	barometer	**palō·meka*
kelo·kokile	crocodile	**kelō·kokile*

Why these mismatches? Possibly for this reason: most loanwords now in the language were borrowed long before long vowels were consistently marked. If these words were passed on not by ear but by eye (for example, through the Hawaiian language newspapers), new readers, perhaps not knowing the source, might have misinterpreted them. Still, that answer is only guesswork, and there doesn't seem to be a way to confirm it.

CAN WE PREDICT WHAT A LOANWORD WILL SOUND LIKE?

When linguists study any part of a language, whether it's connected with the sound system or the grammar, they try to find patterns—that is, "rules." The more data a rule covers, the more powerful (or satisfactory) it is said to be.

Will the patterns sketched here allow us to predict with 100 percent accuracy the form of a Hawaiian borrowing from English? In other words, will they explain the form of every English loanword in P-E or *Māmaka Kaiao?*

The short answer is no. Naturally, the rules are based on the data and will therefore explain the forms of many of the loanwords. But here are some reasons why the rules don't always work.

1. If you look at the sound-to-sound rules presented above, you can see that some of them offer a choice. For example, sometimes an English /e/ sound was interpreted as Hawaiian *e* but other times as *ei.* Similarly, sometimes an English *f* was borrowed as Hawaiian *h* but other times as *p.*
2. Even if the missionaries had not imposed their own rules that dictated which vowels to insert and add, the patterning of such vowels would only *tend* to be regular. For example, sometimes an added vowel doesn't seem to be related to the consonant it follows, but

instead it seems to "echo" another vowel in the word. For example, note the boldfaced vowels in the following words:

*'**e**m**e**paia*	empire	*'**e**m**e**pakekoa*	ambassador
*'**e**m**e**pake*	embassy	*'**e**m**e**pela*	emperor[27]

One might have expected the second vowel in each word to be a *u* (between the bilabial sounds *m* and *p*). Instead, it seems to echo the first *e*—or perhaps it is simply following the imposed practice of inserting *e* between consonants in the middle of a word (see the discussion above and "Verbatim" below).

3. English words were, and still are, pronounced differently by people from different areas. For example, some speakers pronounce a syllable-final *-r* after a vowel; others don't. These differences are often reflected in the form of the borrowed word. For example, in the following three forms on the left, English *-r* is reflected by Hawaiian *l*. However, in those on the right, the lack of an *l* suggests that the English model didn't have *-r*.

Dialect with -r		Dialect without -r	
'akele[28]	acre	*'ana·kā*	anchor
hola[29]	hour	*kinika*	ginger
Hōmela[30]	Homer	*'eme·paea*	empire

4. We can tell by their spelling that some words were borrowed by eye, not by ear. For example, the word *hīmeni* 'hymn' suggests that the spelling influenced the form: *n* appears in the English spelling but not in the pronunciation.[31]

---

27. The inserted *e* in this word might also reflect the policy described by Bingham—breaking up consonants with *e* and adding an *a* at the end of the word.

28. The form of the word suggests that it was based on spelling, not on pronunciation. *'Eka* is almost invariably used today and was used in some land titles in the 1800s (Keao NeSmith, pers. comm., January 2009).

29. Although P-E identifies this word as a borrowing from English, it could possibly be from Latin *hōra*.

30. **Homa* would have been a better fit, as would **kini·kā* for 'ginger'.

31. But reappears in the word *hymnal*.

Another example is *ʻaloe* ʻaloeʼ. In spite of its Polynesian-looking spelling, this word came into English (through Greek and Latin) about AD 1400. It is pronounced [ælo] ([æ] represents the vowel in *cat*). In Hawaiʻi, even in an English context, we can often hear it with the three-syllable Hawaiian pronunciation.

5. The forms of some words suggest that certain vowels might have once been pronounced long, but because the *kahakō* wasn't written until recently, those who learned the words only from their written form didn't know the pronunciation. The word *ʻenemi* ʻenemyʼ is an example; **ʻenemī* would have been closer to the English form.
6. Sometimes, the form closest to the English pronunciation might clash with an existing word. Although *kaona* was a common literary device, one could imagine that if missionaries were involved in creating words for Bible translation they might not accept a new word with a risqué meaning. Here's a hypothetical example. Suppose the closest phonetic form of a borrowing from English, meant for some theological or educational concept, turned out to be *kolohe* ʻnaughtyʼ, *lepo* ʻdirtyʼ, or *lapuwale* ʻworthlessʼ. Most likely the translators, in their role as word makers, would choose a different word.[32]

BORROWED WORDS AND AFFIXES

To show that some borrowings are treated no differently than native words, we need only look for words that have been reduplicated or have added other types of affixes. The following example shows the results of reduplication:

kula	school	*ku-kula*	go to school

The next example, mentioned in chapter 12, contains the causative prefix *hoʻo-*, one of the most productive in Hawaiian:

male	marry	*hoʻo-male*	ʻperform the marriage ceremonyʼ

For some other derivatives, not in P-E but found in texts, readers need to check the context and the meanings of the suffixes:

32. See the earlier discussion (chapter 7) of *lama* vs. *rama*.

kuke	cook	*kuke-na*	(nominal?)
		kuke-a	(passive?)
		kuke-hia	(passive)
		kuke ʻia	(passive)
pela	spell	*pe-pela*	?

LOANWORDS AS GENERALIZERS?

Most of the examples in this chapter show borrowed words filling an obvious need—for example, terms for introduced items of material culture, biblical concepts, Western educational concepts, or names of people and places outside Hawaiʻi. But how does one explain loanwords for concepts such as ʻuncleʼ or ʻsisterʼ, which already exist?

Perhaps loanwords can serve a less obvious function—to avoid the preciseness that certain Hawaiian cultural relationships make necessary. Within the semantic area of kin terms, often native terms are quite specific. There are different words for ʻuncleʼ, referring, for example, to ʻyounger brother or cousin of the father or motherʼ, or ʻolder brother or cousin of the father or motherʼ. The loanword *ʻanakala* is more general, referring to any of these.[33] Similarly, the Hawaiian terms for ʻsisterʼ make distinctions of age and sex, whereas *kika* or *tita* refers to the general concept.

Another possibility is that as the culture has changed, younger speakers of Hawaiian no longer make the distinctions that once existed.

An example outside the area of kinship is *pālamu* ʻpalmʼ, which refers to introduced palms (pers. comm., Puanani Anderson-Fung, 11 September 2013).[34] Does *ʻailana* ʻislandʼ (mentioned earlier) allow the speaker to be less specific—or perhaps avoid the pitfalls of ambiguity, because a large number of compounds with *moku* now refer to different kinds of ships? Does *baila* (also mentioned earlier) refer to the general idea of ʻboilingʼ,

33. In local English, it is also a term of address for a male at least a generation older than the speaker.

34. Neither *palamu* nor *pālamu* (short or long vowel) appears in the Hawaiian-English section of P-E, but the English-Hawaiian section has *pāma* and *pālama,* the former reflecting the more common spoken form of the English word and the latter the written form.

as opposed to a more specific procedure, 'ancient method of boiling by placing hot stones in a bowl containing water' (P-E 404)?

John Charlot (pers. comm., December 2015) added this example: "*hale / home.* Hawaiians may have adopted the loanword because they *felt* a difference between the two referents; that is, a home was much more a center of living rather than just a part of a whole land complex." Could this idea explain the choice of *home,* and not *hale,* in the song "Ku'u Home o Kahalu'u"? Or does *home* convey associations that *hale* lacks?

BORROWING IN THE OTHER DIRECTION: HAWAIIAN AS A WORD DONOR

Perhaps this topic deserves a chapter of its own, but it should be noted that Hawaiian has been the donor, as well as the receiver, of borrowings. Here, I treat only those found in three major reference works.

1. Chapter 8 analyzed Merriam-Webster's pronunciation guide for Hawaiian words borrowed into English. The data, perhaps underrecorded, include 180 words, not unexpectedly consisting of a large number of plant, fish, and bird names and geological terms specific to Hawaiian (such as *pāhoehoe* and *'a'ā*).
2. The *Dictionary of American Regional English* (Cassidy 1985–2013), in its section on English in Hawai'i, recorded 212 Hawaiian words out of a total of 316 words and phrases. It is not clear whether the primary data were from spoken or written sources. For example, it is unlikely that the spelling *alii* (from *ali'i* 'chief'), even in an English context, represents a form actually pronounced without an *'okina.*
3. As for Hawaiian words used in Hawai'i Creole English, the glossary in *Pidgin Grammar* (Sakoda and Siegel 2003) includes 98 Hawaiian words out of a total of 317.

Summary

If we examine the Hawaiian vocabulary for concepts both native and introduced, it is easy to see that as other languages have done, Hawaiian has added to its stock of words in several ways. That is, it has made up new words, assigned new meanings to existing words, expanded the meaning of existing words through affixation and compounding, and adapted words from other languages. All these processes are still functioning today, proof of Hawaiian's flexibility and vitality.

VERBATIM

In 1836, still in the early days of the mission, Lorrin Andrews (1836b:20–21) discussed its unofficial policy of finding new words or adapting old ones for new concepts introduced into the language.

> With regard to new words in a language just reduced to writing and where improvements, or what is the same thing, where new ideas are brought in, there are two methods of proceeding. One is to introduce new words from other languages to express new ideas; the other is, to give new definitions to words already in use. Both of these methods have been pursued in the Hawaiian. New words have been introduced as noticed above. Caution however will be necessary lest words should be unnecessarily introduced, or such as are no more significant than some that are already in the language. The number of the words to which new ideas have been attached is not yet large, but will probably be greatly increased when moral, religious, and scientific studies shall be more extensively and systematically pursued. *Naau,* the heart, *uhane* the soul, and *Akua* God, and several other words, have ideas attached to them now in the minds of the more intelligent natives that they had not a few years ago.

Earlier in the chapter I cited Bingham's imposed rule for added vowels. The following quotation contains that passage in full, as well as other matters concerning the form of borrowings (Bingham 1847:155):

> Though five vowels and seven consonants would well express the Hawaiian language, unmixed with foreign terms, yet there were reasons for introducing other letters, abounding in kindred Polynesian dialects, and in the names of persons, places, and things in other countries, with which the Hawaiians needed to become acquainted. Eleven or twelve letters must be too limited to be the representatives of general knowledge. To preserve the *identity* of foreign or scripture names, was deemed of some importance. We could not, in good conscience, throw out every consonant in the names of Obed, Boaz, Ruth, David, Ezra, Russia, and Gaza, and nearly all out of such names as Sabbath, Christ, Moses, Joseph, Boston, and Genessaret, simply because such

consonants could be dispensed with in writing the words familiar to the people. The following additional consonants, therefore, were adopted: *b, d, f, g, r, s, t, v,* and *z.* These form the third class of letters in the Hawaiian alphabet, which is arranged according to ease and importance, allowing the native pupil to learn to spell and read pure native words first.

Compound consonants, recommended by J. Pickering, Esq.,[35] for writing the Indian languages, are not adopted in the Hawaiian, though the basis of his alphabet, in respect to vowel sounds, is followed. C, J, Q, and Y we omit. To preserve the identity of a foreign name embracing a compound consonant which cannot well be omitted, we take the more important or practicable part of the power—as *p,* for *ph* or *phi; t,* for *th* or *theta; k,* for *ch* or *chi,* &c. When two consonants joined in a foreign word, need both to be preserved, we interpose the vowel *e,* and after a final consonant add usually the vowel *a*—as Bosetona for Boston.

As mentioned earlier, this ad hoc rule, apparently made without examining the patterns in words that had already been borrowed, explains why the expected combinations—for example, *mu, pu, ka, lo, ni,* and *ti,* in both added and inserted vowels—are not nearly as common as they are in English borrowings in Tongan and Fijian (Schütz 1970, 1978a).

35. See chapter 7, note 9 for an identification.

PART V

CHANGES

PAST, PRESENT, AND FUTURE

CHAPTER 14

HOW IS HAWAIIAN CHANGING?

> Since the time of Kamehameha the Great the Hawaiian tongue has been almost revolutionized, so many idioms have crept in and so many English expressions with Hawaiian spelling and pronunciation have been adopted. The old fashioned natives living in the country districts have an extensive vocabulary of words with which the younger generation in the city are wholly unfamiliar. A venerable native came over from Kauai a short time ago to visit his son, who is pure Hawaiian, and after they had conversed a few minutes the elder one exclaimed in Hawaiian: "You talk like a foreigner!"
>
> —"The Hawaiian Language," 1903

This quotation, from over a century ago, touches on the most obvious way that a language can change: new words are added (discussed in chapters 12 and 13), and some old words are forgotten as the culture moves in a different direction. However, the vocabulary isn't the only part of the language affected by the passage of time and by influence from competing languages. Because most speakers of Hawaiian today have learned the language not at home but in the classroom, some features of grammar, as well as vocabulary, have been lost and others introduced. Such changes, which you can notice if you compare the language in nineteenth-century texts with that in today's textbooks, suggest a concept likely to have been imposed from the outside: a "standard" language.

But how do we know what Hawaiians considered "correct" or "incorrect" in their language? Nineteenth-century reports tell us what outsiders observed, such as the (apparently) poor language skills of the Hawaiians who had spent years away from the islands, or the inability of some speakers to translate from English to Hawaiian. And as the quotation that begins the chapter suggests, urbanization had a similar effect.

But those complaints did not touch on the matter of standards. Take pronunciation and vocabulary as examples. In the first decades of the nineteenth century, many people interested in the language commented that consonants varied from island to island. Some reported that words varied as well. But was one of these dialects a standard? Did the speakers themselves favor one type of pronunciation or the vocabulary of a particular region? Or did "standardization" depend on the outcome of warfare? The answers elude us.

Still, although there is little evidence for such attitudes and opinions in precontact time, the nature of classroom instruction and reference materials often demands that a uniform kind of Hawaiian be taught. For example, the decision made in 1826 to eliminate certain consonants from the alphabet (chapter 7) was the first attempt to standardize the language—at least its spelling. Have there been others?

This chapter touches on four areas—pronunciation, spelling, vocabulary, and grammar—in which Hawaiian has either changed in the past, appears to have changed, or is changing now.

PRONUNCIATION

It is hard to separate pronunciation from spelling, especially for people who confuse sounds and letters. In order to understand how and why Hawaiian pronunciation may have changed as a result of the revised alphabet of 1826, we must first be reminded of why it was not practical to continue using an alphabet that, in at least three instances, wrote a single phoneme (distinctive sound) in two or even three ways. This practice was in direct opposition to the main criterion for an alphabet: that one phoneme be represented by one letter. In chapter 7, the principle was explained as follows: "So long as *kapu* and *tapu,* for example, mean the same thing, it doesn't matter whether you write *k* or *t.* But writing both is extremely inefficient. And to insist that both are necessary is to impose the English sound system on Hawaiian."

However, some people who don't understand this principle have reacted emotionally to the streamlined alphabet, feeling that the language itself has been violated. In 1990 one critic called the result of eliminating the unnecessary consonants "a simplified, impoverished, trivialized Hawaiian language."[1] In 1993 another suggested that although performers were striving for authenticity in the hula, "little is ever said about restoring the Hawaiian language to its pre-1829[2] form." It was then, the writer asserted, that "the missionaries changed the language drastically to suit their European ears."[3] Finally, he proposed using a Tahitian dictionary to help "learn the Hawaiian language in the easy-to-speak manner that existed before the meddling."[4]

These points of view are, of course, linguistic nonsense. Keeping the unneeded consonants in the alphabet would have made printing or writing the language extremely cumbersome, requiring learners to memorize individual spellings for thousands of words.

But in a way, the revised alphabet did eventually change one aspect of Hawaiian pronunciation—but only gradually and only for some speakers. Although, as mentioned in chapter 7, the missionaries did not intend to limit the range of pronunciation for the consonants that varied, perhaps they underestimated the power of the printed word. It is likely that many speakers continued to use, for example, the [t] variant of *k;* certainly this practice continued on Niʻihau. But as literacy became more common and more Hawaiians learned English, they may have tended to pronounce written *k* as [k], discarding the [t] variant. As mentioned in chapter 5, perhaps the tapped [ř] was largely replaced by [l] because [l] is closer to the original pronunciation than an American English *r.* As for the pronunciation of /w/, Keao NeSmith (2002:13) noted that language learners tend to pronounce the sound consistently as [v], rather than as the range of pronunciations (from [v] to [ß] to [w][5]) that existed in the nineteenth century. Changes such as these were reinforced when Hawaiian was learned not as a first language but as a second language—and from written textbooks and nonnative speakers in the classroom.

---

1. *Ka Leo o Hawaiʻi,* 3 October 1990.

2. In Elbert 1954:5, 1829 was written in error for 1826; some later works repeated that mistake.

3. Actually, the change was for exactly the opposite reason—to discount how the language sounded to English hearers.

4. *Honolulu Advertiser,* 11 May 1993, A-13.

5. See chapter 7, Schütz 1994:120–21, and Schütz 1981:28–33.

In addition to these changes, due mostly to the standardization of the alphabet, NeSmith noted other types of pronunciations that differed from those of native speakers. Many of these stem from the differences between the sound systems of Hawaiian and English. For example, many pairs of Hawaiian words can be distinguished by the contrast between final unaccented *-i* or *-e;* English, however, has no such contrast. Therefore, some learners don't make this distinction. They may also turn long vowels into diphthongs, pronouncing *ē* as [ey], *ī* as [iy], *ō* as [ow], and *ū* as [uw].[6] Finally, some learners fail to learn the [ʌ] variant of *a* before *i* and *u,* pronouncing, for example, the first vowel in *pali* 'precipice' with an "ah" sound rather than the more native-sounding "uh."

Aside from confusing final *-i* and *-e,* these changes do not affect communication. But they do serve to distance "textbook" Hawaiian from Native Hawaiian, creating a social barrier.

A different kind of study (Piccolo 2005) was an instrumental phonetic comparison of diphthongs and short vowels between the speech patterns of a native speaker of Ni'ihauan Hawaiian and those of a fluent speaker of what she called UH (University of Hawai'i) Hawaiian, whose first language was American English. Piccolo concluded, "The two varieties of Hawaiian have followed different paths. Niihauan Hawaiian has not been significantly influenced by American English in phonetic terms. UH Hawaiian, instead, has been, as illustrated by the results of the present study" (2005:23).

Occasionally we see changes in the pronunciation of individual words, not patterns that affect certain types of sounds. As an example, I chose the picture of *he 'īlio* 'a dog' to decorate the chapter heading. For some unexplained reason, sometimes the word is pronounced *'ílio* (with the only accent on the first syllable)—an accent pattern that is at odds with the Hawaiian system.

SPELLING

We have already described the missionaries' efforts (with the help of native speakers) first to form an alphabet and then to fine-tune it. Settling for one consonant from each of the groups was a change that affected a large

6. The reason for this practice is that the English vowels closest to Hawaiian, *ē, ī, ō,* and *ū* are not pure vowels but diphthongs.

part of the total vocabulary: the number of words that contain one or more of the consonants *k, l,* or *w* is considerable.[7] Later, writing *kahakō* and *ʻokina* was also a sweeping change, affecting many words in the total vocabulary.

However, more recent spelling changes have been more individual in nature, in some cases affecting only a few words.

One of these changes eliminated an unnecessary *w* added after *o* and *u* in a few words. The problem was noted early; Lorrin Andrews wrote, "The letter *w* could, in many cases, be dispensed with, as *o au* would be the same as *owau.* Some Hawaiians write *o Akea,* the name of one of the ancient gods; others write *o Wakea*" (1838:395).

In his revision of Andrews's dictionary (1922), Henry H. Parker was more outspoken in condemning some of these *w* spellings. To the entry for *aui* [*ʻaui*] 'to bend, decline', he added: "Auwi is a corrupt form of this verb."

However, the *w* spellings persisted until recently. In a paper proposing a number of spelling changes decided by the ʻAhahui ʻŌlelo Hawaiʻi (Wilson 1978), it was recommended that this extraneous letter be deleted in certain words. As Andrews had suggested, *o wau* [*ʻo wau*] was changed to *o au* [*ʻo au*]. Similar examples are *auwe,* ⁻ 'alas' and *kauwa,* ⁻ 'slave', which are now spelled *aue,* ⁻ and *kau,* ⁻. The 1986 edition of P-E lists both spellings, but those without *w* are listed first.

Several other spelling changes treated in Wilson's paper are more specific than general. Some involved correcting vowel length wrongly marked in a number of words in the edition P-E then current,[8] regularizing capital letters in certain types of words, suggesting letters to be used for non-Hawaiian sounds in some words, eliminating the apostrophe formerly

---

7. Elbert and Pukui 1979:34 contains frequency counts for both vowels and consonants, based on texts (Elbert 1959), but they do not tell us how many words in the *Hawaiian Dictionary* contain the consonants *k, l,* and *w.* However, Steve Trussel came up with the following figures, including *hoʻo-* forms (pers. comm., 10 June 2013):

Total words:	30,121
words containing *k, l,* or *w:*	15,480 (51.39%)
words containing *k:*	13,365 (44.37%)
words containing *l:*	13,370 (44.39%)
words containing *w:*	3,283 (10.90%)

8. For example, even in the 1965 edition, *kū* was spelled *ku.*

used to indicate "dropped" letters,[9] making (partially) arbitrary decisions on writing vowel length in certain function words (markers), and clarifying rules for using hyphens, writing compounds,[10] and deciding whether certain forms are one word or two.[11]

One of the phrases in the paragraphs that open this chapter suggests that there may be a part of Hawaiian that "*appears* to have changed." It is in the area of spelling that this phrase is appropriate. In spite of some opinions to the contrary, changing how Hawaiian words are written does not—*on its own*—change the language.[12] Writing is only a way to represent language; it is not the language itself. Including *ʻokina* and *kahakō* in the alphabet only helps to reflect Hawaiian's sound system more accurately. Similarly, neither replacing *kauwā* with *kauā* nor *ku* with *kū* changes the spoken language.

Of the changes mentioned here, especially the recommendations from 1978, the only ones that might possibly affect the pronunciation of the language—and therefore change the language—are those connected with the vowel length of certain grammatical markers. Legislating some as long and some as short might possibly obscure the subtle patterns that already exist. The following example is from Elbert and Pukui 1979:136: "The possessive prepositions are *a* (or *ā*) and *o* (or *ō*), and *kā* and *kō*. Long *ā* and *ō* precede syllables containing long vowels and diphthongs, short *a* and *o* occur elsewhere."

Thus, the underlying form of such a marker would contain a long vowel, not a short one, and the difference would be conditioned by the environment in which the preposition occurs. Students who learn these words from books rather than from native speakers are likely to pronounce them as written, not as spoken by a native speaker.[13]

---

9. For example, *ke liʻi,* not **ke ʻliʻi.*

10. Because there are no phonological clues to distinguish a Hawaiian compound from any other two-word combination, the committee (*ʻahahui*) used semantic criteria—that is, the concept of an idiom—to define compounds. See note 3, chapter 11.

11. Briefly, the committee recommended whether to write certain combinations of two grammatical markers as one word or two: for example, *me he* versus *mehe, a me* versus *ame,* etc.

12. For example, if writing *k* instead of both *k* and *t* eventually affected the pronunciation of Hawaiian, it was because those Hawaiians who knew English had become accustomed to perceiving two distinct sounds.

13. Research on this topic, outlined as a proposal, has not yet been carried out.

VOCABULARY

Chapters 12 and 13 discussed two major ways in which Hawaiian can add to its word stock, but it was from a mainly formal point of view: that is, examining the ways that Hawaiian builds words by combining different kinds of morphemes and by borrowing from other languages.

I now look at those topics from a different point of view, adding more detail about the motivation for adding to Hawaiian's vocabulary.

As noted earlier, the missionaries in the 1820s and 1830s were faced with a dilemma when they chose new words for foreign concepts. Should they adapt a word already in use and run the risk of confusing the old and new senses? Or should they borrow a word from English, Hebrew, or Greek and mar what some people thought of vaguely (and futilely) as the "purity" of the language?

While the previous two chapters showed the mechanics of making new words, here I touch on some of the other matters involved: language policy and perhaps a bit of linguistic chauvinism.

First I look at nineteenth-century policies connected with expanding the Hawaiian vocabulary—insofar as one is able to find any record of them.

Next, I examine policies from the recent past—that is, the period after the first edition of P-E was published (1957) and before Pūnana Leo and other immersion programs began.

Then, I take a brief look at the kinds of words that are now being consciously added to Hawaiian's vocabulary, the reasons for these additions, and the sources for these words.

Finally, I touch on some of the controversy connected with the deliberate molding of the Hawaiian vocabulary.

Nineteenth-Century Practices

Fortunately, a few of the missionaries who helped translate the Bible recorded how they invented new words, allowing us to see at least some of the principles they used to expand the vocabulary in one semantic field: Western religion. Foremost among them was Sheldon Dibble ([1839] 1909:137–38), who described in detail some of the different ways the missionaries found or created the additional words necessary for translating the Bible. The following quotations are from Dibble.

First, rather than invent a new word, they simply used an explanatory phrase, or, as Dibble described it, "In many instances they succeed, in a measure, but with circumlocution." An example of this kind of "circumlocution" is a phrase that translates 'smallpox': *ma'i pu'upu'u li'ili'i,* literally, 'disease [characterized by] scattered small lumps'. In that phrase, only existing Hawaiian words are used. Although the P-E definition begins with that phrase, it also lists a borrowing, *kamolapoki.*

Another method, discussed in chapter 13, was to combine existing words into compounds with idiomatic meanings: "In others they use a sort of patch-work of native words. For instance: manao [mana'o] means thought, and io ['i'o] means true or real;—so the combination, manaoio [mana'o'i'o], is used for faith. Again, manao means thought, and lana means buoyant,—so the combination, manaolana [mana'olana], is made by us to express hope. Ala means to rise, hou means again, and ana ['ana] is a participial termination;—so we make alahouana [alahou'ana] to signify the rising again, or the resurrection."

Finally, the translators resorted to outright borrowing: "Then again, in some cases we introduce words of English, Greek, and Hebrew origin."

The partial list of borrowings from Lorrin Andrews's dictionary (some of which are included in chapter 13) contains many examples from these three languages—and from some others as well. Incidentally, it is interesting to see that borrowing is the last method that Dibble discussed. Later in this chapter, you can see the same ranking reflected in current policies.

It is no surprise to find that the search for new words did not end once the Bible was translated. The missionaries also taught secular subjects in the local schools, and the curriculum they introduced to Hawaiian scholars abounded with technical terms for concepts that were foreign to Hawaiian culture.

Here are a few examples. In his Hawaiian grammar, Lorrin Andrews (1854) devised his own terms for a grammatical case system (based on Latin grammar). He chose the word *'aui* 'turn aside' for 'case', because that was the meaning of the Latin word *declinare* (as in the phrase 'to *decline* a noun'). Although Andrews's terms are not often used today, his explanation gives us a rare look at the reasoning that lay behind coining these new compounds: "*Aui kumu,* foundation case, i.e. is *nominative. Aui pili,* adhering case. *Aui iki,* so called with reference to the *aui pili,* i.e. *aui pili* adhering, aui iki, adhering a little [more] than aui pili from *iki* little.—*Aui paewa,* uneven case. *Aui alo,* the front case from its relation to the verb. *Aui moe,* lying down case, it often refers to rest *in* or *at* a place. *Aui hea,* the calling case. *Aui hele,* moving case, as *mai* implies motion. *Aui hui,* union case, as *me* signifies *with, in company. Aui ia* passive case; *ia* is the suffix of passive verbs. This case implies the agent after a passive verb" (1854:43). If you look in P-E or *Pocket Hawaiian Grammar* (Schütz, Kanada, and Cook 2005) just below the entry for *'aui,* you'll find the classical grammatical terms that translate these compounds.

In much the same way, the early translators and teachers used the word *helu* 'count' to form compounds for such arithmetic terms as "composite number," "prime factor," "subtrahend," "multiplicand," and several others.[14]

One way to estimate which and how many scholarly terms were needed in the first few decades of mission work is to find out what was taught in the schools. Hiram Bingham's description of the founding of the Lahainaluna "missionary seminary" in 1831 allows us to make such an estimate, for it sketches the curriculum for the four-year school:[15]

1st year. Arithmetic, Geometry, Trigonometry, Sacred Geography, Hawaiian Grammar, Languages to a select class.
2d year. Mathematics, embracing Algebra, Navigation, and Surveying, History, Languages for a select class.
3d year. Mathematics continued, Natural Philosophy, Church History, Languages for a select class.
4th year. Astronomy, Chemistry, Moral Philosophy, Church History, Languages for a select class. (Bingham 1847:423–24)

Bingham elaborated on this outline: "During the whole course, more or less attention, every week, is given to biblical instruction, embracing the interpretation of Scripture, evidences of Christianity, Archaeology, and Sacred Geography, Composition and Elocution. Systematic Theology was contemplated, as soon as sufficient advancement and preparation for it should be made. Music, vocal and instrumental, Penmanship, Drawing Maps, Engraving, Printing, Binding, Carpentry, Turnery, and Mason work, all received some attention" (424).

14. See the examples in chapter 12.

15. Bingham did not state specifically that all the instruction was in Hawaiian, but he made no mention of English.

Figure 14.1. Lahainaluna School

It might be safe to say that new words for this ambitious program would number in the hundreds, perhaps thousands. But we cannot help wondering how widely the new words were used and how many of them found a permanent place in the everyday Hawaiian vocabulary. (Still, the same is true of much of the technical vocabulary in any language.)

How did the textbooks of the period reflect this curriculum? Judd, Bell, and Murdoch's bibliography of Hawaiian imprints (1978) lists texts for the following academic subjects or activities:

reading in general	arithmetic	geography
geometry	quadrupeds	trigonometry
penmanship	astronomy	English grammar
anatomy	algebra	drawing
political economy	moral philosophy	ancient history
punctuation	surveying and navigation	

From the same source one finds that very few new academic texts were printed from about 1860 on. That date coincides roughly with a time that those with political influence disagreed about the respective merits of teaching in Hawaiian or English. In brief, the arguments ran along these lines: Those favoring Hawaiian maintained that the language was necessary to preserve the "nation." The opposing attitude, in contrast, can be seen in these words from the president of the Board of Education in 1884: "Why worry over the quality of teachers in Hawaiian? We shan't need them much longer anyway" (Reinecke 1969:49n.).[16]

The most drastic feature of this struggle was an 1896 law that banned Hawaiian in schools, both in the classroom and on the school grounds.[17] As a result, although Hawaiian continued to be spoken elsewhere and therefore could not have remained static, the flow of new words (at least scholarly terms) into Hawaiian must have been severely reduced when formal coursework in the various academic disciplines ended.[18]

Because Parker's 1922 revision of Andrews's 1865 dictionary contains no English-Hawaiian section, it is difficult to check it for new words for obviously introduced concepts. Part of Parker's commission was to deal with "ancient and modern Hawaiian words" (iii); he is said to have added some 500 words to the original work (Ashford 1987:13); and he noted that "Hawaiianized words derived from foreign speech have their place in the main body of the work" (vi).[19] However, a sample check for the Hawaiian equivalents of the words *telegraph, telephone, motion picture, phonograph, automobile, piano,* and *telegram* found none of these.[20]

Thus, the only way to discover how the vocabulary was keeping pace with technical innovations would be to examine carefully the Hawaiian language newspapers of that period. A half century ago, when I began

---

16. For more detail on the struggle between Hawaiian and English, see Schütz 1994, chapter 16.

17. Except for the school on Ni'ihau.

18. It would be interesting to study the Hawaiian-language newspapers of the following few decades, our major resource for the written language, to see if new words could be identified. Major projects digitizing the newspapers are underway (see below), but it is uncertain how researchers are making use of these data.

19. This statement refers to loanwords in the body of the dictionary, as well as the list of words beginning with "foreign" consonants, appearing at the end of the Hawaiian-English section (see chapter 13).

20. I chose these words because they referred to technology that would have been known in Hawai'i in 1915–1920, the period in which Parker worked on the dictionary. In the absence of an English-Hawaiian section, I used the terms from P-E for the search.

research on nineteenth-century Pacific linguistics, this seemingly innocuous chore involved squinting at yellow-brown pages, handling them with ill-fitting white gloves, and turning pages with a spatula. Microfilm was a welcome advance, but it was hard to search through, get in focus, read, and print. (Recently, it has become possible to copy a microfilm page directly to a thumb drive.) As the following quotation shows, modern technology has put a new spin on that task:

> **2003**. Ulukau, the Hawaiian Language Digital Library project, goes online, making available more than 100,000 pages of searchable newspaper archives, books, dictionaries, the Hawaiian Bible, *Ka Hoʻolina* journal and other source materials in the Hawaiian language.
>
> Bishop Museum's Hawaiian-language newspapers project, *Hoʻolaupaʻi,* starts to digitize pages from 125 different Hawaiian-language newspapers published from the early 1800s to mid-1990s. The longest running was *Ka Nupepa Kuakoa,* in print from 1861 to 1927. It had a total of 125,000 broadsheet pages, or 1 million manuscript pages. (Hale 2013:86)

A more recent project focuses on just the newspapers: "In 2012, [Puakea Nogelmeier] launched the Ike Kūokoʻa ('Liberating Knowledge'), an effort to digitize 125,000 pages of the 19th-century Hawaiian-language newspapers. (Over eight months, 2,700 volunteers from across the globe transcribed 16,000 typed-up newspaper pages.[21])" (Hale 2013:88)

Similar projects are underway at other institutions that focus on making Hawaiian language written material more accessible. For example, another treasure house of such records is the Hawaiian Mission Houses Historic Site and Archives:

> We have begun three projects that provide a basis of documentation for this collaboration. The first is the digital publication of more than 225 letters written by more than 35 Hawaiian aliʻi. This is the first time these letters have been brought together, transcribed, translated, and provided to the public. These letters are significant because they provide the perspective of the aliʻi on what the missionaries were doing with and for them at their request in the nineteenth century. These letters will be available at missionhouses.org on our website by the second week of November. (Woods 2016:1)

21. An anonymous reviewer (February 2016) pointed out that the volunteers were actually transcribing digital scans or correcting the results of optical character recognition scans.

Figure 14.2. Mary Kawena Pukui

The value of these projects cannot be overstated. As the body of native speakers has dwindled to the small number of Niʻihauans and students from immersion projects, the role of written records has become increasingly crucial. Such records represent not only the accumulated experience of cultural treasures such as Mary Kawena Pukui, but also that of many nineteenth-century writers—ordinary people with a variety of specialties.

In this area of study, the passage of time presents a paradox. As the era when the Hawaiian language and culture were flourishing fades further into the past, advancing technology makes the written records of that period more accessible—thus sharpening and widening our knowledge.

New Words in the Pukui-Elbert Dictionary

Since 1957, it has been difficult to separate the topic of Hawaiian vocabulary from P-E. As do most modern lexicographers, Pukui and Elbert considered themselves recorders, not coiners, of words.

Earlier, however, through necessity, people working with Hawaiian were forced to coin new words. The most obvious examples are those needed for Bible translation and for concepts introduced by the influx of

Figure 14.3. Samuel Hoyt Elbert

Western culture—both material and intellectual. And as chapter 8 noted, some grammarians of the period thought that Hawaiian lacked "abstract words and general terms."

Their additions show that even though Hawaiian was nearly dormant in the late 1950s, the vocabulary was still growing. For example, the first edition included words from "texts published since Annexation [including] names for technological advances and including recent vocabulary additions of World War II" (Pukui and Elbert 1957:xi). Later editions contain translations of (for example) *atomic, computer,* and *escalator.* However, the citations for these new words are not given.

The range of the dictionary, although admirably broad in the area of traditional culture, is, of necessity, minimal in some others, reflecting the ban on using Hawaiian as the language of instruction, in place for sixty years by the time the first edition was published.

For example, a casual check of the English-Hawaiian section of the 1986 edition shows that if science teachers in immersion classes confined themselves to words in the dictionary, it would be difficult to talk about trigonometry (with no words, for example, for *sine* or *cosine*) or chemistry (no word for *element,* and from the table of elements, only about fifteen, in common use, appear in the English-Hawaiian section).[22]

However, for many other fields, a great many words were added in editions that appeared after 1957. The preface to the 1986 edition (vii–xi) relates how the compilers changed the dictionary from edition to edition so that it could better serve its users' needs. For example, Pukui and Elbert explained how some of the additions came about: "Hawaiian-language newspapers—excellent sources for names of rains, stars, winds, *lua* fighting holds, and much else—were reexamined, as well as the important old books in Hawaiian by Kelekona and by Nakuina, and volumes 5 and 6 of the Fornander series. Many legal and land terms were uncovered by William H. Wilson and Ray Kalā Enos, as they translated Hawaiian-language documents at the Hawai'i State Archives" (1986:vii).

Nor did its scientific terminology remain static. Many terms were updated, and, with the help of a publication that appeared after the previous edition was published, many Ni'ihau plant names were included for the first time. All in all, about 4,000 words were added.

All these changes point to an important fact about lexicography: every dictionary is a work in progress. And every lexicographer must rely on specialists—not only to supply new entries but also to refine the information in the existing ones.

In summary, Pukui and Elbert were traditional lexicographers, well aware that their main task was to record and define words that already existed. The next section explains that current lexicographers have had to take a different approach to their work.

New Words for the Immersion Programs

While Pukui and Elbert were compiling the first edition of their dictionary and including commonly used loanwords, another major lexicographer in the Pacific, C. Maxwell Churchward, took a different approach to borrowed words in his *Tongan Dictionary* (1959). Not only did he include many English loanwords, but he also engaged in some creative lexicography

22. For example, arsenic, calcium (*puna* 'lime'), carbon, chlorine, copper, gold, iron, lead, mercury, oxygen, phosphorus, (potash), silver, sulphur, tin, zinc. There are no words for aluminum, iodine, neon, nickel, nitrogen, platinum, radium, silicon, uranium, tungsten, sodium, or magnesium—all words that are commonly used even outside a chemistry class.

that took the form of "language engineering." After estimating that "thousands of such [borrowed] words are now in common use," he continued: "Here and there I have gone a step further: after consultation with my native assistant, I have invented a Tonganized form of an English word that has not yet been assimilated but whose assimilation is almost certain to be called for sooner or later. See, for example, *palafini* (paraffin) and *paikeleti* (pikelet). All such words are marked with the sign ‡; and in each case, for the sake of natives using the dictionary, a Tongan explanation of the new word is given in the English-Tongan section" (Churchward 1959:viii).[23]

Even though the Hawaiian and Tongan dictionaries appeared at nearly the same time, the striking difference in their outlook concerning new vocabulary is directly related to the status of the languages in the 1950s: Tongan was flourishing, but Hawaiian was nearly moribund.

However, the status of Hawaiian was changing. In the 1980s and 1990s, in contrast to only three or four decades earlier, the main thrust of Hawaiian lexicography shifted from recording existing words to coining new ones. In other words, its philosophy had made a full circle since the mid-1800s. This change is a direct result of new developments in Hawaiian language policy.

As noted earlier, because few classes were taught in Hawaiian for nearly a century, the vocabulary needed for various subjects had not been kept current. Before the renaissance and the dramatic growth of interest in the language, dormant vocabulary growth was not a problem. But with the increasing number of immersion programs and their need for words relevant to elementary and secondary school subjects, the teachers of these courses were faced with the same task that the early Bible translators found so daunting. The introduction to *Māmaka Kaiao* (1998) stated the problem as follows: "The first Lexicon Committee was established in 1987–1988 to create words for concepts and material culture unknown to our ancestors. Committee members were native speakers of Hawaiian—most of them elderly—who saw the value in and the need for creating new Hawaiian words." The need for new words leads to two questions. First, what kinds of words are needed? That is, which school subjects need a vocabulary update or overhaul? Next, how should new words be formed?

23. The promise was not always kept. I chose ‡*kapaleta* at random; the entry for English *carburetor* (Commonwealth spelling) consists only of the borrowed Tongan form. In contrast, the entries for *kāpasa* and *compass* contain a short explanation.

What Words Are Needed?

Language planners must decide on a policy that defines the scope of new vocabulary. Is it realistic to try to find or invent Hawaiian words for all semantic fields? At first, one is tempted to answer, no. But on the other hand, as the immersion programs grow, new words will be needed to cover the progress that the various sciences have made since schoolbooks were translated in the nineteenth century. As a result, this question is not easy to answer.

Even classifying the words into existing scholastic disciplines can be difficult. One might think that records from the past would allow us to compare the current curriculum with that of over a century ago. But during the elapsed time, some familiar subjects have taken on unfamiliar names. For example, instead of courses in public speaking, rhetoric, debate, and grammar, one might find all these subjects (and more) grouped under "language arts" or "communication." History and geography, prominent in the Lahainaluna curriculum of the 1830s, were later called "social studies."

Even if a current subject was also taught in the nineteenth century, new words are needed to reflect how that discipline has changed. For example, some of the basic concepts from the field of grammar have trickled down to the language arts. But many of the terms are new. An English teacher may have used (and understood) the term *transitive* in 1860, but the idea of the *phoneme,* as we know it today, did not come into general use among linguists until the 1920s or 1930s, and even now it is not well known outside the field.[24] And although phonetic terminology expanded greatly from the 1840s on, most of it has never been in general use. Still, such terms are widely used in many language-teaching textbooks.

Another development is that entirely new disciplines have emerged as primary and high school curricula have changed. Who could have predicted, even as recently as the 1980s, that computer terminology would be needed at the elementary school level?

In 2003, students in the Hawaiian Language Immersion Program chose from among the following courses:[25]

---

24. The earliest (and only) citation in the *Oxford English Dictionary* is 1894.

25. Mahalo to Puanani Wilhelm for supplying this information (3 November 2003). Some of the courses are required for graduation and others are elective. Still, all of them require Hawaiian terminology.

Algebra	English	Hawaiian Language Arts
Algebra II	Geometry	Modern Hawaiian History
Biology	Guidance	Physical Education
Chemistry	Health	Physical Science
Civics	U.S. History	World History

In 2017, there was no difference between requirements for Hawaiian immersion students and mainstream students to graduate from high school. However, one difference is that for the immersion schools, Hawaiian satisfies the two-year language requirement. One or two schools offered another language, but at the time it was difficult to find teachers fluent in Hawaiian who were also qualified to teach another language.[26]

One has only to compare this curriculum with that from the samples given above for Lahainaluna in the 1830s, and the fields represented by the textbooks published in the next decades, to see the problems that face language planners.

For example, the following words from *Māmaka Kaiao* represent only a small sample of the new vocabulary proposed (reflected by most of the examples beginning with *a-*):

Natural science

au·kahi	electric current	*au makani kikī*	jet stream
au mā·ʻalo·ʻalo	AC		

Social science

au·pana	rhythm (speech)

Material culture

aeʻo·lele	pogo stick	*ahi·kao*	rocket
aho ʻea	monofilament		

Computers

ahu hoʻo·koe	cache	*awa ala pili·pā*	parallel port
haka·haka·pā	disk space	*awa ala pū·kaʻina*	serial port

26. Mahalo to Keao NeSmith and Kalehua Krug for this information (April 2017).

Here is a more informal treatment of some of the semantic fields covered in the new glossary (with only the English translation for a sample term):

athletics (*fast break*)
botany (*hawthorn*)
food (*frozen yoghurt*)
mathematics (*function*)
physiology (*cochlea*)
geology (*fault*)
literature (*nonfiction*)
astronomy (*planetarium*)
forestry (*watchtower*)
communication (*airmail*)
highways (*asphalt*)
modern life (*pollution*)
construction (*four-by-four*)
linguistics (*fricative*)
geography (*Grand Canyon*)
mineralogy (*turquoise*)
education (*workshop*)
cinema (*movie studio*)
animal husbandry (*stable*)
zoology (*carnivore*)
playground equipment (*monkey bars, jungle gym*)

Most of the examples above represent current or recent culture. And as culture continues its inevitable change, more words will be needed in the future.

A recent example reflects not a cultural change but a biological one. Beginning in 2010, scientists and landowners noticed that an icon of Hawaiian forests was being severely affected by the spread of a new disease—rapid *ʻōhiʻa* death (Two new species of fungi that kill ʻōhiʻa trees get Hawaiian names 2018). The cause was found to be two new species of fungi, and their names were chosen to describe their effect on the *ʻōhiʻa:* "*Ceratocystis huliohia* (changes the natural state of ʻōhiʻa), and *Ceratocystis lukuohia* (destroyer of ʻōhiʻa)."[27] Choosing the names was a collaborative effort between the scientists and Hawaiian cultural experts. One member of this team, Kekuhi Kealiʻikanakaʻoleohaililani of the the Edith Kanakaʻole Foundation, explained, "The names are necessary because the 'thing' we need to confront and remove from our reality must have a name."

27. *Huli* 'to turn, reverse . . . '; *luku* 'destroy, lay waste . . . ' Note that in the second part of the binomial nomenclature, spelling rules do not allow an *ʻokina* or a *kahakō,* both of which are necessary to spell the name *ʻōhiʻa.*

How Should New Words Be Formed?

In general, the new words proposed by the committees and published in various editions of *Papa Hua'ōlelo* and *Māmaka Kaiao* follow the patterns described in chapters 12 and 13, although the language planners seem to have made an effort to avoid outright borrowings unless absolutely necessary. For example, there are

1. compounds made of wholly indigenous words:
   hale ho'oikaika kino 'fitness center' (lit., house for bodily strengthening)
   kula ho'owela wai 'water heater' (lit., container for water heating)
   kukui hāweo 'fluorescent light' (lit., glowing light)
2. compounds made up of an indigenous word plus a borrowed word:
   waiu pauka 'powdered milk'
3. straightforward borrowings:
   'amakila 'armadillo' *naelona* 'nylon'
   'alakeka 'alligator' *kiniki* 'zinc'
   'aluminuma 'aluminum'
4. and new combinations of borrowings:
   mīkini panakō 'automated-teller machine' (lit., bank machine, both borrowings).

In addition, some new coinings are based on forms in other Polynesian languages. For example, in their search for a word for "arrow" as an indicator, not a weapon, coiners may have avoided the term *pua* because the form represents so many different words (homonyms) in addition to "arrow." They chose *nahau,* a new form based on Proto-Polynesian **ngāsau.*[28]

One must be careful, however, not to coin a new word for a particular concept when one already exists. As noted in chapter 13, Andrews warned against such a practice. Perhaps new grammatical terms can serve as an example. *Māmaka Kaiao* has introduced a number of new grammatical terms for concepts that can be found in Andrews 1865 or P-E. However, the new terms do have one advantage over the older ones: they are shorter. It may have been felt that single-word terms were easier for students to remember (and use) than phrases.

---

28. Cf. Fijian *gasau.*

As mentioned above, the committee seems to have avoided borrowing from English whenever possible.[29] But many other language-policy bodies have similar policies. Perhaps one of the most extreme is the French Académie, which has tried (sometimes unsuccessfully) to prohibit using such words as *weekend* and *drugstore* in French. In general, speakers tend to ignore strictures against borrowing.

Legislating the Vocabulary?

Although we might not think that adding to the store of words in a language would be controversial, it can actually turn out to be a linguistic land mine. Not only do some people disagree about the source of new words, but they also criticize the very act of adding to the vocabulary. Some users will fault a dictionary for being too conservative, others for being too lenient, and still others for being too authoritarian. They fault it for including some words and excluding others.

Hawaiian dictionaries have not escaped such criticism. The Reverend Lorenzo Lyons, commenting on Andrews's dictionary, wrote, "There were some bad words that ought not to appear in a dictionary" (1878). Another missionary objected to its including "old pule and mele words not understood now even by the oldest" (Elbert 1954:16).

Just as some critics objected to these old words, others have objected to new ones. In the mid-1950s, when P-E was underway, Elbert gave this sensible rejoinder to such complaints: "Some have said that loan words should be omitted because they are not really Hawaiian. According to such reasoning, an English dictionary should be limited to words of Germanic origin" (1954:15). Continuing on that theme, if we were to purge English of borrowings (mainly from French—a result of the Norman Conquest), we would lose about 383 of our 1,000 most commonly used words.

Elbert continued, "If we omitted the Hawaiian words that have come from English, Greek, or Hebrew, we would have to go back to the days before Captain Cook. We could not telephone, tell time, marry, get baptized, read the Bible, drink coffee, spend money, or use soap" (1954:15).

The introduction to *Māmako Kaiao* contains this eloquent passage: "The root of any culture is its language. For Hawaiian culture to survive,

---

29. For a description of a similar policy for Māori, see Harlow 1993.

the Hawaiian language must flourish. Use these new words and make them part of your life. Let us continue resolutely to carry forward the precious gift that is the native language of Hawaiʻi into the dawning of a new era" (2003).

However, the year 1997 saw an attempt not to adapt Hawaiian to a *new* era but to keep it in an *old* one. According to reports in the Honolulu newspapers, a trustee dictated that in the Hawaiian language program at the Kamehameha Schools, teachers should use no words that were not in P-E 1986.[30]

It is difficult to find any justification for such a constraint. Would it protect the "purity" or "authenticity" of the language? For the most part, such terms are meaningless when applied to vocabulary.

Suppose, for example, that the 1957 edition of the dictionary had been chosen. As we saw earlier, the available stock of words would have fallen by about 4,000.

If the attempt to restrict the vocabulary was an effort to limit Hawaiian words in the classroom to those found in traditional stories, chants, or legends, it was doomed from the start. No Hawaiian dictionary, from Andrews's *Vocabulary* (1836a) to the various editions of P-E, has followed such a policy. Here is what Pukui and Elbert wrote on that topic in the preface to the first edition of their dictionary:

> The implications of the descriptive approach pervade every aspect of the lexicographer's trade. He is permitted no personal predilections for words of native origin as opposed to words from foreign sources, for ancient words as opposed to newer ones, for words of one standard dialect as opposed to another, for pronunciations conforming to the spelling as opposed to pronunciations heard in the fast colloquial conversation of cultivated speakers. He must not frame condemnatory definitions of customs of which he may not privately approve, nor on the other hand may he glorify the past or purge from it what he may deplore. Nor may he blanch at risqué terms. In short, he is a reporter and in his role of lexicographer he never takes the part of teacher, missionary, innovator, or purist. (1957:ix)

Their attitude is in stark contrast to that of Lyons, quoted earlier in this section, who objected to the "bad words" in Andrews's dictionary.

As for the attempt to limit the Hawaiian used in language classes to words in a particular dictionary, it was also counter to common sense. No language can be frozen in time—and expect to live.

---

30. See Daws and Nā Leo o Kamehameha 2009:127–45.

GRAMMAR

Although spelling changes and new words in Hawaiian are often easy to notice, changes in the grammar are harder to pin down. Still, people closely connected with language teaching have noticed them and have commented on them.

How do such changes come about? It is possible that translating from English to Hawaiian fixed in the minds of many nonnative Hawaiian speakers (including teachers) a number of misconceptions about Hawaiian grammar and style. For example, consider these assumptions, generally true for English grammar:

- Every sentence must have a subject and a predicate.
- Every count noun must be marked for number (i.e., singular and plural).
- Every verb must be marked for tense.

Although it would be hard to find such explicit statements applying these rules to Hawaiian, they are often implied, especially in older grammars written by nonprofessionals. But the writers of even some twentieth-century grammars seem to have ignored all the linguistic advances of the period. The following quotation is from a textbook for the territorial schools:

> THE NOUN
>
> The Noun may be qualified as to Gender, Number, and Case.
>
> Gender: Masculine, Feminine, or Neuter.
>
> As in English, only living creatures are masculine or feminine; all other nouns are neuter.
>
> Gender may be expressed by the use of a different word:
>
> He elemakule. An old man.
>
> He luahine. An old woman.
>
> Gender may be expressed by applying the terms "kane" or "wahine":
>
> He popoki kane. A tomcat.
>
> He popoki wahine. A she-cat. (Atcherley 1930:23–24)

The problem here is that Hawaiian does not have grammatical gender, and the difference between, for example, *pōpoki kāne* and *pōpoki wahine* has little to do with grammar.[31]

Misinterpretations of another grammatical category—tense—are more subtle. Andrews was careful to warn the reader that the "grand divisions of past, present and future are somewhat distinctly marked; but in practice they run into each other" (1854:103). In other words, we can't apply the categories of English or Latin to Hawaiian without making many changes.

But when Henry P. Judd produced his so-called *Complete Grammar*, he categorized verbs neatly into present, past, perfect, pluperfect, and future (1939:8–11). In particular, the aspect marker *ua* was called a perfect tense marker.

However, the function of *ua* is more complicated than that. When used with a verb of action, it does show that the action has been completed. For example, *Ua hele au i nehinei.* 'I went yesterday.' But when used with a verb that shows a state (such verbs are sometimes called statives or adjectives), *ua* shows that the state has been attained, and moreover, that it contrasts with a previous state. For example, *Ua ola au.* 'I'm well (now, but was previously ill).'

Elbert and Pukui's treatment of tense (1979:57–58) is more sophisticated, but it still tends to confuse the topics of "time" and "tense"—in other words, semantics and grammar. This confusion is illustrated by the following sentence: "Time words may make past tense of any verb" (58). For example, the word *nehinei* 'yesterday' in a sentence makes it clear that a state or action occurred in the past. But the term itself has nothing to do with grammar.

At first, an incorrect and scanty grammatical description may seem to have little effect on changing Hawaiian grammar, but the topics are connected. For example, if grammarians describe and teach *ua* as a required tense marker to students, some of whom will eventually be language teachers, then successive generations of students may learn it and use it that way—and only in that way.

---

31. In 1812, William Marsden wrote in his Malay grammar, "The absurdity of attributing difference of sex to things, or to the names of things not organized by nature to reproduce their kind, did not suggest itself to the framers or methodisers of the Malayan tongue." He suggested that such distinctions "are best sought for in a dictionary."

Apparently, such changes are a real problem. In the speech style he called "Neo-Hawaiian," Keao NeSmith observed "consistent use of *ua* (*verb*) . . . in expressing English past-tense in the active voice" (2002:15).[32] In contrast, he noted that the other traditional methods of expressing similar ideas were not used.

Similarly, some speakers now are using the stative verbs *loaʻa* 'found, gotten' and *maopopo* 'understood' as active verbs ('find, get'; 'understand').[33] But it is not clear whether this change is an innovation by immersion school students or a variation that has existed for much longer. For example, it is found (but rarely) in some old texts (NeSmith, pers. comm., January 2009).

Summary

Language change and variation are signs of vitality, for only dead (or unused) languages remain the same. Argument and disagreement over grammar and vocabulary are natural. And speakers often exhibit the two opposing forces of conservation versus innovation.

Earlier it was noted that one scholar suggested that one form of Hawaiian, Niʻihauan, might be expected to exhibit fewer changes, with less influence from outside. But that study focused on phonetics. Other reports, on different areas of the language, showed different results. For example, Jeffrey Kapali Lyon learned in Ipo Wong's ʻŌlelo Niʻihau course that some minimal pairs for *t* and *k* had developed. He also noticed that in church services, oral reading of the Bible used only *k* (as written), and not *t*.

Perhaps these two examples show that conservation can affect some parts of the language, while innovation can affect others.

Even though some critics use the terms "University Hawaiian" or "UH dialect" for the type of language learned through tertiary instruction, it is impossible now to teach exactly the kind of Hawaiian that was spoken two centuries ago. The language *has* changed and will continue to do so,

32. Early Bible translations into Fijian exhibit the same tendency with *sā*, a marker that functions similarly to Hawaiian *ua*. Atcherley (1930:44) treated *ua* as an indicator of both the pluperfect and perfect tenses.

33. Jeffrey Kapali Lyon added (pers. comm., 30 March 2017), "While *maopopo* might have real examples in the nineteenth century as a rare transitive, I don't think this is so of *loaʻa*."

so long as it is still spoken. Some people interested in the language, such as linguists, are concerned primarily with documenting those changes. Others, sometimes termed "language planners," are concerned more with influencing the direction and extent of the changes. Still others are concerned that new words are being coined without adequate research in nineteenth-century sources for words that escaped the notice of dictionary compilers. Finally, some new words simply appear in scholarly works without the background information that would allow scholars to document their etymology.

VERBATIM

Most of this chapter has focused on changing the vocabulary of Hawaiian by adding to it. But there has been another kind of change that is harder to deal with—loss. Often one feels that so much more of the language could be documented if we could go back in time. For example, in 1836, Lorrin Andrews felt that the Hawaiians' knowledge of their language—especially poetic language—was intact. He wrote, perhaps naively, "There is no probability as there is no evidence, that the Hawaiian language has undergone any material changes for many generations. The *meles* and *kaaos* [*ka'ao*] (songs and legends) of the ancients are understood and recited by the people of the present time" (Andrews 1836b:14). These comments should be taken with several grains of salt. When Andrews made them, he had been in Hawai'i less than a decade. Moreover, there was no way to prove or disprove his assertion that this part of the language had not changed, because there were no written records to consult. Finally, certain branches of comparative linguistics were in their infancy, and we have no idea how much Andrews knew about them.

However, thirty years later Andrews's opinions had changed. By 1865, he had realized that unless someone recorded Hawaiian songs and legends, such material might be lost—at least to outsiders. In the later years of his life, he began translating "the ancient meles, *Haui ka lani* and *Kualii*" (*Missionary Album* 1969:27), noting that certain types of specialized vocabulary had not been recorded in a form that non-Hawaiians could use. Near the end of the preface to his dictionary, he expanded on that theme:

> There are several departments of the language the words of which are but feebly represented in this Dictionary. That which relates to the imaginative

in the Kaaos or Legends of different classes,—that which relates to what may be termed their philosophical views, i.e., their mode of accounting for natural phenomena, as the creation of their own islands,—the Origin of their Religious rites,—and especially the power of imagination displayed in their Meles and the consequent richness of their language for expressing the nicest shades of love, of hatred, of jealousy and revenge, and the language employed by the priests when drawing on their gods for assistance, are but partially presented in the definitions of this Dictionary. The Kaao of Laieikawai [*Lāʻieikawai*] is almost the only specimen of that species of language which has been laid before the public.[34] (Andrews 1865)

In 1865, however, there were few signs that the poetic language would not continue to be transmitted in the usual way. Had Andrews been able to look into the future, he might well have been concerned not only that the richness of poetic language be denied to Hawaiian readers, but also that its very survival was threatened. Andrews continued, "*Many fine specimens have been printed in the Hawaiian periodicals, but are neither seen nor regarded by the foreign community* [emphasis added]. Volumes more of the same quality as Laieikawai might be collected and printed and whose moral influence would be no worse on Hawaiian minds than the famous Scott's Novels are on English readers."

In recent years, these periodicals have been recognized as a treasure trove of language and culture, and—as noted earlier—scholars are making more and more newspapers available online in a searchable format.

As for changes in the dictionary, the following quotation highlights its evolving nature from edition to edition:

In addition to entirely new entries and meanings, many changes have been effected that, we hope, will increase the usefulness of the book. These include a means of showing stress groups to facilitate pronunciation of words with more than three syllables; indication of Hawaiian parts of speech; scientific names of plants changed since the early 1950s; additional ancestral reconstructions; classical origins of Hawaiian borrowings; corrections of previous entries that were made as knowledge of the language progressed; and many more cross references that, when consulted, should enhance understanding of words and their many nuances. (Pukui and Elbert 1986:vii)

34. A recent dramatization of this story was mentioned in chapter 10.

CHAPTER 15

EXPANDING BILINGUAL DICTIONARIES

Hawaiian has an extremely rich vocabulary, which was and is used by speakers. Not all Hawaiian words have been collected, and Pukui-Elbert, excellent as it is, needs to be supplemented by wider reading. Hawaiian was a very productive language, and reduplicatives, for instance were easy to create. The chanter of the KL [*Kumulipo*] seems particularly fond of reduplicatives. The reader should not be surprised to find forms that are not in the dictionary or that are there but with different meanings.

—Elbert and Pukui, *Hawaiian Grammar*

Moreover, dictionary glosses are the products of interpretation, and the tendency has been to include as many glosses as possible to cover all possibilities. Not every gloss is relevant. Not every meaning of a word is intended to be felt in every use.

—John Charlot *A Kumulipo of Hawaiʻi*

In the field of language preservation, many linguists and language teachers have written about the success of Hawaiian immersion programs. Often, these programs have inspired similar work in other language families as well.[1]

1. For example, an article on revitalizing some Native American languages (Nijhuis 2003:38) notes that programs for Māori and Hawaiian have served as models for similar attempts to ward off language death.

Here, I discuss not the programs themselves but the materials that support them—an often-neglected area that I consider to be one of the cornerstones of any language revitalization effort. I will examine some existing materials and propose others that might be needed for the future.

BASIC PEDAGOGICAL MATERIALS

Reference materials for teaching Hawaiian fill two main needs. First, as the section heading implies, they form an essential part of language teaching and learning. Next, they can act as a repository of information to be drawn on if human resources, such as knowledgeable elders, are scarce or completely missing. In other words, such materials can be the cornerstones of language documentation, necessary for recording endangered languages and fostering their preservation. In the following sections, I suggest some areas in which older Hawaiian lexicographic works might be reorganized and new ones developed.

Updated and Improved Bilingual Dictionary

Although apparently unnoticed as a significant date, 2007 marked the fiftieth anniversary of the publication of the first edition of Mary Kawena Pukui and Samuel H. Elbert's *Hawaiian-English Dictionary* (abbreviated here and elsewhere as P-E). This work has served as an invaluable resource for nearly all aspects of the Hawaiian "Renaissance." *Kāhuna* (in the sense of 'experts') from activities ranging from the *Hōkūleʻa* to *hālau hula* to *mele* have acknowledged their debt to this essential reference work.

But no work of this kind is so nearly perfect that it cannot be improved. It has been suggested that criticizing some aspects of P-E was inappropriate, because many Hawaiians considered it the "Bible of the present Hawaiian language movement." Such an attitude is puzzling, because as the last chapter noted, the compilers themselves changed the dictionary significantly through its several editions.

Moreover, further changes might be made if the Hawaiian scholarly community is fortunate enough to find lexicographers with the combination of knowledge and dedication that Pukui and Elbert had. Possible changes fall into the following categories, phrased as questions:

1. How do we define a word?
2. What constitutes an entry?
3. How can nineteenth-century printed material increase the word count?
4. What minor changes are necessary to improve the accuracy and utility of the dictionary?

How Do We Define a Word?

What does it mean to define a word? (In other words, how do we define *define?*) This question sounds simple, but the form of a definition depends mainly on whether it appears in a bilingual or a monolingual dictionary. As the term *bilingual* implies, this type of dictionary lists headwords in one language and gives their meanings (i.e., equivalents) in another language. For most headwords, it means simply translating them into the other language. This can be called the *translating mode;* for example, *hale* 'house'. However, this approach assumes that for every word in Hawaiian, one can find a matching word in English. Lexicographers warn against taking such an assumption for granted: "Linguists and lexicographers have recognized that, except for some scientific and technical vocabularies, many lexical items in any language are culture-specific or culture-bound, and that, consequently, one must be cautious about assuming the absolute equivalency of *any* [emphasis added] two items in different languages" (Benson 1990:43).

Although this point of view is extreme, it is theoretically correct. Even with words that represent common items shared by both cultures, we could not defend the idea that the meanings of, for example, Hawaiian *hale* and English *house* are identical.[2] This practice illustrates a major shortcoming of P-E: to assume implicitly that a translation can serve as a definition or explanation.

For some entries, minimal changes within the definition would make it more professional. For example, P-E's definition of *kahuna* begins "Priest, sorcerer, magician, wizard, minister, expert in any profession . . ." Simply changing the order would produce this improved version: "Expert in any profession, such as priest, sorcerer, magician, wizard, minister."

2. See the *hale/home* example in chapter 14.

Even with the existing dictionary, users can flesh out the basic definition by scanning following entries. Returning to the *hale* 'house' example cited earlier, one finds that the main entry is followed by 162 phrases or compounds beginning with *hale.*

Although the translating mode is not ideal, many items in the Hawaiian lexicon can be defined that way—for example, names of plants, animals, fish, and body parts. But how does a bilingual dictionary deal with an idea or an item that is not shared by both cultures and languages? To answer this question, one must first examine how a monolingual dictionary defines a word. In the simplest terms, a monolingual dictionary defines by putting the item in a class and then distinguishing it from other members of that class. For example, consider the following definition (*Merriam-Webster's Collegiate Dictionary,* eleventh edition [2003]): "**cat**: a carnivorous mammal (*Felis catus*) long domesticated as a pet and for catching rats and mice." *Mammal* names the class and also tells something about its form. The rest of the definition distinguishes *cat* from other members of the class (mainly by the words *domesticated* and *pet*) and by identifying its function ("catching rats and mice"). The scientific name adds information as well. This entry is an example of the *defining mode.*

As a Hawaiian example of the defining mode used to explain a culturally specific term, note Andrews's (1865) definition of *kapu,* in which he first established a class:[3] "A general name of the system of religion that existed formerly in the islands . . ." and then distinguished it from others in that class by listing some of its characteristics: ". . . and which was grounded upon numerous kapus or restrictions, keeping the common people in obedience to the chiefs and the priests." Finally, he switched to the translating mode by adding synonyms: "The word signifies prohibited, forbidden, sacred, devoted to certain purposes."[4]

Compare Andrews's treatment with the P-E definition of *kapu,* which does not name the class but begins in the translating mode: "Taboo, prohibition; special privilege or exemption from ordinary taboo, sacredness; prohibited, forbidden; sacred, holy, consecrated; no trespassing, keep out." With the exception of one explanatory phrase, this "definition"

3. Earlier (1836a), Andrews had compiled a 132-page "vocabulary" of Hawaiian.

4. John Charlot noted (pers. comm., 16 March 2014) that Andrews's definition reflects the missionary, not the Hawaiian point of view.

consists entirely of translations. Note also the compilers' tendency to list a string of synonyms.[5]

Perhaps one of the clearest examples of P-E's focus on translating, to the exclusion of defining, is its treatment of the word *aloha:* "Aloha, love, affection, compassion, mercy, sympathy, pity, kindness, sentiment, grace, charity; greeting, salutation, regards; sweetheart, lover, loved one; beloved, loving, kind, compassionate, charitable, lovable; to love, be fond of; to show kindness, mercy, pity, charity".

As another example, note Andrews's definition of *poi.* Encyclopedic in nature, it gives us information about *kalo* and its importance in the Hawaiian diet: "***poi*** The paste or pudding which was formerly the chief food of Hawaiians, and is so to a great extent yet. It is made of kalo, sweet potatoes or breadfruit, but mostly of kalo, by baking the above articles in ovens under ground, and afterwards peeling and pounding them with more or less water (but not much); it is then left in a mass to ferment; after fermentation it is again worked over with more water until it has the consistency of thick paste. It is eaten cold with the fingers."

The P-E definition uses the defining mode (possibly because there is no simple one-to-one translation): "***poi*** The Hawaiian staff of life, made from cooked taro corms, or rarely breadfruit, pounded and thinned with water." (However, even the name of the class, "staff of life," is an idiom that younger readers may not be familiar with. Andrews's phrase, "chief food," is more direct.)

Judd-Pukui-Stokes 1945 used the translating mode, but not very wisely. Only someone who already knows what *poi* is and how it is used could understand the following definition: "***poi:*** taro paste."

In defense of P-E's approach to defining, one should remember that every dictionary is a product of its time. When the project began in 1949 (Pukui and Elbert 1957:viii), it is unlikely that either compiler (or anyone else then, for that matter) could have foreseen the linguistic and cultural revival that was to begin in the 1970s.

One phrase reveals the compilers' view of the future of Hawaiian: Elbert described the work as "what will probably be the last of the many Hawaiian dictionaries" (1954:17). With interest in Hawaiian at an all-time low in the 1950s and 1960s, it is reasonable to suppose that the compilers thought

---

5. As James T. Collins suggested (pers. comm., October 1992), such a definition reads like an English thesaurus.

Figures 15.1. Cultivating and harvesting *kalo,* the "staff of life"

Figures 15.2. Cultivating and harvesting *kalo,* the "staff of life"

Figures 15.3. Cultivating and harvesting *kalo,* the "staff of life"

Figure 15.4. Pounding poi

that the main use of the dictionary would be a resource not for promoting the growth of the Hawaiian language in the future but instead for viewing the past by helping to translate the legends, folklore, and genealogies that had been preserved. (As a matter of fact, this use is still an important one.)

*

The next suggestion for improving the bilingual dictionary investigates what looks deceptively like a simple matter—whether certain forms are all the same word or different words—but it is actually a problem for many languages.

What Constitutes an Entry?

It is important to remember that in a sense, P-E began as a revision of Andrews's dictionary (1865) and, by extension, of the version compiled by Henry H. Parker in 1922. But it was much more than just a revision: "It soon became apparent that thoroughgoing changes were necessary in the Andrews-Parker dictionary if it were to be in line with present-day lexicography, and that it would be neither accurate nor ethical to call the new work a revision of the previous dictionary" (P-E 1957:viii).[6]

Still, Andrews's dictionaries—both the original and Parker's revision—served as starting points for the new work. But many changes had to be made. For example, in the original, Andrews did not recognize long vowels or *'okina*. Although Parker attempted to remedy this fault, his lack of knowledge of even the rudiments of phonetics and phonology made the pronunciation transcription after each headword nearly useless.

Nor was Elbert satisfied with Parker's concept of what constituted an entry. He explained, "The entire concept of a 'word' in Andrews-Parker seems questionable. Phonetically similar items with *different* meanings are grouped together under one entry if they are a single part of speech, but phonetically similar items with the *same* meaning are listed as *separate* entries if they occur as different parts of speech. Thus a single entry has items with different meanings, and separate entries have the same meaning" (1954:15).

To illustrate the problem, I begin with the original source (Andrews 1865) and its six entries (unnumbered in the original) for what was written as *U-A*. The modern spelling appears in the right-hand column. (Abbreviations for both Andrews and Andrews-Parker are as follows: v. = verb, n. = noun, adj. = adjective, adv. = adverb, dem. = demonstrative, pron. = pronoun. Preterite = past.)

---

6. The compilers retained Parker's, not Andrews's alphabetical order.

WORD	PART OF SPEECH	ENGLISH GLOSS	MODERN SPELLING
1. **U-A**	v.	to rain	**ua**
2. **U-A**	n.	rain	**ua**
3. **U-A**	adj.	vain	**ʻuʻa**
4. **U-A**	adv.	in vain	**ʻuʻa**
5. **U-A**	dem.	that	**ua**
6. **U-A**	tense	preterite	**ua**

First, if one relies on the English glosses, it is evident that there are two entries for ʻrain'—one a verb, and the other a noun. Similarly, there are two entries for ʻvain'—one an adjective, and one an adverb. Such a practice, repeated throughout Andrews's dictionary, reflects a pattern in Hawaiian grammar: many words can serve two or three different functions without changing their form. The following examples illustrate this feature:

Noun	*ʻIke ʻoe i ka* ***hula****?*	ʻDo you know (how to dance) the *hula?*'
Verb	*E* ***hula*** *ana ka wahine.*	ʻThe woman is dancing the *hula.*'
Adj.	*He kumu* ***hula*** *ʻo ia.*	ʻ(S)he is a *hula* master.'

In the first example, *hula* appears after the article *ka,* which marks it as a noun. In the second, it appears in the progressive/continuative[7] frame *e . . . ana,* which indicates that it is a verb. In the third, it appears after a noun and modifies it, which identifies it as an adjective.

Andrews dealt with this property of the language by making separate entries for words that could serve as different parts of speech. For example, he divided the word *maikaʻi* ʻgood' into three entries: one each for the word's use as an adjective, a noun, or a verb.

As noted in Elbert's assessment above, Parker continued that approach in his revision and compounded the confusion because he (like Andrews) was unable to recognize vowel length or the glottal stop at the beginning

7. This construction indicates that an action is in progress but has not been completed.

of a word. Following Andrews, he listed six *ua* entries. The pronunciation band includes symbols for the glottal stop, vowel length, and accent. The modern spelling appears in the right-hand column, and the order has been changed to match the one that Andrews used:

1. **ua** (ū′-a)	v.	to rain	**ua**
2. **ua** (ū′-a)	n.	rain	**ua**
3. **ua** (u'a)	adj.	useless	**'u'a**
4. **ua** (u'a)	adv.	in vain	**'u'a**
5. **ua** (ū′-a)	adj., pron.	aforementioned	**ua**
6. **ua** (u′-a)	prefix	perfect tense [i.e., aspect]	**ua**

(Note that although 1, 2, 5, and 6 have the same pronunciation, Parker transcribed 1, 2, and 5 with a long vowel in the first syllable.)[8]

In summary, just as in Andrews's earlier treatment, there are two phonological forms—*'u'a* and *ua*—and the latter represents three separate words that just happen to have the same shape. In short, there should be four headwords—(1, 2), (3, 4), (5), (6).

In light of Elbert's criticism of the Andrews-Parker concept of a "word" (see the quotation above), how did the compilers of the new dictionary handle this problem? First, because of their careful attention to the *'okina,* especially at the beginning of a word, where it was hard for speakers of English to hear,[9] they gave *'u'a* its own entry.[10]

But what of the three separate words with the same spelling—*ua?* Here is a truncated copy of the entry from P-E (many example phrases and sentences have been omitted): "**ua. 1.** nvi [noun, intransitive verb] Rain; to rain; rainy. See **rain** . . . **2.** demon [strative]. Aforementioned, the one talked of . . . **3**. Common part[icle] preceding verbs and denoting completed or recently completed action; to become." Typographically, at least, one is forced to assume that these three subentries all belong to the

8. Perhaps he perceived *ua* 6 as different because it is never accented in a phrase. Before accent and vowel length were well understood, they were often confused.

9. See the discussion of Gaussin in chapter 8 and in Schütz 1994:145.

10. However, another meaning was added to that entry: *'u'a* 2: 'A coarse mat or tapa'. Is there any obvious connection to the meaning 'useless'? Surely this word should have had its own entry.

"same word": they appear in the same entry (and the same paragraph), separated only by subentry numbers. However, the meanings are as disparate as 'rain', 'aforementioned', and perfective aspect. Moreover, notice how the types of meanings differ. It is inconvenient and misleading for the user to see content forms and function forms listed under the same headword. If this entry represents the P-E concept of "word," then it is just as suspect as that of Andrews and Parker.[11]

Many other entries present the same problem. For example, the marker *i* has a number of different functions—some related and others quite distinct. In P-E, they are all treated under one headword (and in one paragraph) and in four subentries.

As another example, under the headword *'ī* we find the following meanings: 'to say', 'supreme', 'stingy', interjection of scorn, and 'the letter *i*': five completely different words under one headword. And note that the entry for *uhi* contains six unrelated words.

The solution to this problem is simple: separate obviously distinct words into separate entries. Admittedly, it is not always easy to do, for there are often gray areas. A close look at the translations and explanations of the marker *i* in P-E or *Pocket Hawaiian Grammar* would illustrate the problem.

How Can Nineteenth-Century Printed Material Add to the Word Count?

Chapter 14 noted how computer technology has increased both the size and searchability of the previously untapped supply of printed Hawaiian.

---

11. Pairings of homonyms, discussed in the next chapter, might justify Elbert's decision to put all identical forms in one entry. But he did not suggest such a reason, especially in his 1954 article. Still, reworking the entries into their proper forms would not obliterate any pairing: because of the way entries are alphabetized, the words would be in adjacent entries. Perhaps this arrangement could serve as an argument for the P-E alphabetization (which follows the English order) as opposed to that in *Māmaka Kaiao* (which follows the Hawaiian order—i.e., the vowels first, and then the consonants, including a separate section at the end for words beginning with an *'okina*). Although the latter has the advantage of treating the *'okina* as a separate consonant in the alphabet, the former shows words without and with the *'okina* next to each other—valuable for understanding material written without it, such as Hawaiian-language newspapers.

TABLE 15.1 WORDS NOT FOUND IN P-E OR ANDREWS, FROM KĀNEPUʻUʼS "HAMA NALAU"

Word as it appears	Possible variations in spelling and thoughts on possible meaning	Quote from *moʻolelo* 'story, tale'	*Helu* 'volume' in which it is found	Results of search in nupepa.org
16. Ma-ae-ae	*Māʻaeʻae.* Prob. prefix *mā* + *ʻaeʻae* "soft like feathers" Or *mā*+ *aeae* "a prolonged sound." The passage is about how the voice sounds.	ua palale paha ka leo, a ua pa-aheahe, aole hoi ke koikoi pono e like me ko kaua leo ko ke kanaka, he okoa hoi ka leo o ka poe e-epa au e nana iho ai, he ma-ae-ae wale no.	*Helu* 7, Feb. 8, 1868, *NK*	Nothing

However, researchers using this material—especially the Hawaiian-language newspapers—have occasionally found words that do not appear in either older or current dictionaries. If they are unfamiliar to the relatively few native speakers left today, they can present two problems: meaning and pronunciation/spelling.

Based on her reading of Hawaiian-language newspapers and other Hawaiian material, Noenoe Silva has been compiling an open-ended list of words not found in P-E or Andrews 1865, along with possible interpretations and the context. Note the example in table 15.1. Marking the headword **ma-ae-ae* would signal to the user that any vowel might be long, and any vowel not preceded by another consonant might actually be preceded by a glottal stop. Silva's explanation of possible meanings reduces the number of potential forms.

Often, the meaning can be recovered from the context. But because the *ʻokina* was rarely written, and the *kahakō* was never written, the form—the pronunciation—is another matter, unless the words appear in older audio recordings.

The main source for such recordings is the Bishop Museum's audio collection. "The repository is one of the finest of its kind in the world, comprising recordings of Native Hawaiian oral traditions over a period of sixty years from the early 1920s to 1980s and including rare examples of the Hawaiian language spoken by some who first learned the language over 100 years ago" (Collections 2011:13).

In 2011, the Museum completed a two-year digitization project. Its description reads like a chronology of audio-recording technology: "Audio recordings originally on a variety of media such as wax cylinders, discs, steel wire, reel-to-reel, and cassette tapes are now preserved in digital format and available for patrons to access . . . The audio collection is a rich source of Hawaiian history, culture, language, and cultural practices" (ibid.).

Figure 15.5. "Dorothy Barrère and Eleanor 'Ele' Williamson interview Mary Kawena Pukui in Bishop Museum's Hawaiian Hall; 1954" (Collections 2011)

What Minor Changes Could Improve the Accuracy and Utility of the Dictionary?

After the most recent edition of *Hawaiian Dictionary* appeared in 1986, from time to time small errors have been corrected in reprintings. Here, we suggest two such types of changes.

Correcting Mistakes in Marking Accent Measures

One of the innovations in P-E (and later in *Māmaka Kaiao*) is a system of dividing a headword into measures—accent units that show which syllables in longer forms are accented (1986:xvii–xviii).[12]

It is understandable that P-E contains some errors in marking measures. Proofreading a dictionary is one of the most difficult chores in publishing. Therefore, a copy that is free from errors is more often wished for than achieved. If the proofreaders know Hawaiian, they will be able to correct spelling or typographical errors. However, errors in accent measure marking are more subtle, for they involve only the presence or absence of a period in the middle of a word.[13] Moreover, its proper placement involves special linguistic knowledge. A rough check of the dictionary showed about seventy errors of the following two types:[14]

a. Examples with missing measure marking:

Present marking	Correct marking
auē	au·ē
lūpō	lū·pō
lēʻia	lē·ʻia
aka·ʻōlelo	aka·ʻō·lelo
ʻauina	ʻau·ina

12. The concept of accent measures was introduced in chapter 11.

13. A useful innovation of *Māmaka Kaiao* is that the periods are raised, making it easier to separate them from punctuation marks.

14. Besides my own notes, I also had access to ʻŌiwi Parker Jones's list from his searching through *Ulu Kau,* the online version of P-E. (See Parker Jones 2009a, b).

b. Examples with unnecessary or incorrect measure marking:

ko·ʻū	koʻū
ma·leila	maleila
Ka·ʻula	Kaʻula

These changes are noncontroversial and could be made without altering the integrity of the work.

After sending these and other corrections to the publisher, with no response, I found that for the present at least, P-E is being kept in print but not updated.[15] One possible reason is that changes could appear in supplements such as *Māmaka Kaiao.*

This policy is reminiscent of a similar one from a major publisher of dictionaries of American English. In 2001, Random House announced that its unabridged dictionary would no longer be updated, but that it "intended to continue to be 'a major player in the dictionary market' and that all titles would be 'aggressively marketed'" (Random House Dictionaries 2001:1).

Maintaining Grammatical Consistency

Earlier in this work (chapter 10), Kaʻahumanu was quoted as saying, '*Ua loaa [loaʻa] iau [iaʻu]*' when she had a eureka moment, suddenly understanding the nature of the relationship between a letter and a sound. A literal and grammatically appropriate translation is not 'I've got it' but 'It's gotten by me'. Yet P-E defines *loaʻa* as 'to find, get, obtain, discover'. Another example is *maopopo,* which means not 'to understand' but 'to be understood'. P-E defines *maopopo* as 'to understand, recognize, realize'. For consistency, the grammatical forms of the headword and the definition should match.

THE COMPUTER AND THE *COMBINED HAWAIIAN DICTIONARY*

Until recently, the number of entries in a dictionary of an Oceanic language did not stretch the limitations of a traditional bound book. For

15. But do all buyers of P-E 1986 know this fact? Perhaps caveat emptor is appropriate here.

example, counting the front matter, the last edition of P-E totals 600 pages (printed area of each page is 5 x 7¾ inches) and is bound so that the pages can lie flat when the book is open. As a result, the book, weighing only a little over 2 pounds, is convenient to use. Such is not the case with the Fijian monolingual dictionary, *Na Ivolavosa Vaka Viti* (2005), which runs to 1,024 pages (4½ x 7 inches) and weighs over 3 pounds. If it had been properly bound and printed on the right kind of paper, its length would not be a problem—*Merriam-Webster's New Collegiate Dictionary* has about half again as many pages and opens flat. However, on many pages of the Fijian dictionary, words next to the binding are difficult to read, and on some, impossible. Moreover, the book will not lie open.

An obvious solution to the problem of a dictionary that is too large (other than printing it in multiple volumes) is to abandon the printed version for an electronic one. Along these lines, what is the trend for unabridged English dictionaries? In August 2010, the publisher of the *Oxford English Dictionary* (*OED*) announced that the third edition, now underway, was likely not to duplicate or expand on the present 20-volume print format, but it might be available only in an electronic format.

Hawaiian dictionaries have also been affected by such trends. For several years, the online Hawaiian data repository, Ulukau, at www.wehewehe.org, has provided scholars and students access to digital versions of four Hawaiian dictionaries—Andrews 1865, Andrews-Parker 1922, P-E 1986, and *Māmaka Kaiao* (*MK* 2003)—both as PDF pages and text (HTML). Moreover, the site provides a search form that can display results from these dictionaries and provide access to the *MK* addendum (2010) as well.

Because these dictionaries are now accessible online, Stephen Trussel recognized the potential of combining them into a version that could be browsed through. Thus, in early 2011, he began the project, the *Combined Hawaiian Dictionary* (*CHD*).[16] Technical details can be found on the following Web site: www.trussel2.com/HAW. But in summary, this method of comparing the various dictionaries allows users, for the first time, to have a vast array of lexical information literally at their fingertips.

---

16. In this section, the description of the *Combined Hawaiian Dictionary* is based almost entirely on notes supplied by Stephen Trussel, 22 August 2013, and amended from time to time. Trussel, the architect of the Web site, is a software developer, student of Hawaiian, and graduate of the University of Hawai'i at Mānoa's Department of Linguistics.

Here's an example of how useful the *CHD* can be. In a recent search in several Hawaiian dictionaries for names of various diseases, I assumed that many would be compounds formed with *maʻi* 'disease'. Outside the world of computers, one might visualize this task as thumbing through three or four dictionaries, spread out on a desk.

Searching through these dictionaries, one by one, I found these problems:

1. First, as mentioned earlier, P-E treats homophones under one headword and in a single entry. Thus, in addition to *maʻi* 'disease', the entry also defines and gives examples for *maʻi* 'private parts'.
2. Because P-E uses the English system to alphabetize entries, many types of *maiʻa* 'banana' interrupt the search.
3. Adding *MK* for comparison presented a different kind of problem. Because of the position of the *ʻokina* in the Hawaiian alphabet, *maʻi* is alphabetized at the end of *ma-* words, not after *mah-* words.
4. The third dictionary on the desk is Andrews 1865. Here, as in *MK*, the alphabetic order must be taken into account: because the *ʻokina* is not recognized, the spelling *maʻi* does not appear at all, and there are seven entries spelled *mai*. Also, *mai-* spellings follow *mae-*, not *mah-*.

In contrast, the *CHD* allowed me to look at all *maʻi* entries in the three dictionaries, including compounds, in one continuous list.

So far, the innovations in the *CHD* could be viewed as rearrangements, which present the information scattered through a number of conventional dictionaries in a form that is much more convenient for the user.

However, unlike existing dictionaries, the *CHD* can be expanded beyond the limits of a bound book. The following list shows some of the information it contains beyond the usual categories:[17]

1. ***ʻŌlelo Noʻeau.*** Material from Mary Kawena Pukui's classic work (1983) has been incorporated into the entries, and previously appearing material has been marked for this source.
2. **Pre-1820 word lists**. Twelve word lists have been added, most of them collected by explorers or beachcombers before the missionaries arrived in 1820. They include the following:[18]

---

17. Adapted from Trussel's description.

18. The date refers to when the list was collected, not necessarily when it was published.

Anderson 1778
Lisiansky 1804
Martínez 1789
Campbell 1809
Samwell 1779
Gaimard/Arago 1819
Beresford 1787
Bishop/Ellis 1825
Santeliz es Pablo 1791
Botta 1828
Quimper 1791
Dumont d'Urville 1834

Each list duplicates the original spelling and translation. Annotation includes the historical background and the modern spelling and translation (see Schütz 1994:33–39).

3. **Proto forms.** The 1986 (and final?) version of P-E includes approximately 2,000 proposed reconstructions of earlier forms of Hawaiian words in the Austronesian language family.[19] Recent research by the Polynesian Lexicon Project Online (POLLEX) has allowed these forms to be updated or corrected, and 700 or so forms have been added. Here's an example. The URL http://www.trussel2.com/haw/haw-a.htm#akeloa will yield this added form: **akeloa** [ake·loa] *n.* spleen. *lit.,* long liver. [PPN ***ʻate-loa**, *spleen (Clk)*].

   Research on POLLEX is ongoing, and the body of data is increasing. However, this additional material cannot be incorporated into P-E, since there are no plans to revise the dictionary. This situation itself is one of many reasons for students of Hawaiian to familiarize themselves with the *CHD.*
4. **Reorganized headwords.** The different senses that had been included under single headwords[20] have become new headwords.

19. See chapter 3.

20. See the discussion earlier in the present chapter in the section "What Constitutes an Entry?" Also, note the discussion of the *maʻi* entry, just above.

5. **Example sentences.** The example sentences and phrases within entries are redisplayed as lists.
6. ***Ho'o-* forms**. These forms, indicating causative and some other functions, are now listed under *h* as well as in the entry for the base word.
7. **Missing entries**. Many Hawaiian words in the English-Hawaiian section of P-E that are missing in the Hawaiian-English section have been added and identified by a special font. Variant spellings in the English-Hawaiian section are treated similarly.
8. **Images.** Some 200 images have been added to illustrate entries, particularly those for plants, birds, and fish.[21] These are shown as small thumbnail images at the left of the headwords, which are links to larger images and the image source, linked to the online page where additional scientific and descriptive information about the item can be found. This feature is open-ended; more images can be added.
9. **Bible concordance.** A complete concordance of the Hawaiian Bible is connected to the *CHD.*
10. **Place name concordance**. The Hawaiian-language place names in Pukui, Elbert, and Mookini 1974 have been alphabetically integrated into the work.
11. **Derivational information.** For a small but growing number of words, sets of derived forms (that is, words formed by adding a prefix or suffix to a base form or reduplicated forms) have been added and can be accessed.
12. **Topical lists.** In another important respect, *CHD* ventures beyond the boundaries of a conventional alphabetized dictionary into the area of semantic domains.[22] The following categories are a few topics that are treated separately:

    fish names

    plant names

    English loanwords

    place names

    nouns that take *ke* (rather than *ka*)

    causatives

---

21. P-E 1986 was supposed to include line drawings as illustrations. For some reason, that project was abandoned.

22. See, for example, Kent 1986 and the discussion in Schütz 1994:207.

One important consideration in a printed commercial dictionary is saving space. With an online dictionary, that measure is no longer necessary. For example, to save space in P-E and *MK,* measures[23] were marked on the headword; in the *CHD* they appear in brackets after the headword, similar to the pronunciation band in an English dictionary. This convention makes it clearer to the nonprofessional user that the measure divisions are not part of the normal spelling.

As another example, conventions such as "same as x" or "see x" can be avoided, because entries can be expanded to include as much information as necessary. Moreover, cross-references can be treated as links—immediately accessible.

Such links can include material that is now available online—such as Ulukau, *Place Names of Hawaii,* or the Bible—and take the user directly to the corresponding chapter or section of the text.

Trussel ended his description with this note: "The *CHD* is a work in progress, and many of these modifications are ongoing. The current revision date is displayed at the top of each page." Readers can keep up to date by visiting the Web site, which is repeated here: www.trussel2.com/HAW.

INTERNET TRANSLATION

Echoing the rapidly changing technology of the computer world, in mid-February 2016 Google announced a translation service for Hawaiian (Hurley 2016). One reviewer (Lanakila Mangauil) praised it in philosophical terms, noting that it "marks another milestone for a language that was close to extinction only a couple of decades ago." Another (Puakea Nogelmeier) commented (*Honolulu Star-Advertiser,* 19 February 2016, A-17), "I appreciate their awareness of Hawaiian as a living language." However, he criticized how it functioned, finding that some structures beyond simple sentences could not yet be translated accurately. Thus, it might be best regarded as a work in progress.

Laiana Wong raised a different kind of objection, one consistent with a theme treated in the next section. He expressed doubts about relying on a translation rather than "actually learning the full context of the language." Moreover, he added, a translation into English imposes "an English world view."

---

23. Accent units; see chapter 11.

Still, the project is likely to improve in accuracy. As for the conflict between original and translated material, it should provide a useful service for users—scholars and others—who need to be able to understand previously untranslated Hawaiian material but cannot devote a lifetime to developing a native-like control of the language.

THE UNTRANSLATABLES: DEFINING IN A BILINGUAL DICTIONARY

The main difference between a monolingual and a bilingual dictionary lies in the terms themselves: one language versus two. However, perhaps the most important distinction between these two major types is connected with the very nature of definition. One might oversimplify the point in this way: a monolingual dictionary *defines;* a bilingual dictionary *translates.*

However, these seemingly simple statements are complicated by certain general features of language. Even for cultures that are rather similar, it can be difficult to define—that is, translate—from one language to the other. The German word *gemütlich* is often used as an example. Sometimes it is translated into English as 'comfortable', sometimes 'cozy'. But neither word fits perfectly. The following passage treats this word, along with some others with hazy counterparts in another language: "One should note that to be *bourgeois* is not at all the same thing as to be middle-class; the former word connotes a precise set of attitudes, prejudices, preconceptions, life options, and political views. Styles of self-satisfaction vary from country to country, just as to be bored is not the same thing as to suffer from *ennui.* The condition of feeling *einsam* is not identical with being lonely, and *gemütlichkeit* is to be distinguished from comfiness" (Lanchester 1996:42).

When the two languages in question represent cultures that are very different, translation becomes even more difficult. Thus, at points at which the cultures diverge, we must move from the translation mode back to the definition mode. This topic—the cultural aspects of lexicography—is both interesting and challenging for anthropological linguists charged with compiling a dictionary. As suggested earlier, if the lexicographer fails to shift the mode, the result is a so-called definition that reads like a list of synonyms. P-E's definition of *kapu,* discussed earlier, is an example. A definition of that type shows that this particular dictionary was intended more as an aid to translating than as a window into Hawaiian culture.

In the next chapter, we can find more examples of "untranslatables," especially terms that are closely connected with a Hawaiian rather than an English worldview.

PLACE NAMES: UPDATING ANOTHER BASIC REFERENCE WORK

The most recent professional study of place names in Hawaiʻi now exists in three forms: *Place Names of Hawaii* (1966), *Place Names of Hawaii* (1974), and *Pocket Place Names of Hawaiʻi* (1989). Mary Kawena Pukui and Samuel H. Elbert were the primary authors for all three; Esther T. Mookini was a coauthor for the second and third editions.

Although the last volume was compiled after the 1986 edition of P-E, which divided headwords into measures to show the accent patterns (see chapter 11), that system was not used. As a result, even though local place names are possibly the Hawaiian words most often used by visitors and others who are not familiar with the language, there is no reference work that shows how these names are pronounced.

In the works above, the entries are divided into morphemes (units that have meaning).[24] By coincidence, such a marking might hint toward the pronunciation, as in the following:

Entry form	Measure division
Puʻu-makani (lit., windy hill)	puʻu·makani

But often it doesn't help. As a matter of fact, it might lead to a wrong pronunciation. Note the following three examples:

Entry form	Measure division
1 *Ke-ʻanini*	keʻa·nini
2 *Ka-ʻuiki*	kaʻu·iki
3 *Ka-ʻena*	kaʻena

24. Thus, even the article *ka/ke,* which occurs with many place names, is separated from the rest of the word.

Even though *ka/ke* in these examples is separated from the rest of the word by a hyphen, it is accented differently. In the first two examples, the article combines with the first syllable of the following word to form a measure on its own, with the first syllable accented. Thus each form has two accented syllables (including the first one), as shown in the second column. But in the third example, the article combines with the shorter noun, and the whole form has only one accented syllable. Because of how this entry is marked, a user might be tempted to give *Ka-ʻena* two accents, echoing one of functions of hyphens in the 1822 primer (see chapter 9). However, Hawaiian does not allow a short syllable, such as *ka* or *ke,* to serve as a measure on its own.

Some spellings and glosses changed from one edition to the next, with no explanation. For example, the common name *Kāhala* (district, shopping center), with that spelling and the gloss of ʻamberjack fishʼ, changed to *Kahala* and ʻthe pandanusʼ in the pocket edition. As Keao NeSmith pointed out,[25] many places are named after fish. On the other hand, the reference cited for the ʻpandanusʼ meaning is Handy and Handy 1972:200, a respected study on Hawaiian plants. Either form *could* be correct; but we need to hear an authoritative native speaker pronounce the name to be sure whether the first syllable is short or long.

If the name cannot be divided into morphemes, there are no hyphens. Consider, for example, the entry for *Keʻeaumoku,* one of the most mispronounced street names in Honolulu. The entry gives no indication of where the accents are, except for the regular accent on the second-to-last syllable. However, if it were written Keʻe•au•moku, the user of the guide would know that this word has three accented syllables (boldfaced), with the last one emphasized:[26] **Ke**ʻe•**au**•**mo**ku. In short, an ideal future Hawaiian gazetteer (a fancy name for a dictionary of place names) should give the user information about (1) the pronunciation and (2) the meanings, including more details on any controversial pronunciations or glosses.

VERBATIM

In "The Hawaiian Dictionaries, Past and Future," Elbert (1954) reviewed previous Hawaiian dictionaries and gave an account of the beginnings and

25. Pers. comm., 28 January 2015.

26. This directive must appear in the guidelines to using the system.

progress of P-E's *Hawaiian-English Dictionary*. This work appeared three years later and served as the foundation for later editions, culminating in the current standard Hawaiian dictionary (1986). Elbert wrote, "On the whole, the task has been far from monotonous. It has been a voyage of constant discovery into the marvelous structure and patterning of the Hawaiian language, and of the beauties, imagery, and amazing richness of the lexicon. I feel most grateful for the privilege of working on the dictionary with Mrs. Pukui. It is an intellectual and emotional satisfaction and joy: intellectual from the standpoint of linguistics, emotional because it is a further tie with the people of whom I am so fond—the Polynesians" (1954:17).

Modesty Can Be Its Own Punishment

In the same article, Elbert, in order to focus the spotlight on Mrs. Pukui's contributions, wrote, "This is her dictionary, a monument to her. My task has been the humble one of technician." Later, he had cause to regret his excessive (but polite) modesty. When he was shown a draft copy of an article on Hawaiian dictionaries, he found that the author had innocently taken him at his word and had treated his role in the *Hawaiian Dictionary* as a relatively minor one. The writer changed the tone of the article when it was explained that the dictionary was truly a collaborative effort.

It was no doubt this episode that prompted Elbert to write the following: "I had once written that the dictionary was Kawena's book and that I was a 'mere technician.' These comments were repeated too many times by people insensitive to Polynesian culture, in which one debases himself in order to praise another. They were unaware of the need for linguistic training in writing a dictionary" (1989:132).

Elbert's earlier self-deprecating description may have been a subtle parody of Samuel Johnson's classic and often-quoted definition of a lexicographer: "LEXICO'GRAPHER. A writer of dictionaries; a harmless drudge, that busies himself in tracing the original, and detailing the signification of words" (Johnson 1755).

A minor extension of this attitude, in a 2013 publication, is a reference to the authors of the dictionary as "Pukui with Elbert."[27] The ultimate

27. Also, the wrong date of publication is given.

reduction, heard from time to time, is "the Pukui dictionary." To diminish the contributions of the second author and then delete them is not only insulting but bibliographically and historically incorrect as well. It is quite possible to praise the contributions of one coauthor without belittling those of the other.

To illustrate (in part) some details that would not appear in the Introduction, Elbert wrote about Kawena and the early days of working on the dictionary (1989:132–33):

> She was indeed Hawaiian. She said yes by raising her eyebrows. She gently scolded me if I stood with my hands behind my back (I might have a club in them). She never thought about money. She avoided confrontation, a virtue apparently lost today. She was a Mormon, but when the Mormons discussed the origins of the Polynesians, she said nothing.
>
> At one point, the Hawaiian activists began to complain. They considered inclusion of Hawaiianized English words in the dictionary a desecration of the language.[28] They said we didn't include enough diacritical marks, thinking of a small early dictionary[29] that had accent marks over every vowel (a confusing mess that we eliminated, keeping only a reversed apostrophe[30] for the glottal stop, and a macron over long, stressed vowels).[31] Kawena said nothing.
>
> At a meeting of the Territorial Education Committee of the Legislature, an activist stood up to say about our dictionary: "With a haole name on it, it won't get anywhere!" Kawena was not there. I said nothing. But Alexander Spoehr and Kenneth Emory of the Bishop Museum spoke in my favor.
>
> Kawena received phone calls from Hawaiians who questioned her knowledge and accused her of exposing the bones of her ancestors (*kaulaʻi nā iwi*

28. See Elbert's mention of objections to loanwords (chapter 14).

29. Probably Judd, Pukui, and Stokes 1945, reprinted (without revision) and marketed as *Handy Hawaiian Dictionary* (1995). Elbert's description isn't quite accurate; in the English-Hawaiian section, there are three types of vowels: unmarked, marked with a breve, and marked with a macron. This practice obviously reflects an erroneous statement in the preface asserting three degrees of vowel length. Some vowels are also followed by an acute accent mark, but the so-called system is far from accurate.

30. The symbol is actually an opening single quotation mark. *Pocket Hawaiian Grammar* (Schütz, Kanada, and Cook 2005) contains the correct description, but the incorrect one appears in some earlier works.

31. This criticism is an interesting contrast with the refusal to use the *kahakō* and *ʻokina* in writing Hawaiian.

o nā kūpuna). Of me, they could say nothing good. That I had been in the Navy during the war was held against me. Kawena wept profusely at the time of these phone calls; her daughter, Pat, told me. But she kept on working.

Because of the respect—almost reverence—accorded today to the *Hawaiian Dictionary* and its compilers, it is difficult to believe that such negative attitudes not only existed but even threatened completing and publishing the dictionary.

CHAPTER 16

THE POWER IN WORDS

The word had power: I ka ʻōlelo nō ke ola, i ka ʻōlelo nō ka make *(in the word is life, in the word is death)*

—Samuel H. Elbert and Noelani Mahoe, *Nā Mele o Hawaiʻi Nei*

Although every student and scholar of Hawaiian is indebted to the lineage of Hawaiian-English dictionaries—from Andrews 1836a, 1865, to P-E 1957–1986 to *Māmaka Kaiao* 1998, 2003—advanced students eventually reach a point at which it might be to their advantage to eliminate an English bridge when learning the meaning of an unfamiliar word.

Although a bilingual dictionary may be essential for most adult beginners, it is not ideal for some other types of learners. As mentioned earlier, even an apparently simple term such as Hawaiian *hale* does not overlap precisely with the English concept of *house.* And terms that are more culture-specific only magnify the problem. In other words, dictionary users need to understand a Hawaiian concept not by taking a detour through English but by going directly to its Hawaiian explanation.[1]

The move from bilingual to monolingual is common in the history of dictionaries. For example, reflecting England's political and religious history, English lexicography began with bilingual works: usually the second

---

1. "The Power in Words" title is close to that used by Gutmanis (1985:24). Elbert and Mahoe used a similar phrase (1970:19). See the quotation below and "Verbatim" in chapter 11.

When my professor, Charles F. Hockett, wanted to find the meaning of a French word, he used a monolingual dictionary, reasoning that through context, he would learn the meanings of additional words, not just the one he was looking up.

language was French or Latin. The first monolingual English dictionary appeared in 1604, a modest work with some 3,000 entries (Landau 2001:45, 48). Compared with the dictionaries that we use today, it was—shall I say—primitive. For example, note the following definition of *apricot* (Cawdrey 1604): "abricot, (k) kind of fruit." Still, users were not forced to learn the meaning of an English word through its Latin or French equivalent.

Even the first version of Noah Webster's *Compendius Dictionary of the English Language* (1806)[2] was not much more detailed or descriptive: "A′pricot, n. a fine kind of stone fruit." It was not until Webster's 1828 edition that his work began to approach the size and scope of today's Merriam-Webster dictionaries. For comparison, here is the expanded definition of *apricot:* "A fruit belonging to the genus Prunus, of the plum kind, of an oval figure, and delicious taste."[3]

Moving back to the original theme, one can see the perils of relying on an inadequate bilingual dictionary through this anecdote, possibly apocryphal, about the sign on the governor's door in the newly built Hawai'i State Capitol Building (completed in 1969), meant to welcome visitors. Apparently, someone who knew little or no Hawaiian looked up *welcome* in the English-Hawaiian section of P-E and found this definition: "*You are welcome,* he mea iki," and *He mea iki* was carved on the koa door.

However, the problem is that this particular *welcome* is a response to *Thank you,* as in 'You're welcome'. Unfortunately, the literal translation of *he mea iki* is '(it's) a little thing'—rather insulting to the occupant of the office. It could have been worse; an alternate phrase is *he mea 'ole* (lit., '(it's) nothing').

The following caveat does appear in P-E :

> Caution is urged in the use of Hawaiian words that one may find in the English-Hawaiian section. Many have two or more meanings, some of which may have unfavorable connotations . . . For this reason one must look up any Hawaiian word listed on the English side and note all its possible meanings before using it . . . remember:
>
> *Mālama o pā 'oe.* 'Be careful lest the result be disastrous to you.' (Saying 2122 in Pukui 1983). (Pukui and Elbert:xxiii)

---

2. Incidentally, this book was not the first dictionary of American English. That honor belongs to one published in 1798.

3. Obviously, Webster liked apricots.

Perhaps the warning would have been more visible at the beginning of the English-Hawaiian section. But even a better placement would not have guaranteed that a casual user would see it or pay attention to it.

A story on the same theme, also possibly apocryphal, involves another Hawaiian translation of *welcome* in that section of P-E. In this vignette, a waiter "welcomes" restaurant guests who are already seated by saying "*E komo mai*"—which actually means 'Come in.'[4] In 2017 I heard the same phrase in the recorded phone message for a local museum, a request that would have been difficult to honor, because I was several miles away at the other end of a telephone line.

Just as the early monolingual English dictionaries reflected an attempt to avoid a detour through another language, members of several Oceanic cultures, as they have sought to explain the meaning of a native word, have opted for a way to avoid the bridging language of English. Monolingual dictionaries have been completed or are underway for at least four Oceanic languages: Fijian (2005),[5] Samoan,[6] Māori (2008), and Palauan (2000). Of course, the status of these languages is very different from that of Hawaiian, in both the number of their native speakers and the prognosis for their survival. Still, a monolingual dictionary for Hawaiian would only strengthen the efforts to preserve the language.

---

4. John Charlot, pers. comm., 20 October 2012.

5. The print version of the Fijian monolingual dictionary is titled *Na Ivolavosa Vaka Viti* (Suva: Institute of Fijian Language & Culture, 996 pages). Another version, by Paul Geraghty (the main compiler), has been enlarged and corrected and appears online. In late 2016, *Na Ivolavosa Vaka Viti* was being converted to a smartphone app (Apolonia Tamata, pers. comm., 21 September 2016).

6. A Samoan monolingual dictionary project, *Pua Gagana,* was begun in 2001 by the indigenous university, Le Amosā o Sāvavau in Sāmoa. The project was later broadened to include other university Samoan programs abroad with coordination from the now discontinued International Samoan Language Commission (Fale'ula o Fatua'i 'Upu o le Gagana Sāmoa). The dictionary project became increasingly affected by internal disputes and lack of coordination. A major bone of contention was whether or not to include glottal stops and macrons in the alphabet, even in the spelling of the headwords. As of August 2016, the current status of the project is unknown (John Mayer, pers. comm.).

HOW WOULD A MONOLINGUAL DICTIONARY DIFFER FROM A BILINGUAL ONE?

Aside from the obvious difference—that a Hawaiian monolingual dictionary would contain no English translations or explanations of Hawaiian words—a more subtle but significant goal is that it should reflect a Hawaiian worldview rather than an English one. This approach can be illustrated by returning to the simplified instructions for "how to define" in chapter 15: (1) put the item in a class and then (2) distinguish it from other members of that class.

Establishing Classes

The two-part answer just above is not as simple as it sounds. For example, how do we decide just what the classes are? Even if we're dealing with concrete, tangible items—say, animal or plant life—the operation isn't simple. Here's an example from my experience with the Fijian monolingual dictionary project. After two native speakers of Fijian had completed two years of linguistic training at UH Mānoa, the time seemed right to learn how to write definitions. I began with *beka*[7] 'flying fox, bat', thinking that a word for an animal would be easy to define. Seeking first to name the class, I naively asked, "What's the Fijian word for 'mammal'?" This approach was a mistake; there's no such category in Fijian. Instead, *beka* is classified as *manumanu*[8] 'bird'. Armed with this information, you can no doubt guess how *vonu* 'turtle' is classified: not as a reptile but as *ika*[9] 'fish'.

Folk Taxonomy versus Scientific Taxonomy

The examples above reflect a difference between two different worldviews—specifically, the ways that two distinct cultures categorize their respective environments. A system with a non-European origin is often called "folk taxonomy" to contrast it with "scientific taxonomy." The former is said to be "generated from social knowledge" and the latter

---

7. Cf. Hawaiian *peʻapeʻa.*

8. Cf. Hawaiian *manu.*

9. Cf. Hawaiian *honu* and *iʻa.*

"objective and universal."[10] However, I find the term "folk taxonomy" slightly condescending, for it seems to imply that the system is inferior to a Western, "scientific" one.

Form and Function

The following English example reflects my own "social knowledge" and differs from a scientific view. It has long been debated whether a tomato is a fruit or a vegetable. Although I know that botanists, using *form,* classify it as a fruit,[11] my own conception, based on *function,* treats it as a vegetable (it appears in salads and not [usually] in desserts).[12] Perhaps I feel the same way about an avocado: in spite of its form, I don't think of it as a fruit.

Still on the topic of food, I return to the *poi* example from chapter 15. In the Hawaiian worldview, the general category of "food" is divided into two parts, as shown in figure 16.1.

It is clear from the examples that the category *ʻai* consists of plants, both processed and unprocessed. The *iʻa* category has more variety, at

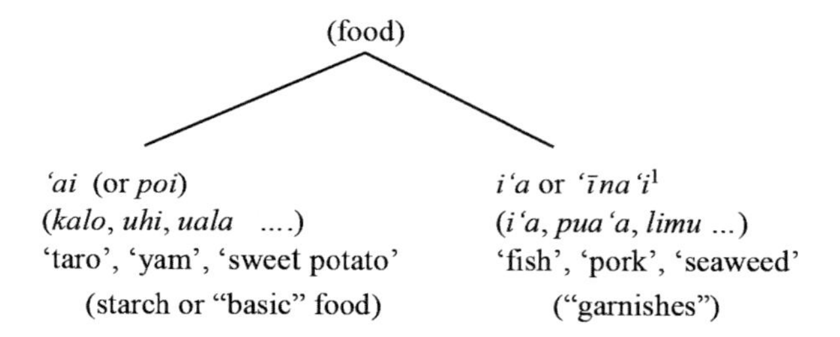

Figure 16.1. Hawaiian classification of food. As related to this topic, these two terms seem to be synonyms. In the following section, I use the term *iʻa* rather than *iʻa* /*ʻīnaʻi.*

---

10. Wikipedia, retrieved 28 February 2008. One might be hard-pressed to define either of those terms in a way that would not be culture-specific.

11. For example, "the usu[ally] edible reproductive body of a seed plant, *esp* : one having a sweet pulp associated with the seed" (*Merriam-Webster's Collegiate Dictionary,* 11th ed.). In 1893, a different kind of authority, the United States Supreme Court, used a functional rather than formal definition to rule that tomatoes were vegetables. See Nix v. Hedden, 149 U.S. 304 (1893).

12. "Knowledge is knowing a tomato is a fruit; wisdom is not putting it in a fruit salad" (from an Internet list of paraprosdokians, retrieved 28 December 2014).

least from a Western perspective. The following comments from David Malo add more detail: "All of the marine life in the sea is called *iʻa*. Those that swim and do not swim [are still called *iʻa*]. There are also several *iʻa* [found in the water upland] on the islands . . . The limu (moss and seaweeds, respectively) [found] in the fresh water and in the sea are considered to be *iʻa*" (Malo:2006:35).[13]

As I look at the categories, I cannot easily dismiss my tendency to give more weight to form when classifying entities. (On the other hand, as noted above, I abandoned form in favor of function when I labeled *tomato* as a vegetable in my own worldview.) However, in Malo's examples, and in the Hawaiian classification of food, form is secondary. Thus, the important defining feature for Hawaiian *meaʻai* 'food' is less the characteristics of the individual items or their contrasting relationship and more the *complementary relationship* of the two classes: *ʻai* 'food' and *iʻa* 'fish'. It is illustrated neatly by the following phrase: *Ua lako i ka ʻai a me ka iʻa* 'be supplied with *kalo/poi* and meat/fish',[14] referring, one assumes, to the whole category of "food." In other words, these are the two components of a complete meal.

Compare these descriptions with P-E's definitions of these terms, along with those of *poi* and *iʻa/ʻīnaʻi:*[15]

> **ʻai:** Food or food plant, especially vegetable food as distinguished from *iʻa,* meat or fleshy food; often *ʻai* refers specifically to poi.
>
> **iʻa:** 1. Fish or any marine animal, as eel, oyster, crab, whale . . . 2. Meat or any flesh food. 3. Any food eaten as a relish[16] with the staple . . . including meat, fish, vegetable, or even salt.[17]
>
> **ʻīnaʻi** (or **iʻa**): Accompaniment to poi [or basic food], usually meat, fish, or vegetable.
>
> **poi:** Poi, the Hawaiian staff of life, made from cooked taro corms, or rarely breadfruit, pounded and thinned with water.

---

13. That is, in the context of eating.

14. Keao NeSmith supplied the example.

15. Some of these definitions were discussed in chapter 15.

16. A. Capell (1941) also used this word to describe a similar category in the Fijian classification of foods. The problem with *relish* as a descriptive term is that most speakers of English would interpret it as a type of condiment.

17. This classification is not included in P-E's definition of *paʻakai* 'salt'.

These definitions capture the connections among the terms fairly well, although the complementary relationship between *ʻai* and *iʻa* is not made clear. Moreover, as the *limu* example in Malo's comments shows, *iʻa* is not confined to food from animals or fish.[18] Nor does the definition of *poi* hint at the important contrast between *poi* and *iʻa*. Finally, some readers may not know the idiom "staff of life."

John Charlot pointed out that context would play a role in the classification as well, noting that certain types of meat, for example, would not be considered *iʻa* if the topic of discussion was sea versus land creatures (pers. comm., February 2015).

The examples given so far show that the broad outlines of the classification system used to define Hawaiian words are similar to the procedure mentioned earlier—putting the item in a class and then distinguishing it from other members of that class. However, the examples also show that although the outlines of the procedure may be similar, the details differ.

A common theme that runs through the examples above—sometimes overtly, other times covertly—is that both similar and contrasting items or concepts are arranged in pairs or larger groups. In the next sections, I discuss different areas in which this worldview is important.

THE IMPORTANCE OF WORD GROUPS IN THE HAWAIIAN WORLDVIEW AND HEALING

I now deal with such widely separated topics as Hawaiian phonology, cosmology, and *lāʻau lapaʻau* (healing), looking for linguistic connections.[19] The unexpected unifying feature of these topics is *word pairs.*[20]

---

18. However, P-E's definition of *limu* doesn't mention its classification as *iʻa* or *ʻīnaʻi*. Another example is *lūʻau* (as in 'baked taro tops', not 'feast'). P-E's definition fails to suggest that it is classified as *ʻīnaʻi* and not *ʻai*.

19. Mahalo to Keao NeSmith, who first suggested this topic and provided some examples (pers. comm., January 2009).

20. Although word pairs are most common in examples of *kaona,* more than two words can be involved. For example, see Noenoe Silva's example of how the spelling *pua* could represent three separate words and figure in "visible *kaona*" (chapter 9.) The topic was suggested by Puanani Anderson-Fung, who found it discussed in McDougall 2016. Where appropriate, I have used the term "word groups" to reflect such a possibility.

Figure 16.2. A source of *pa'akai* "salt"

But not just any two words, chosen at random, are culturally significant. Instead, each group consists of words that are related in some way: identical or similar in sound,[21] similar in function, or contrasting in meaning. These sets play important roles in two cultural areas:

1. Hawaiian cosmology, as revealed in the *Kumulipo* (e.g., Johnson 1981; Charlot 2014) and *Chanting the Universe* (Charlot 1983).
2. Hawaiian healing, through the practice of *lāʻau lapaʻau* (e.g., Gutmanis (1976) 1985, 2013).

The goal in #1 is descriptive/explanatory; that in #2 is functional—that is, medicinal healing.[22]

Cosmology and Worldview: *He Kumulipo*

In the *Kumulipo,* a chant that includes genealogy, procreation, and the universe developing under its own power,[23] pairs of identical or similar names are used to express important relationships.

---

21. Words can be similar in many different ways. Some of these will be examined in a later section, in which the groups are examined from a linguist's viewpoint.

22. There are other literary devices, such as *kaona,* that rely on homonymy, but the two chosen here are perhaps easier to treat in a dictionary.

23. John Charlot, pers. comm., 15 March 2014.

In some lines of this chant, the key words are true *homonyms*—completely identical in form but with different meanings. For example, Charlot cited two lines whose poetic power hinged on these homonyms (2014:14):

pi'o	bent	*pi'o*	marriage of full brother and sister
lani	sky	*lani*	chief

Other examples are as follows:

he'e	octopus	*he'e*	flee
kala	loosen	*kala*	surgeon fish
pili	cling	*pili*	k.o. grass
moi	variety of *kalo*	*moi*	threadfish

The last example reflects an all-important opposition in the study of word pairs: land versus sea. Note similar contrasting elements in these phrases:

> Egg and fish are symbols of land and sea. (Clarice B. Taylor, in Gutmanis 2013:17).

> To ye gods of the mountains (na kulauka) and of the ocean (na kulakai). (Beckwith 2007:184).

The following section gives more examples of this opposing relationship, often listed in the opposite order: sea versus land.

Sea Forms–Land Forms in the *Kumulipo*

This relationship is a recurring theme, primarily illustrating (or defining) an affinity between sea creatures and land creatures expressed by identical or similar names.

Word groups often reflect this connection. The following pairs are from a longer list of living entities that are connected with "the refrain of generation" (Johnson 1981:120–21):

pahaha	mullet	*pūhala*	pandanus
he'e	octopus	*waihe'e*	k.o. shrub
nenue	rudderfish	*lauhue*	gourd

puhi kauila[24]	eel	*kauila*	buckthorn
weke	mullet	*wauke*	paper mulberry
palaoa	whale	*aoa*	sandalwood

In context, such pairs offer further insight into the nature and form of the *Kumulipo* (p. 112): "*Hānau ka Umaumalei noho i kai. Kiaʻiʻia e ka ʻUlei noho i uka.* Born was the *umaumalei* surgeonfish *living in the sea.* Kept by the *ʻulei* shrub *living on land* [emphasis added]." In this example, the terms *umaumalei* and *ʻulei* are bound together by their identical last syllables and by *u* and *ʻu* in their first syllables.

Exceptions to the Sea–Land Connection

Not all pairs show the sea–land opposition.[25] For example, note the following entry from P-E (see figure 16.3: *Lama*): "*Lama* wood [a kind of ebony] was used in medicine and placed in hula altars because its name suggested enlightenment" [*lama:* 'torch, light, lamp', etc.]." The *Kumulipo* also contains pairings not between sea and land creatures but between different species of fish. Johnson wrote, "The fish groups are presented in pairs which emphasize name sounds and roots . . . A list of fish pairs and guardian plants demonstrates the affinity of names irrespective of the classification or relationship between species" (1981:118). Some examples are the following (119):

iʻa	fish (general)	*naiʻa*	porpoise
manō	shark	*moano*	goatfish

Elsewhere, one finds these examples in context (95–96):

Hānau ka iʻa, hānau ka Naiʻa i ke kai lā holo[26]

Born the *fish,* born the *porpoise* swimming there in the sea

Hānau ka manō, hānau ka Moano i ke kai lā holo

Born the *shark,* born the *goatfish* swimming there in the sea

---

24. The spelling has been altered to conform to newer guidelines.

25. Puanani Anderson-Fung, pers. comm., August 2013.

26. The original omits *kahakō* in these examples.

Figure 16.3. *Lama* branch and leaves

Such examples show that whether through historical processes or by accident, two words now pronounced alike, or nearly alike, are felt to have a special relationship.

The examples also show that not all word pairs are perfect homonyms. Many pairs above are forms that are not identical but simply similar to each other. In a later section, I examine the concept of "similar" from a linguistic perspective.

*

The next sections treat word pairs that have a second major and more practical function: to aid in healing.

Lāʻau Lapaʻau—Medicine

I have already discussed the role of word pairs in the Hawaiian worldview. For the most part, this pairing highlights particular features of the Hawaiian view of the universe and its creatures, especially the relationship between those from the sea and those from the land—connected by identical or similar words. Thus, the *form* of the names was all-important.

In the present section, I discuss another key element in word pairs, their *function*—in particular, the role they play in *lapaʻau* 'healing'.[27] In the broadest terms, if healers couldn't find a required substance, they could substitute another whose name was identical or similar. For example, if a certain fish (e.g., *moi* 'threadfish') had healing properties but was unavailable (perhaps it was *kapu* or out of season), similar effects could be derived from a plant whose name sounded the same or nearly the same—in this case, a variety of *kalo* called *moi.*

The following quotations show how this principle was the basis of treatment by a *kahuna lapaʻau* 'healer' who used *lāʻau lapaʻau* (Gutmanis 1985:28).

> The patient was given a special food (*pani*) . . . It was usually something from the sea chosen because of the inter-relationship between marine and land forms of life. The names of the herbs and foods used to treat the patient and those of the closing often shared a common name.[28]
>
> . . . The *pani* was the thing to do or eat at the end of the treatment. Very often it consisted of the *kapukai* (ceremonial sea-bathing), and the eating of the *kala* seaweed or *kala* fish, or any other thing with the word *kala* (freeing) in its name. (Handy and Pukui [1958] 1972:145)

John Charlot added that the "*pani* ceremony restores the balance disturbed by the necessary ingestion of a large amount of the pair-member" (pers. comm., 15 March 2014).

Emphasizing the sea–land relationship, Handy, Pukui, and Livermore wrote (1934:25):

> The prescription of the pani in relation to the drugs used in the treatment appears to be determined by the interrelations of marine forms of life with those on land, as described in the Kumulipo chant of creation. Through this remarkable hymn of the origin of living forms by a process of evolution of higher out of lower types, runs the theme of the *coincidental evolution in the sea and on the land of genera given similar names* [emphasis added].

---

27. In this section I focus not on illnesses or healing procedures per se but on the linguistic aspects of the cures.

28. It wasn't exactly the "same" name, but they were *homophones*—words with the same sound but different meanings.

Note this opposition in the following lines [current spellings are in square brackets]:

> The *akiaki* [*ʻakiʻaki*] moss was born and lived in the sea,
> It was guarded (*kiai* [*kiaʻi*]) by the *manienie akiaki* [*mānienie ʻakiʻaki*] grass that grows in the uplands.
> The *aalaula* [*ʻaʻalaʻula*] seaweed was born and lived in the sea,
> Guarded by the *alaalawainui* [*ʻaʻalaʻulawainui*] that dwells in the uplands.

The following examples stress that language—especially the *sound of words*—was paramount in healing procedures:

> Importance of [ʻ]ōlelo: the spoken word
>
> . . . Hawaiʻi was a culture without written language; the spoken word was all important. *Thus word sound itself could become almost more symbolic than the object it referred to* [emphasis added].[29] This is shown in the sympathetic magic of Hawaiian medical treatment. One ate *limu kala* (a water moss) not because of this physical object's healing powers, but because the word "*kala*" means to "release or free" in a beneficial sense. One used *pili* (a grass) to gain a good memory because the word "*pili*" means "cling." (Pukui, Haertig, and Lee [1972–1979] 2002:178)

Gutmanis explained such relationships further:

> Whether the patient required a special diet to prepare him for treatment, or if the *kahuna* started treatment at once, he immediately removed certain foods from his patient's normal diet. Because of the power in words,[30] the foods removed were usually those whose names had negative meanings. *Limu līpeʻepeʻe,* a seaweed, was typical of a forbidden food. The word *peʻepeʻe* means 'to hide' and consequently, using this food would cause the illness to hide from the treatment.[31] And the octopus, *heʻe,* whose name means "to flee," or the fish, *kualakai,* whose name means "to quiver or quake," would be forbidden. Bêche-de-mer,[32] *loli,* [also] meaning "to turn," might cause the medicine to turn away. (2013:48–49)

---

29. Quoted earlier in chapter 10.

30. This phrase is the source of the present chapter's title.

31. In P-E, under *peʻepeʻe,* one finds "same as *līpeʻepeʻe* but no mention of the medicinal connection.

32. The spelling has been changed slightly.

Handy and Pukui gave a similar reason to avoid *he'e*: "The same kahuna also forbade the eating of *lipe'epe'e* [*līpe'epe'e*] seaweed and the squid (*he'e*) when he was seeking a sign from the gods as the word *pe'e* meant to hide away and *he'e* to flee, hence the gods would hide the information sought after and cause it to flee" (1972:144).

But *he'e* could also have positive connotations, because the act of "fleeing" could apply to negative elements as well, as the following P-E entry shows: "*He'e mahola,* octopus given for sickness caused by sorcery, as octopus (*he'e*) would cause the sickness to flee (*he'e*) or spread out (*mahola*)." Charlot also noted that different healing schools could have different practices—and thus, different classifications (pers. comm., February 2015).

The following examples of healing materials also show relationships different from the sea–land contrast:

> *āholehole* 'young-stage *āhole*'. "Because *hole* means to strip away, this fish was used to chase away evil spirits."
>
> *kala* 'sturgeonfish'. "Given to sick person to loosen (*kala*) the illness."
>
> *loli* 'sea slug'. "Given during an illness to turn or change (*loli*) the direction of the sickness." (Gutmanis 2013:203)

All these pairs show one element from the sea (represented by a noun) evoking an action (represented by a verb). But P-E noted the cultural significance of the pairing only in the entry for *āhole*.

The following description may serve to summarize this section:

> Each form of land-life had a sea-life counterpart and each sea-life form had a land counterpart. Some plants had several forms and many of the plant names reflected these interrelationships. An example was the *kala* of the upland, the *'ākala* raspberry, the *kala* in between, the *puakala* poppy, and the *kala* of the sea, *limu kala,* which the fish feed on. When one of these was required for a ritual or offering and was not available, any one of the others could be substituted. If one of these plants with *kala* as part of its name was used as an opening, the closing would use one of the other forms.
>
> While learning the names of the plants, the trainee also learned all the variations that a plant name might have so that his choice of plants for medical use might utilize the power of the words used for the plant name.

The student also learned that under some circumstances one plant could be substituted for another, usually a *kino lau* of the same *akua*[33] or a land- or sea-form of the preferred plant. (Gutmanis 2013:96–97)

How These Relationships Are Treated in P-E

As just mentioned, for one example above (*āhole*), P-E noted the pairing of terms; for the other two (*kala, loli*), the connection is not mentioned. In some other entries, such relationships are suggested. For example, under *pani,* the connection is noted indirectly: the first meaning is 'to close'. The second is 'Final bit of food closing, a period of treatment by a medical practitioner, commonly but not always sea food'.

In other entries, P-E's treatment is less satisfactory. For example, see the entry for *loli.* The first meaning, 'change, turn', is neither related nor linked to the second, 'sea slug'.[34] And the entry for *kualakai* does not mention a medicinal connection between the meanings of a 'sea creature' and 'quiver'.

Still, in the 1950s, it was probably not among the lexicographers' main goals to indicate every word pair that Mrs. Pukui knew, could be gleaned from Hawaiian practitioners of *lāʻau lapaʻau,* or could be found in written accounts. As mentioned earlier in this book, it was a time when no one could have predicted the increased interest in the language and cultural practices that resulted from the Hawaiian Renaissance.

But perhaps P-E's practice of lumping unrelated words into one entry (criticized in the preceding chapter) could have the unexpected result of highlighting word pairs. For instance, consider the *lama* example (figure 16.3). This entry in P-E contains three unrelated meanings—a kind of tree, light, and the borrowing from English *rum.* It is a confusing practice, but it allowed the writers to mention the medicinal relationship between the first two homonyms. Still, from a professional lexicographic point of view, three separate entries would have been preferable. Because they would have been contiguous, the functional pairing of the first two could still have been easily deduced.

---

33. The original has *ʻakua.*

34. See the section "What Constitutes an Entry?" in chapter 15.

How to Treat Word Pairs

Many unabridged English dictionaries have been compiled with history in mind, especially the *Oxford English Dictionary,* the original title of which was *A New English Dictionary on Historical Principles.* Some dictionaries reflect this philosophy by giving the oldest meaning first. This practice has led some users to consider this meaning the most important or most common, not realizing that it may be obsolete.[35] Still, etymology occupies such an important place in major English monolingual dictionaries that it is usually the third place in the entry, after the pronunciation and the part-of-speech classification.

But remember: etymological information is based on a historical connection, but accidental similarities in form between or among words are ignored.

A Western type of etymology already exists in P-E, for Elbert included those proto-forms that had been reconstructed at the time the dictionary was prepared. (An updated version appears in Trussel's *Comparative Hawaiian Dictionary,* described in chapter 15.) The Hawaiian worldview, especially as exemplified by the *Kumulipo,* does not necessarily contradict such findings, but it looks at the history of words in a different way: it emphasizes function, based on similarity of form, rather than the historical development of the words.

The Linguistic View

It would be convenient (and much easier) to treat the topic of word pairs if the categories could be neatly separated into groups whose names are familiar to linguists: for example, *homonyms* (different words that sound the same); *synonyms* (words with the same or similar meaning); or *antonyms* (words with opposite meanings). But even though these categories do not exactly match the Hawaiian system, they can serve as a starting point.

Homonyms

As with all sets of homonyms, it should be emphasized, again, that each of the example pairs represents not *one* word with different meanings but different words that simply sound alike.

---

35. Such mistakes emphasize the importance of reading the front matter in dictionaries, which should explain the order of meanings within an entry.

Here I will consider how homonyms developed. It is hard to imagine a stage of the language when there were no homonyms. However, some linguistic processes certainly increased their numbers. Chapter 3 discussed the main changes to Proto-Polynesian (PPN) consonants—especially losses and mergers—as that ancestral language developed into Hawaiian. John Charlot described the result of such changes—pairs of words that were either identical or similar in form: "Over the centuries, simplifications, such as the loss of speech sounds, had resulted in a large percentage of homonyms and a much higher percentage of words resembling each other" (1983:42).[36]

As a specific example, consider PPN *r and *l.[37] Their merger into Hawaiian *l* produced a number of pairs of words, once pronounced differently but now the same—that is, as homonyms. Figure 16.4 repeats an example from chapter 3—one form, but with separate meanings and histories. This simple diagram shows how identical forms developed from two separate forms through the falling together of *r* and *l* in an earlier form of the language.

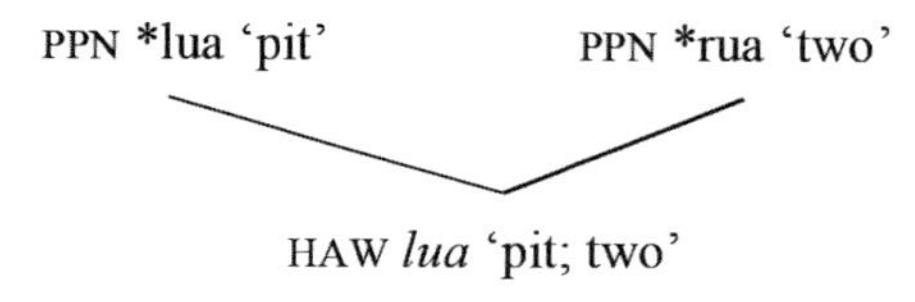

Figure 16.4. The development of Hawaiian *lua*

As another example (mentioned above), the spelling *lama* represents three words (see the P-E entry). If we exclude *lama* 'rum'—a borrowing from English—the set is a pair, consisting of an object (k.o. tree) and a state ('enlightenment'). As is common for such pairs, they are not historically related but can be traced to earlier separate forms.

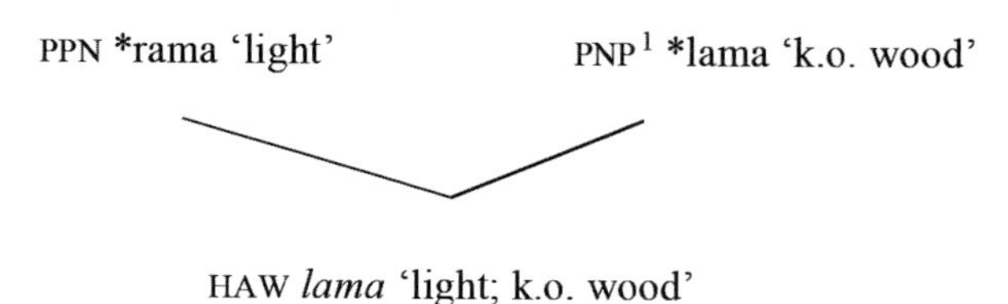

Figure 16.5. The development of Hawaiian *lama*

36. See chapter 3 for specific examples and a sketch of the methodology involved in reaching such a conclusion.

37. Other changes from PPN are the merger of *n and *ŋ and the more complicated relationship among *s, *f, and *w. See chapter 3, figure 3.3.

The *he'e* example in figure 16.6 appears in several descriptions of *lā'au lapa'au.* Again, the homonyms do not share a common history but are descended from two earlier, separate forms:

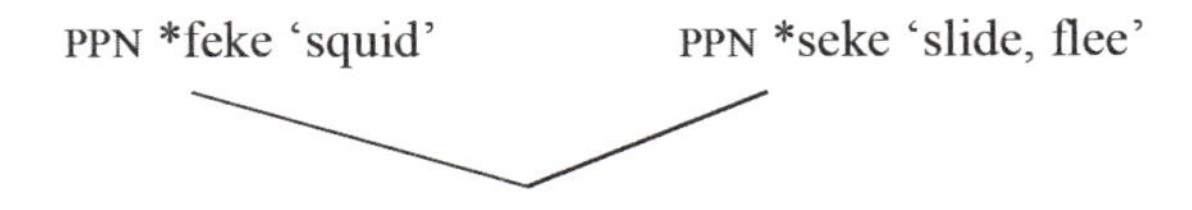

HAW *he'e* 'squid'; 'slide, flee'

Figure 16.6. The development of Hawaiian *he'e*

Further examples of homonyms are listed above in the section "The Importance of Word Groups . . .".

Near-Homonyms

For many pairs, the words are not identical but similar: that is, only parts match. For example,

'awa	kava	*'a'awa*	wrasse fish

'A'awa illustrates *reduplication*, referred to in Charlot 2014:14. In this example, the reduplication is not *full*, but *partial*—that is, only part of the base is repeated.

Figure 16.7. 'Awa

Figure 16.8. Awa, milkfish (*Chanos chanos*)

The following pair shows full reduplication—the entire base repeated:

hala	error	*halahala*	criticism (*PHG* 182)

The next pair shows a different kind of relationship: the words, although pronounced differently, would have been spelled the same before it was common practice to write the *ʻokina*. Thus, the written forms of the words would be identical:

awa [*ʻawa*]	kava	*awa* [*awa*]	milkfish

A similar pair was supplied by Charlot (pers. comm., February 2015): "An old Hawaiian gave me an interesting example. Put an *ʻalā* stone under your pillow, and spirits or ghosts would think that you are *ala* 'awake'.[38] Until fairly recently, these words would have been spelled alike, which reinforced their visual similarity.

In the next pair, a syllable unrelated to the base precedes it (the longer word may be a compound, but it doesn't appear in P-E):

heʻe	squid, flee	*waiheʻe*	k.o. shrub

A different kind of "similarity" is illustrated by the next pair; only the final three vowels in each form match:

palaoa	whale	*ʻaoa*	sandalwood

The following pairs show several different relationships, not easily classified, but all fitting into the category of "similar":[39]

pahaha	mullet	*pūhala*	pandanus
nenue	chub fish	*lauhue*	gourd
weke	goatfish	*wauke*	paper mulberry
ʻulei	k.o. shrub	*umaumalei*	surgeonfish
manō	shark	*moano*	goatfish
hole	strip away	*āholehole*	young *ʻāhole*

38. Charlot added this clarification (pers. comm., December 2015): "Ghosts or spirits attack you when you're asleep, so the point is that the ghosts will think you *are* awake and won't try to attack you in your sleep."

39. The examples have been gleaned from various studies cited in this chapter.

Some of the examples above show relationships that are common and can be easily described, but others may be random. In short, the concept of "similar" or "near-homonyms" is complex and hard to measure, and the category may be open-ended.

One such type reflects not a common *form* but instead a common *pattern* in the Hawaiian vocabulary. It consists of an indigenous word and the same word plus a modifier—producing a compound. (Some of the following examples may not represent pairs that are actually used in healing, but they show how sets of similar words or phrases have developed. See also the section on compounding in chapter 12.)

For example, we begin with the native plant *koa* 'Acacia koa'. For an introduced plant, which at an immature stage resembles *koa,* the modifier *haole* 'introduced, foreign' is added, producing *koa haole* 'Leucaena leucocephala'.

Another example builds on *kalo* 'taro'. A decorative plant, caladium, has leaves that are similar in shape, but they are multicolored—signified by the modifier *kalakoa* (which is borrowed from English *calico*).

In the following example, a plant, whose name was formed in the same way, was used for healing: "When *'awa* was not obtainable . . . a *pōpolo* plant was substituted and called *'awa pōpolo*" (Gutmanis 2013:97).

Figure 16.9. Kalo

Figure 16.10. Caladium

Antonyms

The examples in the preceding sections are based almost entirely on form—that is, they are words that sound alike or nearly alike. Within the *Kumulipo,* however, most of the word pairs are based not on sound but on meaning. Moreover, the individual words are not synonyms, but closer to what linguists call *antonyms*—words with opposite (but related) meanings. Here are some examples:

kāne	man	*wahine*	woman
lani	sky	*honua*	earth[40]

But are the words in these pairs really opposites as are, for example, *good* versus *bad* or *hot* versus *cold?* It is more likely that they have a *complementary* relationship with each other, discussed above in the Hawaiian classification of food.[41] For example *kāne* and *wahine* can be considered the component parts that make up "human being." Similarly, *lani* and *honua* make up a whole entity: "world," suggested by the common English expression "heaven and earth," which doesn't emphasize the differences between the individual words but is the result of combining them. In short, the pairs represent completeness—you can't have one without the other.

The Force of Opposition

In Charlot 2014, one can find, among many examples, the following oppositions:

luna	above	*lalo*	below
uka	inland	*kai*	sea

Other examples from the same source (page numbers in parentheses) are as follows:

ka uka	the interior	*ka moana*	the sea (31)
honua	land	*kai*	sea
Akua	God	*kanaka*	human (27)

40. Moreover, the sky was considered male and the earth female—another contrast (R. Johnson 1981:22).

41. Puanani Anderson-Fung helped develop the concept (pers. com., 14 January 2015).

ʻololī	narrow	*ʻololā*	broad (22)
waiʻololī	narrow stream	*waiʻololā*	broad stream[42]
kī	high note of drum	*pā*	low note of drum (23)
wai-ʻula	lit., red water	*wai-kea*	lit., white liquid (23)

Several examples illustrate the opposition of sea creatures versus plants.

In contrast with pairs containing words that are identical or similar, with the function of healing, these opposing words describe how the Hawaiians' universe is organized. According to Charlot (2014:32), the pairing of opposites could have served as a mnemonic device to help a chanter memorize the massive *Kumulipo,* while also reflecting a particularly Hawaiian worldview.

FUTURE DIRECTIONS

The relevance of the topic of word pairs to Hawaiian dictionaries is simple: for a number of reasons, the relationships between individual terms in a pair—whether similar in form or opposite in meaning—need to be visible in a dictionary if it is to reflect a Hawaiian worldview.

This requirement could be extended beyond paired terms to include almost any Hawaiian concept. For example, P-E's phrase included in the definition of *kalo*—"the staple from earliest times to the present"—only hints at the enormous cultural significance that extends beyond a definition that concentrates on and is perhaps confined to only form and function.

Should a dictionary provide such information? Charlot suggested some essential additions to the types of content that could be added to a traditional entry: "We need an essay describing the word's use . . . with information like antiquity, poetic/prosaic/religious terms, member of a pair, etc." (pers. comm., 16 March 2014).

The idea that an entry should be expanded beyond a mere definition to include more cultural knowledge leads us to a number of possibilities for taking dictionaries outside their usual borders. The first of these involves reexamining a traditional classification whose limits are not clear, but instead, overlap: *dictionary* versus *encyclopedia.*

42. Also representing male versus female (Charlot 2014:23).

Dictionary or Encyclopedia?

First, we need to understand the differences between a dictionary and an encyclopedia—and the similarities as well. The following summary may serve as a beginning:

> A dictionary is a text that describes the meanings of words, often illustrates how they are used in context, and usually indicates how they are pronounced . . . Modern dictionaries often include information about spelling, etymology . . ., usage, synonyms, and grammar . . . An encyclopedia is a collection of articles about every branch of knowledge. Although some articles include definitions, their descriptions go far beyond the information given in a dictionary.
>
> . . . The difference is sometimes stated, perhaps a bit too simply, . . . [as] "Dictionaries are about words, encyclopedias are about things." (Landau 2001:6–7)

"Things" may not capture the essence of the range of an encyclopedia; one might add "ideas" and "people" as well. But the word points us in the right direction—to reach beyond defining merely by using synonyms and paraphrases.

A monolingual Hawaiian dictionary might well be the first step toward a Hawaiian encyclopedia. Moreover, it should be noted that "dictionary versus encyclopedia" is not a dichotomy but a continuum. Consider the changes in Webster dictionaries since the first (1806), which was more like a glossary[43] than a dictionary; or the differences between Samuel Johnson's 1755 English dictionary—itself a milestone in lexicography—and the comprehensiveness of the *Oxford English Dictionary.* Could a merger between the *OED* and, say, the *Encyclopedia Britannica* be possible, especially in an online format?

However, Hawaiian and English lexicography differ in several ways—for example, history, number of speakers, written and oral resources available, and a market for the respective completed projects. But fundamentally, the goals are the same.

An earlier section suggested that perhaps some answers to these vague questions lie in the rapidly changing technology that is moving many standard reference works from print to some kind of electronic medium.[44]

---

43. In a glossary, the "definition" is often just a word or a phrase.

44. For example, see the discussion of the *Combined Hawaiian Dictionary* in the previous chapter.

Aside from ease of access, a number of advantages of the new technologies are related to content.

Two features of such an e-dictionary are especially important: (1) the convenience of correcting and adding to the work and (2) the lack of restrictions on its size. Thus, the already hazy dividing line between a dictionary and an encyclopedia could be further blurred, resulting in a reference work that could be considered not only a dictionary but also an evolving encyclopedia of Hawaiian knowledge.

As an oversimplified example, consider two varieties of *naupaka,* each in the form of a half flower. The romantic legend surrounding the

Figure 16.11. *Naupaka kahakai*

Figure 16.12. *Naupaka kuahiwi*

naupaka kahakai and *naupaka kuahiwi* (shore and upland varieties) personifies the half flowers as parted lovers from different social strata. Is our knowledge of *naupaka* ever complete if we don't know the accompanying legend?[45]

Such widespread and detailed documentation—even though it may deal mostly with Hawaiian's past and present—is especially important if the language is to have a future as well.

*

VERBATIM

As mentioned earlier, sometimes the associative "power" of certain words could differ from case to case. *He'e* 'flee', for example, was described as having both positive and negative connotations. Pukui, Haertig, and Lee enlarged on this theme, giving different examples that could have either meaning. The following excerpt is from the section entitled "*Manō,* the shark":

> To some Hawaiians, the shark is an *'aumakua* in animal form. To others, it is just an object—but one around which many associations cling. For Hawaiians believed that: Some sharks were good; some sharks were bad. Some sharks ate men. Other sharks, especially *'aumākua,* rescued men, even from the jaws of a devouring shark. Sharks were vengeful, angry creatures who, grabbing a man, "tossed him up and down in the sea." Yet, when the first Hawaiians sailed here from Tahiti, "They were guided over the desolate wastes like beloved children by a single great guide, the shark named Kalahiki."
>
> The two-pronged association exists today. To Hawaiians the shark may be, symbolically: bravery, daring, strength, a chief; benevolence, protection, rescue. Or: fright, danger, destruction, death.
>
> The *ānuenue,* the rainbow, also carries conflicting symbolisms. Today, the majority of Hawaiians we know associate the rainbow with death or disaster. It has—and may yet—symbolize good fortune. Varying regional or family interpretations seem to have existed for centuries. Fornander states

45. See Neal (1948) 1965:819–21.

that, "The laws of the priests . . . did not coincide; in the judgement of some, the rainbow was an auspicious sign . . . auguries of the priesthood mentioned in this account were either for good or evil." (Pukui, Haertig, and Lee 1972–1979:178–79)

*

In this book, the example *lama* is repeated, illustrating (1) the potential pitfalls of spelling the early Hawaiianized form of English *rum* with an *l* rather than an *r*, thereby producing unintended images in certain Bible passages;[46] (2) how, through sound change, two earlier forms ended up as one—but still separate words with different meanings; and (3) how the resultant identity of sound and spelling promoted *kaona* in the poetic and symbolic uses of the words.

The following essay—a *mo'olelo* featuring the trees themselves—enriches this linguistic history by adding a physical dimension.

THE *KAONA* OF *LAMA* FOR KAPĀLAMA AND THE ENLIGHTENED LEGACY OF PRINCESS BERNICE PAUAHI AND CHARLES REED BISHOP (BY PUANANI ANDERSON-FUNG)[47]

This is a story about how *kaona* enriches the significance of a project I have proposed—to plant *lama* trees in the *ahupua'a* of Kapālama, on lands now occupied by the Bishop Museum and the Kamehameha Schools.

It begins with *lama,* the Hawaiian name for two species of native trees, known internationally as *Diospyros sandwicensis* and *Diospyros hillebrandii.* In earlier times, the wood of the *lama* was used to build special enclosures for *kapu* 'sacred' purposes (Rock 1913:395). One such

46. See chapter 7.

47. *Mahalo* to Nani for writing this piece at my request. She is a Native Hawaiian ethnobotanist and Kamehameha Schools graduate currently specializing in the science of Hawaiian/Polynesian plant names and how they have evolved as a result of cultural choices, how they compare (favorably) with Linnaean plant names, and what they suggest about the migration of the early Polynesians. When Nani was a teenager, she initiated and directed the restoration of the Waonahele Hawaiian Plant Garden at Kamehameha High School at Kapālama (1974–1977).

structure was used in a ritual, practiced to ensure that the *ali'i* would produce offspring of the highest possible rank. It has been suggested that the *ahupua'a* may have been named Kapālama, literally 'the *lama* wood enclosure', to commemorate this practice, since there is no evidence that it was held in areas other than Kapālama (Kamehameha Schools 1989). Another source, however, says the area was so named because the "high chiefs were protected" at Kapālama (Pukui, Elbert, and Mookini 1974:87), which they define elsewhere as 'the sacred *lama* enclosure' (Pukui and Elbert 1986:308).

Today, a few *lama* trees can still be found on the ridges at the upper end of the *ahupua'a* (Sigrid Southworth, pers. comm., 2016), but most residents have never seen these handsome trees and are unaware of their historical significance to the area. I suggested, therefore, that *lama* trees be planted—and made conspicuous parts of the landscaping—at the Kapālama campus of the Kamehameha Schools and the Bishop Museum.

But the gesture, although appropriate, seemed to be lacking something. I felt that to be better appreciated, the project should also be relevant to contemporary Hawaiian culture and not just commemorate a discontinued practice of an earlier time. Moreover, I thought the project should have a special connection to the two properties that I called upon to enact this proposal.

Here *kaona* enters the picture. The word *lama* also means 'light, torch, lamp' and conveys the connotation of 'enlightenment' (Pukui and Elbert 1986:192). Pairing this word with *lama* 'the tree' means that having *lama* trees on these campuses could also symbolize the remarkable enlightenment of both Bernice Pauahi and Charles Reed Bishop—she, the great-granddaughter of Kamehameha the Great, who donated her lands to build and fund the Kamehameha Schools, and he, who gave his personal wealth to establish a museum to *mālama* 'preserve and protect' the material culture of his wife's heritage and to conserve and study Hawai'i's natural history. Because trees are living things, they would serve as a reminder that the legacy of the Bishops lives on in these two institutions, which are charged with the responsibility of continuing to *light* the way for Native Hawaiians in the generations to come.

At this writing, I am pleased to report that Bishop Museum is very interested in this idea and hopes to adopt this proposal and integrate *lama* trees into the master landscaping plan for the Bishop Museum campus (Amy Marvin, pers. comm., 2017).

As if in tacit agreement to what has been said here, a plaque at the entry to the museum bears the following inscription:

> To the Memory of Bernice Pauahi Bishop,
> founder of the Kamehameha Schools.
> A bright light among her people,
> her usefulness survives her earthly life.
> (Bernice Pauahi Bishop Museum 1915:89)

20 December 2017

REFERENCES

See *Voices of Eden* (Schütz 1994) for more complete annotations and Judd, Bell, and Murdoch 1978 for Hawaiian titles. The symbols < > enclose information about manuscript materials, the symbols { } enclose translations, and the symbols [ ] enclose occasional annotations. For publications with two dates, the earlier date is in parentheses, but the page reference given in the text is from the later edition.

Adelaar, Willem F. H. 1998. The Name of the Sweet Potato: A Case of Pre-conquest Contact between South America and the Pacific. In Mark Janse, *Productivity and Creativity,* 1998:403–12. Berlin, New York: Mouton de Gruyter.

'Ahahui 'Ōlelo Hawai'i 1978. See Wilson 1978.

Alexander, William De Witt. 1864. *A Short Synopsis of the Most Essential Points in Hawaiian Grammar: For the Use of the Pupils of Oahu College.* Honolulu: Whitney. 2 parts. 1871, 2nd ed. (Honolulu: Whitney). 1891, 3rd ed. (Honolulu: Press Publishing). 1908, 4th ed. (Honolulu: Thrum). 1924, 5th ed., revised (Honolulu: Hawaiian News & Thrum). 1968 reprint (Rutland, VT: Tuttle). 1981 reprint (Japan: Charles E. Tuttle Company).

The Alphabet. 1822. O'ahu: Mission Press.

Anderson, Rufus. 1864. *The Hawaiian Islands: Their Progress and Condition under Missionary Labors.* Boston: Gould and Lincoln.

Anderson, William. 1776–77. Directions for the Pronunciation of the Vocabulary. In James Cook, *A Voyage Towards the South Pole and Round the World,* 319–22. <Adm 55/108 (Public Record Office); UHM microfilm 4057, reel 36>

———. 1777. Journal, vol. 1 and 2 (vol. 3 is missing). Great Britain Admiralty Log Books. Captains' logs. 1763–1821. *Resolution* 1776–1780. <Adm 51/4560/203–4; UHM microfilm 4057, reel 23>

———. 1784. Vocabulary of the Language of Atooi, One of the Sandwich Islands. In James Cook, *A Voyage to the Pacific Ocean,* vol. 3, Appendix 5, 549–53.

Anderson-Fung, Puanani O., and Kepā Maly. 2002. Growing Plants for Lei Helps to Preserve Hawai'i's Natural and Cultural Heritage. In Hollyer, Castro, and Evans, *Growing Plants for Hawaiian Lei,* 177–205. Honolulu: University of Hawai'i at Mānoa, College of Tropical Agriculture and Human Resources.

Andrews, Lorrin. (1832) 1834. Essay on the Best Practicable Method of Conducting Native Schools at the Sandwich Islands. Read at the General Meeting of the Mission, June 13, 1832, by Lorrin Andrews, Principal of the High

School at Lahaina. Appendix 3 of the *Annual Report of the ABCFM read at the 25th Annual Meeting* (1834), 156–68.

———. 1836a. *A Vocabulary of Words in the Hawaiian Language.* Lahainaluna: Press of the High School.

———. 1836b. Remarks on the Hawaiian Dialect of the Polynesian Language. *Chinese Repository* 5 (May 1836 to April 1837), Article II:12–21.

———. 1838. Peculiarities of the Hawaiian Language. The *Hawaiian Spectator* 1(4):392–420.

———. 1854. *Grammar of the Hawaiian Language.* Honolulu: Mission Press.

———. 1864. Value of the Hawaiian and English Languages in the Instruction of Hawaiians. *Hawaiian Evangelical Association's Proceedings* . . . 3 June to 1 July 1863, 94–107. Boston: Marvin.

———. 1865. *A Dictionary of the Hawaiian Language, to Which is Appended an English-Hawaiian Vocabulary and a Chronological Table of Remarkable Events.* Honolulu: Whitney. 2003 edition, with an introduction by Noenoe K. Silva and Albert J. Schütz. Honolulu: Island Heritage.

Andrews, Lorrin, and Henry Hodges Parker. 1922. *A Dictionary of the Hawaiian Language.* Revised by Henry H. Parker. Bernice P. Bishop Mus. Spec. Publ. no. 8. Honolulu: Board of Commissioners of Public Archives of the Territory of Hawaii.

Arago, Jacques. 1823. *Narrative of a Voyage Round the World in the Uranie and Physicienne Corvettes, Commanded by Captain Freycinet, during the Years 1817, 1818, 1819, and 1820* . . . London: Treuttel and Wurtz. Reprinted in 1971 as Bibliotheca Australiana no. 45, New York: Da Capo. [See Gaimard 1823.]

Ashford, Marguerite K. 1987. The Evolution of the Hawaiian Dictionary and Notes on the Early Compilers, with Particular Attention to Manuscript Resources of the Bishop Museum Library. *Bishop Museum Occasional Papers* 27:1–24.

Atcherley, Mary W. 1930. *First Book in Hawaiian.* Honolulu: Published for the Territory of Hawaii by the Hawaiian Board of Missions.

Au, Kathryn H., and Julie Kaomea. 2009. Reading Comprehension and Diversity in Historical Perspective: Literacy, Power, and Native Hawaiians. In Gerald G. Duffy and Susan E. Israel, eds., *Handbook of Research on Reading Comprehension,* 571–86. New York: Routledge.

Baker, Tammy Haili'ōpua. 2015. *Lā'ieikawai.* Play performed at Kennedy Theatre, University of Hawai'i at Mānoa, opening on 20 February 2015. [Baker wrote: "For the play I used 1864 Hale'ole and 1888 Bolster & Mehe'ula, both from the *Nūpepa 'Ōlelo Hawai'i.*"]

———. 2019. *'Au'a 'Ia: Holding On.* Performed at Kennedy Theatre, University of Hawai'i at Mānoa, 27, 28 September; 4,5, and 6 October.

Beaglehole, John Cawte, ed. 1955. *The Journals of Captain James Cook on his Voyage of Discovery.* Vol. 1. *The Voyage of the* Endeavour *1768–1771.* Hakluyt Society Extra Series no. 34. Cambridge: Hakluyt Society. [See also Hawkesworth 1773.]

———. 1961. *The Journals of Captain James Cook on his Voyage of Discovery.* Vol. 2. *The Voyage of the* Resolution *and* Adventure *1772–1775.* Hakluyt Society Extra Series no. 35. Cambridge: Hakluyt Society. [See also Cook 1777.]

———. 1966. *Exploration of the Pacific.* Third ed. Stanford, CA: Stanford University Press.

———, ed. 1967. *The Journals of Captain James Cook on his Voyage of Discovery.* Vol. 3. *The Voyage of the* Resolution *and* Discovery *1776–1780.* Hakluyt Society Extra Series no. 36. Cambridge: Hakluyt Society. [See also Cook 1784.]

———. 1974. *The Life of Captain James Cook.* Stanford, CA: Stanford University Press.

Beckley, Fred W. 1923. The Hawaiian Language in the Schools. In *Hawaii's Public Schools: Being the Biennial Report of the Department of Public Instruction, Territory of Hawaii, 1921–1922.* Honolulu: Published by the Department (Advertiser Publishing Co.).

Beckwith, Martha, ed. 2007. *Kepelino's Traditions of Hawaii.* Foreword by Noelani Arista. Bernice P. Bishop Museum Bulletin 95. Honolulu: Bishop Museum Press.

Bellwood, Peter. (1978) 1987. *The Polynesians: Prehistory of an Island People.* London: Thames and Hudson.

Bennett, Wendell Clark. 1931. *Archaeology of Kauai.* Bernice P. Bishop Museum Bulletin 80. Honolulu: Published by the Museum. [*Heiau:* pp. 30–53; 44: "Site 23. Keaalii heiau, at Keaalii on the west side of the Waimea river, behind the first Japanese temple."]

Benson, Morton. 1990. Culture-Specific Items in Bilingual Dictionaries of English. *Dictionaries* 12:43–54.

Beresford, William. 1789. *A Voyage Round the World, but More Particularly to the North-west Coast of America: Performed in 1785, 1786, 1787, and 1788, in the King George and Queen Charlotte, Captains Portlock and Dixon . . .* By Captain George Dixon. London: Goulding. [Although Dixon is listed as the author, he was actually an editor; the forty-nine chapters appear as letters signed "W. B." HAW word list, pp. 268–70.]

Bernice Pauahi Bishop Museum. 1915. *Bishop Museum Handbook.* Part I: *The Hawaiian Collections.* Honolulu: Bishop Museum Press.

Biggs, Bruce G. 1971. The Languages of Polynesia. In Thomas A. Sebeok, ed., *Current Trends in Linguistics 8: Linguistics in Oceania,* 466–505. The Hague: Mouton.

Bingham Family Papers. See Jimerson and Weiss.

Bingham, Hiram. 1819. Notes on George Tamoree (Kaumualii) found in a manuscript letter of Rev. Hiram Bingham in 1819 when he was contemplating service in the new mission to the Sandwich Islands. To Mr Samuel Worchester D. D. Salem Mass., from Goshen [Connecticut] May 11 1819. [In the same letter, Bingham expressed his objections to using numbers in the provisional vowel system.]

———. 1847. *A Residence of Twenty-one Years in the Sandwich Islands; or the Civil, Religious, and Political History of Those Islands; Comprising a Particular View of the Missionary Operations Connected with the Introduction and Progress of Christianity and Civilization among the Hawaiian People.* Hartford, CT; Huntington; New York: Converse. [Later editions in 1848, 1849, 1855, 1969, and 1981.]

Bingham, Hiram, and Elisha Loomis. 1823. Letter to Jeremiah Evarts. <Houghton Library, Harvard, ABC 19.1, vol. 1 (141–56)> [Letter describes orthographic problems and requests special type, including diacritics, vol. 1:141–56.]

Bingham, Sybil. 1823. Select Hawaiian Phrases / Sentences Rehearsed at Table / July 1823. (Title on cover: Selections for the Table.). Bingham Family Papers, Series I, 2–34, Yale University Library, Manuscripts and Archives. Published in 1996: Introduction and typesetting by James Rumford; translation assistance by Puakea Nogelmeier. Honolulu: Mānoa Press.

Bishop, Artemas. 1824–. Correspondence. Library, Hawaiian Mission Houses Historic Site and Archives.

Bolster, Jas. Henry. See Meheula, Sol. 1888.

Borg, Jim. 1997. The History Within: Genetic Research Offers New Views of Polynesian Migrations. *Hawaii Magazine* (February):36–41.

Botta, Paolo Emilio. 1841. Word list, collected in 1828. In Auguste Bernard du Hautcilly (A. Duhaut-Cilly), *Viaggio Intorno al Globo, principalmente alla California ed alle Isole Sandwich, negli anni 1826, 1827, 1828, e 1829 . . .* 2 vols. in 1. Torino: Fontana. [HAW word list, 360–65.]

Boyd, Lou. 2001. Lou Boyd Revisited. *Honolulu Advertiser* 31 October.

Brigham, William Tufts. 1911. *Ka Hana Tapa: The Making of Bark-Cloth in Hawaii.* Honolulu: Memoirs of Bishop Museum 3.

Brumaghim, Wayne H. 2011. The Life and Legacy of Heneri ʻŌpūkahaʻia / Hawaiʻi's Prodigal Son. University of Hawaiʻi at Mānoa MA thesis.

Buck, Peter (Te Rangi Hiroa). 1938. *Vikings of the Sunrise.* New York: Stokes.

Campbell, Archibald. 1816. *A Voyage Round the World, from 1806 to 1812; in which Japan, Kamschatka, the Aleutian Islands, and the Sandwich Islands, Were Visited. Including a narrative of the author's shipwreck on the island of Sannack, and his subsequent wreck in the ship's long boat. With an account of the present state of the Sandwich Islands and a vocabulary of their language.* Edinburgh: Constable; London: Longman; Glasgow: Smith. 1967 ed., Honolulu: University of Hawaiʻi Press for Friends of the Library of Hawaiʻi. 1969 ed.: Amsterdam: Da Capo.

Capell, Arthur. 1941. *A New Fijian Dictionary.* Sydney: Australasian Medical Publishing Co. 2nd ed. (1957), Glasgow: Wilson Guthrie. 3rd ed. (1968), Suva: Government Printer. 4th ed. (1973), Suva: Government Printer.

Carr, Denzel. 1951. Comparative Treatment of Epenthetic and Paragogic Vowels in English Loan Words in Japanese and Hawaiian. In W. J. Fischel, ed., *Semitic and Oriental Studies . . . [for] William Popper.* University of California Publications in Semitic Philology 11:13–25.

Cassidy, Frederic G., ed. 1985–2013. *Dictionary of American Regional English.* Cambridge, MA: Belknap Press of Harvard University Press.

Cawdrey, Robert. 1604. *A table alphabeticall conteyning and teaching the true writing, and vnderstanding of hard vsuall English wordes, borrowed from the Hebrew, Greeke, Latine, or French, &c. With the interpretation thereof by plaine English words, gathered for the benefit & helpe of ladies, gentlewomen, or any other vnskilfull persons. Whereby they may the more easilie and better vnderstand many hard English wordes, vvhich they shall heare or read in scriptures, sermons, or elsewhere, and also be made able to vse the same aptly themselues.* London: I. Roberts for Edmund Weaver.

Charlot, Jean. 1976. *Two Hawaiian Plays.* Laukiamanuikahiki (Snare-that-lures-a-far-flung-bird). Na lono elua (Two Lonos). Honolulu: Privately published, distributed by the University of Hawaiʻi Press.

Charlot, John. 1983. *Chanting the Universe: Hawaiian Religious Culture.* Honolulu: Emphasis International.

———. 2005. *Classical Hawaiian Education: Generations of Hawaiian Culture.* Electronic Book, CD. Lāʻie, HI: Pacific Institute, Brigham Young University–Hawaiʻi.

———. 2014. *A Kumulipo of Hawaiʻi. Comments on Lines 1 to 615 of the Origin Chant.* Sankt Augustin, Germany: Academia Verlag.

Churchward, C. Maxwell. 1959. *Tongan Dictionary.* London: Oxford University Press.

Clark, Ross. 1979. Language. In Jesse D. Jennings, ed., *The Prehistory of Polynesia,* 250–70. Cambridge, MA; London: Harvard University Press.

Cogswell, Bill, Tommy Harrison, and Johnny Noble. 1933 (1950). My Little Grass Shack in Kealakekua Hawaii. In *Songs of Hawaii.* Chicago: Miller Music Corp.

Collections: Hāpai i nā Leo: Preserving Bishop Museum's Audio Collection. 2011. *Ka ʻElele: The Messenger/The Journal of Bishop Museum* (fall):12–13.

Cook, James. 1777. *A Voyage Towards the South Pole and Round the World: Performed in His Majesty's ships the Resolution and Adventure, in the years 1772, 1773, 1774, and 1775.* Vol. 2. London: Strahan and Cadell.

———. 1784. *A Voyage to the Pacific Ocean, undertaken by the Command of His Majesty, for Making Discoveries in the Northern Hemisphere.* London: Strahan, for Nicol & Cadell. See Beaglehole 1967, vol. 3.

Cook, James, and James King. 1785. *A Voyage to the Pacific Ocean . . . in His Majesty's Ships the "Resolution" and "Discovery"; in the Years 1776 . . . 1780,* 2d ed. London: H. Hughs for G. Nicol and T. Cadell, vol. 1, xxxiv.

Dalrymple, Alexander. (1770–1771) 1967. *An Historical Collection of the Several Voyages and Discoveries in the South Pacific Ocean.* Volume 2, *Containing the Dutch Voyages.* [Vocabulary unpaginated, but 7 pages, following "Conduct of the discoverers in the tracks they made choice of."] London: Printed for the Author.

Dana, Richard Henry. N.d., ca. 1870s. Misc. letters . . . 187-, Yale University Library.

Davidson, Janet M. 1979. Samoa and Tonga. In J. D. Jennings, ed., *The Prehistory of Polynesia,* 82–109. Cambridge, MA: Harvard University Press.

Davies, John. 1810. *Te Aebi no Taheiti / e te / Parou Mata Mua / i Parou Hapi / Iaitea te Perini e te Ridini / te / Parou no Taheiti.* London: Printed for the Missionary Society by Townsend, Powel, and Co.

Davies, John. 1823. *A Grammar of the Tahitian Dialect of the Polynesian Language.* Burder's Point, Tahiti: Mission Press.

———. 1839. The Polynesian Nation. *Hawaiian Spectator* 2 (January):49–51.

———. 1851. *A Tahitian and English Dictionary, with Introductory Remarks on the Polynesian Language, and a Short Grammar of the Tahitian Dialect: With an appendix containing a list of foreign words used in the Tahitian Bible, in commerce, etc., with the sources from whence they have been derived.* Tahiti: London Missionary Society's Press.

Davis, Chelsea. 2014. *Hokule'a* [*Hōkūle'a*] and her sister vessel *Hikianalia* set sail. *Hawaii News Now.* Retrieved 2014-05-20. From Wikipedia article "Hokulea," retrieved 6 October 2016.

Daws, Gavan, and Nā Leo o Kamehameha. 2009. *Wayfinding through the Storm: Speaking Truth to Power at Kamehameha Schools 1993–1999.* Honolulu: Watermark.

Day, A. Grove. 1991. An Early Hawaiian Vocabulary. *Hawaiian Journal of History* 25:21–30. [Historical background for and reproduction of Martínez's 1789 HAW word list. Some items identified (with ENG glosses) and respelled, 28–29.]

Day, A. Grove, and Albertine Loomis. (1973) 1997. *Ka Pa'i Palapala: Early Printing in Hawai'i.* Honolulu: Printing Industries of Hawaii. 1997 edition: Honolulu: Mission Houses Museum.

de Brosses, Charles. 1756. *Histoire des Navigations aux Terres Australes: Contenant ce que l'on scait des moeurs et des productions des Contrées découvertes jusqu'à ce jour et où il est traité de l'utilité d'y faire de plus amples découvertes et des moyens d'y former un établissement.* Paris.

Dell, Brad. 2015. "Lā'ieikawai": The Largest Kennedy Mainstage, and the First Hawaiian One. *Ka Leo o Hawai'i: The Voice* 109(34) (16–22 February):12–13.

Dibble, Sheldon. 1838. *Ka Mooolelo Hawaii: I Kakauia e Kekahi mau Haumana o ke Kulanui, a i Hooponoponoia e Kekahi Kumu o ia Kula* {The History of Hawaii: Written by Some Scholars of the High School and Corrected by One of the Teachers of This School}. Lahainaluna: Mea Pai Palapala no ke Kulanui.

———. (1839) 1909. *History and General View of the Sandwich Islands' Mission.* New York: Taylor & Dodd.

Dilworth, Thomas. (1740) 1793. *A New Guide to the English Tongue.* 52nd ed. Gainsborough, England: Mozley. Facsimile reproduction: 1978. Delmar, NY: Scholars' Facsimiles & Reprints.

Di Piazza, Anne, and Erik Pearthree. 2007. A New Reading of Tupaia's Chart. *Journal of the Polynesian Society* 116(3):321–40.

Donne, M. A. [1866]. *The Sandwich Islands and Their People.* London: Society for Promoting Christian Knowledge.

Drechsel, Emanuel J. 2014. *Language Contact in the Early Colonial Pacific: Maritime Polynesian Pidgin before Pidgin English.* Cambridge Approaches to Language Contact. Cambridge, UK: Cambridge University Press.

Druett, Joan. 2011. *Tupaia: The Remarkable Story of Captain Cook's Polynesian Navigator.* Auckland: Random House.

Dumont d'Urville, J. S. C. 1834. *Voyage de Découvertes de l'Astrolabe, éxecuté par ordre du Roi, pendant les années 1826-1827-1828-1829, sous le commandement de M. J. Dumont d'Urville.* Paris: Ministère de la Marine.

Dwight, Edwin Welles. (1818) 1968. *Memoirs of Henry Obookiah, a Native of Owhyhee, and a Member of the Foreign Mission School; who died at Cornwall, Connecticut, February 17, 1818, Aged 26 years.* 1968: Honolulu: Woman's Board of Missions for the Pacific Islands, the Hawai'i Conference, the United Church of Christ. 1990: Honolulu: Women's Board of Missions for the Pacific Islands.

Elbert, Samuel H. 1951. *Conversational Hawaiian.* Honolulu: University of Hawai'i Extension Division. Mimeographed. [5th ed., 1965. University of Hawai'i Press.]

———. 1953. Internal Relationships of Polynesian Languages and Dialects. *Southwestern Journal of Anthropology* 9 (summer):147–73. [Written in collaboration with William H. Davenport, Jesse W. Dykes, and Eugene Ogan.]

———. 1954. The Hawaiian Dictionaries, Past and Future. In *Sixty-Second Annual Report of the Hawaiian Historical Society for the year 1953,* 5–18. Honolulu: Hawaiian Historical Society.

———, ed. 1959. *Selections from Fornander's Hawaiian Antiquities and Folklore.* Honolulu: University of Hawai'i Press.

———. 1989. Kawena: A Personal Reminiscence. *Honolulu* 24(5):130–33, 177.

Elbert, Samuel H., and Mary Kawena Pukui. 1979. *Hawaiian Grammar.* Honolulu: University of Hawai'i Press.

Elbert, Samuel H., and Noelani Mahoe. 1970. *Nā Mele o Hawaiʻi Nei: 101 Hawaiian Songs.* Honolulu: University of Hawaiʻi Press.

Ellis, William. (1825) 1979. *Journal of William Ellis. Narrative of Tour of Hawaii, or Owhyhee; with Remarks on the History, Traditions, Manners, Customs, and Language of the Inhabitants of the Sandwich Islands.* Boston: Crocker and Brewster. 1979 edition, Rutland, VT, and Tokyo: Charles E. Tuttle.

Extracts from a General Letter of the Missionaries, dated 1 July 1833. *Missionary Herald* 30 (1834):285.

Finney, Ben. 1994. *Voyage of Rediscovery.* Berkeley: University of California Press.

Fischer, Steven Roger. 1995. Preliminary Evidence for Cosmogonic Texts in Rapanui's Rongorongo Inscriptions. *Journal of the Polynesian Society* 104(3): 303–21.

———. 1997. *Glyphbreaker: A Decipherer's Story.* New York: Copernicus.

———. 2001. Mangarevan Doublets: Preliminary Evidence for Proto-Southeastern Polynesian. *Oceanic Linguistics* 40(1):112–24.

Forbes, David W. 1992. *Encounters with Paradise: Views of Hawaii and Its People, 1778–1941.* Honolulu: Honolulu Academy of Arts.

———. 1999–2003. *Hawaiian National Bibliography, 1780–1900.* Vol. 1: *1780–1830;* vol. 2: *1831–1850;* vol. 3: *1851–1880;* vol. 4: *1881–1900.* Honolulu: University of Hawaiʻi Press.

Funk & Wagnalls New Encyclopedia. 1972. New York: Funk & Wagnalls, Inc.

Gaimard, Joseph P. 1823. Word list in Arago 1823. [Translation from the French original. Vocabulary of 236 words and some brief notes on consonant alternation, collected in 1819:291–94.]

Garner, Bryan A. 2003. *Garner's Dictionary of Modern American Usage.* Oxford: Oxford University Press.

Gaussin, Pierre Louis Jean Baptiste. 1853. *Du Dialecte de Tahiti, de Celui des Îles Marquises, et en Général, de la Langue Polynésienne.* Paris: Firmin et Didot Frères.

Geraghty, Paul. 1983a. *The History of the Fijian Languages.* Oceanic Linguistics Special Publication No. 19. Honolulu: University of Hawaiʻi Press.

———. 1983b. Review of Peter A. Lanyon-Orgill, *Captain Cook's South Sea Island Vocabularies. Journal of the Polynesian Society* 92(4):554–59.

———. 1993. Pulotu, Polynesian Homeland. *Journal of the Polynesian Society* 102(4):343–84.

Goodheart, Adam. 1996. Mapping the Past. *Civilization* 3:40–47.

Grant, Glen, Bennett Hymer, and the Bishop Museum Archives. 2000. *Hawaiʻi Looking Back.* Honolulu: Mutual Publishing.

Gutmanis, June. (1976) 1985, 2013. *Kahuna Laʻau Lapaʻau: The Practice of Hawaiian Herbal Medicine.* 3rd ed. Honolulu: Island Heritage.

———. 2013. *The Secrets and Practice of Hawaiian Herbal Medicine.* 2nd ed. Honolulu: Island Heritage.

Hadden, Alfred C., and James Hornell. 1936–38. *Canoes of Oceania.* Bernice P. Bishop Museum Special Publications 27–29. Honolulu: Bernice P. Bishop Museum.

Hale, Constance. 2013. ʻŌlelo Hawaiʻi: Ke Ola ka Make? *Honolulu Magazine* (November):52–54, 55, 76, 78, 80, 82, 84, 86, 88.

Hale, Horatio E. 1846. *Ethnography and Philology.* Vol. 6 in *United States Exploring Expedition 1838–42.* Philadelphia: Lea and Blanchard. Unofficial issue; reprinted 1968. Ridgewood, NJ: Gregg. [Includes "A Comparative Grammar of the Polynesian Dialects," 229–89; a PN-ENG vocabulary, 294–339; and an ENG-PN vocabulary, 341–56.]

Haleoli, S. N. 1863. Kaao o Laieikawai: Ka Hiwahiwa o Paliuli, Kawahineokaliula. Kakauia mailoko mai o na Moolelo Kahiko o Hawaii Nei. Honolulu, Oahu: Paiia e H. M. Whitney. [One source for Baker 2015.]

Handy, E. S. Craighill, and Elizabeth Green Handy. 1972. *Native Planters in Old Hawaii: Their Life, Lore, and Environment.* Bernice P. Bishop Museum Bulletin 233. Honolulu: Bishop Museum Press.

Handy, E. S. Craighill, and Mary Kawena Pukui. 1958. *The Polynesian Family System in Kaʻū, Hawaiʻi.* Wellington, NZ: Polynesian Society. Originally in *Journal of the Polynesian Society* 61(3,4): 243–82. 1972 edition, Rutland, VT: Tuttle.

Handy, E. S. Craighill, Mary Kawena Pukui, and Katherine Livermore. 1934. *Outline of Hawaiian Physical Therapeutics.* Bernice P. Bishop Museum Bulletin 126. Honolulu: Bishop Museum.

Hargraves, Orin. 2015. Trademarks and the Lexicographer in the Digital Age. *Dictionaries* 36:88–99.

Harlow, Ray. 1993. Lexical Expansion in Maori. *Journal of the Polynesian Society* 102(1):99–107.

The Hawaiian Language. 1903. *Paradise of the Pacific* 16(11):7–8.

Haweis, Thomas. 1795–1802. Collection of Papers *re* early South Seas Missions. Mitchell Library (Public Library of New South Wales, Sydney). Haweis Papers, MSS. 4190x. CY 933.

Hawkesworth, John. 1773. *An Account of the Voyages Undertaken by the Order of His Present Majesty for Making Discoveries in the Southern Hemisphere and Successfully Performed by Commodore Byron, Captain Wallis, Captain Carteret, and Captain Cook, in the* Dolphin, *the* Swallow, *and the* Endeavour*: Drawn up from the Journals which were Kept by the Several Commanders, and from the Papers of Joseph Banks, Esq.* 2d ed. 3 vols. London: Strahan and Cadell.

Helbig, Ray. 1970. *Let's Learn a Little Hawaiian.* Honolulu: Hawaiian Service, Inc.

Heyerdahl, Thor. 1952. *American Indians in the Pacific: The Theory behind the Kon-Tiki Expedition.* London: George Allen & Unwin Ltd.

Hockett, Charles F. 1958. *A Course in Modern Linguistics.* New York: Macmillan.

Hunt, Terry. See Kubota 2011.

Hurley, Timothy. 2016. Google Service Translates Hawaiian. *Honolulu Star-Advertiser,* 28 February 2016, B1, B3.

Hymes, Dell H. 1983. Lexicostatistics and Glottochronology in the Nineteenth Century (with Notes toward a General History). In Hymes, *Essays in the History of Linguistic Anthropology,* 59–113. Amsterdam/Philadelphia: John Benjamins.

Na Ivolavosa Vakaviti {The Fijian Dictionary}. 2005. Suva: Institute of Fijian Language and Culture.

Jacobs, Julia. 2018. Remote Hawaiian Island Largely Wiped Out by Hurricane. *Honolulu Star-Advertiser,* 28 October 2018, B3.

Janse, Mark, ed. 1998. *Productivity and Creativity: Studies in General and Descriptive Linguistics in Honor of E. M. Uhlenbeck.* Trends in Linguistics. Studies and Monographs 116. Berlin, New York: Mouton de Gruyter.

Jimerson, Randall C., and Rena R. Weiss. n.d. Bingham Family Papers. <Yale University, Sterling Memorial Library Manuscripts and Archives. Ms. group no. 81.>

Johnson, E. 1844. *Ke Ao Spela; he Palapala ia e Ao aku ai i na Kamalii i ka Mahele Pono ana o na Huaolelo a me ka Hai Pololei ana o na Hua.* {The speller: A book to teach children in the division of words, and in the correct pronunciation of words.} Honolulu: Mea Pai Palapala a na Misionari.

Johnson, Rubellite. 1981. *Kumulipo: The Hawaiian Hymn of Creation.* Vol. 1. Honolulu: Topgallant.

Johnson, Samuel. 1755. *A Dictionary of the English Language.* London: Strahan. Facsimile ed., 1979. London: Times Books.

Judd, Bernice, Janet E. Bell, and Clare G. Murdoch. 1978. *Hawaiian Language Imprints 1822–1899: A Bibliography.* Honolulu: Hawaiian Mission Children's Society and University of Hawai'i Press.

Judd, Bernice, and Helen Yonge Lind. 1974. *Voyages to Hawaii before 1860: A Record, Based on Historical Narratives in the Libraries of the Hawaiian Mission Children's Society and the Hawaiian Historical Society, Extended to March 1860.* Earlier edition by Bernice Judd (1929) enlarged and edited by Helen Yonge Lind. Honolulu: University of Hawai'i Press for Hawaiian Mission Children's Society.

Judd, Henry P. 1939. *The Hawaiian Language and Hawaiian-English Dictionary: A Complete Grammar.* Honolulu: Star-Bulletin Ltd. 5th printing: 1944. 10th printing: 1961. Honolulu: Hawaiian Service.

Judd, Henry P., Mary Kawena Pukui, and John F. G. Stokes. 1945. *Introduction to the Hawaiian Language.* Honolulu: Tongg Publishing Company. Reprinted as *Handy Hawaiian Dictionary,* 1995. Honolulu: Mutual Publishing.

Judd, Laura Fish. 1880. *Honolulu: Sketches of Life Social, Political, and Religious in the Hawaiian Island [sic] from 1828 to 1861.* New York: Randolph & Co.

Kahn, Jennifer G., Timothy M. Rieth, Patrick V. Kirch, J. Stephen Athens, and Gail Murakami. 2014. Re-dating of the Kuli'ou'ou Rockshelter, O'ahu, Hawai'i: Location of the First Radiocarbon Date from the Pacific Islands. *Journal of the Polynesian Society* 123(1):67–90.

Kamakau, Samuel Mānaiakalani. (1866–1871) 1961. *The Ruling Chiefs of Hawaii.* Translation of *Ka Moolelo o Kamehameha I* and *Ka Moolelo o na Kamehameha,* by Thomas G. Thrum, Lahilahi Webb, Emma Davidson Taylor, John Wise, and Mary Kawena Pukui (translation reviewed by MKP). Honolulu: The Kamehameha Schools Press. Rev. ed., 1991. Introduction by L[ilikalā] K. Kame'eleihiwa.

Kamehameha Schools. 1986–1989. Kapālama. In *Hawaiian Place Names: The Significance of Hawaiian Sites, their Locations, and Interpretation of their Names* 4(1). Honolulu: The Kamehameha Schools / Bernice Pauahi Bishop Estate, Extension Education Division, Hawaiian Studies Institute.

Kanahele, Elama, Kimo Armitage, and Keao NeSmith (editors and translators). 2007. *Aloha Niihau: Oral Histories by Elama Kanahele, Emalia Licayan, and Virginia Nizo.* Waipahu: Island Heritage.

Kanahele, George. 1982. *Hawaiian Renaissance.* Honolulu: L Project Waiaha.

Kāretu, T[īmoti]. S. 1984. *Concise Māori Dictionary: Māori-English, English-Māori.* Compiled by A. W. Reed, revised by T. S. Kāretu. Wellington, NZ: A. H. & A. W. Reed Ltd.

Ke Kauoha Hou me Ka Buke o Nā Halelū a me Nā 'Ōlelo Akamai a Solomona {The New Testament with Psalms and Proverbs}. 2014. Honolulu: Booklines Hawaii Ltd.

Kendall, Joshua. 2012. *The Forgotten Founding Father: Noah Webster's Obsession and the Creation of an American Culture.* New York: Berkley Publishing.

Kendall, Thomas, and Samuel Lee. 1820. *A Grammar and Vocabulary of the Language of New Zealand.* London: Church Missionary Society.

Kent, Harold Winfield. 1986. *Treasury of Hawaiian Words in One Hundred and One Categories.* Honolulu: Masonic Public Library.

Kerr, Robert. 1814. *General History and Collection of Voyages and Travels,* v. 10. Edinburgh: Ballantyne. [Le Maire and Schouten voyage, 162–91.]

King, James. 1778. Portrait of Anderson. In Beaglehole 1967, Part 2, Appendix 3, King's Journal, 1429–30.

Kirch, Patrick Vinton. 1985. *Feathered Gods and Fishhooks: An Introduction to Hawaiian Archaeology and Prehistory.* Honolulu: University of Hawai'i Press.

———. 2011. When Did the Polynesians Settle Hawai'i? A Review of 150 Years of Scholarly Inquiry and a Tentative Answer. *Hawaiian Archaeology* 12:3–26.

———. 2015. *Unearthing the Polynesian Past: Explorations and Adventures of an Island Archaeologist.* Honolulu: University of Hawai'i Press.

Kolbert, Elizabeth. 2016. Into the Wild. The *New Yorker,* 12 September 2016:25–26.

Korn, Alfons L. 1976. Some Notes on the Origin of Certain Hawaiian Shirts: Frock, Smock-Frock, Block, and *Palaka. Oceanic Linguistics* 15:14–38.

Kratz, Henry, ed. 1986. *A Voyage around the World with the Romanzov Exploring Expedition in the Years 1815–1818 in the Brig* Rurik, *Captain Otto von Kotzebue, by Adelbert von Chamisso.* Translated and edited by Henry Kratz. Honolulu: University of Hawai'i Press.

Krauss, Bob. 2006. First Footsteps of Polynesians' Ancestors Tracked. *Honolulu Advertiser,* 23 July 2006.

Krupa, Viktor. 1982. *The Polynesian Languages: A Guide.* Vol. 4: *Languages of Asia and Africa.* London: Routledge & Kegan Paul.

Kubota, Gary T. 2011. Rats Helped Ruin Isle, UH Researcher Finds. *Honolulu Star-Advertiser,* 5 July, B2.

Kumulipo. See R. Johnson 1981.

O ke Kumumua na na Kamalii: He Palapala e Ao aku ai i na Kamalii Ike Ole i ka Heluhelu Palapala. 1835. Oahu: I mea Pai Palapala a na Missionari. [Notation: by Hiram Bingham (per R. Anderson).]

Kuykendall, Ralph Simson. 1938. *The Hawaiian Kingdom.* 3 vols. Vol. 1: *1778–1854: Foundation and Transformation.* Honolulu: University of Hawai'i Press. Reprinted 1947, 1957, 1968, University of Hawai'i Press.

Laccetti, Silvio. 2012. Hawaii Not Just a Single Paradise, but Rather Quite a Few. *Honolulu Star-Advertiser,* 19 July 2012.

Laimana, John Kalei. 2011. The Phenomenal Rise to Literacy in Hawai'i: Hawaiian Society in the Early Nineteenth Century. University of Hawai'i at Mānoa, MA thesis.

Lanchester, John. 1996. *The Debt to Pleasure.* New York: Picador.

Landau, Sidney I. 2001. *Dictionaries: The Art and Craft of Lexicography.* 2nd ed. Cambridge: Cambridge University Press.

Lanyon-Orgill, Peter A., ed. 1979. *Captain Cook's South Sea Island Vocabularies.* London: Lanyon-Orgill.

Le Maire, Iacob. 1616. See Dalrymple 1770–1771.

Lisiansky, Urey (Lisianskii, Iurii Fedorovich). 1814. *A Voyage Round the World, in the Years 1803, 4, 5, & 6; Performed, by Order of his Imperial Majesty, Alexander the First, Emperor of Russia, in the Ship* Neva. English translation by the author. London: Booth. [Ca. 170 HAW words collected ca. 1804, 326–28.]

Lobschied, D. 1872. Ethnological and Philological Notes Respecting Hawaiians. *The Friend* (January):4.

Loomis, Albertine. (1951) 1966. *The Grapes of Canaan: Hawaii 1820.* New York: Dodd, Mead & Company. 1966 ed.: Honolulu: Hawaiian Mission Children's Society.

Loomis, Elisha, and Maria Loomis. 1819–27. *Journal.* Albertine Loomis's copy. Library, Hawaiian Mission Houses Historic Site and Archives.

Low, Sam. 2013. *Hawaiki Rising: Hōkūle'a, Nainoa Thompson, and the Hawaiian Renaissance.* Honolulu: Island Heritage.

Lyon, Jeffrey Kapali. 2004. Memoirs of Henry Obookiah: A Rhetorical History. *The Hawaiian Journal of History* 38:35–57.

Lyons, Lorenzo. 1878. Comments on Contents of Andrews's Dictionary. *The Friend,* 1 August 1878.

Maddieson, Ian. 1984. *Patterns of Sounds.* New York: Cambridge University Press.

Malo, Davida. 1951. *Hawaiian Antiquities (Moolelo Hawai'i).* Translated by Nathaniel B. Emerson, 1898. 2nd ed. Bernice Pauahi Bishop Museum Special Publication 2. Honolulu: The Museum.

———. 2006. *Moolelo Hawaii.* Translated by Malcolm Nāea Chun. Honolulu: First People's Productions.

Māmaka Kaiao: A Modern Hawaiian Vocabulary. 1996. By the Kōmike Hua'ōlelo: Larry L. Kimura et al. Hilo: Hale Kuamo'o a me ka 'Aha Pūnana Leo. 2nd ed., 1998.

Māmaka Kaiao: A Modern Hawaiian Vocabulary: A Compilation of Hawaiian Words That Have Been Created, Collected, and Approved by the Hawaiian Lexicon Committee from 1987 through 2000. 2003. Kōmike Hua 'Ōlelo, Hale Kuamo'o, 'Aha Pūnana Leo. Honolulu: University of Hawai'i Press.

Marck, Jeffrey C. 1999. Revising Polynesian Subgrouping and Its Culture History Implications. In R. Blench and M. Spriggs, eds., *Archaeology and Language IV: Language Change and Cultural Transformation,* 95–122. London: Routledge.

———. 2000. *Topics in Polynesian Language and Culture History.* Canberra: Pacific Linguistics 504, Research School of Pacific and Asian Studies, the Australian National University.

Marsden, William. 1812. *A Grammar of the Malayan Language with an Introduction and Praxis.* Vol. 2 of *A Dictionary and Grammar of the Malayan Language.* London: Cox and Baylis. Reprinted 1984, Singapore: Oxford University Press.

Martínez 1789. See Day 1991.

McDougall, Brandy Nalani. 2016. *Finding Meaning: Kaona and Contemporary Hawaiian Literature.* Tucson: University of Arizona Press.

McGuffey's First Eclectic Reader, Revised Edition. 1879. Cincinnati and New York: Van Antwerp, Bragg & Company. [Other editions: 1896, 1907, 1920.]

Facsimile edition 1972: New York, Cincinnati, Chicago: American Book Company.
Meheula, Sol., and Jas. Henry Bolster, eds. 1888. *Ka Moolelo o Laiekawai, a o ka mea i kapa ia Kawahineikaliula.* Honolulu: Papa pai mehu "Bulletin." [One source for Baker 2015.]
Merriam-Webster's Collegiate Dictionary. 2003. 11th ed. (CD-Rom version). Springfield, MA: Merriam-Webster.
Merriam-Webster's Collegiate Encyclopedia. 2000. Springfield, MA: Merriam-Webster.
Merriam-Webster's Geographical Dictionary. 3rd ed. 1997. Springfield, MA: Merriam-Webster.
Merriam-Webster Unabridged. 2018. [Online electronic dictionary.] https://www.merriam-webster.com/dictionary/humuhumunukunukuapuaa. Accessed November 7, 2018.
Mills, Peter R. 1997. Historical Ethnography and Archaeology of Russian Fort Elisabeth State Historical Park, Waimea, Kaua'i. *Kroeber Anthropological Society Papers* 81:157–86.
Missionary Album: Portraits and Biographical Sketches of the American Protestant Missionaries to the Hawaiian Islands. 1969. Enlarged from the edition of 1937. Sesquicentennial ed. Honolulu: Hawaiian Mission Children's Society.
Missionary Herald. Publication of the American Board of Commissioners for Foreign Missions. Boston: Samuel T. Armstrong.
Missionary Letters [typed copies] from the Sandwich Islands Mission to the American Board of Commissioners for Foreign Missions, 1819–1837. 8 vols. [The volume count is apparently for the original; the typed copies are contained in 3 vols. "Supplementary to the letters published in the Missionary Herald for the same dates."] <HMCS 266.858/M69.>
Monaghan, E. Jennifer. 1983. *A Common Heritage: Noah Webster's Blue-Back Speller.* Hamden, CT: Archon.
Mookini, Esther T. 1974. *The Hawaiian Newspapers.* Honolulu: Topgallant.
———. 1985. *O Na Holoholona Wawae Eha O Ka Lama Hawaii, or The Four-Footed Animals of Ka Lama Hawaii.* Introduction by Samuel H. Elbert. Honolulu: Bamboo Ridge Press.
Morgan, John S. 1975. *Noah Webster.* New York: Mason/Charter.
Neal, Marie. 1948. *In Gardens of Hawaii.* Bernice P. Bishop Museum Special Publication 40. Honolulu: Bishop Museum Press. New and rev. ed., 1965. Bernice P. Bishop Museum Special Publication 50. Honolulu: Bishop Museum Press.
NeSmith, Richard Keao'ōpuaokalani. 2002. Tūtū's Hawaiian and the Emergence of a Neo-Hawaiian Language. University of Hawai'i at Mānoa MA thesis.

Newbrand, Helene L. 1951. A Phonemic Analysis of Hawaiian. University of Hawaiʻi MA thesis.
New Chair Professor of USTC: Prof. JIAO Tianlong. 2013. University of Science and Technology of China. 23 March 2013.
New Edition of Bilingual Bible Available. 2014. *Honolulu Star-Advertiser,* 18 October, B4.
Nijhuis, Michelle. 2003. Tribal Talk. *Smithsonian* (November):36, 38.
Notes on the Discovery and Settlement of Polynesia. 2011. *Mālamalama,* 21 April.
Oliver, Douglas L. 1958. *The Pacific Islands.* Decorations and maps by Sheila Mitchell Oliver. Cambridge, MA: Harvard University Press.
ʻŌpūkahaʻia, Henry. Ca. 1817. *Hawaiian Grammar, Vocabulary, Speller.* See Ruggles (1819) 1993.
Orthography of the Hawaiian Language. 1826. Typescript copies of original letters at HMCS, made by Bert N. Nishimura, 1936. <Photocopy in UHM Hawn. PL6445. 078>
Papa Huaʻōlelo. 1994. Hilo: Hale Kuamoʻo, Kikowaena ʻŌlelo Hawaiʻi, Kulanui o Hawaiʻi ma Hilo.
Parker, Henry H. 1922. See Andrews 1922.
Parker Jones, ʻŌiwi. 2009a. Loanwords in Hawaiian. In Martin Haspelmath and Uri Tadmor, eds., *Loanwords in the World's Languages: A Comparative Handbook,* 771–89. Berlin: Mouton de Gruyter.
———. 2009b. Hawaiian Vocabulary. In Martin Haspelmath and Uri Tadmor, eds., *World Loanword Database.* Munich: Max Planck Digital Library.
———. 2018. Illustrations of the IPA: Hawaiian. *Journal of the International Phonetic Association* 48:103–15.
Pawley, Andrew K. 1966. Polynesian Languages: A Subgrouping Based on Shared Innovations in Morphology. *Journal of the Polynesian Society* 75(1):39–64.
Pawley, Andrew K., and Kay Green. 1971. Lexical Evidence for the Proto-Polynesian Homeland. *Te Reo* 14:1–35.
Pawley, Andrew K., and Roger Green. 1973. Dating the Dispersal of the Oceanic Languages. *Papers of the First International Conference on Comparative Austronesian Linguistics. 1974—Oceanic. Oceanic Linguistics* 12(1):1–68.
Pennybacker, Mindy. 2016. In Their Own Words: More than 200 Letters Written in Hawaiian by Alii in the 19th Century Are Translated into English. *Honolulu Star-Advertiser,* F1–F4.
Piccolo, Fabiana. 2005. Where Is the Hawaiian Language Headed? A Phonetic Study. *University of Hawaiʻi at Mānoa Working Papers in Linguistics* 36(1) (March). Department of Linguistics Web site, under "Research."
Pickering, John. 1820. *An Essay on a Uniform Orthography for the Indian Languages of North America.* Cambridge, MA: University Press—Hilliard and Metcalf.

Pike, Kenneth L. 1947. *Phonemics: A Technique for Reducing Languages to Writing.* Ann Arbor: University of Michigan Press.

Pollock, Nancy J. 1986. Food Classification in Three Pacific Societies: Fiji, Hawaii, and Tahiti. *Ethnology* 25:107–19.

Polynesian Colonization Was Sudden and Swift. 2011. *Mālamalama* 36(2):6 (April).

Pukui, Mary Kawena. 1983. *ʻŌlelo Noʻeau: Hawaiian Proverbs & Poetical Sayings / Collected, Translated, and Annotated by Mary Kawena Pukui.* Illustrated by Dietrich Varez. Honolulu: Bishop Museum Press.

Pukui, Mary Kawena, and Samuel H. Elbert. 1957. *Hawaiian-English Dictionary.* 2d ed., 1961; 3d ed., 1965. Honolulu: University of Hawaiʻi Press.

———. 1964. *English-Hawaiian Dictionary.* Honolulu: University of Hawaiʻi Press.

———. 1966. *Place Names of Hawaii.* Honolulu: University of Hawaiʻi Press.

———. 1971. *Hawaiian Dictionary: Hawaiian-English, English-Hawaiian.* Honolulu: University of Hawaiʻi Press. Revised and enlarged edition: 1986. Reprinted in 1991 with corrections.

———. 1986. See Pukui and Elbert 1971.

———. 1992. *New Pocket Hawaiian Dictionary, with a Concise Grammar and Given Names in Hawaiian.* With Esther T. Mookini and Yū Mapuana Nishizawa. Honolulu: University of Hawaiʻi Press.

Pukui, Mary Kawena, Samuel H. Elbert, and Esther T. Mookini. 1974. *Place Names of Hawaii.* Revised & expanded edition. Honolulu: University of Hawaiʻi Press.

———. 1989. *Pocket Place Names of Hawaiʻi.* Honolulu: University of Hawaiʻi Press.

Pukui, Mary Kawena, E. W. Haertig, and Catherine A. Lee. (1972–79), 1983, 2002. *Nānā i ke Kumu (Look to the Source).* Honolulu: Hui Hānai, an Auxiliary of the Queen Liliʻuokalani Children's Center.

Quimper, Manuel (Manuel Quimper Benítez del Pino). 1822. *Islas de Sandwich. Descripcion sucinta de este Archipiélago, Nombre que les Dió su Célebre Descubridor el Captain Cook, reconocidas por el teniente de fragata de la armada nacional.* Madrid: E. Aguado.

Random House Dictionaries: The End. 2001. *Dictionary Society of North America Newsletter* 25(2):1, 3.

Reinecke, John Ernest. 1969. *Language and Dialect in Hawaii: A Sociolinguistic History to 1935.* Stanley M. Tsuzaki, ed. Honolulu: University of Hawaiʻi Press.

Reland, Hadrian. 1706. Dissertatio de linguis insularum quarundam orientalum. [Based on the vocabularies of Oceanic languages collected by Willem Schouten and Jacob Le Maire in 1616.]

Renfrew, Colin. 2009. Where Bacteria and Languages Concur. *Science* 323: 467–68.

Rensch, Karl Heinz. 1991. The Language of the Noble Savage: Early European Perceptions of Tahitian. In Robert Blust, ed., *Currents in Pacific Linguistics: Papers on Austronesian Languages and Ethnolinguistics in Honour of George W. Grace*, 403–14. Pacific Linguistics, C-117.

———. 2000. *The Language of the Noble Savage: The Linguistic Fieldwork of Reinhold and George Forster in Polynesia on Cook's Second Voyage to the Pacific 1772–1775.* Canberra: Archipelago Press.

Reyes, Daniella. 2015. 'Lāʻieikawai' a Cultural and Linguistic Triumph: Kennedy Theatre's First Hawaiian Language Play Premieres. *Ka Leo o Hawaiʻi: The Voice* (23 February):28.

Richards, William. 1828. Letter to Rufus Anderson, Boston, 20 May 1828. Library, Hawaiian Mission Houses Historic Site and Archives 266.858/ Sa5a.

Rock, Joseph F. 1913. *The Indigenous Trees of the Hawaiian Islands.* Honolulu: Published privately.

Rolle, Nicholas, and Donna Starks. 2014. Vowel Length in Niuean. *Oceanic Linguistics* 53(2):273–99.

[Ruggles, Samuel]. (1819) 1993. *A Short, Elementary Grammar of the Owhihe Language.* Introduction by James D. Rumford. Honolulu: Manoa Press.

Rumford, James D., ed. 1993a. Introduction to Ruggles's Grammar (1819), attributed to ʻŌpūkahaʻia.

———. 1993b. Authorship of the Henry ʻŌpūkahaʻia Hawaiian Grammar. *Hawaiian Journal of History* 27:245–47.

———, ed. 1996. *Select Hawaiian Phrases & Sentences Rehearsed at Table.* Ms. by Sybil Moseley Bingham. Translation assistance by Puakea Nogelmeier. Honolulu: Mānoa Press. <Original manuscript held at Yale University Library, Manuscripts and Archives, Bingham Family Papers, July 1823.>

———. 1997. The Hawaiian Syllabary Circa 1830. *Hawaiian Journal of History* 31:205–8.

Sachdeva, Meena. 1985. Teacher Creates a Learning Tool in Hawaiian History and Language. *Mālamalama* 9(4):4.

Sakoda, Kent, and Jeff Siegel. 2003. *Pidgin Grammar: An Introduction to the Creole English of Hawaiʻi.* Honolulu: Bess Press.

Samwell, David. 1779. [HAW word list in Beaglehole 1967:1231–34.]

Santeliz es Pablo, Juan Eugenio. 1791. [Vocabulario Castellano Nutkeño, Sandwich, y Mexicano]. Ms. <British Library ADD 17631> [A collection of three word lists: (1) Castellano—Nutkeño—Sandwich—Mexicano, 70 words; (2) Castellano—Sandwich—Mexicano, 216 words; (3) Castellano (this time also called Español)—Nutkeño—Sandwich—Mexicano, 312 words. Each is arranged alphabetically, according to the Spanish gloss. Peter A.

Lanyon-Orgill (1979:182) referred to the Nootka list as a "defective copy" (apparently of Cook's list) and Santeliz es Pablo as a compiler (rather than collector).]

Schütz, Albert J. 1962. A Dialect Survey of Viti Levu, Fiji. Cornell University PhD dissertation.

———. 1970. The Phonological Patterning of English Loan Words in Tongan. In Steven A. Wurm and Donald C. Laycock, eds., *Pacific Linguistic Studies in Honour of Arthur Capell*, 409–28. Pacific Linguistics, Series C. No. 13.

———. 1972. *The Languages of Fiji.* Oxford: Clarendon Press.

———. 1976. Take *My* Word for It: Missionary Influence on English Borrowings in Hawaiian. *Oceanic Linguistics* 14(1):75–92.

———. 1978a. English Loanwords in Fijian. *Bulletin of the Fiji Museum* No. 4:1–50.

———. 1978b. *Suva: A History and Guide.* Sydney: Pacific Publications.

———. 1981. A Reanalysis of the Hawaiian Vowel System. *Oceanic Linguistics* 20(1):1–44.

———. 1985. *The Fijian Language.* Honolulu: University of Hawai'i Press.

———. 1989. 'Op8k3h3'e3's Grammar of H3wie. *Honolulu* 25(5): 126–27, 169–70, 173.

———. 1991. William Anderson's Hawaiian Word List. In Robert Blust, ed., *Currents in Pacific Linguistics: Papers on Austronesian Languages and Ethnolinguistics in Honour of George W. Grace*, 453–64. Pacific Linguistics, C-117.

———. 1994. *The Voices of Eden: A History of Hawaiian Language Studies.* Honolulu: University of Hawai'i Press.

———. 2009. *Webster's Third* and the Pronunciation of Hawaiian Loanwords in English: A Different View of Usage. *Dictionaries* 30:1–17.

———. 2017a. Reading between the Lines: A Closer Look at the first Hawaiian Primer (1822). *Palapala-He Puke Pai no ka 'Olelo me ka Mo'olelo Hawai'i (A Journal for Hawaiian Language and Literature)* 1:1–29, 173–90.

———. 2017b. 'Ōpūkaha'ia, Missionaries in Hawai'i, and Noah Webster: Connections and Puzzles to Solve. In Thomas A. Woods, ed., *Bedroom Annex | Print Shop: Language, Literacy, and Meaning*, 7–24. Honolulu: Hawaiian Mission Houses Historic Site and Archives.

———. 2018. Models for the Hawaiian Alphabet: Polynesian Connections. In *Kōkua Aku, Kōkua Mai. Chiefs, Missionaries, and Five Transformations of the Hawaiian Kingdom*, ed. by Thomas A. Woods, 22–52. Honolulu: Hawaiian Mission Houses Historic Site and Archives.

Schütz, Albert J., Gary N. Kahāho'omalu Kanada, and Kenneth W. Cook. 2005. *Pocket Hawaiian Grammar.* Waipahu: Island Heritage.

Silva, Noenoe K. 2017. *The Power of the Steel-Tipped Pen: Reconstructing Native Hawaiian Intellectual History.* Durham, NC, and London: Duke University Press.

Stevenson, Robert Louis. 1891. *In the South Seas, Being an Account of Experiences and Observations in the Marquesas, Paumotus and Gilbert Islands in the Course of Two Cruises on the Yacht "Casco" (1888) and the Schooner "Equator" (1889).* New York: Scribner.

Tcherkézoff, Serge. 2003. A Long and Unfortunate Voyage towards the "Invention" of the Melanesia/Polynesia Distinction 1595–1832. *Journal of Pacific History* 38(2):175–96.

Thrum, T[homas] G. 1906. Heiaus and Heiau Sites throughout the Hawaiian Islands. *The Hawaiian Annual for 1907: The Recognized Book of Information about Hawaii,* 36–48. Honolulu: Thos. G. Thrum, Compiler & Publisher.

Thurston, Asa, and Artemas Bishop. 1835. Report from Kailua. *Missionary Herald* 31 (1835):376.

Two New Species of Fungi That Kill ʻŌhiʻa Trees Get Hawaiian Names. 2018. UH News. https://www.hawaii.edu/news/2018/04/16/ohia-killing-fungi-get-hawaiian-names. Accessed 20 October 2018.

Vibrant at Ninety: Honolulu Community College. 2010. *Mālamalama* April 2010. [Mentions that two *lama* trees were planted on Arbor Day near the Native Hawaiian Center at Honolulu Community College.]

Wagner, Sigmund. 1821. *Das Leben Malers Johann Weber aus Bern.* Zürich: Künstler-Gesellschaft.

Wahlroos, Sven. 2002. *English-Tahitian Tahitian-English Dictionary / Faʻa-toro Parau Marite/Peritane-Tahiti Tahiti-Marite/Peretane.* Honolulu: Māʻohi Heritage Press.

Wallworth, Mary. 2014. Eastern Polynesian: The Linguistic Evidence Revisited. *Oceanic Linguistics* 53(2):257–71.

Ward, Jack Haven. 1962. Mutual Intelligibility between Certain Polynesian Speech Communities. MA thesis, University of Hawaiʻi.

Webster, Noah. (1783) 1800. *A Grammatical Institute of the English Language.* Boston: Thomas & Andrews. Evans Index 18297–98, 1800 ed., Evans Index 39040.

———. 1806. *A Compendious Dictionary of the English Language.* Hartford: Hudson & Goodwin.

———. 1829. *The American Spelling Book; Containing the Rudiments of the English Language for the Use of Schools in the United States.* New Brunswick, NJ: Terhune & Letson.

Webster's New Collegiate Dictionary. 1977. Springfield, MA: G. & C. Merriam Company.

Webster's Third New International Dictionary. 1961. Springfield, MA: Merriam.

Westervelt, W[illiam] D. 1912. The First Twenty Years of Education in the Hawaiian Islands. In *Nineteenth Annual Report (Twentieth Year) of the Hawaiian Hist. Soc. for the Year 1911,* 16–26.

White, Ralph Gardner. 1967. Onomastically Induced Word Replacement in Tahitian. In Genevieve A. Highland, Roland W. Force, Alan Howard, Marion Kelly, and Yosihiko H. Sinoto, eds., *Polynesian Culture History: Essays in Honor of Kenneth P. Emory,* 323–38. Bernice P. Bishop Museum Special Publication 56. Honolulu: Bishop Museum Press.

Wilkes, Charles. 1852. *Narrative of the United States Exploring Expedition.* Vol. 4. Philadelphia: Lea & Blanchard. 1970 (facsimile reprint), Upper Saddle River, NJ: Gregg Press.

Williams, Herbert William. (1917) 1975. *A Dictionary of the Maori Language.* 7th ed. Wellington, NZ: Government Printer.

Wilmshurst, Janet M., Terry L. Hunt, Carl P. Lipo, and Atholl J. Anderson. 2010. High Precision Radiocarbon Dating Shows Recent and Rapid Initial Human Colonization of East Polynesia. *Proceedings of the National Academy of Sciences* 108(5):1815–20.

Wilson, William H. 1978. Recommendations of the ʻAhahui ʻŌlelo Hawaiʻi 1978 Hawaiian Spelling Project. Typescript copy. Hamilton Library PL6443.W57 1978.

———. 1985. Evidence for an Outlier Source for the Proto Eastern Polynesian Pronominal System. *Oceanic Linguistics* 24(1/2):85–133.

Woods, Thomas A. 2016. Marking the Bicentennial. The *Maile Wreath* (fall 2016) 38(2):1.

ILLUSTRATION CREDITS

All figures not credited in this list are by the author.

Most woodblock prints (the ornaments) are from *O ke Kumumua na na Kamalii: He Palapala e Ao aku ai i na Kamalii Ike Ole i ka Heluhelu Palapala* (First Lessons for Children; a Book Teaching Those Children Who Do Not Know How to Read Books), by John S. Emerson, 1835.

Hawaiian Mission Houses Historic Site and Archives has granted permission for all images from its collection; these are noted in the following list by HMCS.

Fig. 1.1: Left: Courtesy of Stuart Bedford and Matthew Spriggs; right: author
Fig. 1.2: Davidson 1979:85, Courtesy of Harvard University Press
Figs. 1.3–1.5: From Dalrymple 1770–1771
Fig. 1.6: Map reproduced with the permission of CartoGIS Services, ANU College of Asia and the Pacific, Australian National University
Fig. 1.7: David Hall, https://www.gifex.com/images/0X0/2009-12-29-11508/Polynesian_migration_in_Oceania.png, accessed July 16, 2019
Fig. 1.8: Courtesy of Kon-Tiki Museum
Fig. 1.9: Courtesy of Polynesian Voyaging Society
Fig. 2.3: Clark 1979:258, based on Pawley 1966
Fig. 2.4: Based on Wilson 1985
Fig. 2.5: Courtesy of Steven Roger Fischer; adapted from Fischer 2001:122, and Fischer pers. comm., Feb. 2015
Fig. 2.6: Walworth 2014:269
Fig. 4.1: Courtesy of Steven Roger Fischer
Fig. 5.1: From Bingham 1847:217
Fig. 5.2: Courtesy of the Mānoa Heritage Center, Kuali'i Library
Fig. 5.4: Courtesy of Joel Bradshaw
Fig. 5.5: Courtesy of the British Library
Fig. 5.6: Courtesy of the British Library, London, MS 17227, no. 18v
Fig. 5.7: Courtesy of the British Library
Fig. 5.8: Admiralty Records on microfilm, courtesy of Hamilton Library
Figs. 6.1–6.2: Courtesy of HMCS
Fig. 6.4: From Dwight 1990 (1819), courtesy of Hawaiian Historical Society
Fig. 6.5: Courtesy of HMCS
Fig. 6.6: Wikimedia Commons
Figs. 7.1–7.2: Courtesy of HMCS

Fig. 7.3: Courtesy of James Rumford
Fig. 7.4: Courtesy of Jean Charlot Foundation
Figs. 7.5–7.9: Courtesy of HMCS
Fig. 8.1: From Bingham and Loomis 1823
Figs. 8.2–8.3: Courtesy of HMCS
Fig. 9.1: Courtesy of HMCS
Fig. 9.2: From Webster's *American Spelling Book* 1829
Fig. 9.3: Courtesy of Hawaiian Historical Society
Fig. 10.1: Courtesy of Honolulu Academy of Arts
Fig. 10.2: From Bingham 1847:295
Fig. 10.3: Courtesy of Hawai'i State Archives
Figs. 10.4–10.6: Courtesy of HMCS
Fig. 10.7: From Bingham 1847:615
Fig. 10.8: Courtesy of Chelsey Cannon
Fig. 11.1: Courtesy of Jean Charlot Collection, Hamilton Library
Fig. 13.1: Courtesy of HMCS
Fig. 14.1: Courtesy of Honolulu Academy of Arts
Fig. 14.2: Courtesy of Patience Bacon, Bishop Museum Archives
Fig. 15.5: Courtesy of Bishop Museum Archives
Fig. 16.3: Courtesy of Puanani Anderson-Fung
Fig. 16.8: The Fish Site, www.thefishsite.com
Fig. 16.10: Courtesy of Forest and Kim Starr
Figs. 16.11–16.12: Courtesy of Mānoa Heritage Center

INDEX

ABOUT THE AUTHOR

Albert J. Schütz is professor emeritus of linguistics at the University of Hawaiʻi at Mānoa, where he specializes in descriptive linguistics, field methods, lexicography, Fijian and Hawaiian grammar, and the study of Fijian, Hawaiian, and other Austronesian languages. His first fieldwork in Fiji, a dialect geography, involved collecting and analyzing data from 105 villages. In 1971 he was appointed director of a monolingual dictionary project in Suva, Fiji. Schütz's publications on Hawaiian include more than thirty works—not only scholarly articles but also booklets that explain the language to visitors and full-length treatments such as *The Voices of Eden*, which has been used as both a textbook and a reference work.

THE *KAONA* OF THE COVER ART

Arman Tateos Manookian titled his painting *Discovery*—an obvious play on words—pairing the literal sense of the word with the name of one of Cook's ships. But rather than follow the ethnocentric view that it was the Europeans who "discovered" the Hawaiians and the Hawaiian islands, the artist focused on the *mutual* discovery of the two cultures. Moreover, one views the scene from the Hawaiian perspective—standing behind the stylized vegetation on the shore and looking over the shoulders of the Hawaiians to the huge sailing vessel, the longboat and its crew, and the second vessel in the distance.

The canvas is almost equally divided: the Hawaiians and native flora are clearly delineated and dominate the left-hand side. In contrast, the imposing ship—Cook's *Discovery*—dominates the right-hand side, with the *Resolution* less prominent in the background.

The European figures standing in front of the ship are only sketched in outline form, but I would like to think that one of them represents the philologist William Anderson. In chapter 5, you can read how his imminent death and his missing Waimea journal ensured that the details of his life and work would also remain a sketch, perhaps never to be completely filled in.